POLITICS AND RELIGIOUS CONSCIOUSNESS IN AMERICA

POLITICS AND RELIGIOUS CONSCIOUSNESS IN AMERICA

GEORGE ARMSTRONG KELLY

Transaction Books
New Brunswick (U.S.A.) and London (U.K.)

Library of Congress Catalog Number: 83-9284
ISBN: 0-87855-484-X (cloth)
Printed in the United States of America

Library of Congress Cataloging in Publication Data

Kelly, George Armstrong, 1932-
   Politics and religious consciousness in America.

   Bibliography: p.
   Includes index.
   1. Church and state—United States—History.
2. Christianity and politics.   3. United States—
Church history.   I. Title.
BR516.K36 1984   306'.2   83-9284
ISBN 0-87855-484-X

To Faith and to Loyalty
in a time when they are made difficult but not impossible

L'homme écrit son destin jour à jour, mot à mot,
avec la grosse encre noire de la vie, et en même
temps Dieu écrit dans les interlignes avec une
encre encore invisible.
—Victor Hugo

Contents

Acknowledgments

This book came about in a rather fortuitous way. In 1977 Aaron Wildavsky, then president of the Russell Sage Foundation, New York City, asked me to join the foundation's "citizenship" project for a year. Out of that particular venture came only some in-house working papers and an essay later published in *Daedalus*, together with a meeting on citizenship sponsored by the Conference for the Study of Political Thought and the Graduate Center of the City University of New York, of which I was program chairman. But many new ideas were prefigured by the experience. I am indeed indebted to Aaron Wildavsky, as well as to my Sage colleagues Mary Douglas, Elaine Spitz, and Herman van Gunsteren for the earliest impulses to the present work.

At some moment during my time with the Russell Sage Foundation I became convinced of the need to give special attention to the religious dimension of my citizenship project. The result was that I became absorbed in it. No doubt it was hazardous for a historian of French and German political thought to transfer his focus to an exceptionally complicated American problem, but that was the long road I set out to travel. An indispensable benefit now came my way: a fruitful and busy year (1979–80) of research, reflection, and writing at the School of Social Science of the Institute for Advanced Study in Princeton. I am most grateful for the warm hospitality of Professors Albert O. Hirschman and Clifford Geertz and for the generosity of the National Endowment for the Humanities, which partially funded my stay in Princeton.

I had a further opportunity to refine my thoughts and focus when I delivered public lectures and a seminar on some of this material to audiences at the University of British Columbia in Vancouver during January 1981. Professors E.V. Hundert and Stephen Straker were my most obliging hosts for the occasion. By summer's end of 1981 I had basically achieved the form and substance of the book presented here. In the spring of 1982 I had the good fortune to be asked by Dr. Stephen R. Graubard, the editor of *Daedalus*, to submit a paper on politics and religion to an advisory conference in prospect of a special number of that journal. The result was my essay "Faith, Freedom, and Disenchantment: Politics and the American Religious Consciousness," *Daedalus* 111 (Winter 1982), which incorporated parts of the present first, second, and sixth chapters. I thank the publisher of *Daedalus* (Journal of the American Academy of Arts and Sciences, Cambridge, Mass.) for permission to reprint this material; and I am most grateful to Stephen Graubard and to my fellow conferees for their useful comments and suggestions.

At least three other scholars, none of whom is responsible for this book's deficiencies, must be mentioned as important inspirations to *Politics and Religious Consciousness in America*. My colleague at Johns Hopkins, Timothy L. Smith of the History Department, has shared his extensive knowledge of evangelical Protestantism with me in several conversations. My Harvard teacher Louis Hartz early on provided a contextual and intellectual excitement for me that has never dimmed. Although Louis Hartz did not write about American religion, I am sure that his work created part of the mystery that led me on this voyage. And my dear friend Judith N. Shklar—also my teacher—has long been my example of a wise and probing intellect, graceful and resolute at the same time.

A book of this kind, synthetic, diagnostic, and theoretical but non-encyclopedic, necessarily has indebtednesses to many previous writers. I cannot of course list all the works that have, in small ways, influenced my own. But I should like to call attention to some that were especially valuable in constructing my own frame of reference: Sydney E. Ahlstrom's *A Religious History of the American People* (New Haven: Yale University Press, 1972), for its bulging store of information; Cushing Strout's *The New Heavens and the New Earth: Political Religion in America* (New York: Harper & Row, 1974), for raising and discussing a number of vital issues; William A. Clebsch's *American Religious Thought* (Chicago: University of Chicago Press, 1973), for stimulating me to think about Emerson and James in some ways quite different from those of that author; Paul C. Nagel's *This Sacred Trust* (New York: Columbia University Press, 1971), for helping to disclose some of the materials of nineteenth-century American nationalism; and, not least, the various writings of Robert N. Bellah, which figure importantly in chapter 7 and elsewhere. A considerable intellectual debt to Reinhold Niebuhr, a political theorist of stature and no mere political theologian, is cheerfully acknowledged.

For a long while Irving Louis Horowitz has been an important intellectual voice and catalyst in the United States. It is especially agreeable to be associated with him and with the staff of Transaction Books in this venture.

My wife Joanne has practically willed this book from pen to press while listening to more than a fair share of yowls and complaints. *Dux femina facti*, chérie.

Introduction

The United States is today in a very hazy predicament involving both spiritual and political self-understanding. Troubles in both spheres are more commonly related than is generally supposed, and no therapy can be ventured without a candid recognition of these relationships. The purpose of this book is to show how our current orthodoxies have come to be what they are and how our forfeits have taken place, not by revisiting the case books of constitutional law but by telling the deeper story of how religion and politics crossed in America.

If the recovery of self knowledge and some practical means of remedy is, as one must hope, available in our storehouse of native themes, that reservoir of myth and history is also a Pandora's box of illusions and misleading memorabilia. That we must be guided to a franker and more unflinching examination of our ideological and institutional past is scarcely an original exhortation: Louis Hartz proclaimed it, after a fashion, in his theory of the "liberal fragment." I am certainly unwilling to let this stand as a mere taunt. Preliminary truisms cannot be made very interesting or compelling without detailed, though selective, reference to social theory and to the facts of the case. However, I have felt that, by way of transition, a brief exposition, akin to what the eighteenth-century French were fond of calling an *enchaînement des principes,* will help to guide the reader before I start unpacking the strange and parallel mutations of American religion and politics.

What follows by way of introduction will be fully fleshed out in the substantive portion of the book. We begin, as I think we must, with some rudimentary propositions about the connections of politics and religion in occidental and Christian civilization, enclosed in a heuristic philosophy of history. Briefly put, politics and religion have had both competing and collaborative functions in the control of society and in

1

the stimulation of certain durable qualities of human conviction. The authoritative power of religion rose, crested, and waned (or became "secularized" and "privatized") well in advance of that of politics. However, the two forces were never involved in anything approximating a zero-sum game. Although the worldly purposes of the sacred and the profane are discrete, their careers, both as institutions and as reservoirs of conviction, show enough similarity to be profitably compared. Practically speaking, this means that if we can understand religious evolution, we can make progress toward understanding political evolution and even perhaps doing something about it.

In the United States the pathological features of politics and religion—their decline of power and virtue—seem more closely linked in time and substance than elsewhere. I expound historical reasons for this particularity, although I have neither the wit nor the space to enlarge my study to comparative proportions. On the other hand, it is in the United States that we recognize the most full-blown example of what I call, following Peter Berger, the "Protestant paradigm." This is a paradigm of sectarianism and fragmentation that seems applicable not only to contemporary Christianity but also to profane cosmopolitan world views like liberalism and Marxism. Thus the United States in itself possesses interpretive resources for a wider examination, although not in the fashion proclaimed by Tocqueville. More importantly for our subject, it is able to provide its own general theory of interpretation.

Tocqueville intercepted the history of the United States at a moment of vigor and prudent optimism when it was evidently possible to speak of the "harmonization of heaven and earth." It was a moment sustained by geographical expansion, promised abundance, and a peculiar ideology whereby providence and progress would shortly become affectionate partners. On closer examination, however, Tocqueville's America had no intrinsic eschatological properties. Millennialism surrounded him but it did not color his theory. A variety of millennial residues persist today—mostly as nostalgia, and often as delusion. Our proper mode of historical understanding is irony (a contribution of Reinhold Niebuhr) and our best logic of action is Stoicism. But these qualities are not much in vogue.

One glaring deficiency of Tocqueville's vision was his failure to estimate the power of denominational Protestantism over politics and the community-making resources of sectarian religious frenzy. His moderate view of "the slow and quiet action of society upon itself" was somewhat misplaced. From a distance, Hegel saw these things differently. He portrayed America as an inchoate and "young" nation, rather than as a "new" and vanguard nation. Hegel's interpretation seems more durable than Tocqueville's on this issue.

Although it is less evident today than it was fifty years ago, a great deal of the American ethos—in politics as well as in manners and morals—was created by a complex interweaving of Puritan Calvinism and Methodist Arminianism. The balancing action of the one in the sphere of faith and the other in public affairs underlay the "harmonization" theme of Tocqueville's theory. Eventually Calvinism was defeated: an Arminian faith suited to an Arminian republican politics contributed the outstanding impulse to the expansion and unification of the country.

Multiple sectarianism, basic to the generative logic of Protestantism, has been another prominent national feature, resolving itself occasionally in denominational structures. However, it has not characteristically or lastingly—up to now—captured the sources of political practice. American culture has experienced a dialectic of sects and solitude, the rigor of the community and the estrangement of the individual. Shading off into cultism—which is of course different— this phenomenon is close to the quick of the destiny of the American intellectual. Emerson and James were key examples. One might say that prophetism is the stance of intellectual sectarianism, while alienated elitism is the stance of cultism.

Many volumes have been written on the *idée-force* of American providentialism, of America's putative mission as a sacred or profane redeemer nation. The roots of this attitude are very deep and tangled, but in acknowledging this powerful strain of native hubris, distinctions need to be observed and certain constraints need to be given their just due. American manifest destiny is a major theme, but it is not the exclusive theme of the crossing patterns of religion and politics.

More than a few readers may find it quaint that a book about religion and politics in America has so little to say about Lincoln—that it gives him less space than Emerson, Horace Bushnell, or even Grover Cleveland. For this, two explanations will be given. First, this work does not purport to be a comprehensive history. It is, rather, an interpretation of developing clusters of political attitudes within a religious matrix. Much is deliberately omitted. Second, I have come to the radical conclusion that we live now in an America that bears few of the traces of Lincoln's presence, and that the experiment of studying this range of problems without Lincoln is defensible. The critic may judge this point at the end of the examination.

Like other Western nations, America has had to endure what Max Weber called "disenchantment." But the mood arose differently here because of our relative isolation from the misfortunes of war and "foreign contamination," and also because religion maintained itself here more robustly by voluntarism and by yielding to diverse pressures of secularization. This has meant, among other things, that the careers of religion and politics in the United States are more congruent and more inseparable than elsewhere. Nevertheless, disenchantment has struck America, too. In this sense we have rejoined common Western civilization: our institutions and attitudes (as I interpret them through Hegel and Reinhold Niebuhr) will increasingly reflect this destiny. Our politics parallels our religion in this regard. We seem generally unable to assess the position we are in or its implications.

From fairly early on—perhaps since the dissipation of Calvinist-inspired republicanism—Americans have progressively developed an infatuation with the imperial prerogatives of the "self"—abetted by Arminianism, by the types of religious experience commended by William James, and by waves of psychologism active in our culture. This intoxication, reaching its zenith in the "affluent society," has been equally destructive of politics and religion, of their social meaning, and of their delicate balance.

Disenchantment should be taken to include technological secularism, existentialism, religious and political consumerism, and current nostalgias, be they utopian or fundamentalist, as well as the thirst for "civil religion" that came over a part of the academic community in the past generation. Not only was this civil religion modified out of existence by scholarly debate, but it scarcely touched the common citizen. It was a despairing intellectual panacea for a country confused in both its spiritual and political motives. If a civil religion ever really existed in postindependence America, it was probably in the period 1865-1918.

Religion and politics have two dimensions: the interior and the exterior—the believer and the church, the citizen and the state. Both must be adequately accounted for, particularly within the "Protestant paradigm." To speak only of the inner dimension, we can discriminate between the sources and requirements of "faith" and "loyalty." Although crossbred in action, each is distinct. There can be no effective outer shell of religion and politics without them. But the ideologies of present-day America cheapen and delegitimize both. The writings of Josiah Royce on this subject, imperfect as they are, can assist us in recovering a balanced orientation. But it will be difficult,

perhaps impossible, to plan the task of reconstruction unless we relin-
quish deeply ingrained notions of political aptitude and divine blessing
and set about the job with a minimum of illusion.

My work here is archaeological, analytical, and diagnostic. It argues for an understanding and not for a program; however, deep concern is etched into most of these pages. I am especially intent on
making the arguments of this book clear at the outset to my colleagues who investigate and write the history of political thought or
who theorize improved political societies. It seems to me that a diffi-
dence toward the percolating presence of religion has long been a
feature of most research done on politics and the state. But my special hope here is not to capture a new mood; it is to restate an old
truth.

1

The Sacred and the Profane

It was laid low without pardon.
Only the cleverest archivist, the shepherd,
The fool of God, could replace the stones,
The vines, the garden. Biased
By sun and stream, the heresy
Of nature's radical designs
Becomes a self-fulfilling but self-healing
Prophecy. Pascal's page of fire
Arrives in a dream. We learn not to mix
Religion and politics.

—"Port-Royal-des-Champs," by the author

It is a short walk along a woodland path from the parking lot to a dilapidated ticket stall that also sells a few postcards. Only minutes from the Paris urban sprawl, in the gentle Vallée de Chevreuse, Port-Royal-des-Champs, the citadel of Jansenism until its destruction in 1710,[1] is a humble rustic ruin, belonging to another world, another mental space, another projection between the obvious and veiled spheres of existence. Not much there is left standing: only the old *colombier*, a reconstructed *oratoire* turned into a midget museum, and the leveled quadrilateral traceries of this passionate core of Christian ferment. It is not a ruin like others. It was demolished not by the Vikings but by the political acts of a Most Christian King.

And so religion and politics do mix. Both the overt and the underground histories of Jansenism furnish a rich example of their multiple entanglements.[2] Yet the subject I am raising has passed into relative neglect in the mainstream of modern political writing: "Religions appear to be virtually untouched. Certainly no American political scientist has provided a noteworthy analysis of the idea-system (or idea-systems) that characterizes religion in general. Neither has an

7

American political scientist carefully explored the significance for legal government of the belief-system, organization, and rituals we call Christianity.''[3] There are the legions who analyze and prescribe the constitutional and statutory conditions of political-religious separation in contemporary Western countries. But there is little in our literature—unless it is written from an explicitly religious position: Maritain, Yves Simon, Reinhold Niebuhr, Voegelin when he is least idiosyncratic—that attempts to get to the heart of the matter.

I take the heart of the matter to be the character of religious conviction publicly expressed, the character of secular and civic conviction, the manifold crossings of these effects, and the manifold distinctions among them. This problematic or core of interest is generated from conviction and gains public significance by the aggregated convictions that appear in collective practices, positive institutions, and social structures. In other words, while "behavior" in politics or "experience" in religion are not the specific phenomena on which we want to focus, they are, in a sense, our necessary points of departure. Also, we should avoid confusing political-religious relations with the literal normative status of existing rules and institutions in either sphere, although we will wish to study their tension. Broadly speaking, we shall be dealing in such tender as functions, goals, collaborations, hostilities, dichotomies, tradeoffs, misunderstandings, and the like. Amid these complexities we shall be trying to construct an understanding of the "citizen" and the "believer."

Two fundamental theoretical assumptions separate these profiles. The first of these is the common enough notion, elucidated by Durkheim, that religion, if it means anything at all, is the sphere of the *sacred* (supernatural, transempirical, etc.), while politics, at least when it is not committing lofty transgressions, would seem to lie in the realm of the *profane* (mundane, natural, perishable). The second is that of the famous nineteenth-century cleavage of *man* and *citizen* (prefigured by Rousseau's indictment of modernity), which would appear to vault religious practice and belief out of the explicit public or civic space and lodge it, together with a host of other societal activities, in a differentiated and, so to speak, private or depoliticized nexus of relations. Karl Mannheim, for instance, writes of "the gradual *recession into privacy* of certain spheres previously public (the spheres of life in which personal and religious feelings prevail)" as being "in the nature of a compensation for the increasing rationalization of public life in general—in the workshop, in the market-place, in politics, etc."[4] These issues will be taken up in greater detail in the course of the essay. Still, they need to be mentioned at the outset because they underscore obstacle of both definition and historical analysis in our exploration.

This essay will be restricted to the American experience, and that only selectively. Although politics and religion are universal concepts that frequently make universal claims, we can no longer profitably study their connection *urbi et orbi*. The first great theorist of American institutions Alexis de Tocqueville was astonished by the fertilization that politics had received from religion, and he opened up numerous vistas on the subject. A century and a half later, certain features of American life—among which I would include its qualities of sectarianism, shallow religiosity, secularization, and civic privatism—favor the experiment I intend to conduct. Moreover, a great deal of work has been done on American religion. To unite the substance of that work with political theory is almost in itself a religious challenge if we agree with William James in describing the religious dimension of life as "the art of winning the favor of the gods."[5]

This chapter began with the theme of religion in ruins—laid low by politics. That of course happened in old Europe and not in the New World, in a site and circumstance far from our national experience. But there is a growing tendency in America to glimpse ruins, if not to venerate them. Religious vigor, variously dissected by Tocqueville and many successors, may be among the ruins. Indeed, political vigor—a far more controversial case—may itself be passing into decline. Whether or not this is so and however it may be happening, ruins in America seem to be created by a rather different process than the gutted but enshrined monuments of Europe. Invaders have not ravaged our territory except in brief instances (we have little more to mention than the first city of Washington, the Alamo, and the U.S.S. *Arizona*). Civil strife has done better, but its primary leavings are consecrated battlefields, and rarely ruins. Our ruins tend to be the skeletal remains of hasty habitation, overgrown by the forest or neglected by the redeveloper. Our spiritual and conceptual ruins are of a similar order, shelters abandoned in the headlong trek of what Louis Hartz has described as a "culture of flight"[6]—flight along the "American road," variously symbolized by the Cumberland Trail, the "pony express," Herbert Hoover's speeches, or the once-famous novel by Jack Kerouac. Perhaps today this frustrated questing has brought a fatigue to our restlessness and raised our consciousness of native ruins.

Europeans perceived them earlier. On a journey through upstate New York Tocqueville recalls reaching "the shores of a lake which was embosomed in forests coeval with the world" and discovering "a small island" that "formed one of those delightful solitudes of the New World, which almost led civilized man to regret the haunts of the savage" and where he was "far from supposing that this spot had ever been inhabited, so completely did Nature seem to be left to herself." He found one Indian canoe. But at the center of the island he stumbled upon a European's desolated cabin, with a fallen chimney, a blackened hearth, and "the very props . . . intertwined with living verdure." "I stood," he relates, "for some time in silent admiration of the resources of nature and the littleness of man; and when I was obliged to leave that enchanting solitude, I exclaimed with sadness: 'Are ruins, then, already here?'"[7]

The text seems especially poignant because of its placement in the chapter entitled "Causes Which Maintain Democracy," for a principal cause of that, in Tocqueville's opinion, was religion. A ruined religion could lead to a ruined social order, to the democratic tyranny that Tocqueville feared. But this sophisticated visitor needed only a few moments' reflection to conclude that man inevitably leaves ruins in his wake, even in the depths of the primeval forest. No locale is exempt from these fatalities. The tumbled-down cabin, turned into a bower of wild shrubs, was neither Volney's "solitary ruins . . . sacred tombs, and silent walls" whose "presence appalls and chills the souls of tyrants with electric horror and remorse,"[8] nor was it the trampled vestiges of Port-Royal, but it was melancholy—a melancholy still to be mortgaged by a century of optimism. That century has now fallen due. It may be time, guided by Tocqueville's sober and comprehending spirit, to revive the problematic of religion and politics in a democracy along certain lines he could discern and others he could not foresee, for he did not, as another distinguished observer, Harold J. Laski, uncharitably put it, "[write] less with his mind than with his heart" on this issue.[9] Following other writers—notably Montesquieu and Rousseau—he posed questions that still await an answer and opened lines of inquiry that continue to command respect.[10]

We need here to say something more general about religion, politics, and their interconnection. It is consonant with the scope of this inquiry that most of the following will be slanted toward Judaeo-Christianity and Western politics, although I do not intend, as yet, to deal in narrower institutional categories. Church and state are relatively venerable Western institutions that developed mutual identities and relationships from the late Middle Ages on.[11] They are the vehicles within which, for the most part, our religious and political practices have taken place. Most of the exceptions can also be explained with reference to them: revolution is antistatism; antinomianism and sectarianism are antiecclesiastical. However, religion and politics are positively primeval activities in the life of the species. By contrast, church and state are historical and territorial instances of the wider notions. To deal consequently with our own experience, we are committed to analyzing specific institutional forms and not simply recognizing types of universal activity. But I wish to begin here with some observations on the general nature of religion and politics.

In dealing with religion I shall leave open the question of whether it is "true," in what sense it might be true, and—except by way of neutral discussion—its connection with a world beyond our immediate knowledge. My position is simply that religion is pervasive and important—too important to be treated theoretically as a deceit or a delusion demanding deliberate exorcism. Therefore when I cite atheists or apologists it will be to promote some interpretation, never for the sake of proving or disproving the existence of the divine. No doubt the majority of scholars writing about religion today—sociologists and anthropologists as well as engaged theologians or ecclesiologists—have a curiosity and respect for religious belief even though they may not share that belief. Tocqueville, to whom we shall refer often, was such a person: a formal, nonpracticing, highly skeptical Catholic with an obvious admiration for some aspects of Protestantism. But there were also Marx and Freud, who minced no words about their repudiation of religious values.[12]

In my general overview of religion, I shall dwell on three spheres where it would seem to operate with stubborn enracination: as a justification and consolation for the most wrenching human tragedies and, especially, the doom of mortality;[13] as a guide to one's dignity of place and meaning in the cosmos, especially in view of personal inadequacy and the need of expiation; and as a primary bond of social cohesiveness, usually expressed in rituals or ceremonies that link human beings with one another and with the sacred.[14]

The first of these points would seem to need little elaboration. Man, alone among the creatures of nature, knows he must die. As between man and animal, Edgar Morin writes, forethought of death is the occasion for "a rupture far more astonishing than the tool, the brain, or the power of speech."[15] "Man," writes Unamuno, "is an animal that preserves his dead."[16] However, Christian theology, for example, conveys to believers the message that death is not only the end of worldly life but an end in the sense of accomplishment: " . . . the dissolution which brings mutable and mortal things to their death is not so much a process of annihilation as a progress toward something they were designed to become."[17] Tocqueville is penetrated by this perception:

> Man alone, of all created beings, displays a natural contempt of existence, and yet a boundless desire to exist; he scorns life, but he dreads annihilation. . . . Religion, then, is simply another form of hope, and it is no less natural to the human heart than hope itself. . . . Unbelief is an accident, and faith is the only permanent state of mankind.[18]

It should be noted that Tocqueville immediately warns that religion forfeits its inexhaustible strength, "risks that authority which is rightfully its own," when it strikes bargains with the temporal power and attracts to itself the enmity of all who oppose that power. Yet we must, I think, be especially careful to distinguish between religion's facilitation of contact between the sacred and the mundane (which inescapably touches politics) and its transgression of the sacred at the behest of the profane. If death is indeed the ultimate problem that we call upon the sacred to resolve, it may also be understood as a constant mundane happening. This is why, at a watershed of Western thought, the *Encyclopedia* of Diderot and d'Alembert considered death under two discourses, the rubrics of theology and natural history.[19]

   The conjugation between the mystery (and perhaps horror) of death and its inescapable social and worldly presence is well expressed by the sociologist Peter Berger:

> Death radically challenges *all* socially objectified definitions of reality—of the world, of others, and of self. Death radically puts in question the taken-for-granted, "business-as-usual" attitude in which one exists in every day life. . . . Insofar as the knowledge of death cannot be avoided in any society, legitimations of the reality of the social world *in the face of death* are decisive requirements in any society. The importance of religion in such legitimations is obvious.[20]

He goes on to add: "The power of religion depends, in the last resort, upon the credibility of the banners it puts in the hands of men as they stand before death, or more accurately, as they walk, inevitably, toward it."[21] Berger's insight, stated by others in different ways, prepares us for the important notions of social function and legitimation. Suffice it for now to note that religion is preeminently the mode of life that deals with death and severe affliction in both the private and the public spheres. While it is quite true that death can be neglected or "bracketed," it can never be completely ignored. As Pascal wrote

against the *libertins:* "Men, since they could find no cure for death
. . . determined, so as to make themselves happy, not to reflect on it
at all."[22] But, as Solzhenitsyn reminded us recently: "If humanism
were right in declaring that man is born only to be happy, he would
not be born to die."[23] It is not the common lot of men and societies
to be able to sustain happiness.

Religion would also seem to provide for a sector of the symbolic
language and expressiveness of human beings, a widened access for
their sense of worth and a glimpse of true worth.[24] It snatches meaning as well as man from the threat of annihilation. In some sense, this
could be regarded as the positive complement of the consolation
given for empirical annihilation. The proper reference here is, I think,
to something stronger than, say, Emerson's intuitive vision of natural
harmony or William James's "testing of religion by practical common
sense and the empirical method [which leaves] it in possession of its
towering place in history."[25] It is further still from John Dewey's
"criticism of the commitment of religion to the supernatural"[26] and
reduction of it to an "attitude" that is an "effect produced [by a]
better adjustment in life and its conditions, not the manner and cause
of its productions."[27] If *supernatural* is a suspect word, let us call
this notion of religion ineffable or extraordinary, without destroying
the connection between mundane event and higher modes of perceiv-
ing reality. As Clifford Geertz writes: "The religious perspective dif-
fers from the commonsensical in that . . . it moves beyond the
realities of everyday life to wider ones which correct and complete
them. Its defining concern, moreover, is not action upon those wider
realities but acceptance of them, faith in them."[28] Moreover, according to his famous definition:

> Religion is a system of symbols which acts to establish powerful, per-
> suasive, and long-lasting moods and motivations in men by formulating
> conceptions of a general order of existence and clothing these concep-
> tions with such an aura of factuality that the moods and motivations
> seem uniquely realistic.[29]

This I take to be akin to Paul Tillich's famous association of religion
with "matters of ultimate concern."[30] "Religion as ultimate concern," Tillich writes, "is the meaning-giving substance of culture, and
culture is the totality of forms in which the basic concern of religion
expresses itself: religion is the substance of culture, culture is the
form of religion."[31] My preferred emphasis would be on Geertz's
"powerful symbols" and not on Tillich's totality of "culture," which

is at the same time too vague and too imperializing. The unmodified linkage of religion and culture (abstract as these words are) legitimately gives rise to Hannah Arendt's taunt: "I must confess that the notion that one can or ought to organize religion as an institution only because one likes to have a culture has always appeared to me as rather funny."[32] Quite clearly, in our own time religion and culture are not exactly running the same footrace. This does not, however, mean that Tillich's indication of their form of interaction is wrong.

In some sense, ultimacy of concern comes back to symbolic acts and structures of belief that reconcile us with events beyond our control: much of the tension of culture is born from this experience. In some beautifully crafted words, Michael Oakeshott affirms that religion as a dialectical meaning-system rises above even the assuagement of guilt and the pain of death:

> While religious faith may be recognized as a solace for misfortune and as a release from the fatality of wrongdoing, its central concern is with a less contingent dissonance in the human condition: namely, the hollowness, the futility of that condition, its character of being no more than "un voyage au bout de la nuit." What is sought in religious belief is not merely consolation for woe or deliverance from the burden of sin, but a reconciliation to nothingness.[33]

This impressively states the theme of "ultimate concern." Though the level of analysis in the present essay is not designed to deal with what Oakeshott calls "aventures . . . encounters with eternity,"[34] it might be added here that if religion amounts to a "reconciliation to nothingness," politics would appear to be a "reconciliation to facticity." As we spiral downward to less lofty things, we shall begin to discover ways in which these two "reconciliations" themselves manage or fail to be reconciled.

This starts to become evident the moment we take up our third issue: religion as linchpin of social cohesiveness. For here, partly because of a shift in emphasis away from experiences most easily grasped as personal, and partly because of a displacement of the question from the metaphysical why to the instrumental how, religion, too, approaches facticity, and in so doing, approaches politics as a system implementing behavior. At very least, we are distanced from the notion of isolated acts of communication between the believer and the divine; we have forsaken—and I think properly—William James's definition of religion as "the feelings, acts, and experiences of individual men in their solitude."[35] Whether or not solitude is the supreme access to the religious mode of being, and despite the fact that "privatism" infects a good deal of Christianity today, our present perspective raises issues that are mostly germane to collective life. The "inner life" certainly depends on contacts with the "inter-life." We should not, however, confuse a perspective with a dogmatic equation of the human, the religious, and the social.

The Christian churches have always been highly self-aware of their role as vicariously or spontaneously operating sources of social definition and behavioral control through initiations, interdictions, power, and persuasion. The modern difference is that what was once assumed—and given divine sanction even if its consequences were crudely political and mundane—became problematic with the waning of the spiritual power, the disintegration of *sacerdotium,* and the rise of secular criticism. By the eighteenth century Montesquieu declared that he would write about religion not as a "théologien" but as an "écrivain politique,"[36] and he was of course neither the first nor the boldest to have done so (after all, Marsiglio's *Defensor Pacis* dates from 1324). It is, however, only in the late seventeenth century that a critical view of religion, apart from its truth content, as a socially *useful* institution began to preoccupy the intellectuals. Bayle greatly stimulated the debate by asserting that atheists might be as useful citizens of a commonwealth as Christians (after all, even Machiavelli had acknowledged the pragmatic contribution of religion to civic virtue, *so long as it was not Christian).* The beginnings of the comparative study of religions (Voltaire and Montesquieu) did much of the rest.

It took a rather higher degree of specialization and momentum in the social sciences, and a wider context of secularization than the Enlightenment afforded, for religion to receive a treatment largely disburdened of the priest vs. *philosophe* controversies of that age. Durkheim assiduously studied Montesquieu as a "forerunner of sociology" in his 1892 *thèse complémentaire* for the University of Bordeaux and found him wanting in rigor and positivism.[37] Paradoxically, it seemed that the supremacy of the scientific approach could allow religion to be redeemed as a cardinal element of social theory, if not as a living part of the educated man's understanding of his own universe. Proper methods of inquiry and detachment allowed agnostics to "get inside" religion: it was understood that religion should not get inside the inquirer. The nonbeliever Durkheim was able to define religion as "a unified system of beliefs and practices relative to sacred things . . . which unite into one single moral community . . . all those who adhere to them"[38] and as "a system of ideas with which the individuals represent to themselves the society of which they are members, and the obscure but intimate relations which they have with it."[39] If it was true of so-called primitive societies that religion could be regarded as the centerpiece of social solidarity, what of complex modern societies? It is largely this problem that later led Talcott Parsons, whose theorizing was much in debt to Durkheim, to rebalance the construction by asserting that "society is a religious phenomenon."[40] This was also, in part, a Weberian response. Weber had made religious conviction important in his models of authority and his notion of a "calling." Durkheim had made social groups into totemic objects. Parsons was concerned with what religion did for a social system and referred religious symbols away from concrete structures toward "aspects of 'reality' significant to human life and experience, yet outside the range of scientific observation and analysis."[41] This move, together with Parsons's assignment of religion to a paramount place in what he designated a "cultural system," suggests the general tendencies of the "structural-functional" approach and has certain connections with the descriptive theories of Geertz and Tillich mentioned earlier.

The purpose here is obviously not to canvass the history of the sociology of religion, of which I have given only the most truncated *aperçus,* but to suggest the generation of a secular body of theory that, in the waning of theology, has endowed religion with new credentials and new weapons. Most of all, I want to suggest that the "reality" (implying indestructibility) of religion as an indispensable social practice and symbolic system received support from a redoubtable body of scholars, although they scarcely went unchallenged by other powerful intellectual groups. Parsons's frequently complacent assertions regarding the integrative functions of religion in contemporary society, accelerated social "differentiation" notwithstanding,[42] led to damning retorts by other sociologists like Berger: *"The social irrelevance of the religious establishment is its functionality. . . .* It is functional precisely to the degree in which it is passive rather than active, acted upon rather than acting. It is in this capacity that it meets many important psychological needs of the individual."[43] Berger's point, and that of his sometime collaborator, Thomas Luckmann, was that "differentiation" has not affirmed the social strength of religion but has compressed and "privatized" it into a constricted sphere where isolated individuals "consume" sacred values like merchandise by comparison shopping among the denominations, or else construct their own systems of meaning.[44]

I have not taken up the manifold capacities of religion to express and sustain social cohesion through ritual and ceremony, for the point seems obvious and the catalogue endless. These phenomena may be extremely public and flamboyant (like the "baroque Christianity" studied by Ariès, Chaunu, Vovelle, and others)[45] or comparatively simple and muted (like a fundamentalist Protestant baptism), they may be as austere as a novena or as raucous as a camp meeting, but they have been a constant of most history. I would simply make one special point here. It might seem that in contemporary Western culture the meaningfulness of public observances was diminishing, with religion becoming privatized and ritual secularized. Indeed I take this to be true. Yet it is possible that the religious base of collective ceremony is merely hidden from our eyes because we have not been looking for the right religion. At least the Durkheimian-Parsonian notion of religion as the core of a society's meaning system has flourished with new vigor in the writings of men like Sidney Mead and Robert Bellah. Religion has done this essentially by inhabiting a common space with politics. Mead explicitly followed the theoretical interpretations of Parsons, but far more prescriptively. For Mead the traditional denominations were just as hostile to healthy norms of society as Berger would claim them to be, but the true "meaning system" was reinforced and legitimated by the kind of Enlightenment deism or theism professed by Jefferson and other founders, a "religion of the republic."[46] Bellah then trumped Mead to claim the heretofore veiled existence and potency of an "American civil religion," thereby providing the focus for much lively controversy over the past decade and a half.[47] Since we shall return to these matters at much greater length, it is appropriate here only to point out that the notion of religion as a binding and value-giving force is alive. Whether it is well in the "polity" is problematic. It is evidently not so in the traditional denominations, where faith seems increasingly muddled and shallow. It has taken on renewed vigor in the sects and in cults outside specific Judaism or Christianity.

I shall spend less time on politics, since its major properties are more familiar to most readers. Indeed, I shall dwell rather exclusively on those features of politics that appear to concern the present discussion most directly, taking as my point of departure our own radical disjunction between religion and politics, which has not been eternally the case in human societies. Put more simply, I shall be speaking of politics *for us*.

It seems to me, first of all, that there can be no vital dispute over the "truth" of politics in the same sense that there seemed to be one over religion. There can only really be disputes about the truth of kinds of politics. Of course religious practice is not less a fact than political activity. But the validation of politics in general proceeds directly from the fact that its conduct, institutions, and rationale lie within the *profane* sphere and in a civilization that takes (or acts as if it takes) that sphere to be the highest reality. This omnipresence of politics compels us to acknowledge its "truth" or even to seek for truth in it.

Politics is the principal and ultimate control system in the realm of the *profane,* just as religion is in the realm of the *sacred.* The former assertion is certainly less tautological than the latter, for in the sphere of the sacred religion would appear to have no competitors except for naturalistic ethics, aesthetic joy, or obscure "atheistic theologies," in brief, according to one of our established uses of the word, "humanisms." It could plausibly be argued that to deny religion is to deny the sacred. However this may be, no such statement would hold with politics, for it occupies only a portion of the profane or mundane sphere of thought and activity. The reality or necessity of politics may be denied, as by anarchists, without in the least threatening the existence of the profane: other human institutions or instincts, redeemed from the shackles of authoritative control, would then somehow provide for the ongoingness of life in common. The sacred need not enter into the picture at all unless one insists on the "deification of society" and uses Durkheimian images to describe a hypothetical condition at the antipodes of the one that was Durkheim's speculative point of departure. A good deal of this manipulation, I would argue, depends on the deeply enrooted myth that what was once primitively undifferentiated, integral, and "just" can again become so at a level of extraordinary complexity.[48] Even if this were true—which we may be permitted to doubt—politics would need to be the midwife of the new birth and would indeed become "another form of hope," the phrase Tocqueville used to describe religion. Politics—perhaps the "great politics" of Nietzsche—would be the royal carpet of the human prince that rolled itself up with the sovereign's tread and vanished.

At present, however, politics is the principal control system of the *profane.* Another clarification is needed here, for it will be instantly observed that, ancient cosmogonic politics aside,[49] political forms are known to us that have claimed not only to regulate but to embody the sacred: Constantinian empire, divine kingship, Mazzinian democracy, and (somewhat less coherently) the Third Reich. But we are attempting to speak here of the reality of politics, not its terrible pretensions. The pretensions were themselves political. Neither King James I nor, for that matter, King David asserted his sacral authority in order to replace Jehovah; they did so in order to rule their countries with an ultimate form of legitimacy that even the semiprofane or institutionalized agents of religion would not be able to challenge.[50] Usurping the vestments of the sacred to dazzle the multitude and prevail over all competing authority has not been an uncommon happening in the profane world.

In whatever form we study it, politics is presumed to be preservative—the technique of maintaining the state or commonwealth—regardless of the sometimes disastrous outcome of particular policies. Politics is of course an arena of winners and losers, often playing for incredibly high stakes. Moreover, as it is said, the winners write history and in a manner to assert that the losers were depraved and foolish. And we may be certain that politics is often a slaughterbench. But this is not its major tendency or purpose despite the intractable evidence of international relations. In theory at least, whether we refer to the polis, to the patriarchal kingdom, to the Hobbesian state, or to the constitutional democracy, the notion of the preservation of the whole stands out. The means legitimated to achieve this vary widely, as do the judgments regarding the priority of what or who is worth saving in order that the whole may survive. And of course this in itself provides a vast enough area for grave disputes and even civil strife, for those disputes affect not only persons and ranks, goods and territory, forms and functions but also the self-images and values of those who compose the whole. Still, the purpose of politics is to preserve these things, according to the prevailing priority, in the sphere of the profane. Its purpose is not to save souls; though souls were often "saved" by the performance of political acts in bygone times, we should not forget that the sale of indulgences was one of the factors that triggered the breakup of the *respublica christiana*. Neither is it the purpose of politics to "save the world" in some transcendental sense; it is, more humbly but more realistically, to maintain the profane world in being.

Liberal government, with its Christian-Stoic natural law antecedents and its extension toward political and social democracy, confronted the *political* problem of preservation in a radically new ordering of priorities. It proceeded not only from the idea of the preservation of the whole but that of the "preservation of all" in the profane sphere, a notion for various reasons downplayed by the city-state, feudal, and absolutist mentalities.[51] This may in part be accounted for by a shift in ground between the sacred and the profane: despite some ancient texts to the contrary, it had been previously held with far greater conviction that persons could be "preserved" in the next world or in the glory of the annals of their city.[52] The political responsibility of "preserving all," gradually expanded and worked out in the course of centuries, led of course to countless humane reforms, to a cherished dignity of the human person embodied in laws and constitutions and in a "softening of manners," and to a condition that many, at least until recent times, could unblushingly call "civilization." The profane indeed took on many of the burdens of the sacred, while remaining distinct from it (except in occasional texts like Rousseau's famous *Social Contract*, IV, viii, one really has no difficulty in distinguishing blasphemy from treason—though the *ancien régime* had a category of divine *lèse-majesté*—or damnation from deprivation of civic rights—though Roman law had provided a category of *mors civilis*).

The perplexity or tragedy of the great liberal achievement is twofold: it failed to prevent intolerable carnage in which it was not clear that the resolution to preserve "all" had much to do with preserving the whole, hence an emergency resort to tougher creeds; and it produced ever-expanding material demands by the "all" (first the middle, then the working classes) in view of a comfortable preservation, it developed an economic system that, while catering to these needs, stimulated an acute sense of social injustice over the distribution of the preservative surplus, and it then overloaded the state by multiplying claims centers and ideologies.

Politics is, accordingly, a system of preservative control operating in the here and now. It is not in danger of "compromising with the world"; its danger lies in disfiguring the world. Its preservative control may be understood in the basically negative sense of seeing to it that a certain range of destructive and unlawful acts do not take place or are duly punished with empirical penalties (which might include reprimand and probation as well as fines or incarceration or loss of life). The idea here is to protect some from others. The element of authoritative coercion distinguishes politics from other systems of preservation, such as ethical suasion, charitable distributions, and the healing arts. But politics is also a competition of those who aspire to control the system, and the biases of the control. Hence the politics of "free governments" necessarily contains a dialectic between the functions of preserving some from others and of preserving "all" from the preservers, usually rationalized in constitutional guarantees and their mechanisms of redress. A third possibility is that the "whole" might need to be preserved from agitations among the "all" (to recur to Rousseau's dilemma of actualizing the general will), but this is a prospect clearly out of sorts with democratic ideology, where the largest part of the "all" is said to represent the whole. That is the democratic problem; the liberal problem is concerned with preserving each of the "all" from the whole.

Preservative political control may also be understood affirmatively as the stimulation of the parts of the whole to actions and a division of labor that benefit and strengthen the whole. The poles of this enterprise are individual self-realization and national power. The correspondence between these individualistic and holistic conceptions of politics is obscure: they may be, and often are in our discourse, seen as antithetical values, or they may be linked by the purposefulness of intermediary structures. Citizenship in pluralistic societies is complicated by this kind of dilemma. As Harold Laski wrote more than half a century ago: "[The nation] no longer enfolds and absorbs the allegiance of the individual; his loyalties are as diverse as his experiences of life."[53] There is no ready theoretical answer; empirical politics as a control system oscillates in the middle range, at best "settling" but never "solving" the issue. On the face of it, the problem appears to resemble the religious one, where individual salvation and collective providence are often either opposed or mediated through church organization and discipline. The difference is that politics is entirely of this world.

While politics is not strictly reducible to power (i.e., not all political action is power-seeking), theorists of justice would do well to conjure with power in even their ideal formulations if they are serious about "taking men as they are."[54] Yet if politics is to mean anything more than the "tough" side of the human character, it is equally inadequate to make power the central issue and great folly to try to measure politics as power. This is not simply a recalcitrant idealism. If power is the coin of the realm, the immediate consequence is a behavioral reductionism that makes any act of power political.[55] And that is nonsense, for it completely collapses all distinctions between the public and the private: child-beating is then as political an activity as ratifying a constitution. Power cannot be ignored (any more than it can be in religion, where it is likely that the metaphor originated), but it should be balanced, as it was, for example, in Montesquieu's *De l'esprit des lois,* against other elements, even at the risk of some conceptual messiness.

We turn next to general conditions of political and religious interaction, some of which have been hinted at in the previous remarks. This summary can be introduced with reference to two axes: (1) conflict-collaboration; and (2) conviction-organization. Reference to them will underlie and reinforce my treatment of other categories. Briefly put, there are historical and cultural situations where religious and political values or the institutions in which they are embodied are in relative harmony or in relative collision. There may even, in some situations, be something approaching a center of indifference. At the same time, there is an enduring tension in both politics and religion between the belief systems of the loyal and the faithful ("citizens" and "believers") and the positive structures in which conviction is mobilized and organized for worldly action. This tension is, to be sure, far greater in the religious sphere, where extramundane feelings must be adjusted to mundane controls. But it is not absent from politics whenever gaping disparities between values and institutions occur; hence the production of utopias or the resort to rebellion (once couched in the phrase "appeal to heaven"). Moreover, in secularized times, where much of the literal coercion has been removed from pluralized or privatized religion, the tensions in politics may be correspondingly greater.[56]

Some of these relationships are canvassed in a threefold descriptive typology by J. Milton Yinger.[57] In Yinger's first classification, religion and politics tend to be mutually reinforcing. The beliefs and practices of the former help to socialize individuals to common norms, to inhibit crime, to reduce tensions caused by the pursuit of scarce goods, and even to curtail the oppressiveness of rulers (cf. the function of religion in Montesquieu's "despotism"). Yinger suggests that this scheme is most typical of stable primitive societies, but its residues are found even in "mobile and complex" ones. As we have seen, it is on precisely this point that the critics of functionalism have unloaded some of their bluntest language because they believe that "the integrative function of religion" is simply a disguise for its passivity, its thralldom to materialistic and unjust values. As Harold Laski wrote of America a generation ago: "The pervasiveness of the Churches . . . comes in large degree from the subtle compromise they have made with the world rather than from a defiant proclamation of their doctrine. They have not been able seriously to compete with the growing secularization of American life."[58]

In Yinger's second classification, we find "societies where social differentiation and social change are important." Here, the "integrative relationship" is disturbed, characteristically by the secular rulers who seek to use religion for their purposes, turning it into an added means of political coercion. Still, Yinger perceives functional controls to this experience, because it is impossible to achieve a consummate *Gleichschaltung* between politics and religion without destroying the usefulness of the latter. The result, then, is a compromise tilted toward the secular: the religion learns to live with "a *selective* application of its doctrines . . . emphasizing those that enhance the power of the rulers." This would seem to be a quite accurate description of Protestant Erastianism or Japanese Shinto; it covers less well the complicated situation of Catholicism, where a temporal ruler has also been spiritual pontiff of a transnational *ecclesia*.

Finally, there may be a sharp cleavage between religion and politics. As Yinger points out, the founders of the great world religions and their immediate successors either propounded radical solutions to life without reference to politics or claimed the allegiance of persons in such a way as to contradict political requirements.

What is one to make of these classifications for present purposes? One striking feature about them is that from today's vantage point they do little to clarify the empirical situation: interpretations of American religion in the context of politics partake of all three of them. The first strategy is "to leave traditional doctrine understated and, wherever possible, unmentioned . . . because [this] leads to a minimization of religious differences and promotes what Martin Marty terms [pejoratively] the fourth great American religious faith, 'religion-in-general.'"[59] This creates at least the semblance of an integrative religion that, while neither deep nor demanding, can live with politics and even perhaps give it some moral tone. The second strategy is that of the "American civil religion," at least in its most Erastian interpretation, *"the transcendent universal religion of the nation."*[60] As for the cleavage with politics, it can transpire along two entirely different lines: withdrawal and challenge. The tone of withdrawal is well conveyed as follows:

> One of the world's oldest axioms is that radical ideas suffer the translation from ideology to practice. The very fact that contemporary religion is little involved in that translation may mean that it is better able to maintain its integrity in serving the no less valuable function of providing new insights and nurturing old truths beyond the arena of politics.[61]

Challenge we may find variously contained in the "prophetic" side of civil religion developed by Bellah in writings subsequent to his famous article, especially in his book *The Broken Covenant,* in some of the "new breed" writings, and in the acerbic books of Peter Berger, who claimed that it was impossible to identify American values with the Christian faith.[62]

The distinctions between politics and religion, starkly expressed in the concepts *sacred* and *profane*, are conceptually quite clear. But it has emerged from the previous discussion that the literal line of demarcation is in fact blurred. The most obvious reason for this is that there are overlapping concerns in the behavioral control of persons or groups, in justice and punishment, and in cultural definition. In these enterprises the two forces may be collaborative, as when Pilate (reluctantly) had Jesus scourged and executed at the behest of the Jewish religious authorities or when Jeanne d'Arc was delivered by the civil power to the ecclesiastical bonfire. At moments in history, politics and religion have shared the load (religion being more commonly responsible for education, public morals, and records keeping in addition to the supervision of worship and care of souls); frequently religion loaned personnel to politics (the Carolingian clerks, Wolsey, Richelieu, Mazarin, Loménie de Brienne, Gioberti, Archbishop Makarios) although, at least in Christendom, the reverse was not usually the case.[63]

Religion and politics have also, over the centuries, been staunchly competitive, not only because they sought to exercise power in disputed territory but also because their world visions were not the same. Guelphs and Ghibellines were the symbols of this rivalry. The case was especially true when the controllers of either the sacred or the profane reformed themselves or were shaken internally. In both the "age of faith" and the later embattled period of "church and state" we have countless illustrations, so many that essential collaborations sometimes go unperceived. In today's world of disestablished, pluralized, and secularized religion, the linkage of formidable *credenda* like science with the state and with the profane order in general has caused a clash in what have been called "plausibility structures."[64] The competition is now one-sided—even in the sphere of public morals—making it altogether proper to call religion "decadent" if that world is intended in a neutral sense. Yet even in secularist times it is quite obvious that religion possesses three major assets that give it competitive strength or collaborative value: a considerable host of believers whose sensitivities politics cannot ignore; an access to "ultimate concern" that politics (*pace* our handful of intellectual polis-enthusiasts) cannot claim; and a residual power of legitimation that is very useful to politics.

In *Democracy in America* Tocqueville wrote: "For my own part, I doubt whether man can ever support at the same time complete religious independence and entire political freedom. And I am inclined to think that if faith be wanting in him, he must be subject; and if he be free, he must believe."[65] Since I intend to deal more thoroughly with the issue of faith and freedom later, I shall use the passage here to introduce two other issues. The first is that religion and politics have a complementarity and a rivalry not only as control systems but as sources or stimulants of conviction. This occurs both through the private communication of symbols and messages and through the public profession of creeds, oaths, or other articles of belief. In the case of politics we call the effect loyalty or patriotism; in the case of religion we call it faith or piety. Whatever may be said about the radical distinction between sacred and profane, it is likely that these mechanisms of conviction obey a similar logic, although the religious is probably the more powerful. The clash of these convictions can lead to situations of relentless tragedy (cf. Antigone and Creon). Coupled, they will be redoubtable. Much of the fervor of modern nationalism has fed from the twin sources, often in an abusive way.[66] In Jacksonian America Tocqueville saw a groundwork of religious conviction supporting a free, though often small-minded, politics that was relatively passive toward it. He might well have mentioned the reverse possibility, for he was to record some of its effects indelibly in his souvenirs of the 1848 revolution. Cases of "conviction organized" have rocked the world many times.

Second, Tocqueville also seems to suggest in the passage cited that faith has a function in liberating the person not only for a life of hope but from the need for a repressive politics: the control of the secular authority is a harsher bondage than the discipline of faith. This recalls Montesquieu's interesting hypothesis: "Since both religious and civil laws should principally contribute to making men good citizens, we can see that when one of the two strays from its goal, the other should be more firmly fastened on it: the less religion disciplines (sera réprimante), the more the civil laws ought to."[67] The question of the inverse proportionality between religious and political control (or, if one likes, repression)—which of course assumes theoretically that human beings cannot outgrow the need for control—is interesting enough to be pursued more deliberately than has been done to date. Modern evidence suggests that political intervention increases where the quality of public discipline falters in family, church, or school. But the matter is difficult to get a handle on, if only because of the incompatibilities of the profane and the sacred. At very least, it would prove to be ironical if the lapse of human control in those centers where people are most familiar with each other and united in common tasks of instilling and acquiring learning and morals turned the commonwealth into a distant, despotic guardian of perpetual minors and suppliants.

Montesquieu, writing as an "écrivain politique," seems to be exclusively concerned with religious "positivity," not with the autonomy of the believer and the believer's moral capacities for self-control. His concern is with how religion contributes to citizenship, not salvation. This comes out very clearly in his argument against Bayle (and, by implication, Machiavelli):

> [Bayle] dares maintain that true Christians would not form a durable state. Why not? They would be citizens totally enlightened about their duties and very zealous in performing them; they would be well aware of the rights of national defense; the more they thought they owed to religion, the more they would think they owed to their country (patrie). Being engraved in the heart, the principles of Christianity would be immeasurably stronger than that false honor of monarchies, those human virtues of republics, and that servile fear of despotic states.[68]

Is the skeptical Montesquieu being serious about all this? Most assuredly so: "He who has no religion at all is that terrible animal who can only feel his freedom when he is destroying and devouring."[69] Though Montesquieu's expectation of liberty is never complacent, his attachment to it is profound. And for him "the peoples of the North have and will always have a spirit of independence and liberty denied to the peoples of the South."[70] The peoples of the North are Protestant; those of the South, Catholic. Obviously Protestantism did not make the Northerners what they are, but it befits both liberty and the republican experience, that is, it favors virtue. Both Calvinism (closest to the teachings of Christ) and Lutheranism (closest to the deeds of the apostles) are to be admired in this respect.[71] There is no reason to doubt that this hardy statement (published in a country where Protestants were denied legal marriages and civil rights)[72] lies at the base of Tocqueville's favorable assessment of the influence of religion in America (which he perceived as sectarian, though informed by the Puritan spirit). But it must be remembered also that Montesquieu's enthusiasm comes from the perspective of an "écrivain politique," examining the "benefit that one obtains from [religion] in the civil condition."[73] The point is clear: Protestantism can help to make citizens.

In recent times we have been far more exercised to know whether or how Protestantism made capitalists. Since the reign of capitalism has seemed to many to inaugurate a climate hostile to citizenship, Montesquieu's (and Tocqueville's) point is apt to strike one as quaint. However, it is the kind of question raised by contemporary works like Michael Walzer's The Revolution of the Saints, and it was part of a common nineteenth-century assumption by the older settlers of

America, when the Calvinist tradition was not yet the *bête noire* that
it has since become. H. Richard Niebuhr is categorical about this
strength of the Puritans: "They attempted to translate the dialectical
movement of Christian life into a stable, organized synthesis in which
church and state represented the two aspects of Christian society,
sainthood and citizenship, the two directions in personal Christian
life."[74] As is well known, the Calvinist regimes in Massachusetts and
Connecticut were not "theocratic" but secular: the ecclesiastical and
civil governments were not coterminous, although "saints" were presumed to possess indispensable qualities of leadership. "Of all the
governments in the Western world at the time, that of Massachusetts
gave the clergy least authority."[75] Swanson's quantified examination
of forty-one regimes studied *"at the time of their final Reformation
settlement"* discloses that those we would deem today to have the
most expanded public participation (the "balanced" and "heter-
archic"—e.g., New England—types) were virtually all Calvinist.[76]
Other sociologists—e.g., Andreski and Stark—have found Calvinism
hospitable to "civic virtues" while, because of its spiritual temper,
hostile to political excess.[77] In its harshest "Old Light" form Calvinism certainly possessed little of that "douceur" that recommended
the Christian religion to Montesquieu. Neither did its repressive instincts confine themselves to the sacred. But it did favor a structured
politics of involvement that, once liberated from its worst rigidity,
could nourish a proportionate liberty. Parrington's description of Calvinism as "a composite of oriental despotism and sixteenth century
monarchism, modified by the medieval conception of a city-state" is
a polemical caricature.[78] Under Calvinism collaboration was more
pronounced than conflict (although the conflicts have been made famous), and conviction and organization reinforced each other. Politics was, in a sense, possible because religion was far less a private
experience (despite the requirement of "conversion") than a property
of the community.

I would like to take up one other point in conclusion. It is common
in politics for regimes to seek legitimation through an appeal to transcendental values—and not infrequently values associated with the
sacred. If the regime is newly established (e.g., after a revolution),
the appeal serves to fortify its precariousness, justify its novelty, and
create a deeper bond among those who made the new order. If the
regime is old and stable, such an appeal provides prescriptive force to
existing arrangements and cements traditions in the face of periodic
disturbances. Religion is not, of course, the single agent of political
legitimation; Charlemagne and, a thousand years later, Napoleon

were especially anxious to compel popes to coronate them, but this is
not the exclusive method of obtaining authoritative credentials in the
sphere of the profane. Other appeals have been to ancestral custom,
fundamental law, the will of the people, historicist ideology, and so
forth. But behind all these practices there are usually to be found the
ceremony, however slight, and the symbols of sacred investiture. Political rule and conflict must be justified by majesty: glimpses of it are
to be perceived in the toss of the coin at a football game as well as in
the swearing of oaths of office.

Legitimations of this sort cast bridges between the sacred and the
profane systems of control discussed earlier. Despite the retraction
of its claims and powers as a legitimizing source of social practices
in contemporary Western civilization—its gradual cession of these
claims and powers to an abstraction called "society"—religion itself
does not seem to have to be "legitimated," although new religions
must of course be justified as some new and persuasive apprehension
of the divine. But politics—both because it is "profane" and prone to
acts that are morally disreputable—needs a legitimizing source of
strength and receives it most powerfully from the symbolism of the
sacred.

I shall take up the question of legitimation in greater detail ahead,
concentrating here on the historical relationship of the two control
systems in view of the way that legitimation appears to connect them.
When I suggested earlier that the psychological generation of conviction in the spheres of religion and politics bore a resemblance, I was
laying the ground for the hypothesis that they may practice ideological justification by similar kinds of appeals to faith and reason and
that they may even have analogous cycles of strength and weakness
within a given culture. Or it is possible that they represent opaque
sides of the same historical dilemma. In raising this issue I do not
intend to launch our inquiry on a Toynbeean adventure or to conclude—since my conclusion will be pessimistic—that we are simply
dumb brutes drawn to bottomless vortices or mired in implacable epi-
sodes of *longue durée*.

Marx wrote a peculiar sentence to Ruge in 1843: "Just as *religion* is
the catalogue of the theoretical struggles of mankind, so the *political
state* is the catalogue of its practical truths." [79] At this moment Marx
was reaching toward political economy through a critique of Hegel
that used Feuerbachian transformative categories: the words *philosophy* and *class struggle* would shortly replace the key substantives employed here. But we are not concerned with Marx's evolution. We
are interested in his curious juxtaposition of concepts in 1843. The

relation of politics and religion expressed here conveys, albeit from a humanist point of view, the kind of dichotomy suggested by *sacred* and *profane*. Marx was on the verge of committing himself to a "philosophy of *praxis*," but he had not quite arrived at that position. He still could have endorsed Hegel's declaration: "Every day I am more convinced that theoretical work brings more to pass in the world than practical work. Once the realm of thought is revolutionized reality can scarcely hold out."[80] In my earlier discussion of religion I underemphasized the fact that religion had long been the category in which Western man *thought* the world. Marx recognizes this. And since he believes that previous, and especially Hegelian, philosophy is an arcane statement of religion, he can justly regard religion as a text, the prime text, in which man's mind plays out the struggles of existence. Similarly, politics and its embodiment in the state have been the sphere of *doing:* the modern state is a distillation of action, "frozen action" we might say in deference to Marx's later notion of machines as "frozen labor." Marx is, of course, pejorative: he is seeking to abolish the obfuscations that have pertained "up to now." He will replace them with his own interpretation of *thinking* and *doing* and his own vocabulary of concepts. My interpretation, by suggesting that religion is the "control system of the sacred" and politics "the principal control system of the profane," takes this essential Marxian insight back behind Marx.

It seemed to Marx that theology and the Hegelian state were at one in being the theoretical and practical manifestations of an occluded human vision. However, it may be more nearly the case that in Western society religion and politics were detached to the extent that their cycles of conviction, though similar or comparable, were incongruous.[81] This thesis depends on an acknowledgment of both the competitive and collaborative possibilities latent in their institutional forms: both were fountainheads of authority, both managed populations through conviction as well as contrivance, both sustained traditional conduct and assumptions, both played their part in forming the public visage of human society. But to this we may add a discriminating feature: their patterns of ferment, ascent, and decline have not, it seems, taken place concordantly. The most authoritative expansion of religious conviction and its supporting institutions historically preceded the cresting of political authority, which, after the groundwork laid by the centralizing monarchy, occurred in the nineteenth-century nation-state. By this time religious authority had been jolted and religious conviction had itself withdrawn into "civil society."[82] It is not simply that the shrinkage and fragmentation of religion was in part caused by the widened control of politics—which, allowing for complex mediations, is no doubt true—but that politics itself may have been doomed to repeat the experience. In other words, both spheres alike may have been susceptible, though with a lag, to similar challenges to their structure, legitimacy, and morale.

In the first instance, we have become accustomed to calling the process "secularization"; in the second instance, terms like "legitimation crisis" or "crisis of authority" have lately come into fashion.[83] In both cases it is common to speak of apathy or "alienation." Though the "death of God" was already implicit in Feuerbach and *fait accompli* in Nietzsche, no one, to my knowledge, has yet pronounced the "death of Leviathan," even though it has long been a resolute dream of certain liberationists and anarchists. Yet it was Camus, neither a religious believer nor a state worshipper, who proposed the connection between "deicide" and "regicide," to which today's political pessimist might be tempted to add the further stage of "publicide."[84]

Of course, as I have elsewhere argued,[85] there is no evidence that the shell of our public structure—the empirical state—is on the way to disappearing; rather, it would seem to be growing more and more inflated. But it is overloaded with assignments that increase its fragility and cause it to lose respect. The Hellenistic age presented a similar spectacle: a wide but feeble political articulation combined with privatistic attitudes and the multiplication of salvationary sects. The democratic welfare state expresses some of these weaknesses in a changed technological climate. If its liberal-constitutionalist predecessor allowed for some of the conditions in which faith in the sacred was induced, in the superficial sense, to operate in a kind of economic market of civil society and, in a deeper one, to withdraw to the refuge of private feelings, there are some signs that today's *Etat vache à lait* is imposing a similar transformation on the political, fulfilling, but in a bitter and barren way, the visions of system-builders like Auguste Comte.[86] It is also sobering to remember that we live amid, and in the memory of, flagrant examples of the messianic tendencies of nation-building. This is why the destiny of religion is wholly relevant to the destiny of citizenship. If the currents of thought and human discoveries, made available for massive and unreflective daily use that seem to have reduced religion to privatized belief and social pressure-group action, are of the same sort as those that challenge the profane community and the dignity of public life, then both of our institutions (or control systems) that traditionally defined justice, virtue, and other-regardingness are endangered.

Our traditions may mislead us on this point. The implications of what I am proposing clash with the residual hypnosis of both Whig and Marxist historiography, the thought-schemes that continue to shape our politics, govern our vocabularies, and supply our ideals of public conduct. My position argues for a skepticism and a pessimism that are unbecomingly seditious in the company of Western humanism. This is admittedly painful; those values are, for the most part, my own, even though I think that the customary ways of examining them will no longer serve. The notion that history, despite horrors, has been a narrative of the expansion of freedom; that freedom should be essentially defined as the maximalization of security, comfort, and personal choice; that the principal vehicle of freedom has been the progressive domestication of religion and politics (intolerant and coercive by nature) and their probationary release to the guardianship of "society" needs to be examined very critically. This needs to be done not on behalf of "culture" (as against "anarchy," in the sense of Matthew Arnold), nor on behalf of "order" (though an unreflective contempt for order could mean the end of our planet), nor on behalf of "ruling elites" (though these, like the poor, will be always with us), but on behalf of our own intellect and practice.

A respondent might reply that, however well meant, all this is an encouragement to forces that have little love of freedom. I can only refer him to the judicious writings of Tocqueville and to the analysis I shall undertake in the remainder of the essay.

It might also be argued that the notion of a "lag" in the evolutions of religion and politics is a nonsense; that, broadly speaking, Reformation ecclesiology—if not theology—and liberal democratic politics have had intimate and corresponding connections. This is undeniable in a sense. In the final breakup of the *respublica christiana* in the sixteenth century, there were no doubt many common evolutions in religion and politics. This can be shown—although there is contrary evidence, too—in the way that both politics and reformed religion harvested earlier scholastic and juristic themes, not least conciliarism.[87] It scarcely needs to be said again, as a broad generalization, that modern political individualism and the revolt against papal authority are connected. Nor is it any accident that there was an easy passage from scriptural to secular arguments in many of the treatises of the seventeenth century. Congregational church worship and political voluntarism have intimate connections. So do Calvinism and the theory of mixed government.[88]

But there is also a giant lag between modern religion and modern politics. It can be expressed in terms of passion and commitment.

The religious rebels of the Reformation and their successors were ablaze with anguish and "alienation." No doubt the political passion against arbitrary government became a very deep sentiment (the case of Algernon Sidney is striking)—though counterbalanced by the *politique* plea for peace—but the religious *cri de coeur,* when it sounded, was by far the more bowel-biting, whether it came from the pulpit or the scaffold. We did not, I think, have a political John Bunyan or Pascal. Machiavelli never threw his ink pot at the devil. And some two centuries later, Crusoe's momentary dread in the "state of nature" could scarcely compare with the stricken terror of those who populated John Wesley's diaries. It would require more time for politics to become terrorized or alienated (despite the Year Two), to probe its own roots of conviction with fear and trembling.

This is why the "Protestant paradigm" seems to me to provide a crucial vista on the present predicaments of secular politics—the confusions of citizenship, the withholding of conviction from public authority, and sectarian challenges to the public life. Peter Berger writes brilliantly of a worldwide theological crisis characterized by secularization and pluralism. He then goes on to add:

> Indeed, it makes sense to include in the same overall crisis the difficulties faced by the legitimators of non-religious *Weltanschauungen,* particularly that of dogmatic Marxism. In a very real way, however, the Protestant development is prototypical, to the point where one can even say that quite possibly all other religious traditions in the modern situation may be predestined to go through variants of the Protestant experience.[89]

To gain political insight from such a paradigm means, of course, to take it even further than Berger intended. In this case, it means to apply it to the political conditions and destinies of the American state. This, like other subjects we shall treat, is ironic, for it is not usual in "normal" social science to seek basic understandings of a nation or culture in "superstructural" patterns. In the present case, analytical neutrality suggests this approach. There are good reasons for thinking that America is the land of Protestantism consummated or, to use Martin Marty's term, "post-Protestantism."[90] If America is "post-Protestant," it is very likely, in some curious sense, "post-religious," despite its bulging tabernacles, for—with all due respect for the Catholic and Jewish faiths—Protestantism, in both its fundamentalist and liberal forms, has been normative in American society. There is also, however, the question of a "civil religion" to contend with. The meanings of such convictions (or lapse of them) need to be adjusted to the political perspective. We must rethink the relationship of the *sacred* and the *profane*. Tocqueville provides us with some of our clues. Regarding Tocqueville, Cushing Strout's excellent book on the subject, which has yet not managed to say the last word, concludes: "He looked to republican religion for a way of keeping that necessary discord [of liberty] from collapsing into mere fragmentation or uncivil anarchy. His remedy, always a historically limited one, does not now shine with the promise he saw in it."[91] The intention here is not to repeat Strout's analysis, but to deploy some of the same themes differently, with a main focus on the anatomy of conviction and the recovery of citizenship. Only at the end can we judge whether we have been rummaging in ruins.

Notes

1. Port-Royal-des-Champs was a Cistercian abbey for women founded in 1225. From the early seventeenth century on, it was noted for its mysticism and then its cultivation of Jansenist doctrines toward 1650. Arnauld and Pascal were among its defenders. Afterward, its eminence ebbed; but, faced with the hostility of Louis XIV, its inhabitants were excommunicated in 1707 and the institution was suppressed by Pope Clement XI a year later. In 1710 the demolition of Port-Royal, including its cemetery, was ordered.
2. See especially, René Taveneaux, ed., *Jansénisme et politique* (Paris, 1965).
3. Charles S. Hyneman, *The Study of Politics* (Urbana, 1959), pp. 62-63.
4. Karl Mannheim, "Conservative Thought," in Kurt Wolff, ed., *From Karl Mannheim* (New York, 1971), p. 146.
5. William James, *The Varieties of Religious Experience* (New York, 1929), p. 29.
6. Louis Hartz, *The Liberal Tradition in America* (New York, 1955), p. 65.
7. Alexis de Tocqueville, *Democracy in America* (2 vols., trans. Henry Reeve, New York, 1945), I, 306.
8. Charles-Constantin de Volney, *The Ruins* (Albany, 1822; orig. 1791), p. v.
9. Harold J. Laski, *The American Democracy* (New York, 1948), p. 299.
10. These questions have been diligently pursued by Cushing Strout in *The New Heavens and the New Earth: Political Religion in America* (New York, 1974).
11. For an account, see Walter Ullmann's *A History of Political Thought: The Middle Ages* (Harmondsworth, 1965).
12. Cf. Karl Marx, "Bruno Bauer, 'Die Judenfrage,'" in T.B. Bottomore, ed., *Karl Marx: Early Writings* (New York, 1964), p. 17: "The demo-

cratic state, the real state, does not need religion for its political consummation. On the contrary, it can dispense with religion, because in this case the human core of religion is realized in a profane manner. The so-called Christian state, on the other hand, has a political attitude towards religion, and a religious attitude towards politics. It reduces political institutions and religion equally to mere appearances." For Freud, cf. *The Future of an Illusion* (London, 1928), pp. 22-26, where the author describes religion as an illusion derived from man's wishes and compares it with psychic delusion—an essential conflict with reality.

13. There are extreme positions that deny this; cf. Simone Weil, *Gravity and Grace* (New York, 1952), p. 168: "Religion, in so far as it is a source of consolation, is a hindrance to true faith: in this sense atheism is a purification." This is not the common way of regarding the issue. With the mystic there is a fine line between beatitude and the grave indulgence of pride.

14. Not, to be sure, in any comprehensive manner; for one recent treatment, see L.-V. Thomas, *Anthropologie de la mort* (Paris, 1975).

15. Edgar Morin, *L'Homme et la mort* (2d ed., Paris, 1970), p. 7.

16. Miguel de Unamuno, *The Tragic Sense of Life in Men and Nations* (trans. Anthony Kerrigan, Princeton, 1972), p. 46.

17. St. Augustine, *The City of God* (New York, 1950), XII, v. p. 384 (translation slightly altered).

18. *Democracy in America*, I, 321.

19. In the wake of the *Encyclopedia*, and influenced by the methods of the Montpelerin school of medicine, *idéologues* like Cabanis and Bichat stressed only the natural properties of death.

20. Peter L. Berger, *The Sacred Canopy: Elements of a Sociological Theory of Religion* (Garden City, 1967), p. 43.

21. Ibid., p. 52.

22. Blaise Pascal, *Pensées,* ed. C. des Granges (Paris, 1964), No. 168, p. 119.

23. Aleksandr Solzhenitsyn, "The Exhausted West," speech at Harvard University, 8 June 1978.

24. Cf. Kenneth Burke's satirical comments on this notion in *The Rhetoric of Religion: Studies in Logology* (Berkeley and Los Angeles, 1970), pp. 283-84.

25. Williams James, *Varieties of Religious Experience,* p. 368.

26. John Dewey, *A Common Faith* (New Haven, 1934), p. 80.

27. Ibid., p. 14.

28. Clifford Geertz, "Religion as a Cultural System," in Donald R. Cutler, ed., *The Religious Situation* (Boston, 1968), p. 668.

29. Ibid., p. 643.

30. Cf. the empirical attempt of William C. McCready and Andrew M. Greeley to construct and test a model on this basis: *The Ultimate Values of the American Population* (Beverly Hills, 1976).

31. Paul Tillich, *Theology of Culture* (Oxford, 1964), p. 42. For a categorical dissection of this identification, see H. Richard Niebuhr, *Christ and Culture* (New Haven, 1951). For the problematic of a genuinely secular culture, see Bryan Wilson, *Religion in Secular Society* (London, 1966), and below, pp. 176, 179.

32. Hannah Arendt, in "Religion and the Intellectuals: A Symposium," *Partisan Review*, No. 2 (1950), p. 114.
33. Michael Oakeshott, *On Human Conduct* (Oxford, 1975), p. 83.
34. Ibid., p. 85.
35. William James, *Varieties of Religious Experience*, p. 31.
36. Montesquieu, *De l'Esprit des lois*, XXIV, i.
37. See Emile Durkheim, *Montesquieu and Rousseau: Forerunners of Sociology* (Ann Arbor, 1960).
38. Durkheim, *The Elementary Forms of Religious Life* (trans. J.W. Swain, New York, 1947), p. 62.
39. Ibid., p. 257. And cf. Alvin Gouldner, *The Coming Crisis of Western Sociology* (London, 1977), p. 15: "In the course of his studies of religion, Durkheim developed a conception of the requirements of social order which premised that society itself was the godhead and that social order depended on the creation and maintenance of a set of moral orientations that were essentially religious in character."
40. Talcott Parsons, *The Structure of Social Action* (New York, 1949), p. 427.
41. Ibid., p. 421. See the discussion in Roland Robertson, *The Sociological Interpretation of Religion* (New York, 1972), pp. 21-23.
42. On "differentiation," see also Robert N. Bellah, "Religious Evolution," *American Sociological Review* 29 (June 1964): 358-74.
43. Peter Berger, *The Noise of Solemn Assemblies* (Garden City, 1961), p. 103.
44. Thomas Luckmann, *The Invisible Religion* (New York, 1967), esp. pp. 77-117.
45. See esp. Philippe Ariès, "La Mort inversée," *Archives européennes de Sociologie* 8 (1967): 169-95; Pierre Chaunu, *Mourir à Paris* (Paris, 1977); Michel Vovelle, *Piété baroque et déchristianisation en Provence au XVIIIe siècle* (Paris, 1973).
46. See Sidney E. Mead, *The Old Religion in the Brave New World* (Berkeley and Los Angeles, 1977), esp. pp. 68-72, 106-8.
47. Bellak's seminal article "The American Civil Religion" appeared in *Daedalus* 96 (Winter 1967): 1-21.
48. An example is the notion of a civilizational cycle from undifferentiated and "primitive" communism to elaborated and "free" communism found in some of the writings of Marx and Engels.
49. See Henri Frankfort et al., *The Intellectual Adventures of Ancient Man* (Chicago, 1946).
50. It is also suggested by Arnold J. Toynbee that "the ruler's purpose in seeking a religious sanction for his rule outside himself is to find one that will have effective hold upon the imagination and the feelings of his subjects at a stage at which, *ex hypothesi*, their veneration for a god incarnate in an emperor has worn too thin to serve any longer as a prophylactic against assassination." *An Historian's Approach to Religion* (London, 1956), p. 52.
51. Cf. John Locke, *The Second Treatise of Government*, I, ii, 6, in Peter Laslett, ed., *Two Treatises of Government* (New York, 1965), p. 311: "Every one as he is *bound to preserve himself* and not to quit his Station wilfully, so by the like reason when his own Preservation comes not in

competition, ought he, as much as he can, *to preserve the rest of Mankind. . . .*"

52. Cf. Niccolò Machiavelli, "A Discourse on Remodelling the Government of Florence," in Allan Gilbert, ed., *Machiavelli: The Chief Works and Others* (3 vols., Durham, 1965), I, 113-14: "I believe that the greatest good to be done and the most pleasing to God is that which one does to one's native city."

53. Harold Laski, *A Grammar of Politics* (London, 1925), p. 666.

54. I have in mind the formidable array of literature begun and inspired by John Rawls's *A Theory of Justice* (Cambridge, Mass., 1971).

55. See G.A. Kelly, "Politics, Violence, and Human Nature," *NOMOS XVII: Human Nature in Politics* (New York, 1977), passim.

56. I do not mean, of course, that religious coercion has vanished in contemporary Western society. Roman Catholics struggle over church authority and the implications of the *aggiornimento;* as recently as 1952 there were heresy proceedings against a Presbyterian minister in North Carolina (see Duncan Howlett, *The Fourth American Faith,* New York, 1964, p. 17); coercive indoctrination is a feature of militant sects like the Unificationists. But despite this, in the words of Bryan Wilson, "it is not normally open to religious movements to elicit the compliance of their followers by means other than the stimulation of normative commitment" (Introduction to B.R. Wilson, ed., *Patterns of Sectarianism: Organization and Ideology in Social and Religious Movements,* London, 1967, p. 7).

57. J. Milton Yinger, *The Scientific Study of Religion* (London, 1970), p. 409.

58. Laski, *American Democracy,* pp. 296-97.

59. N.J. Demerath III and Phillip E. Hammond, *Religion in Social Context: Tradition and Transition* (New York, 1969), p. 172.

60. Russell E. Richey and Donald G. Jones, eds., *American Civil Religion* (New York, 1974), "Introduction," p. 15.

61. Demerath and Hammond, *Religion in Social Context,* p. 231.

62. See Berger, *Noise of Solemn Assemblies,* pp. 116, 132.

63. For an absorbing fantasy of this kind, see Walter Murphy, *The Vicar of Christ* (New York, 1979).

64. See Andrew M. Greeley, *Religion in the Year 2000* (New York, 1969), pp. 67-70.

65. *Democracy in America,* II, 23.

66. See my models of "Civic II" and "Civil I" in "Who Needs a Theory of Citizenship?" *Daedalus:* "The State," 108 (Fall 1979): 29.

67. *De l'Esprit des lois,* XXIV, 14.

68. Ibid., XXIV, 6.

69. Ibid., XXIV, 2. Bayle had used almost similar words to satirize the presumed ferocity of the nonbeliever: "He is a monster infinitely more dangerous than those fierce beasts, those lions and mad bulls from which Hercules delivered Greece." *Miscellaneous Thoughts on the Comet of 1680,* xxxiii.

70. Ibid., XXIV, 5.

71. Ibid.

72. Lamoignon de Malesherbes, a magistrate and reformer much in the lineage of Montesquieu and the person chiefly responsible for restoring the

toleration of the Protestants in 1788, continually argued that the members of the French Reformed Church would make excellent citizens, if given the chance. See Pierre Grosclaude, *Malesherbes: témoin et interprète de son temps* (Paris, 1961), p. 601.

73. Montesquieu, *De l'Esprit des lois*, XXIV, 1.

74. H. Richard Niebuhr, *The Kingdom of God in America* (New York, 1955), p. 73.

75. Edmund J. Morgan, *The Puritan Dilemma: The Story of John Winthrop* (Boston, 1958), p. 96; cf. Strout, *New Heavens*, pp. 15-16.

76. Guy Swanson, *Religion and Regime* (Ann Arbor, 1967), pp. 49ff. and passim.

77. Cf. Stanislav Andreski, *Elements of Comparative Sociology* (London, 1964), p. 315; and Werner Stark, *The Sociology of Religion: A Study of Christendom*, vol. I: *Established Religion* (New York, 1966), p. 162.

78. Vernon Louis Parrington, *Main Currents in American Thought: An Interpretation of American Literature from the Beginnings to 1920* (3 vols., New York, 1927, 1930), I, 13.

79. Published in the *Deutsch-Französische Jahrbücher* (1844), cited in R.C. Tucker, ed., *The Marx-Engels Reader* (New York, 1972), p. 9.

80. Hegel to Niethammer, 28 October 1808. J. Hoffmeister, ed., *Briefe von und an Hegel* (4 vols., Hamburg, 1952-1960), I, 253.

81. Of course this whole argument presupposes a relative autonomy of politics and religion, and especially the latter. This has sometimes been questioned; cf. Philip Rieff: ". . . from Hobbes to Weber there has been an insistent, ironic voice saying that religious man is really, at bottom, political man. All theologies are metaphors of politics. . . ." "Introduction to Max Weber: 'Science as a Vocation'," *Daedalus* 88 (Winter 1958): 111. But conceivably there is more reason to argue the opposite. However, I suspect that neither a total derivation in either direction nor a total dualism is admissible.

82. See my remarks in *Hegel's Retreat from Eleusis* (Princeton, 1978), pp. 162-63, 169-70, 180-82.

83. There seem to me to be obvious parallels between themes in Jürgen Habermas's *Legitimation Crisis* (trans. Thomas McCarthy, London, 1976) and Berger's diagnosis in the religious sphere, although Habermas is little concerned with religion.

84. Albert Camus connects the renunciation of transcendence with the decapitation of the figureheads of patrimonial society in *The Rebel* (New York, 1956), p. 175.

85. Kelly, "Who Needs a Theory of Citizenship?" pp. 23, 30.

86. It is significant that both Saint-Simon and his followers and Comte became aware that their scientistic "neo-politics" would have to be accompanied by an artificial system of worship. Rousseau had also recommended a civic creed for his republicanism. The difference is that Rousseau was far closer to human possibility and precedent than the technicist visionaries of the nineteenth century.

87. See, in general, Quentin Skinner, *The Foundations of Modern Political Thought*, vol. II: *The Age of Reformation* (Cambridge, 1978), pp. 113-34.

88. The Cambridge Platform of the Massachusetts Church in 1648 called itself a "mixed government"; see Strout, *New Heavens*, pp. 9, 26, the

latter citing John Wise, a religious democrat, who accepted "mixed government" in the state. Also, the analysis by Sidney E. Mead, "The 'Nation with the Soul of a Church'," in Richey and Jones, eds., *American Civil Religion,* p. 52.

89. Peter Berger, *The Social Reality of Religion* (London, 1967), p. 155.
90. Martin E. Marty, *The New Shape of American Religion* (New York, 1959), p. 32.
91. Strout, *New Heavens,* p. 343.

2

Freedom and Control

Tocqueville's treatise on America had the great virtue of distinguishing between the novelty and the history of the country. He knew, more than most of the Americans, that they had a past that fundamentally explained their character. But his perceptions also moved in a panoramic present containing clues so important that they could also designate the unmistakable evolution of the European world, for good or ill. That future would depend on how well men were able to create spaces of freedom to buffer their "passion for equality." Here the American past came into play with hopeful effect: equality of condition and temperament—perilous as a hegemonic principle—had apparently been moderated by the Anglo-Saxon germ of liberty planted in bygone colonial times. This liberty of the English yeoman had itself been purged of feudal trappings and strengthened by a religious faith friendly to the aspirations of republicanism. In New England "the triumph of an idea" had been achieved,[1] for, as Tocqueville argues, "Puritanism was not merely a religious doctrine, but corresponded in many points with the most absolute democratic and republican theories."[2] Many today would challenge this assertion. Indeed, over a century later, Tocqueville's fellow countryman André Siegfried, himself a Protestant, would find in America's Calvinist legacy little but conformism, superficiality, and intolerance.[3] Our point here, however, is that Tocqueville, in the 1830s, explained America's point of arrival in terms of a unique past (as well as unique geographical conditions),[4] while yet subscribing to the generalization that, whether or not shaped by similar factors, endowed or not with a sympathetic religious environment, all of Western civilization would move in the same democratic trajectory.

Tocqueville would not have cared much for Nabokov's *Lolita* as a literary work. Yet, like Nabokov and most European observers up to recent times, he acknowledged the American qualities of restlessness, experimentalism, and innocence. Although Americans did have a past that accounted for their character, they were not a people burdened with memory: the forest, as we have seen, speedily reclaimed their "ruins." Perhaps it could be said that they were simultaneously a mythic and a pragmatic people. History had of course been written in the United States at least as far back as Cotton Mather. And David Ramsay's *History of the American Revolution* (1789) had significantly anticipated Tocqueville's appraisal of the vital connection between Puritanism and the republican spirit: "The clergy of New England were a numerous, learned and respectable body, who had a great ascendancy over the minds of their hearers. They connected religion and patriotism, and, in their sermons and prayers, represented the cause of America as the cause of Heaven."[5] Celebrating the American grip on the past, another writer, George Chalmers, had pointed out: "Of these colonies, it cannot be asserted, as it is of European nations, that their origin is uncertain or unknown; that their ancient history is fabulous and dark; or that their original institutions have come down the current of time, loaded with the disputations of the antiquary."[6] A striking improvement on the merely speculative promises of Vico's thesis that man could know history because he had made it!

Yet the mythic mode—which might be compared to the *Chanson de Roland* or Layamon's *Brut* at the dawn of European nationhood— should not be underestimated. Its most famous illustration was Joel Barlow's quaint epic the *Columbiad,* where the "raptures" of that heroic discoverer are to identify

> . . . a sapient band,
> The torch of science flaming in their hand! . . .
> Superior worlds unfolding to their eyes;
> Heav'n in their view unveils th'eternal plan,
> And gives new guidance to the paths of man.[7]

To see America mythically was an exalted way of beginning afresh with the new covenant of a "redeemer nation." It was for some a clearing in the wilderness. As Jonathan Edwards put it: "When God is about to turn the earth into a Paradise, he does not begin his work where there is some good growth already, but in a wilderness, where nothing grows, and nothing is to be seen but dry sand and barren rocks; that the light may shine out of darkness, and the world be replenished from emptiness."[8] Another mythic device was to sentimentalize the Lockean *tabula rasa:* this appealed to many Old World

writers of the eighteenth century in their appreciation of the New.[9]
Thus the Frenchman Crèvecoeur, who came here to live in the woods
(though, as a Tory, he left America, his property despoiled, in September 1780), declared:

> *He* is an American who leaves behind him all his ancient prejudices and
> manners, receives new ones from the mode of life he has embraced, the
> new government he obeys, and the new rank he holds. He becomes an
> American by being received in the broad lap of our great Alma Mater.
> Here individuals of all nations are melted into a new race of men,
> whose labors and posterity will one day cause great change in the
> world.[10]

Writing in the Jacksonian era, Tocqueville—who was not a Romantic—sought to weigh the traditions and causes that had produced in
America "the image of democracy itself." But he was quite aware of
standing outside the consciousness of his subject and injecting history
into it. "The only historical remains in the United States," he wrote,
"are the newspapers; if a number be wanting, the chain of time is
broken and the present is severed from the past."[11] That was the
pragmatic state of affairs.

The continuities that Americans observed in their public behavior
were not inculcated by ancient lineage and fixed estate, nor by the
jealous hoarding of an old culture. Here there was no aristocracy of
birth. The higher things were not remotely private. As opposed to
Europe, politics was "the end and aim of education,"[12] emanating
from the peace of the domestic hearth.[13] Yet the freedom and initiative of the citizen did have their sources in the probity of the private
man. And that probity, as both privately and publicly expressed,
owed its strength to the diffusion of a religion that, though unregu-
lated by the state, had the most serious public overtones: "In America religion is the road to knowledge, and the observance of the divine
laws leads men to civil freedom."[14]

We have already noted that Tocqueville described religion as "a
kind of hope." How could he then also regard it as "a road to knowledge"? Surely this was not some kind of Kantian architecture connecting the questions "What can I know?" and "What may I hope?"
His point is not so much philosophical as political and sociological; it
returns us to a theme introduced in the preceding section. Religion
was "hope" for Tocqueville because faith was "the only permanent
state of mankind,"[15] a reconciliation of man with his purpose and his
immortality. If you trouble this belief, Tocqueville argued, man will
resolve his public fate in bursts of anarchy or servility. Moreover, he

will be unfit for knowledge and clear vision: "When the religion of a people is destroyed, doubt gets hold of the higher powers of the intellect and half paralyzes all the others." [16] In Tocqueville's view, close to that of Montesquieu, religion, properly understood, promoted liberty by imposing moral self-governance on human beings. [17] In the absence of this control politics would have to substitute servile institutions. Thus, "religion perceives that civil liberty affords a noble exercise to the faculties of man and that the political world is a field prepared by the Creator for the efforts of mind." [18] What had begun in the civic discipline of predestinarian Calvinism bursts into flower in political Arminianism.

Does this mean a religion cast within the cloying confines of Puritanism or a "civil religion" in the sense that that phrase was used by Rousseau or by modern writers like Bellah? Without prejudicing some of the analysis to follow, we can safely reply that it is not the religion of the Massachusetts Bay Colony, though such was its earliest source; [19] it is a congeries of conflicting theologies that, however, produce a single and systematic morality in the world of the profane. As Tocqueville takes pains to insist, American Catholics also adhere to it. [20] Yet, though it is "a democratic and republican religion," [21] it does not seem to be "civil" in the strong sense, for it is not a manipulation of oaths and profane symbols or a Polybian elitist intrigue to keep ordinary men in fear of the gods. It enables civic participation by fulfilling other needs. It dictates values. As Tocqueville notes approvingly: "Those who do not believe conceal their incredulity . . . those who believe display their faith." [22] To borrow Oakeshott's illuminating categories, it has more the quality of a "morality of communal ties" than of a "morality of the common good." [23]

Of course Tocqueville is not examining the "truth" but rather the "use" of this religion: like Montesquieu he is writing as an "écrivain politique." "By the side of every religion," he tells us, "is to be found a political opinion, which is connected with it by affinity. If the human mind be left to follow its own bent, it will regulate the temporal and spiritual institutions of society in a uniform manner, and man will endeavor, if I may so speak, to harmonize earth with heaven." [24] Tocqueville's normative harmonization refers neither to the utopian fantasy of creating a heaven out of profane materials nor to the Hebraizing tendency of many American spokesmen to regard their people as specially "chosen" or their land as one of "milk and honey." Rather, it means that there *is* a religious solution that encourages the wide exercise of civil liberty—approached most closely by the Americans—and that this solution involves a common practice of self-control emanating from private conviction but organized by free churches. When Robert Bellah writes that "every community is based on a sense of the sacred and requires a context of higher meaning. Our nation is a community of fate,"[25] he is somewhat overbalancing the Tocquevillian harmony with somber tones of destiny reminiscent of Lincoln's Second Inaugural Address. Moreover, he is putting the cart before the horse: his community demands the sacred, whereas Tocqueville merely argued that every religion is accompanied by a political tendency. We shall not be surprised, therefore, to find Bellah reaching a position where "republicanism" and "liberalism" are severed and opposed.[26] Tocqueville had used republicanism, American-style, to signify liberalism—although this was not, in many ways, what liberalism has come to mean today—and it was explicitly juxtaposed against the republicanism of Europe, which had already taken on doctrinaire overtones.

It is by now clear that Tocqueville's consuming interest was in the survival and sustenance of civil liberty under democratic conditions and not in religion per se. However, we should not take Tocqueville's "harmonization" to mean that religion was a "noble lie" by which men must live if they are to be free; it is rather that, by giving men both hope and pause, an unknown providence liberates them for cooperative satisfactions in the *res publica*. "What is understood by a republican government in the United States," Tocqueville writes, "is the slow and quiet action of society upon itself. It is a regular state of things really founded upon the enlightened will of the people. . . . The republicans in the United States set a high value upon morality, respect religious belief, and acknowledge the existence of rights. They profess to think that a people ought to be moral, religious, and temperate in proportion as it is free. . . ."[27] What the Americans "profess to think" is apparently identical with the criteria that Tocqueville himself believes necessary to freedom.

In Europe—for Tocqueville was addressing Europeans—it was quite otherwise: "According to [the demagogues], a republic is not the rule of the majority, as has hitherto been thought, but the rule of those who are strenuous partisans of the majority. It is not the people who preponderate in this kind of government, but those who know what is good for the people."[28] Republican doctrine in France was, in the author's view, quite removed from those things the Americans set a high value on, and was laced with hypocrisy and the will to power, besides. He would conjure—or compromise—with this predicament in 1848. The abstract dogmas of the republicans of Europe did not reflect "the prevailing habits and ideas of the people"; it was in unhistorical America that Tocqueville identified "the last link of a chain of opinions which binds the whole Anglo-Saxon world."[29] And it was especially the development of the American religious temper that had made popular sovereignty a plausible system of freedom.

This was of course not out of keeping with what the American Founders, almost to a man, believed. Early on (well before his dalliance with the French Enlightenment), Franklin had written: *"History* will . . . afford frequent Opportunities of showing the Necessity of a *Publick Religion,*[30] from its Usefulness to the Publick; the Advantage of a Religious Character among private Persons; the Mischiefs of Superstition, &c. and the Excellency of the CHRISTIAN RELIGION above all others antient or modern."[31] And Washington's Farewell Address had sounded this same note powerfully: "Whatever may be conceded to the influence of refined education on minds of peculiar structure, reason and experience both forbid us to expect that National Morality can prevail in exclusion of religious principle."[32] Franklin's Christianity was obviously not that of St. Augustine, nor was Washington's "religious principle" specific enough to be at odds with a federal Constitution that had nowhere mentioned any divinity. They, and most of the patriots of the Revolution, were not unaware that "every ardent defense of sectarian Christianity, however unintentional, was by implication an attack on the mainspring of the Republic. . . ."[33] Having engineered the political unification of the states, they could not have been eager to nourish the particularistic claims of the denominations (which, however, continued to enjoy special benefits in the states until the Fourteenth Amendment extended the religious clause of the First Amendment to the subordinate jurisdictions). Yet the core conviction of the Founders accommodated a nation that worshipped the Biblical Jehovah. This was essential to the ideology of their new creation and was, besides, heavily influenced by the vigorous participation of the American pulpits and congregations in the struggle for independence; since God was not, as it seemed to many of the French, a reactionary despot, there was no need for a profane Year One or a Cult of Reason.[34] Indeed, as a modern historian has put it: " . . . the Revolution had been preached to the masses as a religious revival, and had the astounding fortune to succeed."[35] The United States was a nation bound to Providence by repentances and thanksgivings, with a politics respectful of a higher power that was neither the Calvinist deity so repugnant to John Adams nor the remote First Cause of the French deists. Since the Americans were, par excellence, workers on nature and beneficiaries of history, they tended to espouse Jehovah as author of the former and helmsman of the latter.

Service of this God and service of the commonwealth were perceived as harmonious at the republic's moment of truth, and this remained basically the case until the tensions of the 1840s and 1850s. In a nation "conceived in liberty," "Caesar's things" were recast in a way that could provoke no obvious conflicts with "God's things," while the latter, far more ethically than metaphysically interpreted, brought a sacred touch to the profane world. Leavened both by the latitudinarian bent of the century and by the liberation from dogmatics that was an incidental result of the First Great Awakening, the American mind gravitated from the Calvinist "holy experiment" and made the servants of God into citizens of a civil community of republicans under God's protection. Being in but not of the state (as patterned after the Virginia disestablishment of 1785), religion itself—not least because, until after the war, it had been everywhere, even in the liturgical churches, congregational in structure—could be seen as part of the realm of freedom. Precisely because it was "free," it could accommodate to the civil power without that fatal sense of moral conflict that had scarred Europe for centuries. If religion was "reasonable," so was the American constitutional experiment. If it was "revelatory," so was the American "garden in the wilderness." If it was pluralized, so were the areas of settlement and the economic interests.

This does not mean an absence of fustian and fighting among the denominations and sects, soon to be replicated in the politics of the country. However, this bickering never became a deadly quarrel or zero-sum game, nor, as Tocqueville was quick to notice, did it create patterns of moral distinctiveness. It may be that America's religious settlement, over time, produced a kind of sacred shallowness. It may also be that both believers and citizens would, in the long run, have profited from a more lively tension between the life of the spirit and the life of self-interest, from a widened experience, in Barthian terms, of the dichotomy of the "order of salvation" and the "order of preservation."[36] As Martin Marty recently wrote: "Religion in America has paid a price for accommodation to an environment which religionists often regarded as being somehow revelatory and redemptive. I will argue that the price has been paid thoughtlessly and unnecessarily."[37] But that is a contemporary lament. Earlier Americans were not enervated by accommodation nor aware of any damaging compromise. Tocqueville professed to explain the paradox: "Religion in

America takes no direct part in the government of society, but it must be regarded as the first of their political institutions; for if it does not impart a taste for freedom, it facilitates the use of it."[38] Together with freedom, it "reigned in common over the same country."[39] It might be added that Tocqueville was not the only foreign observer to reach this conclusion. At almost the same time Francis J. Grund wrote: "The religious habits of the Americans form not only the basis of their private and public morals, but have become so thoroughly interwoven with their whole course of legislation, that it would be impossible to change them without affecting the very essence of their government."[40]

The power of religion was not to be found in its challenge to the temporal but in its judicious abstinence from the passions of politics. The American clergy, Tocqueville insisted on three occasions in his work, were an integrative and not a partisan force;[41] that was "the pride of their profession." Those same ministers whose predecessors preached independence and supplicated the God of battle "take no share in the altercation of parties, but they readily adopt the general opinions of their country and their age, and they allow themselves to be borne away without opposition in the current of feeling and opinion by which everything around them is carried along."[42] This tendency, projected into the future, would invite the contempt or despair of Abolitionists, Social Gospellers, and the sociological and theological critics of the 1960s. Perhaps it was a bit of an exaggeration. Tocqueville arrived too late in America to experience Congregationalist New England as a last redoubt of Federalism or the Jeffersonian solidarity of the frontier religions. He was also rather blind to the intimate (and democratic) connections between the fervor of the Frontier Awakenings and the Jacksonian consummation of populism.[43] It is not difficult to grasp why. Tocqueville's insight about the close connections between Calvinism and republicanism left him with the somewhat exaggerated notion that the enduring American values had all been created in New England. Acute in discerning the proclivities of American expansionism, he was nevertheless inclined to see the East moving westward and, in time, replicating itself there, rather than the cultural novelties that were being produced beyond the Appalachians. He implied this when he observed that although Connecticut was entitled to only five congressmen, some thirty-six sitting members had been born in that state.[44] Tocqueville paid little heed to two of the major manifestations of American religious life—evangelism and radical sectarianism. Even for one writing principally as an "écrivain politique" and as Cassandra prophesying for Europe, this was an oversight. When Tocqueville encountered the frenzies of evangelism, his reaction was the following: "From time to time strange sects arise which endeavor to strike out extraordinary paths to eternal happiness. Religious insanity is very common in the United States."[45]

There is perhaps a deeper reason that Tocqueville's analysis fails us at this point, even though he traveled through an America where religious convulsions had been stirring for at least two decades and the pursuit of strange creeds—and even strange gods—was gathering steam. If made prominent, all this would be unsettling to Tocqueville's theory of the relationship between religion and republican liberty. For the role of religion, he believed, was to provide men with those inner controls of morality—domestic, municipal, and economic—that made a free public life possible. He did not utopianize the strengths of religious discipline and he acknowledged that "in America religion is perhaps less powerful than it has been at certain periods and among certain nations,"[46] but he expected it "to purify, to regulate, and to restrain," not to release the passions in unlicensed forms.[47] For Tocqueville, the realist, the Dionysiac therapies of evangelism were believed destructive to the rational exercise of freedom. He did not perhaps see that such explosions of the sacred created much of the civil community that was to be had in the sparsely populated wilderness of the West or that the shape of democracy required them as a complement to a new style of politics of which he, seeking for buffering zones between authority and liberty, stood in honest fear.[48] He did not see the resemblances between the stump preacher and the stump politician, and the implications of their common stock of salvationary rhetoric.[49] Another French traveler carefully noted, at exactly the same time (1835), "Religious festivals . . . to which people press with eager delight in spite of the philosophical remonstrances of the more refined sects. . . . Besides the camp-meetings, the political processions are the only things in this country which bear any resemblance to festivals."[50]

Indeed, if Tocqueville's neglect of the emotional pitch of American religion may be interpreted as a distaste for its political consequences, his critical posture is not unique. More than a century later Harold J. Laski, in a work as voluminous though not as perceptive as Tocqueville's classic, was to write: "It is . . . important to realize that the environment of the first seventy years in the history of American religion has left profound traces upon its contemporary character. It has emphasized emotion at the expense of mind."[51] What is most interesting about this juxtaposition of texts written on the near and far sides of immense changes in a giant nation is that Tocqueville essentially wants religion to moralize people in a sober and rational manner so that they may sustain free secular institutions, whereas Laski accuses a sentimentalized religion of moralizing people in the wrong way, at the expense of "reason," "scholarship," and "speculative interest."[52] For Tocqueville, the liaison between religion and civic strength should be affirmed by "self-interest rightly understood," even though this student of Pascal could have had no illusions regarding American religion's intellectual depths; for Laski, their relationship was entirely unfortunate because religion had been obsequious to the shallow concerns of an anti-intellectual and "business" civilization.

Without endorsing either perspective we may conclude that Tocqueville's normative alliance between religion and politics in America changed its character over time. At first their common values were those of the new republican experiment. But years later, after an assimilation of powerful sectarian impulses that Tocqueville mostly passed over in silence, a different kind of partnership was forged. It occurred with the full development of capitalism and in circumstances that were in many respects a violation or extreme caricature of the moderated democratic enterprise that he had conceived. One cannot exactly blame Tocqueville for a deficient vision, for many of his predictions continue to astonish us. If he failed to anticipate the traumas and effects of the Civil War, he saw clearly enough into some of its causes. His speculations on an "aristocracy of manufactures" still carry their bite.[53] But, above all, Tocqueville was not in a position to conjure with technology, urbanization, and the effects of massive later immigrations that today provide the reservoir of much of the American population. Thus there is little wonder that his civic-religious thesis has been jolted out of shape, although it is not *prima facie* obvious that his stipulations for freedom and control in a democratic society were challenged simply because of uncongenial developments. The most hapless result of the recent evolution of America in terms of Tocquevillian theory is that the sectarianism that he saw as voluntarily producing a common moral ideology (common actions, common cautions, common cares) seems, in an age of advanced secularization or in an age where morality is, alternately, torn from its religious roots or enshrined in the bosom of holier-than-thou religions, to have produced a nightmare of hostile and unnegotiable moral pluralism. Although one might reasonably expect that the hostilities will eventually be resolved in some new compromise, the ground under Tocqueville's "harmonization" is greatly shaken. And this is more than a deviance from Tocqueville's republicanism; it is a great irony in its workings.

A striking feature of Tocqueville's discourse about America is his continual reference to "society" and his reluctance to use the word "state."[54] In part this is a convention of far-reaching import in the European political syntax of his time, but more substantially, as we shall see, it is a response generated by special conditions in the curious country where Tocqueville sought "the image of democracy itself."[55] In the Europe of the late 1830s and 1840s a linguistic change was brought about by theorists and advocates of a "social movement," guided by its own metaphysics, that aspired to abolish the political structures of the post-Napoleonic Restoration in favor of expanded dominance or hegemony by the producing and/or laboring classes. Bourgeois liberals were touched by this new language to the extent that it freed their interests from a traditional world view, but it was the socialists, mobilized in revolutionary conventicles, who were the hardiest innovators. Their antistate, which dared not speak its name and was believed, besides, to portend novel political relationships, called itself "society." Initially a kind of profane deification of the "people" organized against the ruling classes (as in Mazzini or Michelet), the concept of society was quickly subjected to the analysis of class struggle and class dominance and to the notion that politics could be defined as social power obedient to natural or dialectical laws of development. Democracy was the formal cornerstone of this theoretical construct. Yet pure political democracy (equality under law, extensive male suffrage, and representative government) was judged abstract and deficient by the socialists unless it led to structural changes in economy and society. This distinction had perhaps first been drawn by the Marquis de Condorcet, who had commended the French Revolution as superior to the American on the grounds that it had been "social" and not merely "political."[56]

Tocqueville's use of the word "society" as well as his appreciation of the irresistible impulse of democracy were no doubt affected by the European background. But they were more deeply influenced by his reflection on the transplantation of Anglo-Saxon liberty to the shores of the new continent. That is, he was more preoccupied by the developing institutions of "liberal" freedom in a hospitable environment where the state was too weak to frustrate the initiatives of the social groups, where although "monarchy was still the law of the state . . . the republic was already establishing in every township."[57] This was not metaphysics, but historical fact—so important a fact that Tocqueville adorned it with hyperbole: "At the present day the principle of the sovereignty of the people has acquired in the United States all the practical development that the imagination can conceive." As if this were not strong enough, he declared, a few lines later:

> In some countries a power exists which, though it is in a degree foreign to the social body, directs it, and forces it to pursue a certain track. In others the ruling force is divided, being partly within and partly without the ranks of the people. But nothing of the kind is to be seen in the United States; there society governs itself for itself. . . . The people reign in the American political world as the Deity does in the universe. They are the cause and the aim of all things; everything comes from them, and everything is absorbed in them.[58]

This testimony to the omnipotence of the people can only sound quaint today. Although in more than a few regards the prerogatives of "society" have been increased by statute or by constitutional inter- pretation since Tocqueville's time, popular sovereignty is surely no longer to be confused with God's jurisdiction over the universe. By the most benign of interpretations, "ruling force" would at least seem to be divided between government and people. Or, on another view, "the democratic method is that institutional arrangement for arriving at political decisions in which individuals acquire the power to decide by means of a competitive struggle for the people's vote."[59] What- ever the verdict regarding the present shape of democracy in the United States, one obvious and drastic change has happened since Tocqueville wrote of the people as "the cause and the aim of all things." That is the rise of a central state, increasingly policy ori- ented, with its bureaucratic sprawl into areas previously designated as "free," i.e., as belonging to "society." The disestablished American religion, while scarcely impervious to politics, has not been an ob- vious casualty of the growth of the state—partly because of deeply rooted taboos regulating permissible contact between the sacred and the profane, partly because of the material and secular biases of power in contemporary life.

In Tocqueville's view, "society" was the arena of liberty, and in the freest of societies religion held sway both as an inner control and as a moderating force in politics. America's unique disestablishment, pragmatically compelled by the need for a sufficiency of unity in the face of competing denominations, released these institutions from the grip of government and from the persecution of one another. Thus religion took shape in America as a force in the voluntary rather than the compulsory sector, as opposed to the state religions in virtually all of Europe.[60] This outcome had been conditioned by the history of settlement in the territories of the republic, by the absence of true religious war in a mainly Protestant land open to expansion, and by the fabricated nature of the central government. Politics and religion were made separate in America. But although congregations and parishes were not the same as townships, they had earlier followed a similar logic, mutually shaping the national character. Linkages would continue to exist.

It is of course not possible here to trace the archaeology of the religious clause of the First Amendment, commenting speculatively on the contributions made by such figures as Roger Williams, William Penn, John Wise, Isaac Backus, and the Founders themselves. As is well known, the First Amendment (later extended to the states by the Fourteenth Amendment) had two principal results: it guaranteed to Americans the "free exercise" of religion and it forbade their national government the establishment of any particular religion. In unbinding church and state the authors of the Bill of Rights were themselves undertaking a political act. The unconditional liberty henceforth enjoyed by any sect, creed, or private belief was politically conditioned by its subordination to the doctrine of the public good. And that liberty was also acknowledged to be a result of a necessary political compromise in matters pertaining to the sacred. This is not to accuse Madison and his colleagues of toying with divine truth for the sake of *raison d'état,* for they were sincerely convinced of the positive and moral dimensions of the solution: they believed that matters of conscience were not affairs of the state and that government, while it might have to constrain men, had no part in making them better or procuring their salvation. I wish only to suggest that the religious settlement was in the logic of the Founders' political science. An extended comment by Lord Bryce on this is still apt:

> The abstention of the State from interference of faith and worship may be advocated on two principles, which may be called the political and the religious. The former sets out from the principles of liberty and equality. It holds any attempt at compulsion by the civil power to be an infringement on the liberty of thought, as well as on liberty of action, which could be justified only when a practice claiming to be religious is so anti-social or immoral as to threaten the well-being of the community.

> The second principle, embodying the more purely religious view of the question, starts from the conception of the church as a spiritual body existing for spiritual purposes, and moving along spiritual paths. It is an assemblage of men who are united by their devotion to an unseen Being, their memory of a past divine life, their belief in the possibility of imitating that life, so far as human frailty allows, their hopes for an

illimitable future. Compulsion of any kind is contrary to the nature of such a body, which lives by love and reverence, not by law.

Of these two views it is the former much more than the latter that has moved the American mind. The latter would doubtless be now generally accepted by religious people. But when the question arose in a practical shape in the earlier days of the Republic, arguments of the former or political order were found amply sufficient to settle it.[61]

There can be no reasonable doubt that this is true. Love and reverence were not at the core of the American arguments for freedom of worship. Indeed, the politics was even more "realistic" than that allowed for by Bryce. When Madison declared that "security for civil rights must be the same as that for religious rights; it consists in the one case of a multiplicity of interests and in the other in a multiplicity of sects," he was applying the impeccable mechanics of "new political science" to politics and religion alike.[62] Jefferson held a similar, if not as tough, position: he felt that there was a safeguard against error in religious diversity, since each sect would perform the office of censor over the other.[63]

But these views did not close the issue. Disestablishment carried in America for much the same reasons as toleration in parts of Europe: the *politique* concern of peace and the liberal issue of conscience. Having secured peace, the Founders were in no rush and in no position to unsettle the states by demanding that they extend absolute rights of conscience, although they may have expected that this would follow. As Madison replied to Patrick Henry in the Virginia debate: "Fortunately for this commonwealth a majority of the people are decidedly against an exclusive establishment. I believe it to be so in the other states."[64] Conscience was, nevertheless, important. It was not, perhaps, quite so entangled with the political argument as Bryce believed it to be. Tenants of an eighteenth-century rational religion that shaded off into deism and was certainly contemptuous of theological mystification, Franklin, Jefferson, Adams, and their kind were believers in a transcendent moral sense that operated outside the prescribed facilities of church and creed. It had, moreover, intimate connections with other private rights that the republic had undertaken to secure. Here the rather dry faith of a few *philosophes* could make contact with the common American religious heritage. As Protestant, that heritage had produced the belief that membership in a specific denomination was not, as the Catholics held, crucial to salvation. America was not ostentatiously religious at this time as measured by church membership; yet it can scarcely be denied that the quality of the average man's spiritual life was often sustained by private encounters with the sacred. These encounters would not be couched in formulas like "my mind is my church" (Paine) or "I am a sect myself" (Jefferson), yet in each case the conscience sought its sense of direction from Nature's God. The turbulence of the First Great Awakening had died down (a second was soon to start), but it had left behind it a questioning of the authorities and the dogmas of traditional Calvinism and a reliance upon private judgment and private emotion. Behind this emotion large quantities of Puritan covenant theology remained.[65] Patriotism blended these elements. The *philosophes* of the young republic tended to favor—if only for political reasons—forms of Protestantism that stressed individualism and detachment from political agitation. Finally, it must be added that much as Jefferson and Madison sought, through disestablishment, to avoid the interference of the sects in politics, the clergy had also come to appreciate a state that showed no disposition to direct the conscience. The Brycean motives for religious freedom were, therefore, somewhat mingled in the American settlement, though the political was surely uppermost.[66]

No doubt the bias of the Founders' religion was polarized between the private[67] and ethical and the public and ceremonial. Attacked frequently as an infidel (in part because of his French sympathies), Jefferson wrote to Adams: "They wish it to be believed that he can have no religion who advocates its freedom."[68] This was the private side, evidently indebted to Locke, Toland, and Hutcheson. The ceremonial side—in which contemporary writers detect the stirrings of "civil religion"—was a public sharing of good fortune and calamity directed by the chief magistrates of the nation through proclamation or the austere pomp appropriate to a Protestant and republican land. It is certain that early presidents, as well as later ones, used biblical imagery, common Christian forms, and the appeal to God to promote national unity and concord. It is less certain that, in so doing, they were consciously founding what is sometimes called today a "fourth religion." At very least, it is possible that late twentieth-century sociologists, armed with the theories of Durkheim and Parsons or simply with their own formulas for revitalizing the spiritual energy of the nation, encounter some difficulty in partaking of the eighteenth-century *Zeitgeist,* that atmosphere of ethical religiosity where the attenuated latitudinarianism of the intellectuals and the dedogmatized emotionalism of ordinary men and women, shaped in part by the Great Awakening and in part by "self-interest rightly understood," could meet in common Christianity.

To be sure, this was not the Christianity of Niebuhr, Tillich, Bonhoeffer, or John Courtney Murray. It was a Christianity of Hutcheson's moral sense, of Lockean empiricism applied to the evangelistic conversions of Jonathan Edwards and his followers, and a nervous belief in God's providence. These were not shallow forms imposed on the public consciousness by crafty ideologists. Already, on 12 June 1775, the Continental Congress had issued a dispatch asking the thirteen colonies that 20 June be universally observed as "a day of publick humiliation, fasting, and prayer"

> that we may with united hearts and voices unfeignedly confess and deplore our many sins, and offer up our joint supplications to the all-wise, omnipotent, and merciful disposer of all events; humbly beseeching him to forgive our iniquities, to remove our present calamities, to avert those desolating judgments with which we are threatened.[69]

It is not artifice but profound pathos that prompted President Adams in 1798 to call the nation to confession, fasting, and repentance in the hope that "humiliation might foster renewed kinship among the citizens."[70] Nor was it sham when the politic President Madison, in the depths of the War of 1812, spoke of "the sacred obligation of transmitting entire to future generations that precious patrimony . . . held in trust by the present from the goodness of Divine Providence" and proclaimed days of national thanksgiving to praise "the Great Disposer of Events" for opportunities rather than for success. Madison also proclaimed national humiliations in 1812, 1813, and 1815.[71]

Tocqueville was right on two counts: in sensing the pervasive religious spirit that defined the American character and in stressing its connection with the liberties proclaimed by the Founders. This was effectively confirmed in a presidential message of the "infidel" Jefferson in 1801: "The liberties of a nation [cannot] be thought secure when we have removed their only firm basis, a conviction in the minds of the people that their liberties are the gift of God."[72] Parrington's myth of the wicked Calvinism "that it needed two hundred years' experience in America to disintegrate,"[73] the venal potions of utilitarian Whiggery (now called "possessive individualism"), and the generous infusions of "French romantic theory" (sc., Rousseau) all boiling in the national cauldron provide gripping drama, but it is not a faithful recording of how matters stood when Tocqueville disembarked on our shores. It is not surprising that Parrington's *Bildungsroman* of the American cultural trek ended with a summons to memory and on a note of despair: "Liberals whose hair is growing thin and the lines of whose figures are no longer what they were are likely to find themselves today in the unhappy predicament of being treated as mourners at their own funerals. . . ."[74] For the "goodness of man" in which Parrington so fervently believed, despite much evidence to the contrary, provided for a democracy that was more anarchic than civic in its caress of liberty and for a religion that glorified liberty but could never be the source of it.

That was not quite what the Founders, even Jefferson, had in mind, nor did it adequately measure the cultural forces present at the creation. However we may be tempted to view the American spiritual predicament today—a combat between capitalist lucre and social idealism à la Parrington, between liberal mechanics and republican faith à la Bellah, between arrogant denominationalism and Enlightenment à la Sidney Mead, or between bovine accommodation and radical witness à la Peter Berger—neither the Founders nor Tocqueville doubted that this was a Christian community. If the new political science developed at the Convention of 1787 was worldly and mechanical, its spirit was still infused with faith in the divine grounding of human law. For well over a century Americans continued to believe this of their Constitution. A Missouri Supreme Court decision of 1854 puts this nicely: "We must regard the people for whom it [i.e., the Constitution] was ordained. It appears to have been made by Christian men. The Constitution on the face of it shows that the Christian religion was the religion of its framers."[75] Today, when this transcendent connection has disappeared from the articulate public consciousness, it may seem correct to agree with Max Lerner that "instead of finding their democratic faith in supernatural religion, Americans . . . tended to find their religious faith in various forms of belief about their own existence."[76] But this had not always been so. The genius of the Founders' religion had been to leave the popular religion untouched, that is, unconstrained, and, in so doing, to clear a space for its further avatars, hoping for a harmonization of heaven and earth.

We have thus far analyzed Tocqueville's theory of freedom and control in a democratic society and examined some of the evidence that he elicited from the American experience to support it. Put in simplest terms, Tocqueville held that religious belief was inseparable from free government and free public life because it was the channel of a self-imposed moral restraint that shaped and, in so doing, liberated the individual for participation in the republic. There were, to be sure, other mediating or moderating institutions that promoted public responsibility, but Tocqueville prominently stresses the dyad *religion* and *liberty* from the outset of his work.

His argument was, as he claimed, part of a new political science.[77]

Thus, the religion that he described was not particularly severe and otherworldly, nor was the freedom that he applauded especially indebted to the virtue of the ancient polis. Both smacked of utilitarian concessions. Neither was, in the strong sense, exemplary in the spheres of the sacred and the profane, but both were held sufficient to the task in the new age of democracy. Religion was judged valuable not for its theological virtuosity but for its ability to domesticate "self-interest, rightly understood," to turn self-regarding actions into a public concord of liberty. Religion itself was never described as "free," except by virtue of disestablishment: it was the source and enablement of secular freedom. That freedom, in turn, was largely expressed in "society," that is, in the relations and transactions that people enjoyed exclusive of government. But it was also expressed in political intelligence and participation and in law-abidingness. Government "of the people" was essentially weak government, and government could be weak because the people, relatively equal in condition and concerted in values, exercised moral self-governance from religious motives. What Tocqueville arrived at was a kind of conflation of the theories of Rousseau and Benjamin Constant, with, to be sure, more affinity for the latter than the former.

While it seems obvious that Tocqueville's theory could only have been articulated in the empirical presence of America, it was not simply intended to explain the relative success of that nation's institutions but also to set norms and furnish warnings for the inevitable democratization of France. Its origin, therefore, is not in an induction from the American experience but in a conundrum which that experience had been called on to solve, for in Europe everything seemed topsy-turvy. Tocqueville makes this clear in his introduction:

> Where are we then?
>
> The religionists are the enemies of liberty, and the friends of liberty attack religion; the high-minded and most noble advocate bondage, and the meanest and most servile preach independence; honest and enlightened citizens are opposed to all progress, while men without patriotism and without principle put themselves forward as the apostles of civilization and intelligence.[78]

In Europe, as the poet Yeats would later put it, "The best lack all conviction, while the worst/ Are full of passionate intensity." Tocqueville implores God's Providence (perhaps only rhetorically) to assure him that the course of history cannot intend such anomalies to persist. From such a point of departure, we might expect America to burst on the scene as a kind of utopia inherited from the popular genre of the "extraordinary voyage." It is a testimony to Tocqueville's great percipience, analytical skill, and realism that little of this distortion clouds his work. But we are already alerted that he has an axe to grind. Many will ask today, and many have asked: Is it so strange that the friends of liberty should attack religion? Tocqueville was therefore under some pressure, as an "écrivain politique," to find some kind of religion that could underwrite the necessity of religion *tout court* while still promoting a political development that seemed inevitable.

Tocqueville had not been historically alone in this undertaking. As we saw previously, Montesquieu had laid its groundwork in the *Spirit of the Laws,* and others, like Constant and various German thinkers, had carried it forward. Years later, the functional sociologists had used the same problematic framework for their research into the mechanisms of social stability. It is of even greater interest to note that Bryce, who observed an America vastly changed in the half-century since Tocqueville's visit, still felt bound by the same civic-religious hypothesis and was disposed to generate a theory from it:

> America is no doubt the country in which intellectual movements work most swiftly upon the masses, and the country in which the loss of faith in the invisible might produce the completest revolution, because it is the country where men have been least wont to revere anything in the visible world. Yet America seems as unlikely to drift from her ancient moorings as many countries of the Old World. . . . The more democratic republics become, the more the masses grow conscious of their own power, the more do they need to live not only by patriotism, but by reverence and self-control, and the more essential to their well-being are those sources whence reverence and self-control flow.[79]

Already the moorings are "ancient." Some of these comments may surprise: especially the lack of reverence for things in the visible world, given that this is now the age of unrestrained capitalism. But Bryce is evidently speaking of the "average man," for whom "religious teaching, though it has become less definite and less dogmatic, is still . . . the source whence he believes himself to have drawn his ideas of duty and content."[80] He acknowledges that such is not the case everywhere: "In the cultivated circles of the great cities one finds a good many people, as one does in England, who have virtually abandoned Christianity."[81] Yet, toward the end of the century Washington Gladden was optimistic about the state of affairs: "A considerable part of the life of civilized society is controlled by Christian principle. We have come to a day in which it does not seem quixotic to believe that the principles of Christianity are soon to prevail; that all social relations are to be Christianized."[82]

It is probably not the view of many contemporary critics that religion has continued to underwrite public liberty in America. Either religion is of little consequence in determining how Americans perform in the public sphere, or it has connived with forces of reaction to distort that expression, or it has lost its soul in shallow patriotism, or there is increasingly less liberty in the Tocquevillian sense for it to sustain. Without prejudging any of these attitudes, but with full awareness that *Democracy in America* opens issues that cannot be easily laid to rest by Tocqueville, we are obliged to pick up the threads.

It is possible that Tocqueville saw virtually all of the essential in his remarkable work. But since his technique for stabilizing a democratic society appears not to be operating successfully in contemporary America, we may be justified in asking: What did Tocqueville miss? I do not mean to imply that he should have seen things that were not there to see, but that he missed certain features of his surroundings. One of his negligences, as I have said, was his underestimation of the power of emotional religious currents that were perhaps beyond the ken of a European aristocrat. Another, I think, was a failure to evaluate the multiplier effect of total disestablishment. Tocqueville knew that there were sects aplenty in America, and he was shrewd enough to see that, *grosso modo,* they preached the same morality, but he had little idea of how they would spangle the American horizon with their organizational, theological, and personal explosions, in perfect liberty but not as a source of liberty. Finally—and the point is inseparable from the previous ones—I think that Tocqueville failed to estimate the political implications of the action of Arminian doctrines (especially as embodied in Methodism) upon the civic roots of Calvinism, a process that was taking place even as he traveled and scrutinized the country. Obviously these are not the only issues that might be raised here, but they will serve to launch our subsequent discussion.

Notes

More than two years after I wrote this chapter, I was very interested to read James T. Schleifer's "Tocqueville and Religion: Some New Perspectives," *Tocqueville Review* (1982): 303-21. Drawing upon Tocqueville's unpublished manuscripts deposited at Yale University, the author reaches virtually the same interpretation as that presented here.

1. *Democracy in America,* I, 33.
2. Ibid.
3. See André Siegfried, *Les Etats-Unis d'aujourd'hui* (Paris, 1927), pp. 32, 52-55; and his *Tableau des Etats-Unis* (Paris, 1954), pp. 89-92, passim. A decade before the visit of Tocqueville, William Ellery Channing had this to say: "By shocking, as it does, the fundamental principles of morality, and by exhibiting a severe and partial deity, it tends strongly to pervert the moral faculty, to form a gloomy, forbidding, and servile religion, and to lead men to substitute censoriousness, bitterness, and persecution for a tender and impartial charity." *Unitarian Christianity* (New York, 1957), p. 25.
4. *Democracy in America,* I, 298ff.
5. David Ramsay, *The History of the American Revolution* (2 vols., Philadelphia, 1789), I, 199.
6. *Political Annals of the Present United Colonies,* quoted in Wesley French Craven, ed., *The Legend of the Founding Fathers* (New York, 1956), pp. 53-54.
7. Joel Barlow, *The Vision of Columbus,* bk. VII, ll. 220-21, 226-29 (Paris, 1793), p. 220.
8. Jonathan Edwards, "Thoughts on the Revival of Religion in New England," in *Works* (4 vols., New York, 1868), III, 315.
9. Cf. Gilbert Chinard, *L'Amérique et le rêve exotique dans la littérature française au XVIIe et XVIIIe siècles* (Paris, 1913), passim.
10. J. Hector St. John Crèvecoeur, *Letters from an American Farmer* (Gloucester, 1968), p. 49.
11. *Democracy in America,* I, 219.
12. Ibid., I, 330.
13. Ibid., I, 315.
14. Ibid., I, 43.
15. Ibid., I, 321.
16. Ibid., II, 22.
17. Montesquieu had written of the religionless person as a "terrible animal." Benjamin Constant added: "Religious peoples can be slaves, but no irreligious people has ever been free." *Du Polythéisme romain considéré dans ses rapports avec la philosophie grecque et la religion chrétienne* (2 vols., Paris, 1833), II, 91-92.
18. *Democracy in America,* I, 46.
19. Cf. ibid., p. 45: "The settlers of New England were at the same time ardent sectarians and daring innovators. Narrow as the limits of some of their religious opinions were, they were free from all political prejudice."
20. Ibid., I, 311-12. Max Weber saw very little to distinguish the American sects. Of his trip in 1900, he wrote: "It does not matter whether one be a Freemason, Christian Scientist, Adventist, Quaker, or what not." H.H. Gerth and C. Wright Mills, eds., *From Max Weber: Essays in Sociology* (New York, 1967), p. 307.
21. *Democracy in America,* I, 311.
22. Ibid., I, 324.

23. Michael Oakeshott, "The Moral Life in the Philosophy of Thomas Hobbes," in *Hobbes on Civil Association* (Oxford, 1975), pp. 76-77.
24. *Democracy in America,* I, 310.
25. Robert N. Bellah, "American Civil Religion in the 1970s," in Richey and Jones, eds., *American Civil Religion,* p. 270.
26. See Bellah's "Religion and Legitimation in the American Republic," *Society* 15 (May-June 1978): 16-23.
27. *Democracy in America,* I, 433.
28. Ibid.
29. Ibid., I, 434.
30. Franklin was of course writing only for Pennsylvania. See below, p. 216.
31. "Proposals Relating to the Education of Youth in Pennsylvania" (1749), in *The Papers of Benjamin Franklin,* ed. Leonard W. Labaree (21 vols., New Haven, 1961), III, 413.
32. Washington's "Farewell Address," in *The World's Great Classics: Orations of American Orators* (2 vols., New York, 1900), I, 40.
33. Mead, *Old Religion,* p. 79.
34. In the atmosphere of the Boston Massacre orations, Catherine L. Albanese detects a trend toward Roman paganism and invocations of the Goddess of Liberty, but the mood seems rhetorical and transitory. See her *Sons of the Fathers: The Civil Religion of the American Revolution* (Philadelphia, 1976), pp. 73-78 passim.
35. Perry Miller, "From the Covenant to the Revival," in J.W. Smith and A. Leland Jamison, eds., *The Shaping of American Religion* (Princeton, 1961), p. 353.
36. See Karl Barth, *Community, State, and Church* (New York, 1960), esp. pp. 122-48.
37. Marty, *New Shape,* p. 118.
38. *Democracy in America,* I, 316.
39. Ibid., I, 319.
40. Francis J. Grund, *The Americans* (Boston, 1837), pp. 163-64.
41. *Democracy in America,* I, 314-15, 320; II, 28-29.
42. Ibid., II, 29.
43. See, on this, Strout, *New Heavens,* pp. 111-13.
44. *Democracy in America,* I, 304; cf. I, 32, on New England as norm. It is not in dispute that many New Englanders moved west, into upper New York state, and later into the states of the Northwest Territory, and that the majority were from Connecticut; one source estimates 800,000 migrants between 1790 and 1820. See William Warren Sweet, *Religion on the American Frontier, 1783-1840* (Chicago, 1939), p. 13. But the Connecticut phalanx did not recreate New Haven and Hartford.
45. *Democracy in America,* II, 143.
46. Ibid., I, 323.
47. Ibid., II, 27. Perhaps Tocqueville should have given more heed to a text of Bayle, probably known to him (Article "Drusius," *Dictionnaire historique et critique,* 16 vols., Paris, 1820, VI, 37): "It is not in the temporal interest of a religious communion that all its members should be reasonable. The violent spirits, who adhere to it solely out of factiousness, perform for it, humanly speaking, a thousand valuable services. So it is

useful that hotheads of this sort should be found in its ranks; this is a necessary evil."

48. See I. Scott Miyakawa, *Protestants and Pioneers: Individualism and Conformity on the American Frontier* (Chicago, 1964), p. 215.

49. Tocqueville did have some apposite remarks on American vocabulary and rhetoric *(Democracy in America,* II, 94-98), but not in this connection.

50. Michael Chevalier, *Society, Manners, and Politics in the United States* (1838; reprint, New York, 1969), p. 317.

51. Laski, *American Democracy,* p. 270.

52. See ibid., p. 266.

53. *Democracy in America,* II, 168-71.

54. Of course Tocqueville often refers to the "states" of the Union. He points out (ibid., I, 148-49) that "in America the real power is vested in the states far more than in the Federal government."

55. Ibid., I, 15.

56. See Marquis de Condorcet, *Esquisse d'un tableau historique des progrès de l'esprit humain* (Paris, 1933), pp. 171-72.

57. *Democracy in America,* I, 43.

58. Ibid., I, 59-60. Although the Tocqueville text just cited sounds almost Mazzinian—and is certainly intended to be provocative—it cannot be regarded as normative without severe qualification. Tocqueville's social pluralism is poles apart from the idea of integrative populism, whose deficiencies receive a painstaking critique in *Democracy in America.* When Tocqueville wishes to warn of the dangers of democracy, he aggregates the public; when he dwells on its advantages, he distributes the public.

59. Joseph Schumpeter, *Capitalism, Socialism, and Democracy* (3d ed., New York, 1962), p. 269.

60. A generalization, of course: Connecticut had an established religion (with toleration) until 1818, and Massachusetts until 1833. Jews and other non-Christians or freethinkers were denied political rights in various states during the first half of the nineteenth century.

61. James Bryce, *The American Commonwealth* (2 vols., New York, 1895), II, 699-700.

62. Federalist No. 51, in *The Federalist,* ed. Henry Cabot Lodge (New York, 1894), p. 326. In Federalist No. 10, differences in religion are also a species of faction.

63. See Strout, *New Heavens,* p. 83.

64. In Jonathan Elliott, ed., *The Debates in the Several State Conventions* (5 vols., Philadelphia, 1901), III, 330.

65. See esp. Miller, "From Covenant to Revival," pp. 341-44.

66. "The disestablishment of religion was neither an original goal nor completely a product of the Revolution. Its roots lay deep in the colonial past, in circumstances that Jonathan Parsons described as 'a random way of settling ministers and churches, together with a vile contempt of creeds and confessions . . . all seem to jumble together, and make mere *hodgepodge.*' These unplanned, unexpected conditions, lacking in completeness and justification, were touched by the magic of Revolutionary thought, and were transformed." Bernard Bailyn, *The Ideological Origins of the American Revolution* (Cambridge, Mass., 1967), p. 271.

67. Private but not "privatized" as the word is used today. A personal religion defended against institutions is not the same thing as a retreat to privacy conditioned by the failure of institutions.
68. Letter to Adams, 15 June 1813, in *The Adams-Jefferson Letters: The Complete Correspondence Between Thomas Jefferson and Abigail and John Adams*, ed. Lester J. Cappon (2 vols., Chapel Hill, 1959), I, 331.
69. B.F. Morris, *Christian Life and Character of the Civil Institutions of the United States* (Philadelphia, 1864), p. 525.
70. Cited by Paul C. Nagel, *This Sacred Trust* (New York, 1971), p. 28. Jefferson abandoned the practice, only to have it reinstated by his successors. See Anson Phelps Stokes, *Church and State in the United States* (4 vols., New York, 1930), I, 489-91. For Jefferson's rather cloudy religious views, see Adrienne Koch, *The Philosophy of Thomas Jefferson* (New York, 1943), pp. 23-39.
71. James Daniel Richardson, ed., *Compilation of the Messages and Papers of the Presidents* (20 vols., New York, 1897-1908), II, 515, 517.
72. Cited in I.A. Cornelison, *The Relation of Religion to Civil Government in the United States of America* (New York, 1895), p. 93.
73. Parrington, *Main Currents,* I, iv.
74. Ibid., III, 401.
75. State v. Ambs, 20 Mo. 216-17 (1854). Cf. Church of the Holy Trinity v. United States, 143 U.S. 226 (1892), which declares that "a volume of unofficial declarations [can be added] to the mass of organic utterances that this is a Christian nation."
76. Max Lerner, *America as a Civilization* (New York, 1957), p. 715.
77. Cf. *Democracy in America,* I, 7: "A new science of politics is needed for a new world."
78. Ibid., I, 13.
79. Bryce, *American Commonwealth,* II, 727.
80. Ibid., 723.
81. Ibid., 718.
82. Washington Gladden, *The Nation and the Kingdom* (Boston, 1909), pp. 7-8.

3

Amazing Grace

In his lectures on the philosophy of history delivered in Berlin in 1830 (the year before his death and Tocqueville's arrival in America), Hegel included a few brief remarks on the United States. He saw there "an unbounded license in religious matters."[1] For Hegel, America was as yet only a rude "civil society" *(bürgerliche Gesellschaft)*, lacking a fully developed "state." A comparison of the thought of Hegel and Tocqueville shows that both allotted religion a crucial mediating function between freedom and control in the profane sphere of politics. Hegel had written: "It is in being . . . related to religion that state, laws, and duties all alike acquire for consciousness their supreme confirmation and their supreme obligatoriness, because . . . in religion there lies the place where man is always assured of finding a consciousness of the unchangeable, of the highest freedom and satisfaction."[2] This is not unlike the mission that Tocqueville assigned to religion in the American republic.[3] But with regard to the respective capacities of "state" and "society" Hegel and Tocqueville were at odds. We have already discussed Tocqueville's derivation of the concept of "society" and its connection with the realm of freedom. For Hegel, society was no more than a precursor or dialectical moment in the development of the true freedom that the state alone could foster through its comprehensive ethical and yet plural unity (supported by a monarchical, not a republican, constitution). According to Hegel, "North America will be comparable with Europe [i.e., as a "state"] only after the immeasurable space which that country presents to its inhabitants shall have been occupied, and the members of the political body shall have begun to be pressed back on each other."[4] A real state can be formed "only after a distinction of classes has arisen, when wealth and poverty become extreme, and when such a condition of things presents itself that a large portion of the people can no longer satisfy its necessities in the way it has been accustomed so to do."[5]

There is no obligation here to prefer either of these analyses. Hegel's cursory remarks cannot, in any case, be reasonably counterpoised against Tocqueville's comprehensive study of American institutions. However, the following might be said. The normative sentiments of a great many Christian Americans (Catholics as well as Protestants, although my emphasis here is on a predominantly Protestant religious culture) operate, and have operated, within the orbit of Tocqueville's liberal view. That is to say, the stress is on religion as voluntary and plural—as emanating from convictions embraced in "society"—and on the public function of religion as a moral prolegomenon to citizenship. The notion of religion as some kind of axiomatic adjunct to state power, although familiar in our patriotic rhetoric since the beginnings of the republic, is usually acceptable to Christians only in the sense that God has intended this relationship and that it has been operable through the voice of the people. But, as I have indicated, there seems to be something empirically wrong or fabulous in this ideal belief, however well it might have described the situation in Tocqueville's time. There is an ironical clash between the Tocquevillian—and American—view of the "new" nation and the Hegelian—and, in the main, European—view of the "young" nation, one that the resources of history are still being called on to umpire.

Tocqueville's point of departure is, however, of immense fertility. We must take issue with Perry Miller's dictum that "his pages on religion in *De la Démocratie en Amérique* are probably the least perceptive he ever wrote."[6] Miller confronts Tocqueville with the tributes to American religion paid, also for the benefit of European readerships, by Robert Baird and Philip Schaff. Baird, who was a missionary agent in France for the Presbyterian Church, published his massive *Religion in America* in 1843. Although, as Miller points out, he differed from Tocqueville in his enthusiasm for evangelical religion, his major point surely was to praise the beauties of the "voluntary principle" of disestablishment, which assured "perfect religious freedom . . . freedom of conscience for all: for those who believe Christianity to be true, and for those who do not: for those who prefer one form of worship, and for those who prefer another."[7] That eminently Madisonian view—though it must be stressed that Baird was passionately hostile to the rationalistic founders, especially Jefferson[8]—was surely aligned to Tocqueville's position. Schaff, a German *émigré* whose role in the development of American theology and religious historiography, centering around the Mercersburg Seminary in Pennsylvania, was of capital importance,[9] revisited Berlin in the 1850s and lectured there on American Protestantism. The result was a book, translated under the title *America,* in which he declared notably that "the United States are by far the most religious and Christian country in the world; and that, just because religion is there most free."[10] It is difficult to see how this conclusion contradicts or surpasses Tocqueville's. Like Tocqueville, Schaff found it possible to conceive of an ecumenical American religion, though grounded in theology rather than ethics, that "will not simply be a continuation of either the English, or the German alone, but the result of the combined action and reaction of both, as applied to the peculiar wants and conditions of American Christianity and society."[11] Miller is of course right in discerning that Tocqueville's treatment of religion (as an "écrivain politique") shortchanged some of its intensity of conviction, but he is ill advised to demean the quality of that analysis. Different as they were in tone from *Democracy in America,* the works of Baird and Schaff were really witnesses to its sagacity.

"America," Schaff wrote, "is, without question, emphatically the land of the future."[12] He intended this in a providential sense, stressing Christianity rather than democracy as *telos.* Strangely enough, this is the same phrase that Hegel had used in his *Lectures on the Philosophy of History.* Interpreters of Hegel later took this to mean that America concealed further and higher manifestations of the world spirit. Yet for Hegel himself, who judged the fullness of *Geist* by speculative philosophy and the consummated political state, America was clearly off the map; for him "future" meant "undeveloped" or "not of present concern."[13] If we wish to measure America by Hegelian standards, we must focus on the America of his future and our present. The evolution that we find is the following. Over time, some of the consequences of becoming a "state" have indeed been fulfilled. The "immeasurable space" has been occupied and, at least in the numerous redoubts of *megalopolis,* citizens have "begun to be pressed back on each other." Evidences of class distinction, extremes of wealth and poverty, and problems in satisfying necessities have long been visible. Corporate conglomerates in the economy and interdependencies of collective life have replaced wide areas of independence and "rugged individualism." While not exactly usurping "society," the state has increasingly penetrated it with regulations, distributions, bureaucracies, and rewards and penalties. There is no American monarchy, as Hegel might have predicted (most European ones have fallen by the wayside), but we may have its functional equivalent in the "imperial presidency" with its trappings of majesty and a host of tributary personnel.[14] Religion is still disestablished and seemingly uninhibited (we would not expect this in the Hegelian model, which favored a restricted denominationalism working closely with the state), but it may be no accident that many of today's critics see the traditional denominations drained of vitality and popular faith concentrated in a belief system of "civil religion," vaguely biblical, vaguely Protestant (despite the rhetorical *politesse* obtaining in a country of forty-nine million Catholics and six million Jews), at least "post-Protestant."[15]

Hegel had applauded (Lutheran) Protestantism as the seed-plot of secular freedom: It had promoted "a sentiment which . . . is the fountain of all the equitable arrangements that prevail with regard to private right and the constitution of the state."[16] Similarly, from the point of view of "society," Tocqueville, for whom all religions encouraged "a political opinion," found Calvinism specifically allied with "democratic and republican theories."[17] Montesquieu had also had good words for both the major branches of Protestantism.[18] The question here is whether the Hegelian analysis takes us further than the others. It surely does not do so in any manner vaguely related to the idiosyncratic career of Lutheranism in America, for that current of faith has been almost as far from the mainstream as Catholicism.[19] However, we can, at least deviously, trace from the development of Hegel's philosophical materials the ideas of "disenchantment" and "civil religion," to be taken up ahead. The former, prefigured in Hegel's *"Aufhebung* of the Christian religion," was further mediated through Feuerbach, Nietzsche, the neo-Kantians, and Weber, as well as through a crisis of faith common to all Western civilization, whereas the latter carries not only the echo of Rousseau and republicanism but also Hegel's idea of religion as the basic manifestation of the spirit of a people *(Volksgeist).*[20]

The original geography of settlement in the North American colonies had scattered the Christian communities so that an implanted and vigorous sectarianism would be played out against the fleeting shadow of establishment. It not only was unlike anything ever before known in Europe, where inclusive churches treated dissenters as civic misfits, but had its own anomalies. The Church of England, theoretically sovereign in the lands of English colonization, had, from the earliest, ceded the de facto principle of establishment to the Congregationalist Puritans of Massachusetts and Connecticut, where, in time, its own communicants received mere civil toleration. In established Connecticut the Congregational parishes drew close to a Presbyterian form of organization, while Presbyterian immigrants from Scotland—accustomed to a state church—received only sectarian standing in their new areas of habitation. The low-church Anglican colonies of the South were swiftly infused with a variety of sects whose growth would inundate the predominance of the Tidewater communities. Proprietary Maryland, governed at first by a Catholic elite, extended complete toleration to its Protestant majority, then endured an Anglican establishment. Proprietary Pennsylvania, a congeries of all the religious movements of the European diaspora, was pluralized from the start. Royal New York, officially Anglican in the populous southern counties, had to accommodate the Reformed Calvinists of New Amsterdam. Occasional antinomianism, of which Anne Hutchinson may be described as the "symptom and prophecy," rippled the waters of conformity. Roger Williams carried a sweeping doctrine of toleration into Rhode Island, creating not only a haven for separatists but a fundamental distinction between the prerogatives of politics and religion that prefigured elements of the later federal solution. Quakerism, which repugned strife but accepted the coercive instrument of civil government, spread the same doctrine.[21] Ingenious liberals like John Wise, in his *Vindication of the Government of New-England Churches* (1717), commenced the amalgamation of Calvinist covenant theology with the more optimistic assumptions of social contract theory.[22] Of such diverse pragmatic materials came the premises of American disestablishment, and from it, in turn, came a further impulsion to the sects, now in a politically liberated milieu, and to the national validation of a secular citizenship practiced by believers. While it is true that "secular tolerance created the social and spiritual diversity that led men to seek community in attacking the community of others,"[23] this *contretemps* was not made starkly apparent until new waves of Catholics and exotic sects outside the Protestant consensus, notably the Latter-day Saints,[24] fueled underlying bigotry and caused religion to blaze up within politics.

As Martin Marty points out, "The first of the great inventions [of disestablishment], and the one which determined life in the others, was the denomination."[25] The *locus classicus* of ecclesiastical typology, Ernst Troeltsch's *The Social Teachings of the Christian Churches,* had dichotomized the religious bodies of the European Reformation into "church" and "sect." Churches tended to be instruments in the state and its ruling classes, inclusive and ascriptive in their membership, endowed with the *mana* of grace and salvation. Sects, on the other hand, were formed by voluntary choice or conversion; havens of the underprivileged and the rebellious, they depended on "actual personal service and co-operation . . . [a] bond of union

. . . directly realized in the personal relationships of life."[26] Whatever the merits of Troeltsch's analysis—and it has been many times criticized—it was unsuited to describe the American situation. No doubt in their secret hearts some of America's competing religious groups aspired to be "churches," thereby underscoring the rectitude of their doctrine and constitution and the normative implications of the same for Christianity. Both Congregationalism and Anglicanism had been established in colonies of North America, as the Presbyterians had been in Scotland, the Reformed Church initially in the Netherlands, and the Lutherans in Scandinavia and parts of Germany. Then there was Roman Catholicism, a "universal Church" and a case apart. But, without form or elaborate complaint—even among America's earliest native Catholic leaders—the status of denomination was tacitly accepted as the logic of a pluralistic society ruled by republican institutions. Again in Martin Marty's words: "The ground rules of the denominational game assured that no church would be favored by the civil power, nor would any people find sanctions taken against them so long as they remained within a very broad and generally approved consensus."[27]

While churches were thus demoted to denominations because of their novel political environment, sects had the opportunity to rise to equivalent status. Long a pietistic "ginger group" within Anglicanism, the Methodist movement of John and Charles Wesley declared its independence only in 1784. From the period of the Great Western Revival to the Civil War its growth in numbers, power, and stature was meteoric. The same can be said, with a slight lag, of the thousands of autonomous congregations calling themselves Baptist, having diverse origins in Europe, New England separatism, and the frontier movement itself. Seventy percent of all Protestant Americans would be affiliated to some branch of these two faiths by 1855.[28] Other sects followed along the path to denominationalism, as measured by social and economic integration in the country and defined by H. Richard Niebuhr as accepting "compromise between Christianity and the world":[29] the Unitarian schism from New England Congregationalism, the Disciples of Christ, and even, in the recent opinion of some, the Quakers, Adventists, Christian Scientists, and Mormons.[30] The denominations were throughout most of their history and up to today's more "ecumenical" times highly fissiparous, except for the Episcopalians, who themselves managed to wage acrimonious controversy between their high- and low-church wings. Ethnic origins, theologies, authority structures, the slavery question, liturgical practices, and the fundamentalist-modernist split all contributed to these cleavages. The denominations were, in truth, "great families," subject to every manner of family quarrel and sometimes more friendly with close neighbors than with siblings. An important kernel of common doctrine and ancestry validated their self-identification, but, as long as America spoke and thought in religious categories, they carried the spirit of sect within them. Created in space and time according to the voluntary principle and with a certain interchangeability of ministry and membership, federalized and pluralized by a heavy dose of local rule, they had something of the nature of America's loose and polyglot political parties, as well as the practical orientation of its social action groups. President Andrew Jackson is quoted as telling Nathan S.S. Beman that his political opponents "don't bother me half so much as do the discussions in the Presbyterian Church." [31] Religion, like politics, fought free of its "era of good feelings." When it rested from its labor of churching infidels and repentants, its debates, quite as impertinent as those among Jackson, Clay, Webster, and Calhoun, were apt to be intramural.

"Denominations" was a word in fashion a hundred years before H. Richard Niebuhr invested it with a sociological imprimatur. Bluntly put, the denominations became the fractious but prudent oligarchs of the Tocquevillian republican religion. Some of them came from sects and they sometimes dissolved into sects, but they achieved a meeting between America's elites and masses and its high and common culture in a way that persistent sectarianism could not (exception partly made for the Quakers). The American democracy was to a considerable degree shaped by these religious oligopolists. When in a world of "secularization" and "disenchantment," spokesmen like Peter Berger liken the denominations to competitive actors in an economic market, they are describing nothing very strange or new. "Allegiance," Berger writes, "is voluntary and thus, by definition, less than certain. As a result, the religious tradition, which previously could be authoritatively imposed, now has to be *marketed*. It must be 'sold' to a clientele that is no longer constrained to 'buy.' The pluralistic situation is, above all, a *market situation*." [32] While it is certainly true that authoritative impositions of religious tradition, strong in the nineteenth century, are feeble today and that religion must compete in its accustomed market with profane merchandisers, the market image has long been fitting, for in all territories, open and settled, from the banks of the Mississippi to the urban centers of the East, the creeds had been accustomed to competitive strategies of growth within a large context of Protestant evangelical solidarity. As an example, it took only sixty years from its founding for the Methodist Church to become the second-largest denomination in recalcitrant New England.[33]

The political aim of religious disestablishment had been to level out and diffuse America's spiritual precocity. Tocqueville observed that this had created a common national morality grounded in a supernatural faith that supported republican values. Yet the sects, in becoming denominations, and the charismatic and prophetic leaders, in creating yet more sects, went far beyond Tocqueville's prescription of harmonizing heaven and earth in a public ordering of self-interests. While the domesticated denominations eventually kindled a republican consensus from their emotional cinders, reinterpreting the national mission in a fervent biblicism alien to the Founders though latent in the mentality of eighteenth-century citizens, new sectarians carried forward the logic of disestablishment. Denominationalism reaped, but sectarianism sowed as the European migrants peopled a continent "from sea to shining sea."

This does not mean that Americans were not as practical and worldly as most reports would suggest or that they were not easily roused by material impulses. The debates about faction in the Constitutional Convention were deadly serious: Americans had their will-to-power, too. Indeed, from the start, political economy had deeply affected their theory of government and their public preoccupations, nowhere more drastically than in the War of 1812.[34] While Massachusetts merchants and New York financiers feathered their nests, in the New West—the West of Henry Clay and Old Hickory—"law, religion, education, culture were pressed into the service of speculation."[35] Tocqueville himself observed that although "America is still the place where the Christian religion has kept the greatest real power over men's souls . . . it cannot moderate their eagerness to enrich themselves."[36] Madison's politics was no doubt an ingenious "preservative control system of the profane." Was the religion authorized on the same principle an effective "control system of the sacred?" To a degree it was: in the sense that Tocqueville cites, the sphere where the sacred made acquiescent contact with the profane, disburdening guilt and thus stirring initiative. But to the degree that religion served its vocation of redeeming human beings in a transpolitical context, it went beyond the sober behavior of checks and balances to preach a new covenant of grace in the youngest of the nations, stressing the abjection of sin, the miracle of conversion, and the majesty of providence. None of this had been quite dreamt of in the Philadelphia debates of 1787. It is difficult for us to grasp that *homo economicus* and *homo religiosus* could exist side by side, and even interchangeably, in an earlier America, without any burning awareness of *mauvaise foi*. The Calvinist God reached toward man, inscrutably, and elected him for sainthood, but the new Arminian man, confounded by his evil ways, reached toward the Lord. Salvation was not severely demarcated from other kinds of acquisitiveness, all of which required faith and toil.

The First Amendment had legislated the "free exercise" of religion, but it had not legislated the religious imagination. That impulse was provided by prophetic evangelists using the vehicle of Scripture. The revivalist had been a fixture of the American scene since the preludes to the First Great Awakening of ca. 1740.[37] At that time both itinerants and local pastors, often to the scandal of their more passive and orthodox clerical colleagues, traversed western New England and the frontiers to the south to regenerate fallen populations with the emotional gospel of conversion.[38] The Scriptures—especially as preached, not read—provided not so much a conclusive set of rules for Christian practices as an immense thesaurus of images, parables, and cautionary texts syncopated by revivalist rhetoric and designed to strike a chord in the hearer's imagination. As H. Richard Niebuhr expresses it, a little primly: "The Scriptures for Protestants are not like what the Constitution is for Americans, but more like the collection of all the documents from Magna Charta to the Atlantic Charter that record the story of secular liberation. The authority of the Bible has been more like that of the prophet than that of the law-giver."[39]

While any reduction of the American civic experience to its religious avatars would be as one-dimensional as any other reductionism, a clue to that experience can be gained by examining the fortunes of theology and evangelism within the paradigmatic careers of the two leading forces—the Calvinists (Congregationalists and Presbyterians) and the Methodists. The American citizen is indirectly a product of this history.

American Presbyterianism shared a single theology with the first New England Congregationalist settlers. What traditionally divided these denominations was their notion of church authority, with the Presbyterians reliant on a hierarchy of presbytery and synod beyond the self-governing features of the individual congregations. In Massachusetts, the Puritans affirmed their congregationalist position in the Cambridge Platform of 1648: affiliation, but no consociation or higher form of government. However, it must not be imagined that in America this distinction played as critical a role as in Commonwealth England, where the parties also had sharp political quarrels. Nor were the New England Puritans—who had founded their "city on a hill" more than a decade earlier—to be confused with Commonwealth "Independency," which was closer to the beliefs of our Separatists and Baptists; this was proved in the antinomian controversy that led to the founding of Rhode Island. In their doctrinal interpretation of Calvinism—with emphasis on predestinarianism, election, original sin, and the efficacy of grace—the seventeenth-century settlers of Massachusetts were closely aligned with both Geneva and the Church of Scotland. Attested conversion was a public, and provisional, testimony of "sainthood."

As distinct from the Congregationalist Puritans, American Presbyterianism had its major root-source in emigrations from Scotland and Ulster in the eighteenth century.[40] These migrants tended to settle in the Middle Atlantic colonies and along the chain of the Appalachian Mountains. Their dogmatic Calvinism rivaled any found in the Bay Colony, but their political arrangements, usually taking place in the company of other sects, were far more pragmatic. In the meantime, especially after the appointment of a royal governor from England in 1684, followed in 1691 by the rechartering of the Bay Colony, both polity and church in Massachusetts were liberalized. The franchise was now based on a property qualification, not on church membership. Arminianism—meaning here the notion that man could earn salvation through his own works—began to penetrate the faith, no doubt because it was congenial to the wealthy commercial class. It was this creeping comfort that the revivalists of the First Great Awakening sought to disquiet with their emotional emphasis on true conversion.[41]

In Congregationalist Connecticut, a more affirmed "clericalism," enunciated in the Saybrook Platform of 1708, had strengthened orthodoxy by introducing a semipresbyterian form of church government.[42] This permanently marked the Connecticut contribution to American Calvinism and promoted closer relations with the Presbyterians of the Middle Colonies. While in the course of the eighteenth century Cambridge and Boston fought the revivalistic impulses of the Awakening, drifting toward rationalistic Arminianism and, eventually, Unitarianism, the bastions of New Haven, Hartford, and Princeton welcomed the theology of Edwards and, albeit with a certain prudence, the fruits of evangelism, though this enthusiasm would swiftly wane in Hodge's Princeton.

American Calvinism was, of course, a house of many mansions, totally impossible to describe in single, sweeping generalizations. Little in American Protestantism—except Lutheranism—was untouched by Geneva. The Episcopal Church itself was not free of Calvinist am-

biguities, Hawthorne's tale of the Roundheads and Cavaliers at Mer-
rymount notwithstanding. The great Arminian sects—Methodism and
Baptism—led one back always to a fundamentally Calvinistic psychology of sin and grace. In rejecting the Massachusetts Bay ecclesiastical polity root and branch, Roger Williams remained "as
passionately Puritan as . . . his persecutors."[43] The gentle Quakers
with their "inner light" were not immune from this syndrome. Even
Unitarianism, the unfaithful child of its parent, was impossible to define without a birth certificate. The same would later be true of Christian Science.

We can grasp both the force and the ambivalence of the notion that
America long remained in thrall to a "Puritan ethic." It most surely
did so if the ethic is made elastic enough to accommodate all these
things, if Benjamin Franklin (à la Max Weber) and hence a good bit of
the American Enlightenment is included in it. The thrift, industry,
and sobriety implied by the ethic could encompass important theological rifts. However, Puritanism did more than describe a character
around which many Americans became polarized; it settled the conditions and issues, sometimes long in advance, for much of American
ethical controversy, indeed for the eventual assault on its own positions. If Martin Marty's term "post-Protestantism" seems to shed
light on our present culture, then the term "post-Puritan" is not out
of place either. "Post-Puritan" should not be taken to mean "anti-
Puritan" so much as "the *Aufhebung* of Puritanism."

The civic development of the American mind and the Tocquevillian
issue of freedom and control in the profane sphere are implicated in
the preceding, for if we now narrow our concentration to the Calvinist core—as represented particularly in the New England and Presbyterian faiths—we are also aware of looking at the germ of a civic
order. That order emanates from the theology expressed in the West-
minister Confession, described by Ahlstrom as "by far the most influential doctrinal symbol in American religious history."[44] It is highly
participationist, even though it is not egalitarian. It is resolutely non-
perfectionist, for never is it suggested that man, whether aided or
unaided by grace, can create a political community in which all can
delight and take their ease. That would have seemed a nonsense to
the Calvinists, for they were convinced that human ills were not due
to bad institutions but to the indwelling presence of evil in human
beings. Indeed, this notion is perfectly Augustinian: the enduring virtue of the human political experiment lies in the natural need for preserving peace and order, but that virtue is negative in comparison to
the true community of saints in the City of God. As a consequence,

and despite other hints by Jonathan Edwards, American Calvinism's greatest theologian, there is a heavy premillennial tendency in this vision of politics: the achievement of the earthly kingdom cannot be a prelude to Christ's coming again.[45]

In the Calvinist city, distinct from the city of heavenly grace, there is a gripping tension between what is licit and what is moral. In the first place, town politics and congregational order are not coterminous. The laws of each would appear to bind men in different ways. However, the divine covenant is always superior to the earthly compact. "Conversion" is the human mechanism by which the first asserts its superiority; what visible signs of grace there are signal likely sainthood. Thus the temptation to "political Donatism" is always present: not only must God's law supersede earthly magistracy but the magistrates themselves should be pious and above reproach. Early New England Puritanism toyed with Donatism, yet the legal strain was at least as powerful, for it repulsed subjectivism on behalf of collective discipline. Moreover, the Augustinian logic of the inscrutability of election and the "two cities" encouraged a positive submission to the law.

But this did not close the issue. For the Puritan "holy experiment" was not Augustine's Roman Empire. It was not the inherited shell of a pagan Babylon but a clearing in the wilderness created by Christian men and women. It contained all the flaws of original depravity in its human material, but its foundations were pious in intent. It had a consciousness of sanctity, a high opinion of itself. It also had a propensity to punish any who breached that sanctity, as well as the public peace. But there was another, more promising, side of the coin. Men were not mute and helpless in the mystery of God's grace, for they were caretakers of the city and gardeners of the wilderness. Having given the city their pious commitment, they had also to give it their political and social effort. Although their distaste for certain forms of culture like the theatre, opera, and liturgical art was notorious, Calvinists set much store in the life of the mind. They were avid and selective readers and confirmed believers in education. As the seventeenth century wore on, philosophical and scientific culture from across the Atlantic (the Cambridge Platonists, Pascal, Newton, Fénelon, and Locke) reached them in a steady flow. Puritans were also connoisseurs of the classics. At Harvard College (and at Yale College in New Haven) they gave their ministers a depth of learning and professionalization.[46] And they educated their citizen bodies to the cares of politics, the "republicanism of the townships" that so impressed Tocqueville. Their politics was direct, widely shared, pre-

ventive, and constitutional in the sense of curbing corrupt man's desire for power.[47]

The Calvinist political conception I have just traced was, in many
respects, alien to the politics that has been generally practiced in later
America. In what respects it has differed depends on the period of
scrutiny. If we look at the political assumptions of 1787, we are
struck by the relative optimism that the Founders placed in secular
values and their translation of effort from human regeneration to the
science of institutional checks and balances. Moreover, the disparity
between the "two cities" had virtually vanished for them. At the
same time, a majority of the Founders—of whom John Adams was
typical—shared with the Puritans a healthy fear of the corruption of
power in human hands. In this they joined "classical republican"
concerns with a religious heritage. They also shared the Puritan con-
noisseurship of useful knowledge and enlightenment, and they derived some of their legalism and constitutionalism from Puritan
sources. But they dismissed the theological doctrines of depravity,
conversion, and election; at least they denied them any part in the
concerns of the profane order. They remained prudent about the millennium, as was appropriate to their preservative politics, a politics
that was Lockean and anti-Augustinian.

In the century and a half to follow (despite the exceedingly somber
tones of the slavery crisis and the war for the Union), politics fed
from a providence that seemed tangibly revealed in the profane
sphere and was often confused with the idea of progress. Wealth,
territorial expansion, technology, and religion all contributed to this
frame of mind. Romantic optimism promoted a semispiritualized,
semipragmatic conviction of America's purpose and power. This syndrome was endlessly complex because of the multiple manipulations
of secular and sacred motives. It was not clear whether America was
supposed to remain pure of the world, to convert the world, or to
bear witness to what the world might become: these complications
will be treated in a following chapter. However, the general movement of the American mind, while immensely indebted to the evangelistic roots of its religion and the velocity of republican dynamism,
progressively abandoned the Calvinist precepts of humility, religious
introspection, and civic cohesion as well as the prudential restraints
of the men of 1787.

In today's politics residues of all these pasts appear—etched into
the precepts of law and morality, conditioned by custom, rhetoric,
and the history books, visible in the monuments and shrines of the
nation. But they are no longer compelling sources of unity. Often felt

as reflex actions, they are also memories that have not managed to achieve synthesis; hence they are memorabilia. The past of the Calvinists, the past of the Founders, and the past of the empire-builders have been subject to exposures that are both salutary and corrosive. But they have not been replaced by a higher criticism, nor have their intimacies and antagonisms been effectively explored in the context of present needs of freedom and control.

This far we have traveled from the sources of what Tocqueville described as a "democratic and republican religion." Tocqueville could not have intended unproblematically that the mental climate of early New England was "free." What he appears to have meant is that Calvinism performed a necessary dual function. Theologically it gave men a discipline and a conditioning for freedom by binding them to each other in a purposeful, yet not extravagant, enterprise. Politically it removed the shackles of birth and estate that threatened Europeans with the absolute choice of equality or freedom. The civil freedom of modernity is perhaps not the most sublime condition that the mind might contrive. But Tocqueville was searching for a specific freedom that could redeem inevitable democracy. For this the regulated will of society was necessary, a political creativeness and indeterminacy that would remain bonded to a remembered discipline and a transcendent judgment. We may call this political will, this operation of the sovereignty of the people, Arminian, because it is explicitly, definitively free in the profane sphere and manifest in its works. But such a force seems to have required, for consistency's sake, an Arminian liberation in the sacred sphere as well. Democratic man needed to be reassured of the worth of his visible works; he needed to feel that his repentant surge toward God's mercy was efficacious; and, above all, he needed the conviction that most persons, unless they flouted God's ways outrageously, would be saved.[48] It was not Catholic absolution, but a sense of renewed innocence, that he needed in order to practice his politics. Ironically, for they upset the premature balancing of Tocqueville's democratic ethos, specific doctrines of Arminianism in the sacred sphere accompanied the tendencies of American secular politics to their fulfillment. Tocqueville himself had of course written that politics was attached to a particular religion "by affinity." But here the causal direction seems to have been from politics to religion.

At this point paradigmatic Methodism enters the picture and merges with the history of paradigmatic Calvinism. From its small beginnings just after the Revolution, the growth of this denomination was staggering: from fewer than 3000 members in 1800, to 30,000 in

1812, to 175,000 in 1830, in the West alone.[49] "By 1844, when the church divided north and south, the Methodists had become the most numerous religious body in America, with 1,068,525 members, 3988 itinerant preachers, 7730 local preachers, and an incalculable number of regular hearers."[50] The potent expansion of the Methodists, followed closely by the Baptists and at a much greater distance by the Presbyterians and other groups, was owed not only to the kinetic spark of revival but also to a feeling prevalent in the second quarter of the nineteenth century that religion alone could unite "the local, jarring interests" of the country and that this was so ordered by the Creator.[51] A conspicuous feature of the spread of Methodism prior to the Civil War was its relatively even distribution throughout America.[52] Even today, with the comparative ebbing of its fortunes, Methodism remains the church with the most solid claim to being "national." This does not seem mere coincidence; we shall try to show that the qualities of Methodism were closely harmonized with the values of the American polity and culture. Indeed, Methodism has been a sensitive barometer of American social mobility and the transformed attitudes of Americans toward the harmonies of the sacred and the profane.

First and foremost, we must glance at the Methodist theology. Its origins need not concern us as much as its exposure to the American scene, but some reference will be indispensable. The background of Methodism was not, like Puritan Calvinism, in an explicit departure from the authority of the national church but in a pietistic reaction—common to other movements in Western Europe—against its rationalistic slumber. If the emotionalism of the religion preached by the Wesley brothers owed much to Spener, Zinzendorf, and the German revivalists, it owed more to the Anglican precepts of Jeremy Taylor and the nonjuror William Law, and to the high-church wing, in general. Such attachments did not, however, lead to a liturgical emphasis, but to a homiletic concern with preaching and conversion and a massive effort to revive the faith of ordinary people. Although John Wesley left the Church of England with great reluctance (after favoring the British cause in the War of Independence) and Charles Wesley never did, the demands of their conviction expressed in theology, preaching, and hymns had long before established a new sect. Since Methodism may be accurately described as a churching technique as much as a doctrine, there were also connections with the revivalist tendencies of Calvinism. The thoroughgoing Arminianism of Methodist theology did not preclude a common emphasis on the centrality of conversion, grace, and salvation. When the Methodizing Anglican

George Whitefield swept the American frontier settlements with his
message in the mid-eighteenth century, his work was welcomed and
joined by Jonathan Edwards and other kindred Congregationalists.
They had a common enemy in religious apathy and laxity. No Calvinist Methodist church ever arose in America; but the existence of one
in Wales, blending Genevan theology with Wesleyan fervor, shows
that the concoction is not unimaginable.

Be that as it may, the theological underpinnings of Methodism are
of great importance to its reception in America—a land of "free"
religion, social restlessness, and democratic politics. The distinctive
doctrine of the Methodists was "perfectionism." It may be further
defined as

> the privilege open to every Christian believer of being perfected in the
> love of God and man, and of being wholly delivered from indwelling sin
> . . . retained by the obedience of faith which became fruitful and effec-
> tive through an abiding union with the crucified and risen Redeemer.
> Indeed, the doctrine of a complete deliverance from all sin was re-
> garded as the logical and experimental outcome of the proclamation of
> a free, full, present salvation as the gift of grace to every penitent
> sinner.[53]

The clash of implications between this doctrine and the Calvinist belief in the transmission of Adamic depravity and in God's election of
the saints needs no extensive comment. Even in the emotional context of revivalism, there is a conspicuous gap between one's image of
the breathless salvation of true repentants through the immediacy of
conversion and the meticulous Edwardsian psychology of tangible
grace, evident in its "twelve positive signs" of sainthood, probabilistic at best and only to be concluded over a long period of time by the
visible scrutiny of the religious community.[54] The political message of
"perfectionism" seems no less clear: democracy can become a kind
of purifying ether in which God's people, sincerely sorry for past
transgressions, deploy *their* will in order to have mercy and restore
the nation to innocence, where all civic sin is reprieved. At very
least, democracy is fidgety in the noumenal presence of saints and
sinners.

We owe it, however, to Wesley's intelligence to clarify his intentions. He was not a democrat, but a monarchist. His emphasis upon a
loving God and the joy of Christ's redemption opposed an Old Testament bleakness and a propensity toward clerical *amour-propre* and
moral authoritarianism that were all too visible in Calvinism. His notion that what the Puritans positively identified as sins could be inter-

preted as "involuntary transgressions" resembled Socratic teaching and conceded that fallible human beings could still be "filled with the love of God."[55] "Arminianism," Martin Marty points out, "has meant many things. But at the heart of them all has been the view of a benevolent deity in tandem with a man who is full of potential . . . to cooperate for bringing about a blissful change in human circumstance. . . ."[56] Wesley's version of Arminianism stressed the supple and mysterious relationship between the human will for true conversion and the free outpouring of God's mercy, never discounting the penalties of sin and disbelief, and never preaching salvation as a doctrine of works (a tendency of the far more optimistic Boston liberals). Wesley and his followers were little occupied with eschatology or the millennium. He rebuked antinomianism and, as a good eighteenth-century Englishman, cautioned against "enthusiasm." In his spiritual formation there was a good deal of Cambridge Platonism. But predestinarianism especially shocked him; it seemed barbarian, as one of the stanzas of Charles Wesley puts it,

> To damn for falling short
> Of what they could not do,
> For not believing the report
> Of that which was not true.[57]

Wesley's precautions were not always, or exquisitely, observed in a trans-Atlantic climate. Or, rather, they underwent modifications that suited them more to a democratic republic unfettered by a state church, characterized by an expanding frontier, and peopled by settlers whose social and religious impulses were not the same as those of the English. Sydney Ahlstrom correctly argues that this "Arminianism set on fire" owed far more of its strength to its Wesleyan theology than to its stature as a "democratic theology" or "frontier faith," and that this theology was a reinterpretation but not a repudiation of the Calvinist mottoes that had served the First Awakening.[58] Indeed, one important feature of the Methodist thrust was its appreciation of both ecclesiastical and organizational discipline, its system of bishops, circuits, and preaching stations and its ability to recruit and employ its ministry for greatest effectiveness. But one consequence of the latter was a widespread use of relatively untrained or virtually unlettered ministers, men ablaze with the spirit and at ease in the vernacular who made speedy contact with their listeners not through learned jeremiads but through fiery gospel preaching. This democracy of the Methodist clergy, rather in contrast to the pastoral elitism of the Calvinists, demonstrated the Arminian spirit of American politics even while it promoted the spread of a compatible theology.

Finally, there was that original mode of "mass religious experience and . . . community morality," where, when the converted soul "found his relief in decision it was in the submission of his inner self and social behavior not only to God but to His believers and their way of life."[59] This was, of course, the "camp meeting," in whose organization the Methodists excelled.[60] The camp meeting bore little resemblance to today's tepid revivals televised from urban coliseums; it was more like a rock concert, although deprived of narcotic aids:

> Held in a wood, near a supply of water, the encampments usually lasted four days or longer. There were several services each day and sometimes four or five ministers spoke at the same time from different parts of the camp ground. The animated evening services of the frontier assemblies, accentuated by pine knots flickering in the dense darkness, were usually tense with excitement and frequently marked by emotional irregularities such as jerking, falling, barking, rolling, and dancing.[61]

Bearing in mind that the frontier revivalism of Bishop Asbury and his colleagues must in more than one sense be distinguished from the Second Great Awakening proper, which is generally held to have arisen in Connecticut, we need now to repay a visit to the Calvinists. We may be authorized to write here "Presbyterians," because, always close in doctrine and drawing ever closer in church organization, the Presbyterians and Congregationalists had framed a Plan of Union in 1801, whose major result for almost the next forty years was an immoderate triumph of the more hierarchic Presbyterian principle. "The effect was that the Presbyterian Church grew phenomenally, largely through the addition of New Englanders. Between 1807 and 1834 the General Assembly reported an increase in communicant membership from 18,000 to 248,000."[62] Since the criterion of "conversion" was still in effect, it may be estimated that a far larger number, perhaps two million, were actually affiliated with Presbyterianism.[63] The union was fairly destroyed by the Auburn (N.Y.) Convention of 1837; however, it was not a resurgence of Congregationalism but a split within Presbyterianism that provoked this rupture of the united front.[64]

The American Calvinist mind harbored within itself two principles deeply rooted in New England history and manifest since the days of the First Great Awakening: (1) the exclusionary tendency of "sainthood," connected with Calvinist orthodoxy in theology, with civil conformity, and with a certain Talmudic vision of clerical supremacy;

(2) the inclusionary tendency of revivalism and evangelism, connected with some slippage of dogma or at least its submersion, with a more secular political stance, and with a more prophetic view of the clergy. One of Jonathan Edwards's miraculous accomplishments had been to weld an aesthetic coherence out of these two impulses, placing dogmatic theory on firmer foundations while opening the way to salvationary and emotional commitment.[65] Indeed, he could be at the same time the precursor of Presbyterian "New School" evangelism and the source of "Old School" theology as it emanated from the seminary at Princeton. Edwards was in no sense a political thinker. Speaking of that period, Parrington is perfectly correct in judging that "theology was still of greater popular interest than politics," although this would not long be the case.[66] Even in a politicized nation, Tocqueville would later comment on the clergy's abstinence from political partisanship.[67] And H. Richard Niebuhr has written that "the function of the church was to prepare men for crisis and for promise by proclaiming to them the gospel of repentance and faith then by persuading them to undertake specific political activity."[68] Yet, in a deeper sense, Edwards was embarked on a political mission: not just that of endowing two schools of Presbyterianism with an available harmony but that of joining the rigidities of the human community of faith with the compassion of God by means of practical experience— a sterner task than Wesley's.

The Edwardsian center could not hold. In Massachusetts he was confronted by liberals and Arminians who were themselves challenged and overtaken by the benevolent Unitarians, while the Princeton theologians, recondite and able, inherited the flair for sniffing heresy.[69] In Connecticut, the home of Edwards's more lineal descendants, liberalized theology and a respect for evangelism *rightly understood* were accompanied by a gust of political conservatism. It seemed to Edwards's grandson Timothy Dwight, a prolific patriotic poet and president of Yale College, that the propaganda of the French Revolution threatened everything that was hallowed in American religious life. "Shall our sons become the disciples of Voltaire, and the dragoons of Marat, or our daughters the concubines of the Illuminati?" he thundered.[70] Out of such stimulants the Second Great Awakening was born. Its author could scarcely have suspected with what intensity and consequences it would leave its polite perimeter, sweeping across upper New York (the "burnt-over district") and the new states of the Northwest Territory, ceaselessly circling and eddying until it issued in calls to free the slaves and to drive the Catholics from political life.

If Timothy Dwight's New Haven evangelism had been only a crusade against the godless French, it would have waned with the fortunes of the Federalists. But, as carried forward by his chief lieutenants Lyman Beecher and Nathaniel William Taylor, it led to revisions in the Calvinism that Edwards had fashioned. This meant liberalization in three respects: first, a prudent extension of fellowship to other (Arminian) denominations, resulting in the disestablishment of Connecticut Congregationalism in 1818; second, a rebalancing of reason (i.e., "common sense") and revelation in the theology of Presbyterianism; and, finally, a retreat from the dark dogmas of depravity and predestination.[71] All these measures were interrelated: disestablishment asserted the voluntary principle so important to true conversion; Taylor's criterion of "common sense," indebted to the Scottish philosophy of Thomas Reid and Dugald Stewart, suited the evangelical mentality by emphasizing the competence of the repentant to decide for Christ on rational grounds; semi-Arminianism, if we may so describe it, fought back Unitarian strictures and made it easier for the evangelist to exhort his audience to an outcome in which they participated in the work of the Holy Spirit. If these matters seem a bit technical, it must be remembered that they energized the emotional response of the revivals. Old School spokesmen attacked them as "Pelagian." But their message, in the words of Albert Barnes, of "the assurance that all that *will* may be saved" and Taylor's motto "Choose ye this day" touched many with new faith, while still lingering on the fringes of Westminster orthodoxy.[72] By these approaches Lyman Beecher and others were particularly successful in launching crusades against drinking and sloth. It was also notably Beecher who tied his evangelism powerfully to the image of a unique American destiny; we shall take that up in greater detail ahead.

"The movement of revival," H. Richard Niebuhr writes, "arises in the midst of ordered and habitual religious action. . . . It seeks only the elimination of those elements in the traditional way that seem corrupt—adjustments made by the church to ways of the world for the sake of survival or success."[73] The Second Great Awakening, like subsequent lesser revivals up to the days of Dwight Moody and Billy Graham, freights this judgment with ambivalence. No doubt revival was not revolution in any commonly accepted sense. Its purpose was purification through the discharge of theological baggage that could no longer be borne. But it also preached a purification through human commitment that, if successful, implied social change. What was distinctive about this social change is that it would be carried out "by converting men one by one, so that societal reform trailed after and resulted from massive individual conversions."[74] This type of connection between spiritual action and the implementation of political reform had roots in the traditions of the Reformed churches. Its efficacy would be challenged by the Abolitionists and later by the Social Gospel, but in the world of ca. 1830 this attitude was normative. Religion's control on freedom consisted in being relatively free of politics itself. This, however, does not mean that revivalism turned its back on "success"—defined as the count of "saved" souls and churched men and women—or despised all the ways of the world in achieving it.

The touchstone and stormy petrel of this enterprise was Charles Grandison Finney, described by Ahlstrom as "an immensely important man in American history by any standard of measurement."[75] Born in Connecticut, trained as a lawyer, at the age of twenty-nine an emotional convert to evangelical Christianity, Finney was licensed as a minister by the Oneida (N.Y.) Presbytery in 1824. Thenceforward he carried the Christian message of salvation in a theatrical fashion across the "burnt-over district" of western New York State to immense public prayer meetings that gathered to hear his preaching. These events became celebrated for Finney's oratorical vulgarity and a number of innovations he introduced to revivalism: the use of advance men and publicity, protracted harangues, the vocal participation of women, and an "anxious bench" where seekers of salvation were exhorted in full view of the congregation.[76] Accounted a charlatan by the Old School, Finney nevertheless worked wonders of conversion. "New Haven theology" was blamed for his departures from orthodoxy. The New England evangelicals were disturbed, but even Lyman Beecher confessed to the "truth and power in the preaching of Mr. Finney," while hoping that "he can be so far restrained as that he shall do more good than evil."[77] Eventually drummed out of Presbyterianism, Finney carried his revivalist gospel to the Midwest, where, as professor of theology and president of Oberlin College, he contributed to female education and the antislavery movement. He was indeed not a man to be bound over to the criticism of presbyteries. As he recounts: "I found myself utterly unable to accept doctrine on the ground of authority. . . . I had nowhere to go but directly to the Bible, and to the philosophy or workings of my own mind."[78]

Finney is best remembered as a showman with shallow notions of theology. Of his extraordinary conversions, he remarked: "A revival is not a miracle, or dependent on a miracle in any sense. It is a purely philosophical result of the right use of the constituted means."[79] To be sure, this recipe bespeaks some of the rationalism of the Connecticut school, makes precarious contact with Edwards's "tangible grace," and looks ahead to the pragmatism of William James. But it is not theology: it is really a statement of political manipulation. Finney, however, would scarcely have placed his conversions in the profane sphere, and it would be misleading to regard him as a mere confidence man. He was one of those "earnest men" whose "language is in point, direct and simple" and whose "sentences are short, cogent, powerful."[80] Finney had at least an antitheology; he had arrived at the "perfectionism" of the Methodists by other means, totally repudiating Westminster standards. He, too, looked upon sin as a voluntary act and sanctification as the consequence of repentance, "hence holiness was a human possibility. . . ."[81] In point of fact, Finney attempted to bestride the apparent gulf between "sinless perfection" and "obedience to God" through his vision of personal holiness[82] and by emphasis on something very close to Lyman Beecher's "moral government of God."[83]

This concept returns us to the Tocquevillian problem of freedom and control; for Beecher, and Finney also, it seems, held that liberty under popular government would be calamitous without proper recognition of God as divine governor and lawgiver.[84] If that interpretation is right, it indicates, according to one scholar, "the growing awareness among ordinary men of the need for an internalizing of ethical standards powerful enough to make them both free and fit for the new life of competitive social and economic achievement that commercial and democratic societies afforded."[85] That the "perfectionists"— Presbyterians who had gone over the edge like Finney, and the Methodists—devised "a highly sophisticated system of theology that aimed at the perfection of man and social institutions"[86] may be doubted. But there is no denying that an emotional and democratic Arminianism was on the way to triumph in both politics and religion.[87] These counterparts fitted the puzzle that Tocqueville had bequeathed, although not in a way that would have reassured him. From this point forward the contours of a mainstream religion suited to a politics of optimism and expansion took shape. "Theologically it was Reformed in its foundations, Puritan in its outlook, fervently experiential in its faith, and tending, despite strong countervailing pressures, toward Arminianism, perfectionism, and activism."[88] That faith may be described as a Presbyterianized Methodism. As for the Presbyterianism, let us not neglect to mention that William Jennings Bryan, Woodrow Wilson, and Norman Thomas all belonged to that church. The twentieth century would record the evisceration of Presbyterianized Methodism.

Perhaps that last sentence is too severe. For a long while, amid the torrents of civil war, industrialization, and social change, the mainstream religion floated. And despite sectarian disorders (most heated among the Presbyterians, who, as late as the 1930s, were split by the fundamentalist controversy and heresy proceedings),[89] these two important denominations, arising from such distinct sources, have seen their destinies join in something approaching an ecumenical solidarity. When the "Arminian fire" of Methodism died down and it became the respectable social vehicle of the middle classes, North and South, the denomination proved particularly hospitable to liberal and semisecular views; it seemed to mirror America's growing aversion to theology. The Presbyterians, somewhat higher on the social scale and in certain religious matters more credulous, nevertheless approximated Methodist attitudes by the second half of the twentieth century. In 1966, 36 percent of Presbyterians and 34 percent of Methodists attended church at least weekly.[90] The Methodist laity proved to be more skeptical on theological issues than the Presbyterians, with the Episcopalians generally scoring in between.[91] On both theological issues and social issues the clergies of the two denominations recorded almost identical percentages, far closer to each other than it could be said of any other two of the Protestant groups surveyed:[92]

| | Agreeing (%) | |
	Methodist	**Presbyterian**
• Creation story is literally true.	18	16
• Authority of Bible is not limited to matters of faith.	13	12
• Myth and symbol are important for understanding Scripture.	77	76
• Jesus was born of a virgin.	40[1]	51[1]
• Jesus rose physically from the grave.	49[1]	65[1]
• After death comes divine judgment.	52[2]	57[2]
• Hell refers to a condition in this life.	58	54
• The demonic is a real force in the world.	38[1]	53[1]
• Man is guilty of original sin.	36	47[3]
• The Church should exist for man.	75[4]	72[4]
• The Church should withdraw from the world.	6	5
• Churches have been inadequate.	76	76
• Christian education should confront urban problems.	74[5]	68[5]

1. The two lowest percentages in the survey; other groups are: Episcopalian, American Baptist, American Lutheran, Missouri Synod Lutheran.
2. Episcopalians score in between.
3. Presbyterians score higher than Baptists and Episcopalians on this fundamental Calvinist issue.
4. All churches except the Episcopal scored within 4% on this.
5. Also 68% for American Lutheran.

But, for the most part, this statistical unanimity is the vagrant ghost of a pre–Civil War turn to Arminianism that affected the fundamental character of Christian belief and action in America as well as the problem of self-monitoring and self-control in a democratic regime. In any case, this excursion into the theology and ecclesiology of two denominations tells only part of the story. There will be yet more to learn by observing *homo democraticus* in his other modes of the sacred, self-consciously private and intensely fraternal.

Notes

1. G.W.F. Hegel, Introduction to *The Philosophy of History* (trans. J. Sibree, New York, 1956), p. 85.
2. G.W.F. Hegel, *The Philosophy of Right* (trans. T.M. Knox, London, 1967), para. 270A, p. 166.
3. Cf. *Democracy in America*, II, 23; I, 43.
4. Hegel, *Philosophy of History*, pp. 85-86.
5. Ibid., p. 86.
6. Miller, "From Covenant to Revival," p. 365.
7. Robert Baird, *Religion in America; or An Account of the Origin, Relation to the State, and Present Condition of the Evangelical Churches in the United States, with Notices of the Unevangelical Denominations* (New York, 1844), p. 38.
8. See Mead, *Old Religion*, pp. 98-99.
9. See, especially, Henry Warner Bowden, *Church History in the Age of Science: Historiographical Patterns in the United States, 1876-1918* (Chapel Hill, 1971), pp. 52-63.
10. Philip Schaff, *America* (New York, 1855), p. xii.
11. Philip Schaff, *Germany: Its Universities, Theology and Religion* (Philadelphia, 1857), p. 9.
12. Schaff, *America*, p. xvii.
13. See my remarks in *Hegel's Retreat from Eleusis*, pp. 184-85.
14. This point is stressed in such works as Samuel P. Huntington, *Political Order in Changing Societies* (New Haven, 1968), pp. 108ff.; and Michael Novak, *Choosing Our Kings: Powerful Symbols in Presidential Politics* (New York, 1974), passim.
15. The point is contentious: the sociologist Will Herberg argued in *Protestant, Catholic, Jew: An Essay in American Religious Sociology* (Garden City, 1955; rev. ed., 1960) that the melding of religion in America had produced an amalgam of indifferentism and shallow unwholesomeness for all of them; "ecumenical" attempts have sometimes reinforced this conclusion. Marty himself, while stressing the term "post-Protestant" to characterize American religious culture, has appeared to agree partly with Herberg in introducing the deprecatory term "religion-in-general": see *New Shape*, pp. 32-44. My own view is that most of us, outside large polyglot cities, do not live in an emaciated Herbergian world; indeed there are many reluctances of Catholics and Jews to see it as such. For example, Henry J. Browne, in "Catholicism in the United States," in Smith and Jamison, eds., *Shaping of American Religion*, pp. 72-121,

stresses the multiplicity of "Catholicisms" and the generally modest contribution they have made to the prevailing culture; so, especially, does Monsignor John Tracy Ellis in "American Catholics and the Intellectual Life," *Thought* 30 (Autumn 1955): 351-88. Milton Himmelfarb, in "Secular Society?: A Jewish Perspective," *Daedalus* 96 (Winter 1967): 230, cautions: "The West has become secular—but not all that secular. From the perspective of Jewish experience and contemporary Jewish reality, the Western secular society is Christian as well as secular—and that includes America."

16. Hegel, *Philosophy of History*, p. 444.
17. See above, chap. 2, nn. 2, 21.
18. See above, chap. 1, n. 64.
19. See Siegfried on this: *Tableau des Etats-Unis*, pp. 82-83.
20. See Hegel's Phenomenology of Mind (trans. J. Baillie, London, 1949), p. 808; Letter to Duboc, 30 July 1822, *Briefe*, II, 326; "Rede zum Antritt . . . ," *Berliner Schriften*, ed. J. Hoffmeister (Hamburg, 1956), pp. 13-14.
21. Some of these anomalies are treated in Robert T. Handy, *A Christian America: Protestant Hopes and Historical Realities* (New York, 1971), pp. 3-18.
22. See Strout, *New Heavens*, pp. 26-27.
23. Ibid., p. 137.
24. For the Latter-day Saints, see especially Thomas O'Dea, *The Mormons* (Chicago, 1957).
25. Martin E. Marty, *Righteous Empire* (New York, 1970), p. 69.
26. Ernst Troeltsch, *The Social Teachings of the Christian Churches* (trans. Olive Wyon, 2 vols., New York, 1931), I, 339.
27. Martin Marty, *Protestantism* (New York, 1972), p. 137. One of the most frequently cited definitions of denominationalism is that given by Winthrop S. Hudson, "Denominationalism as a Basis for Ecumenicity: A Seventeenth Century Conception," *Church History* 24 (1955): 32-50, cited by Russell E. Richey, ed., *Denominationalism* (Nashville, 1977), p. 22: "The word 'denomination' implies that the group referred to is but one member of a larger group, called or denominated by a particular name. The basic contention of the denominational theory of the church is that the true church is not to be identified in any exclusive sense with any particular ecclesiastical institution. The outward form of worship and organization are at best but differing attempts to give visible expression to the life of the church in the life of the world. No denomination claims to represent the whole church of Christ. No denomination claims that all other churches are false churches." This states denominationalism's best intentions, not always its characteristic results.
28. See Timothy L. Smith, *Revivalism and Social Reform* (New York, 1957), p. 22.
29. H. Richard Niebuhr, *The Social Sources of Denominationalism* (New York, 1929), p. 25. Niebuhr also warned that "denominationalism . . . represents the moral failure of Christianity" (ibid.). For a variety of recent views, see Richey, ed., *Denominationalism*.
30. In our own time, out of about 103,000,000 church members in the United States, the Baptists, Methodists, Lutherans, Presbyterians, Episcopalians, Congregationalists, Disciples of Christ, and their close offshoots

account for about fifty million. Over forty million are Roman Catholic. See A. Leland Jamison, "Religions on the Christian Perimeter," in Smith and Jamison, eds., *Shaping of American Religion,* p. 165. Those figures are, of course, somewhat out of date.

31. Cited in Robert Ellis Thompson, *A History of the Presbyterian Churches in the United States* (New York, 1895), p. 109n. Beman (1785-1871) was a leading New School evangelist from upstate New York.

32. Berger, *Social Reality,* p. 137.

33. Sydney E. Ahlstrom, *A Religious History of the American People* (New Haven, 1972), p. 436.

34. See Albert H. Carr, *The Coming of War* (New York, 1960), pp. 335-36; Reginald Horsman, *The War of 1812* (New York, 1969), p. 13.

35. Parrington, *Main Currents,* II, 139.

36. *Democracy in America,* I, 291.

37. Special note should be made of the revivalistic impulses of Tennent and Frelinghuysen with New Jersey Presbyterianism a decade before the New England Great Awakening: see Ahlstrom, *Religious History,* pp. 269-70.

38. Revivalism was countered by the rationalistic denunciations of enthusiasm by Charles Chauncy in his *Seasonable Thoughts on the State of Religion in New England* (1734). On the whole matter, see especially J. William T. Youngs, Jr., *God's Messengers: Religious Leadership in Colonial New England, 1700-1750* (Baltimore, 1976), pp. 113ff.; and James W. Schmotter, "Clerical Professionalism and the Great Awakening," *American Quarterly* 31 (Summer 1979): 148-68. Both these studies expose deep splits in the New England clergy, bickerings between the traditionalists and the congregations, and a ready disposition of many of the latter to welcome nondogmatic evangelicalism.

39. H.R. Niebuhr, "The Protestant Movement and Democracy in the United States," in Smith and Jamison, eds., *Shaping of American Religion,* p. 44.

40. My tendency in this exposition is to focus far more on the colonial experience of New England Puritanism than on Middle Colony Presbyterianism. This may seem a bit quaint, given the announced intention. However, my purpose is chiefly to explore the psychological consequences of a theology, not to pursue religious sociology. For the early history of American Presbyterianism, see Ahlstrom, *Religious History,* pp. 265-79.

41. As Jonathan Edwards said of the Arminians in 1750: "The progress they have made, within this seven years, seems to have been vastly greater than at any time in the like period. . . . These principles are exceedingly taken with corrupt nature and are what young people . . . are easily led away with." "Farewell Sermon," in *Representative Selections,* ed. C.H. Faust and T.H. Johnson (New York, 1962).

42. For the Saybrook Platform, see Williston Walker, ed., *The Creeds and Platforms of Congregationalism* (Boston, 1960), pp. 499-506.

43. Strout, *New Heavens,* p. 16.

44. Ahlstrom, *Religious History,* p. 131.

45. Alan Heimert, *Religion and the American Mind* (Cambridge, Mass., 1966), p. 64f., strongly asserts that Edwards broke with premillennialism;

James West Davidson, *The Logic of Millennial Thought: Eighteenth-Century New England* (New Haven, 1977), p. 151f., gives a more balanced account.

46. On the foundations of Puritan learning, see especially Claude M. Newlin, *Philosophy and Religion in Colonial America* (New York, 1962).

47. See above, chap. 2, p. 42. The numerous writings of Edmund S. Morgan give substantial background to the preceding account.

48. To be sure, this problem had greatly exercised the Calvinist divines with their doctrine of election. For their problems of reaching an optimistic reckoning between the saved and the damned (especially the arithmetic of Joseph Bellamy), see Davidson, *Millennial Thought*, pp. 189-94.

49. William W. Sweet, *Religion in the Development of American Culture, 1765-1840* (New York, 1952), p. 119.

50. Ahlstrom, *Religious History*, p. 436.

51. See Miller, "From Covenant to Revival," pp. 366-67.

52. Ahlstrom, *Religious History*, p. 436. Regarding Methodism's contribution to denominationalism, Russell E. Richey has written: "A movement which at all costs avoided becoming a denomination was, despite its best efforts, to become the quintessential one, not in the details of its polity or ecclesiology but in the principles which, in fact, underlay them." In Richey, ed., *Denominationalism*, p. 176.

53. James Hastings, ed., *Encyclopedia of Religion and Ethics* (12 vols., Edinburgh, 1917), IX, 730.

54. See *Works of Jonathan Edwards*, eds. Perry Miller and John E. Smith (New Haven, 1957), II, 205-383.

55. John Wesley, *Collected Works* (14 vols., London, 1879), XI, 380.

56. Marty, *Protestantism*, p. 92.

57. G. Osborn, ed., *The Poetical Works of John and Charles Wesley* (13 vols., London, 1868-1872), III, 36.

58. Ahlstrom, *Religious History*, pp. 436-38.

59. Strout, *New Heavens*, p. 107.

60. Interestingly enough, it is generally held that the first camp meeting was jointly conducted by Presbyterian and Methodist ministers in Logan County, Kentucky, in July 1800.

61. James Thurlow Adams, ed., *Dictionary of American History* (5 vols. w. suppl., New York, 1940), I, 280.

62. See George M. Marsden, *The Evangelical Mind and the New School Presbyterian Experience* (New Haven, 1970), pp. 11-12.

63. Ibid., pp. 82-85.

64. Ibid., pp. 117-18.

65. See William A. Clebsch, *American Religious Thought* (Chicago, 1973), pp. 14-22.

66. Parrington, *Main Currents*, I, 161.

67. See above, chap. 2, p. 46.

68. H.R. Niebuhr, *Kingdom of God in America*, p. 149.

69. See Ahlstrom, *Religious History*, p. 463.

70. Timothy Dwight, "The Duty of Americans at the Present Crisis" (1798), quoted in Charles Roy Keller, *The Second Great Awakening in Connecticut* (New Haven, 1942), p. 20.

71. See Marsden, *Evangelical Mind*, pp. 12-13, 46-49.

72. See Albert Barnes, "The Way of Salvation: A Sermon Delivered at Morristown, N.J., February 8, 1829," in Maurice W. Armstrong, Lefferts A. Loetscher, and Charles A. Anderson, eds., *The Presbyterian Enterprise* (Philadelphia, 1955), p. 147; and N.W. Taylor, "Concio ad Clerum: A Sermon Delivered in the Chapel of Yale College, September 16, 1828" (New Haven, 1842), p. 37.

73. H.R. Niebuhr, "Protestant Movement and Democracy," pp. 38-39.

74. William R. Garrett, "Politicized Clergy: A Sociological Interpretation of the 'New Breed'," *Journal for the Scientific Study of Religion,* 12 (December 1973): 387.

75. Ahlstrom, *Religious History,* p. 461. Cf. Richard Hofstadter, *Anti-Intellectualism in American Life* (New York, 1963), p. 92, for a similar commendation.

76. Ahlstrom, *Religious History,* p. 460.

77. Lyman Beecher to Asahel Nettleton, 28 May 1828, in Charles Beecher, ed., *Autobiography, Correspondence, etc. of Lyman Beecher* (2 vols., New York, 1865), II, 106.

78. Charles G. Finney, *Memoirs* (New York, 1876), p. 54.

79. Finney, *Lectures on the Revival of Religion* (New York, 1835), p. 12.

80. Finney, *Memoirs,* p. 90.

81. Ahlstrom, *Religious History,* p. 460.

82. See Timothy L. Smith, *Revivalism,* pp. 205-6; and the same author's "Righteousness and Hope: Christian Holiness and the Millennial Vision in America, 1800-1900," *American Quarterly* 31 (Spring 1979): 27.

83. See Marsden, *Evangelical Mind,* pp. 21ff.

84. Lyman Beecher, "The Perils of Atheism to our Nation," *Works* (3 vols., Boston, 1852-1853), I, 115-16.

85. Smith, "Righteousness and Hope," pp. 29-30.

86. Ibid., p. 44.

87. This Arminianism was especially diffused to the young by the presidents of the numerous denominational colleges. See ibid., p. 39.

88. Ahlstrom, *Religious History,* p. 470.

89. See especially Norman F. Furniss, *The Fundamentalist Controversy, 1918-1931* (New Haven, 1954), pp. 127ff.

90. Gallup Poll, *Information Service* 46 (28 January 1967).

91. Charles Y. Glock and Rodney Stark, *Religion and Society in Tension* (Chicago, 1965), chap. 5, tables 1, 2, 4, 5.

92. Jeffrey K. Hadden, *The Gathering Storm in the Churches* (Garden City, 1969), tables 7-15, pp. 40-47; tables 20-23, pp. 57-61.

4

Society, Sects, and Solitude

"Nature," wrote Emerson, "is loved by what is best in us. It is loved as the city of God, although, or rather because there is no citizen. The sunset is unlike anything that is underneath it: it wants men. And the beauty of nature must always seem unreal and mocking, until the landscape has human figures, that are as good as itself. If there were good men, there would never be this rapture in nature." [1] Emerson, who lived much of his life on the fringes of a polite and lettered society and even of sects, like Brook Farm, was, with his friend Thoreau, the American oracle of an unpeopled city of God. [2] Although not a systematic thinker, Emerson was fully conscious of the delicate balance that he was commending to his audiences. In another essay he expressed it thus: "Solitude is impractical, and society fatal. We must keep our head in the one and our hands in the other. The condition is met, if we keep our independence, yet do not lose our sympathy." [3] Emerson's was the consummate morality of individuality achieved in America. His concern was almost avariciously reserved to the self and its soul and their disciplining in the visual presence of nature. In his famous treatment of "self-reliance," he declared that "[man] cannot be happy and strong until he too lives with nature in the present, above time." [4] His extraordinary notion of history was that it was "only Biography. Every soul must know the whole lesson for itself—must go over the whole ground. What it does not see, what it does not live, it will not know." [5]

As with many Romantic individualist thinkers, Emerson's visceral possession of the self in all its idiosyncratic beauty pointed to a transcendental notion of a common humanity, identified by what is best and most natural. In the history essay he also affirmed: "There is one mind common to all individual men. Every man is an inlet to the same and to all of the same." [6] Men, while remaining highly individuated, participated in an "over-soul": "We live in succession, in division, in

91

parts, in particles. Meantime within man is the soul of the whole; the wise silence, the universal beauty, to which every part and particle is equally related; the eternal ONE."[7] Whether Emerson got this idea from Neo-Platonism, the German Idealists, or his ventures into Indic philosophy is not of great importance to our inquiry. We are concerned with its symbolic—and propagandistic—significance to the American cultural experience, for our plan is to come at Tocqueville's essentially political problem of freedom and control from yet another angle.

Emerson represents the quandary of the American intellectual, for he was at the same time a resolute believer in the commanding power of genius with its right to be recognized, and a democrat of the spirit. "Every true man is a cause, a country, and an age," he wrote, ". . . and posterity seems to follow his steps like a procession."[8] Yet, "there is a certain wisdom of humanity which is common to the greatest man with the lowest, and which our ordinary education often labors to silence and abstract."[9] It is a post-Christian humanism gone halfway to an irreverent panlogism that anchors the whole construction: "Ineffable is the union of man and God in every act of the soul. The simplest person, who in his integrity worships God, becomes God; yet forever and ever the influx of this better and universal self is new and unsearchable."[10]

It is in the breadth and implication of such assertions that Emerson merits serious claim as a theologian—a theologian of the intimacy and power of the person against the backdrop of the eternal One. Sydney E. Ahlstrom appropriates Emerson as a major figure in his collection *Theology in America*.[11] And William A. Clebsch treats his religious thought with great comprehension and respect in a volume that also places special emphasis on Jonathan Edwards and William James.[12] The unity of Clebsch's volume is in treating thinkers who "took being at home in the universe to involve ugly discordancies of life by accepting invitations to and gifts of harmony. In this new sense, their religious thought like their own shared spirituality was less doctrinal, was less moral, was less ritual, was less otherworldly than it was esthetic."[13] It is certainly true, within Clebsch's project, that Emerson preached through "nature, the metaphor of God and mankind" a harmonious correspondence of inner human tension and outward cosmic domicile.[14] And it is also true, broadening the canvas to cover most of Romantic Transcendentalism, that the movement may be "most accurately defined as a religious demonstration."[15] It has also been described by Richard Hofstadter as "the evangelicalism of the highbrows."[16]

But, religious consequences or not—and it can be easily shown that Emerson had an explicit religious antecedence proceeding from Jonathan Edwards by way of Samuel Hopkins, William Ellery Channing, Theodore Parker, and the Unitarians, who ordained him and stimulated his apostasy—Emerson's harmony of a benevolent and beautiful nature accessible to kindred spirits also bespoke a fracture or discordancy, a dialectic of sect and solitude, proceeding by way of a construct of society that is praised as an ideal communion of pure spirits and yet deplored as an actuality that "seems to have agreed to treat fictions as realities, and realities as fictions . . . [where] the simple lover of truth . . . finds himself a stranger and alien."[17] The problem, one is tempted to say, is a Romanticism that utterly explodes Tocqueville's grasp of the "individualistic" problem of American democracy, which was that of the *homo privatus,* not that of the *homo religiosus.*[18] With Emerson, it appears, religion is of necessity a solitary act performed by men surfeited with the banality of society in the presence of a nature-surrogate for God, which is nevertheless far from being "nature's God" of the American Enlightenment. Yet the solitary individual is joined speculatively in this worship by a multitude of other disembodied souls who all contribute to the One, to the unpeopled City of God. How strange is Emerson's dilemma that nature seems "unreal and mocking" in the absence of good men and yet that it would lack "rapture" if this were otherwise! To realize nature's rapture is the experiment of solitude; to stifle its mocking is the experiment of sect. This is an aspect of Emerson's principle of "compensation," but it cuts deeper. It would be tempting to leap directly from this unresolved duality to the contemporary predicament of "alienation," and indeed there is a lineage. However, Clebsch seems right when he concludes that our "spokesmen of alienation . . . take their relation to the universe to be unfriendly because *they feel inimical* to the world and God and mankind."[19] Emerson's Romanticism received the counterpoint of man and nature as predisposed to a hospitable, though not complacent, harmony.

There are, as Lovejoy has reminded us, Romanticisms and Romanticisms.[20] Transcendentalism and existentialism scarcely fit together. Neither, for that matter, do all the trends and nuances in American culture that seemed to constitute Parrington's preferred "main current." Yet Romanticism certainly complicated the republican politics of the Enlightenment, just as it troubled its rather prosaic view of religion. Writing almost contemporaneously with Emerson, Kierkegaard declared: "The new development for our time cannot be political, for politics is the relationship between the community and the representative individual. But in our time, the individual is becoming far too reflective to be satisfied with being merely represented."[21] We should not conflate Kierkegaard with Emerson, but the parallel here is suggestive. In both cases, representation in the City of God and representation in profane society have become unstitched. Individualism is the paradoxical prelude to sectarianism because it calls for a peopling of nature's city of God without sacrifice of "rapture." Amid the vagaries of American congestion and American openness, the press of "the lonely crowd" and the flight to therapeutic nature, this irony reaches far beyond Emerson to the beat of our conflicting pulses.

This is a far deeper problem of the individual and the community than any that Tocqueville ever foresaw, or, rather, it transcended the political terms in which he had set his argument. For Tocqueville,

> Individualism is a mature and calm feeling, which disposes each member of the community to sever himself from the mass of his fellows and to draw apart with his family and friends, so that after he has thus formed a little circle of his own, he willingly leaves society at large to itself. Selfishness [on the contrary] originates in blind instinct; individualism proceeds from erroneous judgment more than from depraved feelings; it originates as much in deficiencies of mind as in perversity of heart. . . . Selfishness is a vice as old as the world, which does not belong to one form of society more than another; individualism is of democratic origin, and it threatens to spread in the same ratio as the equality of condition.[22]

There is certainly no disposition in Tocqueville to associate democracy with fraternity; he is far more Platonic in this than the modern prophets of participation. In a powerful hyperbole, Tocqueville insists that "democracy . . . throws [one] back forever upon himself alone and threatens in the end to confine him entirely within the solitude of his own heart."[23] That solitude may have been agreeable to Emerson in his cosmos of the "over-soul"; for Tocqueville, it was clearly a kind of civic hell.

Although Tocqueville's fears of the forfeits of individualism were just as powerful as, and in some ways parallel to, his fear of the "tyranny of the public opinion of the majority,"[24] he felt that America had erected several barriers against this outcome, notably its organs of local participation and its nonpolitical voluntary associations.[25] A progress of public participation is established: "Men attend to the interests of the public, first by necessity, afterwards by choice; what was intentional becomes an instinct, and by dint of working for the good of one's fellow citizens, the habit and taste of serving them are at length acquired."[26] Brute arrangement stimulates what we earlier called a morality of individuality, and finally results in a durable morality of communal ties that is compatible with the common good.[27] This, however, was not the view of Romantics like Emerson, who projected a society in which civic habit and civic duty were either scarcely worth the cost to a man's purity or where their systems functioned so unobtrusively or irrelevantly that they could scarcely threaten the soul's wholesomeness. That was especially true of politics in the rigorous sense.

Emerson deserves to be seen as a religious thinker in part because his politics was essentially religious, and not civil: his enemies were the creeds and the denominations, not the secular parties. "Institutions," as Clebsch writes, "were but derivative, secondary, artificial forms and beliefs that people produced in a futile effort to cast the organic and imaginative aspects of religious experience into static molds."[28] Emerson wanted to take religion out of doors, out of the stuffy cathedral and the stifling pulpit—although he never forgot how to preach—into a kind of macro-Concord of woods and meadows. But very much like Rousseau, who could write the *Rêveries* and still love the civic confines of the small republic, Emerson's aesthetic individualism could be adapted as a program for sects. He was a prophet of the kind of authenticity that carried more than a hint of sectarian rectitude.

His essay on politics is, in this regard, an attempt to draw the arcane perversities of government within the manifold of the comprehending soul. Emerson cared neither for radicals, whom he found generally mean-spirited and unlettered, nor conservatives, who, though better educated and mannered, were timid and self-serving. Like Rousseau, he regarded states as conventional and subordinate to individual wills, and created by single founders.[29] This of course implied that individuals could improve states. There was also some of the dispassionate quality of Montesquieu in his analysis: political institutions spring "from the character and condition of the people." Though Americans "ostentatiously prefer [their own] to any others in history . . . they are not better, but only fitter for us."[30] Actually, says Emerson, returning to the spirit of Rousseau, although "beneficent necessity shines through all laws," "every actual state is corrupt . . . [therefore] good men must not obey the laws too well."[31] "Governments have their origin"—not in sin, conquest, or exploitation—but "in the moral identity of men."[32] However, heretofore all such experiments have been shallow and perverse: "The power of love, as the basis of a State, has never been tried." Individuals *could* rule themselves. But there is presently lacking, "[even] among the most religious and instructed men of the most religious and civil nations, a reliance on the moral sentiment, and a sufficient belief in the unity of things to persuade them that society can be maintained without artificial restraints, as well as the solar system."[33] This is a surprising conclusion for one who also wrote: "It is very unhappy, but too late to be helped, the discovery we have made, that we exist. That discovery is called the Fall of Man."[34] But Emerson did not invite us to ask consistency from him. The point is that he was troubled by the individual and social polarities of existence, while shutting the public and the civil out of that debate. His political musings were those of a sectarian, disabused of all traditional establishments, but still perpetrating a religious mood and a private communicative vocabulary on the realm of the secular. To be sure, he was neither apocalyptic nor exclusionary, like many spokesmen of the sects, but he shared much of their vision of the good and the true against the denominational oligarchs. And he commended the politics of love.

To locate Emerson as an individualist capable of transmitting the sectarian impulse requires some discrimination of "individualisms" and of "sectarianisms." Obviously, he was not the arch-individualist frequently associated with utilitarian free enterprise, the denizen of Mary Douglas's "low-grid, weak-group," which is "a social context dominated by strongly competitive conditions, control over other people, and individual autonomy . . . [where] individuals can transact freely . . . [and] no one in this social environment can expect anyone else to support him if he fails to deliver or sets the wrong price on his services."[35] He was not C. B. Macpherson's "possessive individualist" of the seventeenth century.[36] In some ways he was like Montaigne, who "recommended the course of self-absorption, with only limited and measured involvement in public life."[37] Yet Montaigne's private and rather classical tranquillity (with its traditional distinction between *otium* and *negotium*) was not quite the same as Emerson's Romantic and post-Protestant ethic of self-reliance. Indeed it was clever of Siegfried to write at the end of his reportage of American civilization: "We have the feeling that this country of immense possibilities, complete good intention, and intense sincerity required a dose of classicism. It needed a Montaigne, but an Emerson is what it got."[38] Montaigne placed a high value on the individual for want of a reliable standard by which to measure common human nature; for Emerson that nature was ineluctable and it approached the divine.

The bias of Transcendentalism was toward an anarchic, fissionable, scarcely classical sectarianism.

If there is any connection to be made in anthropological terms between Emerson's sturdy individualism and his sectarian strictures against the "fatality" of society and the constraint of institutions, it is perhaps to be found in Douglas's image of the "hermit" (her *locus classicus:* Thoreau): "Sweet and harmless in his life, his voice is surprisingly raucous, and it is even more surprising to note what attention it earns from people who are trying to achieve very different objectives. The withdrawn cosmology is a perennial source of metaphors of radical social change."[39] As Douglas adds, the hermit's "voice . . . speaks directly to those who have elected to withdraw from mainstream pressures, not alone but in small sectarian groups."[40] This was clearly one of Emerson's functions, together with that of addressing a far wider, much more proper audience of denominationalized Americans seeking native enlightenment and moral exhortations without sabbatarian pain. Moreover, Emerson was the paradigmatic American intellectual of the nineteenth century; and in America intellectuals, if they have not precisely been hermits, have been largely a sect of solitude, from Irving and Cooper through Hawthorne to the Parisian exiles of the 1920s.

What I have been attempting to suggest in my analysis of Emerson is the two-sided nature of the American prophet who has abandoned the religious control system of denominationalism, releasing both the sectarian impulse that, dwelling very deep in the origins of Protestantism, had been magnified by the American experience, and the seemingly contrary result of a religion of solitude. Both seek a purity and a truth that can only be contaminated by institutions, religious or political, by which the attempt is made to regulate or implement a morality of "self-interest rightly understood." Both have been live forces in the development of the American mind and practice, whether their appeals were to nature, to the millennium (combined in images like "The Peaceable Kingdom"), to the naked soul, or to exclusionary brotherhood. Emerson was not, of course, the most idiosyncratic of these truth-seekers—we remember him now as a polite *littérateur* of the lecture circuit—but he may be taken as symptomatic of both "the solitude of the heart" and "the responsibility of the regenerate."

It is an immense task to grasp the strength and meaning of sectarianism in America. John W. Nevin, a conservative theologian of the last century, aptly pointed out that "the idea of a historical continuity in the life of the Church carries with it no weight whatever for the

sect consciousness."[41] As opposed to the "normative" denominations, the sects, since earliest times, have protested against compromise with the profane and have formed conventicles of true belief.
They have also, typically (although not always: cf. especially Christian Science), come from the ranks of the deprived. We have already
noted that some of the denominations grew out of sects and harbored
sectarian urges within them. Those sects that were volatile, evangelistic, or millenarian displayed tendencies that appeared to differ only
in intensity and exclusiveness from the prolific emotionalism of the
more established faiths—at least in the pre–Civil War period. There
were resemblances, moreover, between the fractionalizing drive of
the sectarian mentality and the disdain of the American Enlighteners
for institutionalized forms of religion; some sects, too, were involved
in primitivistic purifications of religion that might have won the ap-
proval of deists and theists. The First Amendment was, among other
things, an emancipation proclamation for sectarian faiths and a recognition—not always practiced—of their inviolability and right to multiply. New dispensations, new prophets, new creeds, and new reforms
abounded in a country formed, so to speak, from virgin land, and an
ocean's distance away from incarnate corruption. To all this should
be added the refugee dimension of the numerous sects, especially
German-speaking, that had sought escape from persecution in the Old
World. Finally, there was the much-noted experimental quality of the
American genius, freed from many of the trammels of the centralized
state, and fully as adventurous in religious fantasies as in technical
improvements. There were, it would seem, profuse vacant lands to be
filled not only with the overflow of ordinary persons, religious or not,
but also with tiny bands of fervid worshippers. Or, ultimately, where
in closer quarters the jostling of orthodoxy grew too great, there were
always men to stand up and dispute the reigning faith. Uninhibited
Protestantism, religious freedom and protection of worship, imagination, unremitting mobility, social distance from government, prophecy, millenarianism—these, then, were some of the reasons for the
extraordinary spread of the American sects.[42]

   The sect was not, of course, an American invention, but it swiftly
became the American phenomenon par excellence: far more sects
have arisen here than elsewhere in Western Christendom, and some
of these—like the Witnesses—have exported their faith with great
success. We must recall here Troeltsch's original dichotomy of
"sect" and "church," which seemed to have little descriptive or ex-
planatory value for American religion.[43] Numerous attempts have
been made to improve on that simple typology.[44] One of the most

successful of these has been that of Yinger, which may be encapsulated as follows: [45]

1. The *Universal Church* (e.g., the medieval Roman Church)—highly inclusive, responsive to both the integration of society and individual needs.

2. The *Ecclesia* (e.g., a national church like the Church of England)—less inclusive, less responsive to both society and the individual.

3. The *Denomination* (as used above)—particularistic, rather open.

4. The *Established Sect* (e.g., the Quakers)—exclusivistic but broadly integrated to society while emphasizing individual needs.

5. The *Sect* (as in Troeltsch)—exclusivistic though voluntary, poor social integration, but very successful in individual satisfaction.

6. The *Cult* (frequently charismatic)—with little orientation to the social order and almost totally involved in servicing individual needs.

In this spectrum of categories of faith—adaptable only to Christianity—we are currently concerned with types 4, 5, and 6. On the subject of "cults," proceeding from the milieu of a Christian, or at least "post-Christian," civilization but sometimes moving very far off the Christian map, I shall have some subsequent remarks to make. Yinger's distinction between "established sect" and "sect" is perceptive with regard to the American surroundings, for it appropriately describes a difference between religious groups whose organization, exclusivism, and theology do not, either for reasons of historical implantation or social respectability, preclude a large measure of interaction with the wider society and those that cannot or do not wish to cross that boundary.

The study of sects themselves has proved to be one of the most popular pursuits of sociologists of religion and even anthropologists. An ideal-type account of sect—without specifications concerning religious, political, or other purpose—has been provided by Mary Douglas in her "grid-group" theory. The characteristics of such a community are derived from its presumed location on a biaxial map of "grid" and "group," expressing, respectively, "a dimension of individuation" and "a dimension of social incorporation," [46] and confirmed by its cosmological value structure, i.e., attitudes toward nature, time, human nature and social behavior, and a number of other rubrics under these heads. [47] What I have been calling sectarianism is exposed in the "weak-grid, strong-group" quadrant, i.e., restricted individuation and strong social incorporation. Among the characteristics of such a situation are these:

> The social experience of the individual is first and foremost constrained by the external boundary maintained by the group against outsiders. . . . Individual behaviour is subject to controls exercised in the name of the group. . . . Instruments for resolving internal conflict are inadequate; only the sanction of withdrawal of the privileges of membership and resulting expulsion from or fission of the group can be effectively applied. . . . The group will tend to be small and hopes for its long persistence disappointed; it will be subject to fission.[48]

It will be seen at a glance—and as a specific investigation of Douglas's "cosmologies" would confirm—that this integral portrait of sectarianism bears a certain resemblance to the American religious experience, while differing considerably from the actual performance of specific sects. Among religious sects boundary constraints vary; so do the modalities of control and the grievance mechanisms or sanctions. Above all, as opposed to certain other kinds of sects, with religion it is presumed that "direct coercion can occur only within the tolerance of the individual's own belief, and whilst, for believers, sanctions can be severe, beyond this a voluntary movement never has at its disposal physical means of exacting compliance. The sanctions applied must themselves be part of the belief system. . . ."[49] Moreover, it is an established fact that, whether from overriding cosmological compulsion or from a permissiveness that American disestablishment has encouraged, numerous sects have known a long persistence.

Douglas's anthropological paradigms were not, of course, designed to carry precise, complex, and dynamic historical loads. In America deviations from such "rules" of sectarian behavior may of course be explained by arguing that many of the American sects have not been, or behaved as, very pure sect-types. Progressively weakened as self-sufficient and belligerent communities, they have been impregnated with general and more secular social values (though not so as to make the denominational leap), and have perhaps unwittingly saved themselves from fragmentation and decay by these concessions: in Douglas's terms they have moved "up-grid." Take, for example, the dilemma of a pacifist sect, as illustrated by Martin Marty:

> These radicals [e.g., the Anabaptists] knew that the state was built on the problem of channeling or suppressing violence, and the police or military power necessary for its perpetuation implied a coercion and other kinds of violence which they felt could not be executed by the regenerate, who lived in a realm of perfection and freedom. . . . [But] that state had not yet arrived, so the state was legitimate as an instrument for the unregenerate. The true believers could not lift themselves out of the world of political order entirely.[50]

The case of the Adventists is of a slightly different order. Their origin was in the Millerite conviction of an imminent millennium, due to occur in 1843. William Miller, ordained as a Baptist preacher, had pondered the Book of Daniel and Archbishop Ussher's chronology of the world with uncanny mathematical aptitude. In fervent preaching conducted between 1840 and 1843 Miller managed to persuade "thousands, no doubt hundreds of thousands" to prepare for the Lord's coming. But 1843 and 1844 passed without visible apocalypse. "The mass movement collapsed amid a general feeling of betrayal, widely circulating charges of profiteering, and harsh disciplining in the Baptist, Methodist, and other revivalistic churches from which the millennial throngs had chiefly drawn."[51] After starting a small congregation in Vermont, Miller died in disillusionment in 1849. But it was not long before fire commenced to rise from the ashes through the visionary vehicle of Ellen G. Harmon White, whose transports and prophecies and views on health and diet, as expressed in her nine-volume work *Testimonies,* helped not only to promote the Seventh Day Adventists as a vigorous and growing sect but also to establish the Kellogg breakfast cereal empire.[52]

Although it is taken as more or less given that sects "seek in one way or another to insulate themselves from the wider society and its influences and . . . tend to regard their theology and ecclesiology as definitely fixed from the beginning of their existence," changes can be legitimated, without schism, by new revelations, new charismatic leaders, or the presence of strong centralized leadership, as among the Jehovah's Witnesses.[53] The possibility of *insulating* rather than *isolating* the community is another tactic. "Insulation of the sect represents an active, 'on guard,' relationship to the wider society. An isolated sectarian community, such as the Amish, may in fact learn to insulate itself, if the penetration of the wider society is not too abrupt."[54]

The abruptness with which society and its law can indeed penetrate the sectarian sanctum in this land of disestablishment has been recently publicized by two widely different cases. On 31 August 1979, Robert L. Bear accosted and briefly kidnapped his wife Gale in Lemoyne, Cumberland County, Pennsylvania. The Reformed Mennonite Church, from which Bear was an apostate but in which his wife remained a believer, had ordered the religious community, including Bear's family, to "shun" him, i.e., to refuse all contact with him whatsoever. This practice drove him finally to his desperate act and to charges of which he was later found innocent in a criminal court—without, of course, his achieving family or community reconciliation.[55] And on 8 January 1979, accused by the California attorney general of "pilfering" millions of dollars of church assets, Stanley Rader, the general counsel, and Herbert W. Armstrong, founder of the Worldwide Church of God (Pasadena, California), were barred from their offices by court-appointed armed guards. The Worldwide Church, an evangelistic sect that had once counted among its adherents the world chess champion Bobby Fischer, disposed of an annual income of nearly $70 million, operated a so-called university, and had a membership of about 70,000.[56]

From the pathetic and the tawdry to the heroic and the altruistic: it has ever been thus with American sects, thwarting all valiant attempts by scholars to pigeonhole them very neatly. The conventional word "sect" carries its terrible burden from the philanthropy of Philadelphia to the horror of Jonestown. But that last hideous expletive should not be left dangling. James Jones had turned what might have originally been a sect, the People's Temple, into a psychopathic projection of his own obsessed mentality, abandoning all religious or salvationary sincerity. As his wife put it in a *New York Times* interview: "Jim had used religion to try to get some people out of the opiate of religion." At the end it was not any kind of liberation. Perhaps no last word can ever be written on Jonestown, but Jean Baechler has said eloquently and persuasively all that is to be argued about the uniqueness of this atrocity outside of any sociology of the sects.[57]

By now it is clear that while we can perceive that a sect is neither a church nor a denomination, and can at least intuitively grasp its nature by the criteria of exclusivity, boundaries, militancy, intensified conviction, and the like, there is still great latitude for multiplicity.[58] That multiplicity may be somewhat domesticated if, as Roland Robertson suggests, we take into account both "the nature of the organization's system of compliance and the socio-cultural base upon which the organization draws its membership," as well as their "degrees of 'fit.'"[59] Such an analysis would, for example, provide for a clear demarcation between the Christian Scientists and the Plymouth Brethren. But such a distinction still cannot express the special qualitative goals of a sect in which we discern its motives for acting and its core of collective belief. It is not just that there is in each sect "a tendency to exaggerate the crucial significance of those [elements of the Christian faith] uniquely held, and to attach diminished importance to those held in common with others,"[60] but that there is an important centrality of emphasis placed in such titles as "Christ, Scientist," "Universalist," "Pentecostal," or "Adventist." Hence, great numbers of sect typologies have been furnished in the literature, of which the following may be taken as representative:

Clark:[61]   1. Pessimistic or adventist
2. Perfectionist or subjectivistic
3. Charismatic or pentecostal
4. Communistic
5. Legalistic or objectivistic
6. Egocentric
7. Esoteric or mystical

Braden:[62]   1. Non-Christian
2. Offshoots from larger denominations
3. Groups exaggerating more orthodox doctrines or practices
4. Transplanted European
5. Personal (i.e., modern) founder
6. Syncretistic cults
7. Humanistic or ethnocentric

Berger:[63]   1. Enthusiastic
2. Prophetic
3. Gnostic

Wilson—I:[64]   1. Conversionist
2. Revolutionary
3. Introversionist
4. Manipulationist
5. Thaumaturgical
6. Reformist
7. Utopian

Wilson—II:[65]   1. Conversionist
2. Adventist or revolutionist
3. Introversionist or pietist
4. Gnostic

The reader may well reel with the categorical profusion. I have introduced it here not to hand it over to impertinent analysis but to show what slippery subjects sects are for sociologists. Three points, however, are to be briefly noted. There appears here to be some confusion of sects with cults, if one adheres to Yinger's wider typology.[66] Sects tend to be defined in terms of how they live and act as well as of what they believe, and the connection is not altogether clear. Sects may be either introverted or extroverted, seeking peace or spreading truth. A good deal of this typological chaos is as much a reflection of American history—the history of culture and mentalities—as it is of intellectual accountability for the essence of an object.[67] We may indeed speak of sectarianism and its spirit; but each of the sects has its peculiar explanation.

Sectarianism has roots in purity, special revelation, or dissent, at least in Christianity. In Catholicism it was contained—through the creation of orders and concessions to prevailing practices—in the Church Universal. In Protestantism it burst the bondage of the control. In America, the great heyday of Protestant sectarianism was the nineteenth century, when sects were created by outpourings of conviction, by bitter theological quarrels, or by the preservation of power for folkways. At this time Americans were less burdened by secular government, more captivated by the sacred, more able to create self-sufficient communities cordoned off from the wider society. However, neither the passage of time nor the exhaustion of the frontier nor the progressive supremacy of an urban and uniform life has done much to destroy the sectarian style and impulse: "The latest edition of the *Yearbook of American Churches* reports a total of no fewer than 258 autonomous religious bodies in the United States. . . . Elmer T. Clark[68] estimates that a really accurate enumeration would swell the total to more than 400 more or less definitely organized bodies."[69] A comparative portrait of the largest and most familiar American sects (some of which have the "sociological" characteristics of denominations) as presented in the *Yearbooks* of 1964 and 1980 shows a 70 percent growth of these bodies in the past fifteen years, a period when the traditional denominations, except for the Roman Catholics[70] and Southern Baptists, have been losing members:[71]

	1964	1980
Churches of Jesus Christ of Latter-Day Saints	1,682,096	2,952,000
Assemblies of God	514,532	1,293,394
Churches of God	485,010	654,244
Churches of God in Christ	419,466	726,000
Pentecostal Assemblies	404,611	663,420
Seventh-Day Adventists	335,765	535,705
Church of the Nazarene	323,491	462,724
Jehovah's Witness	286,908	519,218
Salvation Army	259,955	414,035
Mennonites	164,440	208,920
Reorganized Church of Latter-Day Saints	159,336	185,636
Friends	128,495	95,690
Totals	5,161,105	8,708,986

The sectarian total (with an estimated 300,000 Christian Scientists added and numerically negligible, unclassifiable, or non-Christian sects omitted) approximates the number of Methodists in the United

States and is about one-fifth of the Roman Catholics reported. Those familiar with the current American religious scene will weigh the purely "sectarian" factors in this growth against the broader appeals of fundamentalism and evangelicalism that had been waning in the denominations after the Second World War. Some of the sects have clearly been inhabiting a portion of the old Protestant "mainstream," while others have been of the "fringe" variety. One of our most acute religious historians, William G. McLoughlin, an expert on revivalism and sects, wrote in 1967:

> It seems apparent that the pietistic upthrust by fringe-sect dissenters and come-outers does not in itself constitute the creation of a significant new religious movement in Christendom. Rather the fringe sects appear to be the usual and inevitable emotional and institutional effluvia of a major alteration within Christendom. . . . Upon examination it appears to be the fringe groups that refuse to face reality and try to deny or thwart change.[72]

From the perspective of the moment it might seem that McLoughlin's prediction was a bit complacent in the short run, given the fact that the sectarian impulse and organizing energy show a newly won zeal as well as an abundance of earthly treasure that is injected into political causes. Whether or not these movements "face reality" is a matter to be discussed ahead.[73] It remains true, as McLoughlin well knows, that the denominationalization of sects is an old American story. On the other hand, one of the striking religious phenomena of our times is to find "sect" and "cult" (in Yinger's terms) making distinguishable but noteworthy contacts with material secular reality in ways that both challenge and extend "post-Protestantism."

The sect combinations given above are to some degree confusing. They disguise the autonomies that are to be found within most of them—particularly those that proceeded from Baptist-Separatist traditions—and the psychological expenditure that the voluntary member pays to them (often reflected in commitment of material resources, work, and energy) on account of their exclusive access to the sacred. This also raises the question of the boundary situation between sects and cults. It is fairly obvious where the sects stand in relation to denominations, at least in present-day America: a sect would appear to be a religious group engendered out of Protestantism that resists its identification in any "ecumenical" movement that might suppress its most cherished beliefs and practices. It will be useful to make brief reference to a consummate example in national history of how sects have related, and can relate, to politics—the

Abolitionist movement. Of this much-studied phenomenon Cushing Strout writes:

> The style of the Abolitionist movement was intensely sectarian in several ways: its evangelical concern for an inner transformation on the self, anxious about its purity of commitment; its passion for evangelizing the heathen; its moral suspicion of the worldly surrounding culture, of hedonistic customs and pragmatic authorities; its emotional identification with the lowly and oppressed; its lay participation in leadership roles; and finally its adventist faith in the coming kingdom of God.[74]

The language of William Lloyd Garrison easily makes the point that the Abolitionists were scarcely concerned with problems of slavery in their profane sense, but rather in a wider, sometimes apocalyptic notion of fraternity, equality, nationhood, and the favor of God's Providence:

> By the dissolution of the Union we shall give the finishing blow to the slave system; and then God will make it possible for us to form a true, vital, all-embracing Union from the Atlantic to the Pacific—one God to be worshipped, one Saviour to be revered, one policy to be carried out—freedom everywhere to all the people, without regard to complexion or race—and the blessing of God resting upon us all![75]

Garrison's ringing words on the eve of the Civil War reveal some of the qualities of activist sectarianism in America: (1) the sect takes itself to be a carrier of universal values (antislavery is certainly among the most genuine of these); (2) in so doing, the sect anchors itself around a single principle, held sacred, and brands as idolators those who do not give it their unremitting adherence; (3) the sect attaches itself to a nation and challenges that nation to fulfill itself in its values; (4) in respect to its values the sect adopts a position of *fiat justitia, ruat coelum;* (5) the sect, under full steam, transgresses ordinary religious boundaries, that is, it constantly disturbs the rules of denominationalism, in quest of its *parousia.*

The career of Abolitionism tells us little about most sects—which are often reclusive and little disposed or able to touch politics with their control systems—but it is a leading example of how the spirit of sectarianism enters politics. Ordinarily, with reference to the control system elaborated by Tocqueville, it is the denominations that have had, or shared, power. The sectarian appeal to politics, when it occurs, is characteristically an appeal to justice. The result is positive when both the quality of the religious imagery and the kind of justice demanded have responded to deeply held national values, usually in the mode of revivalism. Parallel with the growth of the Abolitionism one could detect a similar galvanization of the sectarian spirit in the constant and violent attacks against Roman Catholicism, an "antinational" religion.[76] The temperance movement was a later example of this fierce concentration and, in far more recent times, the civil rights, anti-Vietnam, and ecological movements have shown some of the same features. Even though the direct impact of sects on politics in America has been generally slight till recently, the sectarian enterprise deeply affects social movements, even if they do not proceed from an explicit religious base. As Cushing Strout notes: "The problem of distinguishing and relating secular and religious ideas in American reform movements of the late nineteenth and early twentieth centuries is a profoundly puzzling one."[77] This is not only because, as Strout points out, liberal Christianity and secular social science often shared their goals and motives in a common ethical atmosphere but because preaching and perfectionism had long been the stimulus to reform. Even agnosticism, beginning with the remonstrations of Robert Ingersoll, took on the appearances of a sect in America. Atheism has also been so organized, and has been subject to fission as well. Its acknowledged leader, Madalyn Murray O'Hair (American Atheists, with headquarters in Austin, Texas), has recently been challenged by the Freedom From Religion Foundation (Madison, Wis.) and Humanists Quest for Truth (Colorado). Mrs. O'Hair, whose campaigns against church-sponsored bingo games and prayer at public meetings followed upon her triumph in having compulsory prayer banned in public schools in 1963, was charged by dissidents with nepotism, lavish living, autocracy, and anti-Semitism.[78]

Cults are not to be confused with sects. Their appearance and activity can, of course, be traced historically far behind the advent of Christianity, and their existence within the orbit of Christian civilization, unlike that of the sects, is frequently alien to the dominant tradition. Also, unlike sects, they invest little emphasis in solidarity, but rather in the uniquely personal experience of an ecstatic state of consciousness induced, to be sure, in the presence of a community but more surely by the rapport and aid of spiritual intermediaries. The role of the magus or shaman, capable of experiencing or exploring realms of inexpressible meta-reality, is a hallmark of most cultism. Yinger attributes the following traits to cults: small size, the search for mystical experience, lack of organizational structure, a sharp break in religious (not necessarily social) terms with society, charismatic leadership, characteristically local implantation, short life, vexing problems of succession, wide deviation in rite and belief, and almost total concern with individual problems.[79] Another observer, Robert S. Ellwood, Jr., who has done a fundamental study of "new, not normatively Judaeo-Christian, religious movements in America," writes: "The cult stems from the exemplary type of personality possessed by an ecstatic experience, or even by the symbolized or verbalized suggestion of the possibility of such an experience. They seek both to have it as a means of ultimate transformation and to trigger or perpetuate it by direct or symbolic means. It is important that each individual's interest be maintained by the experience itself."[80] Two features that Ellwood particularly stresses are the affinity to shamanism and the syncretic nature of cults (as opposed to sects), their virtuosity in combining traces of traditional and alien religions with scientific, or at least "scientistic," elements.[81] Additional common characteristics are these: a charismatic founder; an experience of possession or travel (e.g., UFOs) by the adept; presence of supernatural helpers; a tendency to use "modern" scientific language; a reaction against orthodoxy; eclecticism; a monistic and impersonal ontology; evolutionary optimism; emphasis on healing; uses of magic; a simple but definite process of entry and initiation; sometimes, a sacred center; emphasis on psychic powers; a tendency to attract isolated individuals; increasing emphasis on corporate participation in ecstatic experience.[82]

"What the cults are doing," Ellwood writes, "is contributing to the formation of a Protean or expansive man whose spiritual life is not tied to a monolithic culture of self-identity. They are changing the meaning of religion from the single commitment to a series of experiences or awareness of a possible series of options whose very presence subtly changes the tone of religious activity even if many are left untried."[83] In brief, the voluntary and pluralistic experience of American denominationalism—overcharged with its own inhibitions, prudences, and irrelevancies—is now giving way to a new religious adventure, implicit in disestablishment and in the wide departures of the sects, where faith will continue on its personalistic trajectory and yet pursue the quest of universalism taken up years earlier by Madame Blavatsky and Annie Besant.

Whether cults are objectively liberating or not is a matter of some dispute. Margot Adler has devoted a sympathetic study to one species of cult—Witchcraft (or, as she calls it, Neo-Paganism)—which has seemed to her "a philosophy that could heal the breach between the spiritual and the material."[84] Others, like Christopher Lasch, see in these movements a manifestation of the "new narcissism."[85] What seems certain is that while these groups harbor persons with political biases, they do not constellate political positions: "In most of what we may still call the 'counterculture,' the split between the political and the spiritual seems to be widening."[86] An exception to the political indifference of cults—and here we might be better advised to call them sects, although the dividing line is fragile—would be in those few examples of politically eschatological movements that have called forth enormous adverse publicity, such as the People's Temple, Synanon, or the Reverend Sun Myung Moon's Unification Church. These doctrinaire and authoritarian cult movements profess the aim of restructuring secular culture and have provided themselves with dualistic public theologies.[87] To use earlier language, they are revolutionist and "post-millennialist." However, they do not represent the authentic cult voice.

That voice is sometimes combined with both a Dale Carnegie-style salesmanship and the subjective Romanticism of the 1960s to produce "educational corporations" like *est* (Erhard Seminars Training), which teaches its clients "to transform your ability to experience living so that situations you have been trying to change or have been putting up with clear up just in the process of life itself."[88] Through 1980, *est* had trained 300,000 persons, a quarter of them in California. In the San Francisco Bay area, one of every nine college-educated young adults has passed through *est*.[89] *Est* is, of course, secular; it is more like a quickie-college with alumni than a church with members or communicants. It attempts to resolve some of the ethical ambiguities of modern times in its cocktail; as such it has resemblances to the mind-cure movement that impressed William James a century ago.

There are, it seems to me, three possible interpretations for the arousal of cults. One is Ellwood's conviction of the Manichaean nature of Western religion, with the submerged cultic tradition ever ready to burst through the surface of polite, rationalized, and consensual belief. A second is the notion that the cultic enterprise itself represents a social *anomie* that, either because of the power of the establishment or because of its own propensities toward escapism, is unable to break forth into the struggle for secular change. A third— which the cults would share with the quietistic sects—is an unbalanced view of the functions of the sacred and the profane in human existence, resulting in the concoction of a spiritualized realm not only hostile to the polity but indifferent to it. The third notion, which implies that for most cults and for many sects Tocqueville's *Democracy in America* would be a far more opaque book than the Bible, not to mention the works of Joseph Smith, Mary Baker Eddy, Rudolf

Steiner, or Gurdjieff, has, I think, a deep vein of truth. The "profane" (with all its implications of normative science, health, brotherhood and peace) can be collapsed into the "sacred," so that they are neither read as glosses upon each other nor assigned different missions in human nature and human history, but that what is held to be sacred literally monopolizes the secular—for the exaltation and true virtue of individuals or for the solidarity of a small community.

Sects, as we have seen, following Yinger, are not cults; in American history, and in Western history in general, they have known moments of political grandeur. In Europe they have done this principally against established churches; in America, they have intermittently baited the denominations or succeeded to denominational importance themselves. Yet, *qua* sects, their structural proclivities toward insulation, tests of true faith, and fractionalization have been serious impediments to their effectiveness in legitimating secular change. However, there have been in America conditions whereby the more cultist aspects of sectarianism have produced a political result. One of these has been their function as an indicator of disaffection and their role in channeling dissent into nonpolitical paths. Another has been in the publicity of charismatic inspiration, as opposed to niceties of doctrine, among a people hungrily looking for new experience—on the road, on film, or in the tabernacle. A third, on which I will place special emphasis in the remainder of this chapter, is in the specific "cultish" influences on American intellectual elites, persons capable of affecting the national values or even the character of politics and secular institutions. This is not so much a matter of the ideological "border" struggling against an established "center," as would be more typical in European intellectual life—but a connivance of the two, validated by the rubric of democracy and yet expressive of an alienation more poignant than any that has ever existed between the rulers and the "clerks" of the old Continent.

We began with Emerson and his attempted manipulation of the polarities of "solitude" and "society" within the scheme of a benevolent nature. A consideration of the status of American sects and cults showed the difficulty of making exquisite discriminations between their origins and peculiarities or of distancing the populist from the more recondite movements. The notion of "cult" helps us to return to the problem that Emerson, and American intellectuals in his wake, faced: the nature of democratic society and institutions in the face of an individualism—i.e., a sectarianism run to personal extremes—that repugned the implanted versions of the Christian religion and yet reproduced their sectarianism at a further remove.

Emerson interests us here as the purveyor of a highbrow sectarianism that was not unmixed with cultism. To argue that Emerson perpetrated this deed on American thought to its lasting regret would be very wrong; but it is surely true that, by means of techniques like those of Emerson, elite and mass culture have been able to coexist as aspects of a single, though complex, natural mind-set, although it has been a fragile concordance for many Americans. For one thing, it has quelled their political appetite to the degree of making them ambivalent about the credentials of their culture and the ways in which they might represent it. In the American democracy intellectual linkages with populism have tended to have sectarian, and not critical, overtones; otherwise, they have seemed "foreign."

William James—who remains terribly important for the understanding of American religion and its contact with the profane—is conceded to have been, in many respects, a successor of Emerson. The character of their intellectual lineage is arguable,[90] but it can be broadly stated that both men were Romantics with regard to the total scope and meaning of experience, that both were individualists who attempted to create the preconditions of a universal harmony by way of the dialectic of solitude and society, that both were sectarians of the higher reaches, and that both were optimists. It goes without saying that Emerson was an inferior philosopher whose formative years were passed neither in the company of Darwinism or neo-Kantianism nor amid the atmosphere of industrial capitalism and its threats to the hospitable value of nature. James, on the other hand, was a thinker of great originality and complexity who bestrode, and made a project of reconciling, the old discipline of philosophy and the new science of psychology, which were tugging in opposite directions.

Still, there was a cultish link between the two sages that stemmed not only from a New England universe in which each of them blossomed intellectually but from the curious mediation of Emanuel Swedenborg (1688-1771). It is difficult to summarize the compendious doctrines of Swedenborg as expressed in his *Worship and Love of God* or the diverse influences of his New Church. To quote Ahlstrom on the subject:

> Powerfully asserting the freedom of man and the promise of the times, he gratified those who would flee Calvinistic doctrines of sin, reprobation, and hell. And in all this he not only made the Bible his constant point of departure but gave a thrilling new impulse to biblical exegesis. Thus each of the major sectarian themes of the day—perfectionism,

millennialism, universalism, and illuminism—had their place in his message. Its popularity, in short, is an essential guide to much that was new in America's great period of religious innovation.[91]

Swedenborg read the Bible as a symbolic, not a literal, document, while upholding its sacred principle; in this sense he taught that the Second Coming of Christ and the foundation of the New Jerusalem had already occurred. He preached neither miraculous conversion nor a rigid ethic. His esoteric visions encouraged the growth of spiritualism. He rebuffed the historical and doctrinal controversies of mainstream Christianity. Most importantly for Transcendentalists like Emerson, he asserted the equation of the divine and the natural in both God and man and featured a doctrine that was not unlike that of Emerson's "over-soul." Ahlstrom comments that "his disdain for tradition encouraged radicalism in every direction."[92]

Emerson was deeply touched by Swedenborg, whom he described in one of his writings as the "last Father in the Church."[93] The whole Emersonian circle was similarly affected. As for William James, his intellect was marked by the fact that his father's spiritual pilgrimage had led him to become a minister of the New Church. No doubt it was the less exotic side of Swedenborg's message that accounted for the conversion of Henry James, Sr. But it was an induced realization of the attainment of selfhood and the refusal to compromise authentic integrity with the demands of institutions that most affected the father. America, he felt, was most suited to the attainment of selfhood because its institutions were voluntary and "having no public prestige."[94] Here an altruistic and cosmopolitan individualism was possible; one could strive to live in "intimate and indissoluble fellowship, equality, and universal brotherhood of man."[95] According to William James, his father's religiosity was based on the immersion of self and on cosmic optimism: "In the first place, he felt that the individual man, as such, is nothing, but owes all he is and has to the race nature he inherits, and to the society into which he is born. And secondly, he scorned to admit, even as a possibility, that the great and loving Creator, who has all the being and the power, and has brought us as far as *this,* should not bring us *through,* and *out,* into the most triumphant harmony."[96]

There was no unproblematic connection between the religious theories of William James and the beliefs of his father. Indeed, no sect captured the son (rather it was the plurality, the "varieties," of religious experience that impressed him). His own grasp of the meaning of religion for himself was won amid the torment of nervous disorders

verging on the morbid and suicidal.[97] Yet for William James, as well
as for Henry James, Sr., the essence of religion as well as the essence
of all valid life experience was that it took its point of departure from
the will of the creative individual. "My belief. . . ," he wrote, *"can't*
be optimistic [experience had, at this time, given him a more tragic,
Sisyphean view of the world than the one bequeathed by his father]—
and I will posit life (the real, the good) in the self-governing *resistance* of the ego to the world. Life shall be . . . doing and suffering
and creating."[98] This basic individualism followed James throughout
his philosophical development; as he wrote later in the wake of the
Dreyfus affair: "We 'intellectuals' in America must all work to keep
our precious birthright of individualism, and freedom from these institutions [of Old Europe]. *Every* great institution is perforce a means
of corruption—whatever good it may also do. Only in the free personal relation is ideality to be found."[99] Mingled in this proclamation
one detects the voices of Swedenborg, Emerson, Henry James, Sr.,
and a descant of the Americanism that Tocqueville distrusted. It is
perhaps not inappropriate that at the confluence of Kirkland Street
and Divinity Avenue in Cambridge, Massachusetts, the diminutive
Gothic Church of the New Jerusalem (no longer used for Sweden-
borgian worship) should look up at the gigantic, pseudo-Japanese William James Hall, a redoubt of sociologists and psychologists.

William James is sometimes attacked as a pied piper of "anti-
intellectualism" because of his emphasis on the practical and noncog-
nitive, the creative will and passions of the "whole man," easily identified with the common man. Many of his passages sustain this view.
"It is almost incredible," he wrote, that men who are themselves
working philosophers should pretend that any philosophy can be, or
ever has been, constructed without the help of personal preference,
belief, or divination."[100] This is a rather commonplace idea in the
world of Weber and Mannheim, but it was not so in an earlier period
dominated by science and Kant. No doubt the philosophy of James,
like that of Nietzsche or Bergson, furnishes some encouragement to
pseudo-intellectuals or to those who prize action above the life of the
mind. In a more serious vein, the thought of James appears (despite
his sophistication, reading, and travel) to be quintessentially American in antecedence and thrust. As a writer on religion, he is thus
implicated in the problematic of freedom and control that Tocqueville
set forth, especially insofar as his is not a closet doctrine but both a
codification and stimulus of the *genius loci*. Tocqueville would not
have been reassured by reading James. One can infer from James that
religion is a psychological and not a social phenomenon; that although

it is but one of the composites of experience that men confront in their world (or, better, is a "world" among many), it suffices the individual privately and never publicly; that it is a way of reaching for the unity of the soul, not for the community of men;[101] and that all true religion rebuffs that "wicked practical partner, the spirit of corporate dominion . . . [whose] spirit of politics and . . . lust of dogmatic rule . . . contaminate the original innocent thing."[102] As James's *frère-ennemi* at Harvard Josiah Royce explained: "James no longer finds in the religious life of communities the novelty and independence of vision which he prizes."[103] This is a radical withdrawal that has also served the purposes of social conservatism.

James might have been more tolerated by the rationalists if he had curtailed his imaginative doctrine of belief and action and veracity to religion alone, for that could be "bracketed out." However, James treated all knowledge as experience and held that experiences contain or create their own significance. Human beings move in multiple worlds, all of which are tested in this fashion: "the world of sense"; "the world of science"; "the world of ideal relations, or abstract truths believed or believable by all, and expressed in logical, mathematical, metaphysical, ethical, or aesthetic propositions"; "the world of the 'idols of the tribe,' illusions or prejudices common to the race"; "the various supernatural worlds"; "the various worlds of individual opinion, as numerous as men are"; "the worlds of sheer madness and vagary, also indefinitively numerous."[104] James's radical pluralism is doubled: it exists both in the needs and acts of the consciousness and in the shape of the worlds required by it. Each man becomes, as it were, a sectarian system unto himself. It is not surprising, therefore, that James placed such a high premium on the "common storehouse of emotion upon which religious objects may draw. . . ."[105] These were at least an integrating feature in the cosmic chaos of the possible personality: "Religious feeling is . . . an absolute addition to the Subject's range of life. It gives him a new sphere of power. When the outward battle is lost, and the outer world disowns him, it redeems and vivifies an interior world which would otherwise be an empty waste."[106]

This special character of religion—plural as it might be in its manifestations and accompanied as it was by other sorts of quests for unity[107]—gave it a role in the harmonization process not far from Emerson's perceptions. Indeed, James discussed and generally praised the anti-institutional Emersonian religion.[108] Near the conclusion of his lectures on religious experience James made it clear that religion, feeling, individuality, and reality itself were collaborative elements of a seamless philosophy:

> By being religious we establish ourselves in possession of ultimate reality at the only points at which reality is given us to guard. Our responsible concern is with our private destiny, after all.

> You see now why I have been so individualistic throughout these lectures, and why I have seemed so bent on rehabilitating the element of feeling in religion and subordinating its intellectual part. Individuality is founded in feeling; and the recesses of feeling, the darker, blinder strata of character, are the only places in the world in which we catch real fact in the making, and directly perceive how events happen, and how work is actually done.[109]

In the lectures, James made confession of his own religion, *"the fact that the conscious person is continuous with a wider self through which saving experiences come."*[110] But it was a religion of the most peculiar sort, owing much, to be sure, to the general method of pragmatism described by Peirce ("Beliefs, in short, are rules for action; and the whole function of thinking is but one step in the production of active habits. If there were any part of a thought that made no difference in the thought's practical consequences, then that part would be no proper element of the thought's significance"),[111] but also to a respect for the experiences and reports of spiritualistic cultism, the mind-cure movement, and mysticism.

Because James made God's reality radically contingent upon human belief and action he had to conjure with the disparity and incongruousness of the human sources, and indeed of the human "worlds." This was, among other things, a kind of Calvinism heretically stood on its head, for it described a sphere of reality in which men and women "elected" their gods, rather than vice versa. These gods were essential to belief and life: "The gods we stand by are the gods we need and can use, the gods whose demands on us are reinforcements of our demands on ourselves and on one another."[112] And gods they were, too—only regulatively and in conformity with the historical accident of the prevailing religion were they One—because the human range of need and belief was too diverse to lead to the conclusion of any single deified object.[113] James was therefore a methodological polytheist—although not of the Olympian sort—who required what he sometimes referred to as "the higher powers." Intersociality as well as psychic need led one to conceive of "a pluralism of independent powers," the melioristic consequence of the adjustment and cooperation of individual lives.[114] The degree to which this conclusion follows culturally from the sectarian and distributive influences of American religion and American life, from its regional and social pluralisms, is of course impossible to pin down. Arguably, it is compatible with that history and has been shunned in most discourse and practice, as many radical implications tend to be. As David Miller writes: "Polytheism is not only a social reality; it is also a philosophical condition. It is that reality experienced by men and women when Truth with a capital 'T' cannot be articulated reflectively according to a single grammar, a single logic, or a single symbol system."[115] Since the normative liberal version of truth is, *faute de mieux,* plural, it might be that a shadowy plural divinity is needed to legitimate plural tolerances and allegiances in the profane world. It may even be that James was implying such a commitment outside the self, one that would implicate politics, competitions, and coalitions— a new Canaan of the "high places." The one-godliness of plural and discrepant life, even within each individual, is perhaps ironic; and James may have been nudging us toward our most authentic logic of worship. Be that as it may, contemporary Americans are far less aware of worshipping separate deities or clusters of them than they are of the general difficulty of divine worship itself.

Regarding his own devout commitment to a pantheon of "higher powers," James left both a hint and a question mark:

> [The larger power] might conceivably even be only a larger and more godlike self, of which the present self would then be but the mutilated expression, and the universe might conceivably be a collection of such selves, of different degrees of inclusiveness, with no absolute unity realized in it at all. Thus would a sort of polytheism return upon us—a polytheism which I do not on this occasion defend, for my only aim at present is to keep the testimony of religious experience clearly within its proper bounds.[116]

If polytheism is a logical result of the convergence of disestablishment, pluralism, and pragmatism, it might exist without our knowing it, since there is no center of authority to decree it or any conveniently common religious discourse available for authenticating plural divinity. Toynbee has written of "the soul's irrepressible appetite for a plurality of gods, to reflect the apparent plurality of natural forces in the Universe."[117] But it is not the Emersonian or the Einsteinian universe that today encourages divine proliferation, nor was it so for James, who saw gods as ruling the "worlds" willed by people. What we can say of James is that in reconstituting the reality of faith he radically relativized religious experience, challenging its institution-alized forms with charges of tyranny and with internal criteria that perhaps achieved the consummation of Hegel's "unbounded license in religious matters" more thoroughly than any Mormon, Pentecostal-ist, or Adventist had ever done. He also, in the terms he had set, made Tocqueville's precious conjugation of religious belief and civic freedom totally irrelevant. His was the antithesis of the Social Gos-pel, which had grown up, side by side, in his own time. By the same token, it was the herald of any intensified private worship in solitude. And to the degree that James's peculiar celebration of sect and soli-tude made itself felt in the religious responses of the culture beyond the narrow boundaries of his own intellectual society, its effects may have had something to do with the irony of calling forth, many years later, the panacea of "civil religion," a City of God peopled by Americans.

Notes

1. Ralph Waldo Emerson, *Essays: Second Series* (Boston, 1857), p. 173.
2. "Concord too was a kind of bohemia, sedate, subversive, and transcen-dental all at once." Irving Howe, "This Age of Continuity," *Partisan Review* 21 (January-February 1954): 10.
3. Ralph Waldo Emerson, *Society and Solitude* (Boston, 1904), p. 15.
4. Ralph Waldo Emerson, *Essays: First Series* (Philadelphia, n.d.), p. 75.
5. Ibid., p. 14.
6. Ibid., p. 7.
7. Ibid., p. 291.
8. Ibid., p. 69.
9. Ibid., pp. 300-1.
10. Ibid., p. 316.
11. See Sydney E. Ahlstrom, ed., *Theology in America* (Indianapolis, 1967), pp. 48-50, 58-62.
12. Clebsch, *American Religious Thought*, esp. pp. 67-111.
13. Ibid., p. 4.
14. Ibid., p. 69.
15. Perry Miller, ed., *The Transcendentalists: An Anthology* (Cambridge, Mass., 1950), p. 8.
16. Hofstadter, *Anti-Intellectualism*, p. 48.
17. Emerson, *Society and Solitude*, p. 241.
18. See below, n. 21.
19. Clebsch, *American Religious Thought*, p. 111.
20. See Arthur O. Lovejoy, "On the Discrimination of Romanticisms," in *Essays in the History of Ideas* (New York, 1960), pp. 228-53.
21. Søren Kierkegaard, *The Journals of Kierkegaard* (trans. Alexander Dru, New York, 1959), entry of 1846, p. 97.
22. *Democracy in America*, II, 104.

23. Ibid., p. 106.
24. See esp. ibid., I, 227.
25. Ibid., II, lllff.
26. Ibid., p. 112.
27. See above, chap. 2, p. 42.
28. Clebsch, *American Religious Thought,* p. 76.
29. Emerson, *Essays: Second Series,* p. 193.
30. Ibid., p. 200.
31. Ibid., pp. 204-5.
32. Ibid., p. 205.
33. Emerson, *Essays: Second Series,* pp. 212-13. Cf. Henri Bergson: "Democracy is evangelical in essence and its motive power is love." *The Two Sources of Morality and Religion* (trans. R.A. Andra and C.H. Brereton, New York, 1939), p. 282.
34. Emerson, "Essay on Experience," in *Essays: Second Series,* p. 77.
35. Mary Douglas, *Cultural Bias,* Occasional Paper No. 35, Royal Anthropological Institute of Great Britain and Ireland (London, 1978), p. 21.
36. See C.B. Macpherson, *The Political Theory of Possessive Individualism* (Oxford, 1962).
37. Nannerl O. Keohane, "Montaigne's Individualism," *Political Theory* 5 (August 1977): 364.
38. Siegfried, *Tableau des Etats-Unis,* p. 342.
39. Douglas, *Cultural Bias,* p. 43.
40. Ibid., p. 44.
41. John W. Nevin, "The Sect System," *Mercersburg Review* 1 (September 1849).
42. I am incompetent—and it is generally outside the scope of this study, though of great importance to American civilization as a whole—to give a critical account of the genesis and career of Afro-American Christianity. See, in general, E. Franklin Frazier, *The Negro Church in America* (New York, 1964); and Joseph R. Washington, Jr., *Black Religion: The Negro and Christianity in the United States* (Boston, 1964).
43. See above, pp. 67-68.
44. See, for example, Howard Becker (adapt.), *Systematic Sociology on the Basis of the Beziehungslehre and Gebildelehre of Leopold von Weise* (New York, 1932), pp. 624-42.
45. J. Milton Yinger, *Religion, Society, and the Individual* (New York, 1957), pp. 142-55.
46. Douglas, *Cultural Bias,* p. 7.
47. Ibid., pp. 22ff.
48. Ibid., pp. 19-20.
49. Wilson, ed., Introduction to *Patterns of Sectarianism,* p. 8.
50. Marty, *Protestantism,* p. 211.
51. Ahlstrom, *Religious History,* p. 480.
52. Ibid., p. 481.
53. B.R. Wilson, "The Exclusive Brethren: A Case Study in the Evolution of a Sectarian Ideology," in Wilson, ed., *Patterns of Sectarianism,* p. 318.
54. Robertson, *Sociological Interpretation,* p. 132.

55. See the account in the *Philadelphia Bulletin,* 30 September 1979.
56. See *New York Times,* 9 January 1979; also 12 April 1978.
57. Jean Baechler, "Mourir à Jonestown," *Archives européennes de Sociologie* 20 (1979): 173-210.
58. B.R. Wilson's is probably the most valiant try at a comprehensive definition ("An Analysis of Sect Development," in Wilson, ed., *Patterns of Sectarianism,* pp. 23-24): "Typically a *sect* may be identified by the following characteristics: it is a voluntary association; membership is by proof to sect authorities of some claim of personal merit—such as knowledge of doctrine, affirmation of a conversion experience, or recommendation of members in good standing; exclusiveness is emphasized, and expulsion exercised against those who contravene doctrinal, moral, or organizational precepts; its self-conception is of an elect, a gathered remnant, possessing special enlightenment; personal perfection is the expected standard of aspiration, in whatever terms this is judged; it accepts, at least as an ideal, the priesthood of all believers; there is a high level of lay participation; there is an opportunity for the member spontaneously to express his commitment; the sect is hostile or indifferent to the secular society and the state." Some, though not all, of these criteria suggest the sectarian origins of early American denominationalism.
59. Robertson, *Sociological Interpretation,* p. 135.
60. G. Willis and B.R. Wilson, "The Churches of God: Pattern and Practice," in Wilson, ed., *Patterns of Sectarianism,* p. 257.
61. Elmer T. Clark, *The Small Sects in America* (New York, 1949), pp. 22-24.
62. Charles S. Braden, *These Also Believe* (New York, 1949), passim.
63. Peter Berger, "The Sociological Study of Sectarianism," *Social Research* 21 (Winter 1954): 467-85.
64. B.R. Wilson, "A typology of sects in a dynamic and comparative perspective," *Archives de Sociologie des religions* 16 (1963): 49-63.
65. Wilson, "An Analysis of Sect Development," *Patterns of Sectarianism,* pp. 26ff.
66. See above, p. 99.
67. This despite the fact that Wilson is English.
68. Clark, *Small Sects,* p. 12.
69. Jamison, "Religions on the Christian Perimeter," p. 162.
70. Catholic fervor and church attendance have, however, rather drastically fallen off. See Wade Clark Roof, "America's Voluntary Establishment: Mainline Religion in Transition," *Daedalus* 111 (Winter 1982): 171.
71. *Yearbook of the American and Canadian Churches,* 1964, 1980.
72. William G. McLoughlin, "Is There a Third Force in Christendom?" *Daedalus* 96 (December 1967): 45.
73. See below, pp. 109-110.
74. Strout, *New Heavens,* p. 163.
75. William Lloyd Garrison, "On the Death of John Brown," Tremont Temple, Boston, 2 December 1859, in *Orations of American Orators,* II, 210.
76. See David B. Davis, "Some Ideological Functions of Prejudice in Ante-Bellum America," *American Quarterly* 15 (September 1963): 124-25.

77. Strout, *New Heavens*, p. 225.
78. *New York Times*, 17 May 1978.
79. Yinger, *Religion, Society, and the Individual*, pp. 154-55.
80. Robert S. Ellwood, Jr., *Religious and Spiritual Groups in Modern America* (Englewood Cliffs, 1973), p. 26.
81. Ibid., pp. 17, 23.
82. Ibid., pp. 28-30.
83. Ibid., p. 199.
84. Margot Adler, *Drawing Down the Moon* (New York, 1979), p. 338.
85. Christopher Lasch, "The Narcissistic Personality of Our Time," *Partisan Review* 44, 1 (1977): 9-19.
86. Adler, *Drawing Down the Moon*, p. 173.
87. Irving Louis Horowitz, "The Politics of the New Cults," in Thomas Robbins and Dick Anthony, eds., *In Gods We Trust* (New Brunswick, 1981), pp. 162-63.
88. From "What is the purpose of the *est* training?" *est*, No. 680-3 (13 January 1976). The reference is from Steven M. Tipton, "The Moral Logic of Alternative Religions," *Daedalus* 111 (Winter 1982): 190.
89. Source: Tipton, "Moral Logic of Alternative Religions," p. 191.
90. Cf. Morton White, "Logical Positivism and the Pragmatism of James," in *Pragmatism and the American Mind* (London, 1975), pp. 118-20, where the author argues that James's later work (especially *Pragmatism*) marks a fundamental break with the inadequacies of the earlier heritage.
91. Ahlstrom, *Religious History*, p. 484.
92. Ibid., p. 485.
93. Rlaph Waldo Emerson, *Representative Men* (Boston, 1850), p. 122.
94. William James, ed., *The Literary Remains of the Late Henry James* (Boston, 1885), p. 187. (I owe these citations and much of the treatment to Clebsch, *American Religious Thought*, pp. 127-33).
95. Ibid., p. 83.
96. Ibid., p. 15.
97. Clebsch, *American Religious Thought*, pp. 138-40.
98. Henry James, ed., *The Letters of William James* (2 vols., Boston, 1920), I, 148. One wonders here if James has been influenced by Fichte.
99. Ibid., II, 100-1.
100. William James, *The Will to Believe and Other Essays in Popular Philosophy* (New York, 1898), p. 93.
101. William James, *Varieties of Religious Experience* (New York, 1929), p. 172.
102. Ibid., pp. 330, 327. James does not, however, completely separate religious experience from radical or ideal political expectations. On this, see *Varieties*, p. 266, where "abstract moral, ideal, civic or patriotic utopias" are held to be "true lords and enlargers of our life." Also, p. 352.
103. Josiah Royce, "Individual Experience and Social Experience," in *Basic Writings*, vol. II, ed. J.J. McDermott (Chicago, 1969), p. 1029.
104. William James, *Principles of Psychology* (New York, 1893), II, 292-93.
105. William James, *Varieties of Religious Experience*, p. 29.
106. Ibid., p. 48.

107. Ibid., p. 172.
108. Ibid., pp. 32-34.
109. Ibid., pp. 491-492.
110. Ibid., p. 505.
111. C.S. Peirce, "How to Make Your Ideas Clear," *Popular Science Monthly* 12 (January 1878): 286.
112. William James, *Varieties of Religious Experience,* p. 324.
113. See, on this, Clebsch, *American Religious Thought,* pp. 158, 164.
114. William James, *Some Problems of Philosophy* (London, 1911), pp. 229-30.
115. David Miller, *The New Polytheism* (New York, 1974), p. 4.
116. William James, *Varieties of Religious Experience,* p. 515.
117. Arnold J. Toynbee, *A Study of History,* vols. VII-X, abridged by D.C. Somervell (New York, 1957), p. 279.

5

Westward the Star of Empire

In no respect have religion and politics more massively borrowed from each other in mythology, rhetoric, and common spiritual incentive than in the powerful theme of American providentialism. From the moment when Cotton Mather scribbled in his diary, *"They are coming! They are coming! They are coming!"* [1] to Woodrow Wilson's distressed, impassioned appeal in Pueblo, Colorado, for the ratification of the Versailles Treaty, where he told his listeners that "nothing less depends upon this decision, nothing less than the liberation and the salvation of the world," [2] there has been a collusion of biblical prophecy and national eschatology.

Those connections are always intricate and frequently fragile. We should be only covering well-trodden ground if we repeated the simple tale of America as God's chosen nation or regarded that self-image uncritically. We need also to assess the intricacy between the sacred and secular components as well as their checks and balances on each other. It is sobering to remember that Tocqueville, our keenest analyst, who awarded such laurels to the religious spirit of the American civil community, dropped this matter completely when he commented on the inevitability of American power and greatness:

> It must not, then, be imagined that the impulse of the British race in the New World can be arrested. The dismemberment of the Union and the hostilities that might ensue, the abolition of republican institutions and the tyrannical government that might succeed, may retard this impulse, but they cannot prevent the people from ultimately fulfilling their destinies. No power on earth can shut out the immigrants from that fertile wilderness which offers resources to all industry and a refuge from all want. Future events, whatever they may be, will not deprive the Americans of their climate or their inland seas, their great rivers or their exuberant soil. Nor will bad laws, revolutions, and anarchy be able to obliterate that love of prosperity and spirit of enterprise which seem to

be the distinctive characteristics of their race or extinguish altogether
the knowledge that guides them on their way.[3]

Tocqueville excluded the providential religious dynamism from the
polity and invested it in the individual's habits of republican self-
control. As Peter Dennis Bathory has recently written: "For Tocqueville . . . the success of liberal democracy is dependent upon *both*
the strength and freedom of individuals and groups within [their pre-
destined] limits *and* a continued appreciation by these same persons
of the Providential nature of the limits. Political institutions can encourage strength and freedom, but they will be more likely to do so if
the moral order which they govern is intact."[4] It is very important to
grasp this sense in which Tocqueville's "providence" operates at the
local and not at the national level. Above all, it must not be confused
with geopolitical inevitability. He most surely would not have agreed
with the raptures of the Presbyterian publicist Robert Baird: "What
elements of power are entrusted to us! These arts of printing that
multiply the Word of God literally with every minute,—these accum-
ulations of capital still active, still accumulating,—these means of
communication over sea and land,—through the broad earth,—who
does not hear the voice of God in all these?"[5] Tocqueville's speculative religious *telos* was equality, not progress and prosperity—and he
advances this proposition with delicate irony: "We may naturally believe that it is not the singular prosperity of the few, but the greater
well-being of all that is most pleasing in the sight of the Creator and
Preserver of men. What appears to me to be man's decline is, to His
eye, advancement; what afflicts me is acceptable to Him."[6] It is by
this subtle and wistful turn of phrase that this giant among nineteenth-
century prophets parts company with the rising messianic discourse
of his time.

Although the great texts of providential mission are to be found
spangled throughout our history, they do tend to "take over" in the
religious and political discourse, as well as in the *belles-lettres,* of the
nineteenth century. But it would be useful to balance the record by
drawing attention to comparable utterances from the "corrupt" world
across the Atlantic, for it was not only the preachers of the American
dream and destiny who used this rhetoric. In other words, a wider
wash of optimism, militancy, and challenge, inextricably tied to nationalism, literacy, and technology, infected all culture and raised all
pulsebeats from the Don to the Mississippi. Three examples should
suffice. The first of these is from Fichte's *Addresses to the German
Nation,* delivered by the philosopher during the French occupation of

Berlin in 1807-1808. After exhorting the Germans to commemorate and restore their past vitality and "play the man," Fichte declared to them: "You will see in spirit the German name rising by means of this generation to be the most glorious among all peoples; you will see this nation the regenerator and re-creator of the world."[7] "A large part of modern humanity," Fichte continued, "is descended from us, and the rest have received from us their religion and all their civilization. . . . The divine plan, I say, solemnly appeals to you to save its honor and existence."[8] Somewhat later, in France, Jules Michelet declaimed: "What Christianity has promised . . . fraternal equality, [France] has taught the world. . . . France is the Pope . . . the organ of a new revelation, its interpreter between God and man . . . through Montesquieu, Voltaire, and Rousseau, by the Constituent, the Code and Napoleon."[9] Dostoievsky added his diapason from Holy Russia: "Every great people believes, and must believe if it intends to live long, that in it alone resides the salvation of the world; that it lives in order to stand at the head of the nations, to affiliate and unite all of them, and to lead them in a concordant choir toward the final goal preordained by them."[10] In his novel *The Possessed* he had Shatov assert that the Russians "are the only God-fearing people on earth, destined to regenerate and save the world."[11] Comparable hyperbole can be found in Mickiewicz, in Mazzini, and in some of the trumpeters of the British Empire; indeed in Marx's claims about the eminence of "German philosophy" and its supersession by the climactic revolution of the proletariat. As Ernest Tuveson has commented: "It was no accident, perhaps, that Marx was writing when millennialism was particularly strong in both Britain and the United States."[12]

The gathering debate between sacred providence and profane progress followed the first settlers across the Atlantic. In America both the sacred and secular themes were joined with the pre-Romantic notion of a discovery of "innocence" in the New World, an idea that the imaginative Europeans themselves, with their increasingly utopian speculation, did much to foist on the colonists. A utopianizing of the American continent could service equally the dreams of the original European settlers who had crossed the sea for reasons of faith and doctrine and the later tastes of the American Enlightenment. In Puritan New England, the sacred motives had sunk deep roots and achieved paramountcy. But, as the texts of early American history show, the "lumières" followed the faith in the eighteenth century. In the soil of the new continent—where the venture was for some a "holy experiment" and for others a secular liberation from dogmatic feudal and ecclesiastical institutions—there was a fertility that could

nourish both the religious longings of the pious and the more pragmatic inspirations of the worldly. What in Europe often seemed like a
pitched battle was umpired in America by a harmony of identities—
the feature that so much struck Tocqueville—for in America religion
was not in bondage to accumulated grievances and servitudes, nor
was Enlightenment perceived as an anti-Christian affair. A century
before Lincoln reused the phrase, Americans, on both counts, were
starting to think of their enterprise as a "best hope."

The ultimate sacred theme is expressed in the concept "millennialism." The millennium is, purely and simply, a central dogma of
Christian faith, which states that the sinful world, as we know it, will
have an end and a judgment heralded by Christ's return. In the narrative of St. John's gospel (xvi.5), in preparation for His ascension,
Christ told the disciples: "It is expedient for you that I go away: for if
I go not away, the Comforter [i.e., the Holy Spirit] will not come unto
you; but if I depart, I will send him unto you. And when he is come,
he will reprove the world of sin, and of righteousness, and of judgment: of sin, because they believe not in me; of righteousness, because I go to my Father, and ye see me no more; of judgment,
because the prince of this world is judged." Christ makes no mention
here of a return. But in the gospel of St. Luke (xxi.25) Christ teaches:
". . . the powers of heaven shall be shaken. And then shall they see
the Son of man coming in a cloud with power and great glory. . . .
When ye see these things come to pass, know ye that the kingdom of
God is nigh at hand."

Likewise, St. Matthew (xxiv.23): "they shall see the Son of man
coming in the clouds of heaven with power and great glory. And he
shall send his angels with a great sound of a trumpet, and they shall
gather together his elect from the four winds, from one end of heaven
to the other." The Revelation of St. John (accepted among the canonical books of the Bible) is an explicit—though confusing—allegory of
the sacred history attending Christ's promised return. Further alle-
gorical expression of the millennium is obtained from the Book
of Daniel and from the so-called Deutero-Isaiah in the Old Testament. The Athanasian creed of Christianity includes the profession:
"And he shall come again, with glory, to judge both the quick and the
dead. . . ." No doubt, by the latter half of the nineteenth century,
millennial awareness and hope had come to seem like an archaic eccentricity to many "liberal" Protestants, but it has remained a fundamental doctrine in the traditional churches as well as the persistent
centerpiece of those sects of the adventist and dispensationalist persuasions.[13] In the fundamentalist unrest following World War I and

lasting into the 1930s, many Protestants, rejecting "the optimism once inspired by the theory of evolution . . . instead focused their hope upon one of the five major points of the Fundamental Creed, the Second Coming."[14]

Aside from the conversion experience itself, the millennial image was probably the most important part of early Puritan religious psychology. Cotton Mather was convinced of the millennium, calculating it first in 1697, then again in 1716: "Until his death in 1728 he continued to pray and hope for the arrival of Christ's kingdom."[15] The tangibility of such a belief axiomatically induced a predilection for the decipherment of sacred history. In 1739 Jonathan Edwards preached a series of thirty sermons, "tracing the divine plan all the way from Adam's creation and fall down to the present times and the coming millennium and final judgment."[16] It is precisely with Edwards, as pointed out above,[17] that the Calvinist tension between "premillennialism" and "postmillennialism" reached its peak. "God," Edwards wrote, "is continually causing revolutions; providence makes a continual progress and continually is bringing forth things new in the state of the world, and very different from what ever were before; he removes one that he may establish another. And perfection will not be obtained till the last revolution, when God's design will be fully reached."[18] Was the coming of Christ to precede or follow the peaceful and holy reign of the saints on earth? In truth, Calvinist New Englanders seemed to be very confused on this issue: "Interpreters failed to find meaning in history through an agreement on the order and arrangement of its last events; and as a result, New England parishioners could hardly have held very consistent or coherent opinions."[19] Millennial understanding was itself laced with irony in this commonwealth of constant expectation. What is certain is that the atmosphere was never drained of millennial resources: the minor earthquakes of 1727 and 1755 provoked jeremiads from the pulpits and a more watchful piety. It is even argued by one historian that the response to the earthquake of 1727 furnished a kind of dress rehearsal for the Great Awakening of 1740.[20]

Though the theological intricacies of sacred history might be muddled, the practical implications of the two millennial views are quite clear. Premillennialism argued for a total divorce between secular and sacred history, giving undoubted primacy to the latter. Postmillennialism, however, encouraged the view that men had an obligation and a power to set their mundane house in order in preparation for Christ's coming; if it did not establish, it at least leaned toward the Arminian and perfectionist tendencies discussed earlier. A thoroughgoing premillennialist could, in effect, be a political quietist, while fervently believing in apocalyptic destruction. Postmillennialism encouraged an equation of the story of redemption with the literal history of mankind, making that history transparent to the sacred errand. Postmillennialism gave positive value to the "lumières" and to society and polity; it authorized the human actualization of the kingdom of God and could therefore open the way to extravagant providential claims for the colonies and for the republic that they later formed. Such views had already been injected into New England Puritanism from England, where that prime text of the dissenters, John Foxe's *Book of Martyrs,* had argued "that the English people were an elect nation and would play a key role in the downfall of the [apocalyptic] beast."[21] In the transformed times of George III it would be a simple matter for Whig eschatology to claim election for the Americans and turn England into that beast.

After somewhat of a cooling-off period in the politically critical 1780s, the theme of millennialism was sounded more forcefully from pulpits and in pamphlets following the outbreak of the Revolution in France. It was, at the minimum, an available language in which the rising American factions could dispute about these events and the role of the new nation in them. At the maximum, it became a sacred gloss upon secular history that was especially favorable to the apocalyptic kind of premillennialism and, as such, a source of nourishment for the Second Great Awakening.[22]

With the political revolution fulfilled and nationhood won, the liberal Calvinist clergyman Samuel Hopkins could unite postmillennialism with secular advance on all fronts: " . . . a time of eminent holiness must be a time of proportionate great light and knowledge. . . . And great advances will be made in all arts and sciences, and in every useful branch of knowledge, which tends to promote the spirit and eternal good of men, or their convenience and comfort in this life."[23] One cannot indeed be certain which millennial line Timothy Dwight was pursuing when he preached: "Forget, then, the little period which intervenes between us and this glorious day. Convey yourselves on the wings of anticipation to the dawn of this Great Sabbath of time."[24] We do know that for Dwight patriotism and providence had very close connections. But in the thought of the progressivist Unitarian William Ellery Channing we become fully aware that the urgent events of secular history are the true landmarks. They have flown free of their Christian moorings; the new role of religion is not to authorize, but to vindicate, human improvement:

At this period [the author is referring to the turbulence of 1830 in Europe], we see a mighty movement of the civilized world. Thrones are tottering, and the firmest establishments of former ages seem about to be swept away by the torrent of revolution. In this moment I rejoice, though not without trembling joy.

I have hope in the present struggle of the world, because it seems to me more spiritual, more moral, in its origin and tendencies, than any which have preceded it.

In such a state of the world, it seems to me of singular importance that Christianity should be recognized and presented in its true character, as I have aimed to place it before you this day. . . . It should come forth from the darkness and corruption of the past in its own celestial splendor, and in its divine simplicity. . . . Let Christianity be thus taught and viewed, and it will act as a new power on human affairs. And unless thus viewed, I despair of its triumphs.[25]

It is this total immersion of the millennial theme in progress—in Channing's case revolutionary progress aimed at social justice; in the discourse of others a more complacent, material, and bourgeois progress—that creates the great flux of secularized (but still heaven-born) providentialism so familiar to the national consciousness. This takeover of apocalypse by the "lumières" was becoming so pronounced by mid-century that Mark Hopkins, the liberal president of Williams College, was moved to declare: "We believe in no *law* of progress that would exclude the providence of God, and in no condition of progress that would exclude the religion of Jesus Christ. . . ."[26]

Premillennialism, in general, could not and cannot make explicit contact with the idea of a "redeemer nation," even if it was believed that some of the cryptic destiny of the apocalypse would be worked out on American soil: rock-hard Calvinist orthodoxy might have founded a "holy experiment," but it was too sensitive to humility, watchfulness, and the terrors of an opaque providence to propel a profane nation into the driver's seat of history. However, postmillennial beliefs could encourage such a confidence so long as the American heart was pure. Even here one must not leap to excessive conclusions. It may well be, as Timothy L. Smith writes, that "millennial expectation . . . was more religious than ideological in character . . . and preoccupied as much with the future of all mankind as with the special role of the United States in securing it."[27] This writer is especially concerned with the role and message of the Connecticut School, of Finney, and of the Methodist perfectionists. Nevertheless, even Smith conceded that "the spread of religious awakenings after 1800 convinced clergymen in all parts of the country that the Spirit of the Lord was mightily at work, ushering in the millennium through the hallowing of America."[28] What remained to be worked out in dialogue, debate, and the train of circumstances was whether the special role of this country would be America as holy experiment, America as example for the world, America as world missionary, or America as preponderate world power, for providence would be preached on all these levels.

We have uncovered at least one obstacle to political messianism: premillennial residues that preached catastrophism as much as optimism. Let us see if we can identify others. Again we must return to the early Puritans and witness the transformation of their attitudes. These men did not believe, as H. Richard Niebuhr points out, "that human reason is sufficiently wise, or human will sufficiently selfless, to make the erection of a perfect society possible." Moreover, "[God's] kingdom was not an ideal dependent for its realization on human effort. . . ."[29] However, somewhat in the same way that St. Thomas Aquinas, forced to conjure with Aristotle in the thirteenth century, restored a considerable autonomy and virtue to civic and secular life, so Puritan writers like John Wise,[30] confronted by Whig doctrines of the Enlightenment, undertook an amalgamation of covenant theology with secular contract theory. "In Wise's thinking," Strout summarizes, "a new respect for man's natural competence pushed into the background his 'moral turpitude,' and the covenant, designed for the control of rebellious unregenerate human nature, became instead a contract, expressing his natural sociability and reasonableness. The state, instead of being a disciplinary institution [the Augustinian interpretation], presupposed the virtue of its citizens."[31] Sociability, reasonableness, and virtue, if eminent civic qualities, are not, by far, a prelude to providential messianism; they establish a kind of barrier or *juste milieu*. However, the politicization of the religious consciousness in itself does create space in which millenarian religious urges can become identified with the fatherland and with secular life. The Great Awakening provided an emotional setting for some of this transfer. Moreover, as Perry Miller has pointed out: " . . . this identification of Protestant self-distrust with confidence in divine aid erected a frame for the natural-rights philosophy wherein it could work with infinitely more power than if it had been propounded exclusively in the language of political rationalism."[32]

As the colonists' clash with England moved closer after 1763, Biblical tones, sometimes independently, sometimes fused with Whig ideology, began to drum in American ears, from the Mosaic vision of the promised land to the prophecies of Revelation. One preacher declared: "Israel were a free, independent commonwealth, planted by

God in Canaan, in much the same manner that he planted us in America."[33] The parallel with Israel was much in vogue, even in secular literature.[34] However, Israel was not itself a part of the American myth of the founding, although it would later be invoked with wild extravagance by the Latter-day Saints and other sects;[35] nor can it really be said that millennial notions specifically contributed to the dynamics of the Revolution. After careful investigation Bernard Bailyn has concluded that religion had "no singular influence on the Revolutionary movement."[36] This is perhaps a bit too blunt. Hatch writes of a "civil millennialism" that fused awakening with opposition to arbitrary government,[37] for considerable religious scenery occupied the stage where a secular drama was played out. Indeed, in 1766 Jonathan Mayhew drew a very fertile idea from a religious analogy: "You have heard of the *communion of churches.* . . . While I was thinking of this in my bed, with the dawn of day, the great use and importance of a *communion of colonies* appeared to me in a very strong light, which determined me immediately to set down these hints, in order to transmit them to you."[38] Such notions of course did not turn the rebellion against England into a holy crusade. Despite identification of England with the Beast of the Apocalypse, Benedict Arnold with Satan, and the Americans with the people of the Exodus, the main rhetoric of the Revolution was republican and patriotic.[39] "If," as Davidson writes, "eschatology influenced the coming of the Revolution, it did so as a rhetoric of history rather than as a blueprint for utopia, as a tale which both comforted the afflicted and at the same time goaded them into action against the enemy they perceived as antichrist."[40] Or, as John Pocock has put it, "the apocalyptic dimension . . . while apparent in the rhetoric of the Revolution, is hardly dominant there. Americans of that generation saw themselves as freemen in arms, manifesting a patriot virtue, rather than as covenanted saints."[41]

As noted earlier, the great majority of the American clergy placed its pastoral offices and powers of exhortation on the patriot side. Its more learned pamphleteers like Nathaniel Niles (*Two Discourses on Liberty,* 1774) fused populistic Puritanism to the new political loyalty. And, as Strout remarks: "Whigs and Pietist Calvinists spoke overlapping but different languages that enabled them to cooperate, but it was the clergy who had learned most from the collaboration by politicizing the gospel to suit the revolutionary case."[42] No doubt the situation had the long-range effect of making the Protestant clergy tenors of the republic, of laying the groundwork for a patriotic providentialism that would burst forth in the rhetoric of Timothy Dwight and Lyman Beecher. Indeed, the New England Baptist Association declared in 1784: "Nor is it at all improbable that America is reserved in the mind of Jehovah to be the grand theatre on which the divine Redeemer will accomplish glorious things. . . . If we observe the signs of the times, we shall find reason to think he is on his way."[43]

However, when the delegates of the states met in Philadelphia to lay the basis for a "more perfect union," nothing could have been further from their minds than the pouring of the seven vials or the coming of a Heavenly Kingdom as a result of their deliberations. They were embarked on a delicate political operation; their language was that of power, political virtue, and natural jurisprudence; their mood was not affected by apotheosis or providence. Yet many of them did share with the Puritans a deep distrust of the human uses of power and a desire to bring those uses under a common control, in this case strictly profane. It was not chiefly the Founders themselves, but the next generation, that had to contend with tracing the lineaments of the American myth, where religion became confounded with national destiny.

Somewhat later, Washington's Farewell Address bespoke a humility and a hope without eschatological bearing. As for the humility: ". . . I am . . . too sensible of my defects, not to think it probable that I may have committed many errors. Whatever they may be, I fervently beseech the Almighty to avert or mitigate the evils to which they may tend."[44] As for the hope, it was moderate and scarcely imperialistic:

> That heaven may continue to you the choicest tokens of its beneficence; that your union and brotherly affection may be perpetual; that the free constitution, which is the work of your hands, may be sacredly maintained; that its administration, in every department, may be stamped with wisdom and virtue; that, in fine, the happiness of the people of these States, under the auspices of liberty, may be made complete by so careful a preservation and so prudent a use of this blessing as will acquire to them the glory of recommending it to the applause, the affection, and adoption of every nation which is yet a stranger to it.[45]

In John Adams's inaugural address, while speaking of "a veneration for the religion of a people, who profess and call themselves Christians,"[46] he declared that "if national pride is ever justifiable or excusable, it is when it springs, not from power or riches, grandeur or glory, but from convictions of national innocence, information, and benevolence."[47] Jefferson's first inaugural was quite in the same tone. He addressed himself to a people "enlightened by a benign religion, professed indeed and practiced in various forms, yet all of them inculcating honesty, truth, temperance, gratitude, and the love of man, acknowledging and adoring an overruling Providence, which, by all its dispensations, proves that it delights in the happiness of man here, and his greater happiness hereafter."[48] These Tocquevillian cadences belie a complicity of the Founders in the encouragement of the *idée fixe* of a providential errand. At very most, the tone here is that of America "as example," with appropriate warnings against complacency. It is true that the Founders believed they had built well, and that this confidence sometimes took the form of native superiority. As Jefferson wrote to Adams in 1816: "We are destined to be a barrier against the returns of ignorance and barbarism [evidently he was referring to the Treaty of Vienna]. Old Europe will have to lean on our shoulders, and to hobble along by our side, under the monkish trammels of priests and kings, as she can."[49] But this waning voice of the American Enlightenment has little or no connection with the far more raucous appeals for a "providential nation" that were simultaneously rising.

A second inhibition, then, to American providentialism was the prudence of the Founders, their abstinence from millennial myth-making, and their experience of the realities of republican politics. Others, very quickly, would create myths where they had built institutions, and would endow those myths (especially the myth of Washington) with the imprimatur of a God working in history.

The creation of the mainstream faith of American providentialism was the work of the nineteenth century. Even when the literal lineaments of the Second Coming began to seem quaint, the ghost in the machine of redemption lingered on among American prophets and patriots. The whole span of rhetoric by which the United States came to feel itself a nation is less important than the *topoi* of providence that these years produced. Essentially two great movements of consciousness were at work. In a first stage, the mythology of the national past and national revolution were integrated into, or symbolized as, trends and texts, exemplary ones, of a sacred history very much touched by the notion of God as a Whig might see him. In a second stage, all the preceding was amalgamated with a quite secular concept of progress—common to the century and to the Western world—that encompassed a number of politically anomalous themes: perfectibility; material, technological, and territorial expansion; prosperity; cosmo-republicanism; sectarian rejections of foreign values; and even utopianism. In the process of these complex developments, millennialism, orthodoxly understood, was gradually pushed back or even out of sight, except for the very pious and some of the dissenting sects. It came to be used as a kind of background music, such as in Theodore Roosevelt's: "We stand at Armageddon and we battle for the Lord."

To illustrate what I have called the first stage, we can consider two texts by John Quincy Adams, son of a Founder and sixth president of the country. Both are speeches; they are delivered at an interval of thirty-five years. In the first of these orations, given at Plymouth, there is a passage of which either Tocqueville or Edmund Burke might have approved for its expression of public and moral sentiment.

> Man . . . was not made for himself alone. No; he was made for his country, by the obligations of the social compact; he was made for his species, by the Christian duties of universal charity: he was made for all ages past, by the sentiment of reverence for his forefathers; and he was made for all future time, by the impulse of affection for his progeny.[50]

This is precisely the kind of language we might expect from a decently pious, decently conservative blue-blooded scion of the most famous of New England stock: it bespeaks traditionalism and continuity, sociability, family, and duty. But perceptibly the tone is changed as Adams advances further into his address:

> Two centuries have not yet elapsed since the first European foot touched the soil which now constitutes the American Union. Two centuries more and our numbers must exceed those of Europe itself. The destinies of this empire, as they appear in prospect before us, disdain the powers of human calculation. . . . Let us unite in ardent supplications to the Founder of nations and Builder of worlds, that what then was prophecy, may continue unfolding into history—that the dearest hopes of the human race may not be extinguished in disappointment, and that the last may prove the noblest empire of time.[51]

John Quincy Adams's providentialism is not the most passionate we shall encounter—indeed it is charged with a certain nervous respect for fortune, which inhibits the total glorification of providence—but it is very characteristic of a mentality that is taking shape. By the 1830s (after a half-century of God's bounty) Adams could well afford to throw caution to the wind. Here is what he told a gathering in Newburyport on Independence Day, 1837:

> Is it not that, in the chain of human events, the birthday of the nation is indissolubly linked with the birthday of the Savior? That it forms a leading event in the progress of the gospel dispensation? Is it not that

the Declaration of Independence first organized the social compact on the foundation of the Redeemer's mission upon earth?[52]

Statesmen could not have addressed audiences in this fashion if such images had not been fiercely preached by the clergy. As Lyman Beecher put it:

> Our own republic in its Constitution and laws is of heavenly origin. It was not borrowed from Greece or Rome, but from the Bible. Where we borrowed a ray from Greece or Rome, stars and suns were borrowed from another source—the Bible. There is no position more susceptible of proof than that, as the moon borrows from the sun her light, so our Constitution borrows from the Bible its elements, proportions and power.[53]

Beecher has been made a hero of Sidney Mead's "religion of the republic"—a kind of Jefferson in clerical garb.[54] But contrary to Mead's assumption, there appears to be little in Beecher's faith and doctrine that has close affinity with Enlightenment deism. No doubt Beecher was a sincere advocate of republican and representative government who nevertheless wished—beyond "political science"—to find in politicians high moral standards of conduct and a "general approbation of the Christian religion and its institutions, as will dispose them to afford to religion the proper protection and influence of government."[55] In Ahlstrom's words, Beecher forged an "intimate association of evangelism in the broadest sense with moral reform and social benevolence."[56] Also, Beecher, like his distinguished colleague Nathaniel William Taylor, was an exponent of "the moral government of God." This was not disguised theocracy, nor was it "civil religion," but rather a clear separation between the civil and sacred orders of authority as well as an appeal to free will and free conviction.[57] Beecher further believed that all (Protestant) churches were tiny replicas of the "moral government" that God had granted freely to man and that, gathered together, they reinforced the providential march to the millennium.[58] Yet he was far from being an optimist; he could thunder: "In our country's bosom lies [sic] the materials of ruin, which wait only the divine permission to burst forth in terrible eruption, scattering far and wide the fragments of our greatness."[59] He had a scathing contempt for the institutions of Old Europe and a conviction that they must be replaced by "revolutions and convulsions" and "violence of nation dashing against nation." Then, "the spirit of God shall move again . . . and bring out a new creation."[60]

Beecher was also fiercely anti-Catholic. His preaching was indirectly responsible for the incineration of an Ursuline convent in Charlestown, Massachusetts, on 11 August 1834. He reiterated his bigotry in *Plea for the West,* a providentialist tract with an antipapist subplot published in the same year.[61] This was not exactly "enlightened," though the mood was common. Beecher's American providence would not be available to Catholics for another half-century. In that regard, the words preached by John Ireland, the Catholic archbishop of St. Paul, on the subject of the Spanish-American War deserve close attention:

> It is a grand fact which all Christians should delight in taking cognizance of that in the midst of the war in which the country has been engaged, the chief magistrate of the nation should request the people of America to pause and acknowledge that above armies and navies there is a supreme power holding in his hand the destiny of nations and disposing of those nations for his own designs.
>
> Almighty God has assigned to this republic the mission of putting before the world the ideal of popular liberty, the ideal of the high elevation of all humanity. . . . As Catholics in America we have the right to sing the Te Deum for America's victories.[62]

Thus were Americans in communion with Rome, now by far the largest church in the nation but culturally outside its mainstream, assimilated to the hosannas of patriotic destiny. But that was not so when the arson was committed against the Ursulines.

Horace Bushnell, Mead's *bête noire,* is also indispensable to our chronicle. Also a product of the "Connecticut school," a generation younger than Beecher, Bushnell ministered to a single congregation, Hartford's North Church, for twenty-six years. By far Beecher's intellectual superior, he is best remembered for forging a new "liberal" theology out of Schleiermacher, Coleridge, the Transcendentalists, and traditional elements, with emphasis on the mediation of the natural and supernatural in the faith of the believer. But he was a political and social conservative who spoke in Burkean tones: "Piety to God, piety to ancestors, are the only force which can impart an organic unity and vitality in a state. Torn from the past and from God, government is but a dead and brute machine."[63]

Bushnell was among those who rhapsodized about the providential greatness of America: "The wilderness shall bud and blossom as the rose before us; and we will not cease, till a Christian nation throws up its temples of worship on every hill and plain; till knowledge, virtue, and religion, blending their dignity and their healthful power, have filled our great country with a manly and happy race of people, and the bonds of a complete Christian commonwealth are seen to span the continent."[64] The danger was the pollution of America's original racial stock; the swarm of new arrivals from Catholic Europe distressed Bushnell greatly: " . . . *emigration, or a new settlement of the social state, involves a tendency to social decline.* There must, in every such case, be a relapse toward barbarism, more or less protracted, more or less complete. Commonly, nothing but extraordinary efforts in behalf of education and religion will suffice to prevent a fatal lapse of social order."[65] If Beecher was anti-Catholic, Bushnell was strongly nativist as well. He believed that God's law and purpose were themselves the essence of the American venture, that America was central to the divine plan.[66] "We are the depositaries of that light which is to illuminate the world," he declared.[67] Providence was very much connected with secular improvement; in collaboration men and God would conquer sin and crime.[68]

But the tragedy of the Civil War scarred Bushnell and pushed him to state the full implications of his political and theological position. With the nation divided against itself, America was enduring a test of "adversity and sacrifice" where great moral and religious ideas were struggling to be born.[69] Republicanism and the "moral government of God" had come unstitched. For Bushnell, the war's deepest causes could be traced to a negligence of religion in the founding of the republic, to a pernicious overbalancing of the infidel doctrines of natural right and social contract against the rights and liberties "shaped historically by our popular training in the church, and the little democracies of our towns and colonial legislatures."[70] It was mainly the fault of Jefferson's "nostrums of Atheistic philosophy." Of the Declaration of Independence, Bushnell concluded: "The doing was grand, but the doctrine of the doing was eminently crude—as Mr. Jefferson very well knew how to be."[71] He dissented from the Constitution "because it affirms the possibility of making a real government over man by man; a government, that is, without ascending into the region of moral and religious ideas."[72] However, "the saws of our current political philosophy . . . could, many of them, be true enough were they qualified so as to let in God and religion or so as to meet and duly recognize the moral ideas of history."[73] He advocated "inserting in the preamble [of the Constitution] some fit recognition of God."[74] And he decried a political union based on consent when "nothing . . . can be needed to end it but a dissent."[75] Thus he held that even popularly elected magistrates governed through God's ordinance, by "divine right." His agnosticism regarding regimes, common enough in much of the history of political thought but almost treasonable in the *novus ordo seclorum,* led him to state: "A born magistracy, however unequal, be it kingly, or noble, is good without consent, if only it rule well."[76]

Bushnell's proposals for theocratic remedy to the American doctrine of political legitimacy were washed away in the Union triumph. He did, however, confront the issue between ultramontane Protestantism and secular government in America. He challenged the adequacy of consent theory and saw the perils of pluralism. And he anticipated coming assaults of atomic individualism. It was an irony of Bushnell's anti-Jeffersonian position that a theistic constitution could be theorized against the economic asperities of naked self-interest as well as the liberties of bourgeois secularism. If God alone could unify the federal nation, it was not far to conclude that the state was God's work and callous laissez faire a distortion of it. As Richard T. Ely, of the Social Gospel, later wrote: "God works through the State in carrying out His purposes more universally than through any other institution. . . . It takes first place among his instrumentalities."[77] The anti-Tocquevillian Bushnell was an eccentric, but important and symptomatic, public theologian.

Despite fatuous complacencies in the Protestant preaching and journalism of the first half of the nineteenth century, there were also sharp punctuations of warning. It was not so much that the nation-building Arminians felt menaced with premillennial catastrophe as that they continued to harbor a lively sense of the excess of selfishness and corruption that might yet disrobe the nation of its mantle of destiny. Secular crises as well as waves of material and moral laxity conditioned these misgivings. Often the piety itself was worse than the symptoms, as we have already observed in the nativism of Beecher and Bushnell. When Andrew Jackson told the Americans in 1837 that "Providence has . . . chosen you as the guardians of freedom, to preserve it for the benefit of the human race,"[78] we should read this passage for what it is, but also as a challenge to moral fibre and as a fear (somewhat like Soviet Russia's "fear of encirclement" in the 1920s and 1930s) that, away from American shores, despotism pretty generally held sway. In 1843 the aged Albert Gallatin, in an address, bound his listeners "by the most sacred obligation to their Country and to their God, to preserve and transmit, unimpaired, to posterity, the invaluable inheritance they have received from their ancestors," for, he proclaimed, "America justly became . . . everywhere the hope of mankind."[79] What is striking about the ebb and flow of optimism (at least in the North) is that—allowance made for "false consciousness" and the like—the spread and triumph of democracy, liberty, and Protestant Christianity were firmly linked in the public mind. America had, as it is said, "no enemies on the Left."

The main question was—and it remained so for a long time— whether America's complicity with providence mandated any kind of world role, and, if so, what role that would be. Our country's first urge to spread the seeds gathered from its fertile garden expressed itself in the missionary impulse—especially as dictated by its continental destiny.[80] Inevitably the missions would work hand in hand with political expansion. But they would not cross the seas profusely until much later in the century. Although America's energies were engaged in the continental adventure, the nation was also given the assignment of sitting in passive but righteous judgment on the older powers. As a Presbyterian clergyman wrote: "What Christianity has done for us, it will do for the world. The movement is as sure as the providence of God."[81] That America could be regarded as a symbol rather than as a means of conversion reflected not only a realistic assessment of the world balance but also a growing acknowledgment of congruence between God's intentions for the human race and the operative evidence of an evolutionary natural law: "Deity has implanted in [man's] nature the seeds of improvement, furnished him with the power and faculties for the cultivation, and to these superadded a sense that the cultivation is a duty."[82]

The complex feelings of the pre–Civil War period are expressed in the chameleon-like views of Emerson. In one of his depressed moods he wrote: "I think man never loved life less. I question whether care and doubt ever wrote their names so legibly on the faces of any population. . . . Old age begins in the nursery."[83] Then, as he toured the country in 1853, he was struck not by its providential visage but by its lack of polish. He ironized that American culture could scarcely soon crystallize in a Michelangelo or a Shakespeare: "America is incomplete. Room for all of us, since it has not ended, nor gives signs of ending in bard or hero. 'Tis a wild democracy, the riot of mediocrities, and none of your selfish Italies and Englands, when an age sublimates into a genius."[84] Yet this same thinker could also declare: "Our whole history appears a last effort of the Divine Providence in behalf of the human race."[85] The noble Transcendentalist even trespassed a cubit on the stock-in-trade of the nativists, to wit a journal entry of 1851:

> In the distinctions of the genius of the American race it is to be considered that it is not indiscriminate masses of Europe that are shipped hitherward, but the Atlantic is a sieve through which only or chiefly the

liberal, adventurous, sensitive, *America-loving* part of each city, clan, family are brought. It is the light complexion, the blue eyes of Europe that come: the black eyes, the black drop, the Europe of Europe, is left.[86]

If America's ideology of providential favor did not charm or impress trans-Atlantic visitors, the American patriot could snarl back: "I love natural, American progress . . . the advance of true happiness and true greatness. . . . But let us not turn back and attempt, what I fear is a hopeless task, to regenerate the old, worn-out, *effete* institutions of Europe."[87] America courted progress with a certain decorum before leaping into bed with her. In 1826 Joseph Story told a learned audience: " . . . though we may not arrogate to ourselves the possession of the first genius, or the first era in human history, let it not be imagined that we do not live in an extraordinary age." Essentially Story's praise of modern achievement was cosmopolitan in scope, although he did recur to "a wholesome consciousness of our powers and our destiny."[88] A generation later, Edward Everett, best remembered for his stentorian style, noted simply that "true progress is thoughtful, hopeful, serene, religious, onward, and upward."[89] Or, as Theodore Parker put it: "The Progress of Mankind is continuous and onward, as much subject to a natural law of development as our growth from babyhood to adult life."[90]

Despite cadences of this optimistic, but somewhat dry, evolutionism—a slightly accelerated version of Enlightenment—something definitely had swollen in the American range of expectations within a decade of Tocqueville's sojourn. A popular, not self-reflectively religious, sense of youth and unstoppable advance had taken hold. One straw in the wind was the success of D. Macauley's volume *The Patriot's Catechism; or the Duties of Rulers and Ruled,* published in 1843 and endorsed by such luminaries as John C. Calhoun and Thomas Hart Benton. *The Catechism,* intended for the young, taught that patriotism must mean surrendering to the nation, as God's law decreed.[91] Far more secular and activist was the "Young America" movement of Edwin de Leon—Mazzinian in name and temper if not in connection—which flourished for about a decade after its founding in the early 1840s, reflective of faith in the energy and perfectibility of the common man.[92] This decade saw, through conquest, purchase, or partition, the completion of the continental land mass of the United States (excluding the Gadsden Purchase and Alaska). President Polk, the architect of this consolidation of empire, sounded the theme without dissemblance in his Second Annual Message to Congress: "The progress of our country in her career of greatness, not only in the vast extension of our territorial limits and the rapid increase of our population, but in the resources and wealth and in the happy condition of our people, is without an example in the history of nations."[93] It is now that a half-forgotten pronouncement by our fifth president was elevated, as "the Monroe Doctrine," into the canonical creed of the nation. A host of literati leaped to this new summons. Orestes Brownson (first incarnation) declared: "We are THE PEOPLE OF THE FUTURE."[94] Walt Whitman exulted: ". . . we are to expect the great FUTURE of this Western world! a scope involving such unparalleled human happiness and national freedom, to such unnumbered myriads, that the heart of a true *man* leaps with a mighty joy only to think of it!"[95] In the meantime, as if to counterpoint this great outburst of secular rapture, the first wagon train of the Mormons, led by Brigham Young, completed its crossing from Iowa and set up an encampment in the Great Salt Lake basin, in July 1847. Two expansions, one of pursuit, the other of flight, the one at home in the world, the other rooted in sacred revelation and patriarchalism, took up housekeeping in the vacant lands. Both would eventually send out their gospels into the wider world.

In 1848, revolution struck Europe, greatly encouraging movements like "Young America" and adding a measure of cheek to the rectitude of the American experiment and the providential and progressive nature of republican institutions. The cry of "progress" reached a pitch in close concert with the American mission. Already in 1845 James Gordon Bennett had declared that the nation "must soon embrace the whole hemisphere, from the icy wilderness of the North to the most prolific regions of the smiling and prolific South."[96] John L. O'Sullivan, in his *New York Morning News* and *United States Democratic Review* coined and spread the phrase "manifest destiny."[97] As *The Independent* of 16 January 1851 proclaimed: "A grand feature of our times is that *all* is *Progress.*"[98] In the decade before "bleeding Kansas" everything seemed to converge on this motto: democracy, which equated progress with both territorial development and moral crusade; conservatism, which viewed progress as confirming its notion of a God of property rights; utopianism in its various forms—Owen, Fourier, the earlier Brownson, Albert Brisbane, Horace Greeley—because it saw progress inaugurating "scientific laws of nature" that would cast down privilege and superstition. The Protestant churches, too, saw their missions vindicated in this effort—except for those deeply troubled by the slavery issue; it would take the newly Catholicized Orestes Brownson to warn: "The age attaches, no doubt, too much importance to what is called the progress of society or the progress of civilization, which, to the man whose eye is fixed on God and eternity, can appear of not great value."[99] There came to be another tremulous collective doubter: the politicians of the South. They could not be enchanted by prospects for the political statutes of the new territories or by gushing fervor for the liberation movements of Europe.

Were there any indigenous American brakes to this mania—with premillennial gloom and the worldly prudence of the Founders apparently forsaken? There was one, of almost religious reputation: Washington's Farewell Address to the Nation. Washington had praised our institutions and issued the hope that they might inspire other peoples; but he had strongly cautioned humility, a trust in moral resources, and an abstinence from all unnecessary interference in the affairs of other nations. The Farewell Address could not, of course, interrupt the continental impulse that Washington's own secretary of the Treasury had foreseen with favor, nor could it curb the lust for material bounties, but it could warn Americans away from a providentially inspired world role.

A fascinating illustration of the power of the address is provided by the Kossuth episode of 1851-52.[100] Louis Kossuth, the defeated hero of the Hungarian rebellion of 1848-49, arrived in America on 5 December 1851 to seek diplomatic aid, arms, and, if possible, military intervention. American sympathy with the Hungarians (not only among the German '48ers but in the population at large) was remarkably strong; Hungary had wished to become a republic and had been crushed by despots. Kossuth received hysterical acclaim in New York, where he was greeted by the mayor in Castle Garden and besieged by shouting and stamping admirers.[101] His tour through various cities of the East and Middle West was equally, if not more, tumultuous: he received honors, and indeed sacred tributes, from many of America's political and religious leaders. For a time the national capital was his. Such American enthusiasm for a foreign guest had burst forth only when Lafayette returned at the invitation of President Monroe in 1824; now, legislation was introduced in Congress to grant Kossuth honorary citizenship and he was invited to address the House of Representatives in open session on 7 January 1852, distinctions previously accorded only to the great French Revolutionary hero.[102] His name was commercialized by fishmongers, restaurateurs, jewelers, button-makers, flag-makers, march and dance composers.[103] Kossuth was known to be a Lutheran; he received the adulation of much of the Protestant clergy, and was glorified as an anti-Catholic crusader, with special fervor in Ohio and Indiana.[104] "The American Bible Society, declaring Kossuth 'a true friend of the Bible,' elected him a vice-president."[105] Above all, he collected many thousands of dollars in gifts and "Hungary bonds," as well as donations of weapons and ammunition. He assiduously cultivated leading politicians like Lewis Cass. There was a very serious possibility that this crowd-pleaser could sway the 1852 election.

Kossuth was astute enough to recognize the main obstacle that lay in his path:

> Only Washington's Farewell Address, and the prestige conservatives could marshal behind the prestige it represented, he believed, could thwart his scheme to drag the United States into the vortex of European politics.
>
> Kossuth's first unceremonial act in the New World was to request a copy of the address, along with a set of Jared Sparks's eleven-volume edition of Washington's writings. For a week afterward, he and his staff closeted themselves with those documents in their few free hours, preparing a definitive attack against the address and admitting publicly that the fate of his entire mission depended upon the success or failure of that attack.[106]

In the end, Kossuth could not demolish Washington. President Fillmore emphasized: "It becomes an imperative duty not to interfere in the government or internal policy of other nations . . . although we may sympathize with the unfortunate or the oppressed everywhere in their fight for freedom."[107] In his Third Annual Message he castigated those who "mistake change for progress and the invasion of the rights of others for national prowess and glory."[108] The Whig Platform, adopted on 19 June 1852, asserted: "Our mission as a republic is not to propagate our opinions, or impose upon other countries our form of government by artifice or force, but to teach by example, and show by our success, moderation, and justice, the blessings of self-government and the advantages of free institutions."[109] Although the Democrats won the election, their platform gave Kossuth no great cause for rejoicing and their weak compromise candidate Franklin Pierce showed little taste for providential republican crusades in Europe. Kossuth quickly left the premises, scourged by the advice of the wise Washington.

Another particular trait of the American political spirit served to curb the providential impulse. This was the consensual (or "social contract") notion of political authority and obligation that the Americans had inherited in part from Puritan sources,[110] in part from

Locke, and in part from the jurisconsults and natural rights philosophers of the Continent, the doctrine decried by Bushnell. For American purposes, the "social compact" implied several things: (1) that secular authority ascended from the people and was symbolized in their "pact of association"; (2) that governments were responsible to and revocable by society; (3) that consent was the token of free government and that allegiance to government was conditioned by the government's capacity to preserve liberty and security; (4) that consent defined citizenship; (5) that the aims of free government authorized by a consenting citizenry were fundamentally preservative and not "providential"; (6) and that there was no surmise, at least in the secular sphere, that human government could ever be superseded by any millennium or utopia.

Compact theory shines only translucently through the Constitution, where the states were the real bargainers; yet Madison, the chief architect of the document, was, as we know, thoroughly schooled by Witherspoon at Princeton in the texts of natural rights philosophy—Grotius, Pufendorf, Barbeyrac, and others.[111] Locke and Burlamaqui were also widely read by the intellectuals of the colonies. The political horizons of contractarianism were, of course, invaded by other strains of thought that ignored the paradigm and stressed moral sentiments, utility, natural sociability, and collective sovereign will—such as we find them in Hutcheson, Ferguson, Hume, Smith, and Rousseau—as well as by the powerful millennial impulse of the evangelical denominations. Yet the ideas of contract and consent provided a capital normative and ideological focus in the pre–Civil War years and were not without lasting influence on the ecclesiastical polity of, especially, the Congregationalists, the Unitarians, the Baptists, and the Disciples of Christ—despite their contributions to providentialism. The contract idea, voluntaristic, moral, and businesslike all at once, also guided most of expanding America away from anarchistic or utopian enterprises.

An illuminating case pivots around the fascinating and complicated personality of Alexander Campbell, the founder of the Disciples of Christ, and, more particularly, his marathon debate of April 1829 with the utopian socialist Robert Owen "on the evidences of Christianity." A man of great scope and curiosity and a powerful and persuasive orator, Campbell was simultaneously a crusader, an educator, a theologian, a populist, and a patriot. Perhaps he may best be summarized as a consummate dissenter. He despised the denominations, having emerged on the scene as a Baptist, and he was scathingly hostile to clericalism in all its forms; his mission, as he saw it, was "to unmask the clergy and their kingdom.'' [112] In brief, he scorned pastoral supremacy over Christian worship and favored the most democratic and austere form of church government. Most certainly he was no rabble-rouser. He desired to return all Christianity to the presumed practices of the primitive Church. Interestingly enough—in view of the argument I shall be developing—Campbell appealed both to the social contract and the Bible to sustain his views concerning proper congregational ordering.[113] He pilloried the pretensions of Presbyterianism and its learned oracles at Princeton, claiming—curiously—that Calvin had been a deist and that all the creeds proceeding from his inspiration were therefore false.[114] He would attack Owen's social system as deviantly influenced by Scottish Christianity. Yet he objected himself to the doctrine of the Trinity, not because it was false but because it was cast in ''unintelligible jargon.'' [115] Methodism was little better; it was freighted with enthusiasm.[116] Later he was contemptuous of the Mormons.[117] Needless to say, he was militantly anti-Catholic, regarding the Roman Church as totally un-American.[118] In the spirit of his day, he professed the primacy of Anglo-Saxonism.[119] Campbell was a patriot: these are the words with which he celebrated the Christian mission he had begun on 4 July 1823:

> It is right that I should keep to the *rights of man,* as I have proposed to wear out one pen on them. . . . This is the fourth day of July, the day on which this nation was born, and the day on which Thomas Jefferson and John Adams died. On this day I wrote the preface to the first volume of the Christian Baptist, and it was the day on which I write the preface to the seventh and last volume of this work.[120]

Indeed, Campbell—a staunch natural rights advocate, an ''agrarian,'' [121] and eventually the founder of a college in Bethany, (now) West Virginia—shared many opinions with Jefferson and admired the sage of Monticello.[122] However, when Campbell visited Monticello in 1855 he was shocked to find the busts of Voltaire and Paine in the statesman's chambers. ''He repudiated the Bible,'' Campbell lamented, ''and he dreamed of making a free and happy people without faith, a hope, or a desire for Christian immortality.'' [123]

Campbell neatly balanced the claims of reason and revelation: ''Reason is exalted a judge over revelation, and its power to *comprehend* made a test of the sound in doctrine, and the pure faith. We have no objection to reason in religion when its use is not perverted. . . . But why should we reject anything in God's revelation because we cannot comprehend it?'' [124] Yet he castigated rationalistic Uni-

tarianism as a hostile creed, proclaiming that "under the government
of Christ, we have a Christology, too." [125] Campbell believed in the
Bible as humanly written but divinely authenticated; [126] he also believed in miracles, at least those of the early Church. [127] Although a
sincere democrat and hostile to slavery (Campbell was not an abolitionist, but he had manumitted his own two or three slaves), he counseled Christians not to take an active role in politics because it was a
corrupting practice. [128] His magazine was politically impartial. [129] He
held a Bushnellian view of God's command of civil magistrates. [130]
Although only "Christocracy" could suffice as the perfect regime,
Campbell came to believe "that the American, of all governments, is
the nearest approximation of Christianity, for it offers 'no utopian
theory of politics or religion' and is more Protestant." [131]

These direction signals prepare us somewhat to consider Campbell's "millennialism" (already shown in salient respects to differ
from the stock in trade of evangelical providentialism), and then to
pass to the implications of the debate with Owen. When Campbell
founded a new magazine in 1830, he called it, auspiciously, *The Millennial Harbinger*. How much of a harbinger was it? As one historian
correctly observes: "The name of the new magazine . . . does not
indicate any special interest in the second coming of Christ in a spectacular way or any marked devotion to either the premillennial or the
postmillennial view. Apparently he uses the term in a quite loose and
general sense." [132] He did at least write:

> *Jesus Christ will yet govern the world by religion only, and that by the
> operation of a single principle.* . . . [When that happens] admirers of
> American liberty and American institutions will have no cause to fear
> it. . . . [It will be] but the removing of a tent to build a temple. [133]

Campbell was old and broken when the Civil War smashed the social compact. But he was in the prime of life when he confronted
Owen. In retrospect, it has seemed to some a tame clash of principles: Campbell was certainly no orthodox champion of the religion
practiced in America. Ernest Tuveson writes: "The most curious fact
is that both contenders were passionate believers in the necessity and
indeed certainty of indefinite advancement; at times the debate seems
to be a bout of straw-men, the agreement is so close. . . ." [134] West
concurs: "The similarities between Campbell and Owen are striking.
Both were nineteenth-century utopians, each with his proposed system to free mankind from prejudices, classes, and sects." [135] No
doubt it would have been more theatrical if Owen had debated the

pope. Both Owen and Campbell were incorrigible optimists and adherents of progressive doctrines. But Campbell opposed a voluntaristic religious program of reform to a rationalistic utopian doctrine that
would demolish all contingency and free will.

Owen had challenged the clergy of New Orleans on 28 January
1826 to a kind of round robin in which he would claim to establish
that "all the religions of the world have been founded on the ignorance of mankind" and are "the real source of vice, disunion, and
misery." The gauntlet was not taken up. "Finally Alexander Campbell, rising out of the dust of the tumbling ecclesiastical structure
which he had attacked, accepted the challenge in 1828." [136] Through
intermediaries Owen learned of Campbell's proposal and agreed,
through the *New Harmony Gazette* of 14 May 1828, to confront
Campbell in a moderated debate before a public audience. That performance was held in Cincinnati, beginning on 13 April 1829 and lasting the better part of eight days, with each of the parties entitled
alternately to the privilege of a half hour's uninterrupted speech. This
was a forensic *tour de force* such as the age of television can scarcely
imagine; as Owen declared, in mid-debate, "There never has been
any antecedent time, in the history of any country, in which any individual has been permitted to speak as I have done." [137] The printed
debate document taken from the stenographic records contains about
a hundred thousand words.

Owen launched the issue uncompromisingly:

> I am now to prove "that all the religions of the world have originated in
> error; that they are directly opposed to the divine unchanging laws of
> human nature; that they are necessarily the source of vice, disunion,
> and misery; that they are now the only obstacle to the formation of a
> society, over the earth, of intelligence, of charity in its most extended
> sense, and of sincerity and affection. And that these district religions
> can no longer be maintained in any part of the world, except by keeping
> the mass of the people in ignorance of their own nature, by an increase
> of the tyranny of the few over the many." [138]

He had bitten off more than he could chew. How could he have pin-
pointed the errors of all the religions of the world, much less those of
the Christian sects? Owen therefore chose to present his own system.
He would prevail "by bringing forth . . . the facts which determine by
what unchanging laws man is produced, and his character formed;
and by showing how utterly inapplicable all the religions which have
hitherto been invented and instilled into the human mind are to a
being so created and matured." [139] He thus chose to deliver a windy

and lifeless lecture on what he called the "twelve laws of human nature," the central one being the sixth: "That each individual is so
created, that he must believe according to the strongest impressions
that are made on his feelings and other faculties, while his belief in no
case depends on his will." [140] "When," Owen declared, "men shall
acquire sufficient wisdom or experience to induce them to abrogate
all existing laws and institutions which are unnatural, and to contend
no longer against the divine laws of human nature . . . then, and not
before, will peace be established on earth, and good-will among mankind." [141] It was the materialist, Helvetian motto of "l'éducation peut
tout."

The competitive outcome of the debate could not be in doubt, for
Owen persisted in his recitation and commentary of the "twelve
laws." It was also clear that Campbell possessed logical and forensic
skills that overmatched his opponent. None of this, however, detracts
from the interest of some of the things that were said. Owen charged
"all governments" with the motive of keeping the governed in abject
ignorance and with extracting from them "the largest amount of their
labour." To this end they always gave political support to what they
called *"the true religion."* [142]

According to Owen it had become possible in the nineteenth century to introduce justice and public rationality, owing to the great
progress in knowledge and scientific power and the wealth they could
generate: "We shall discover that there can be no cause for anxiety,
with regard to pecuniary matters, or rather the means of living in
comfort. . . . There will be a surplus, greatly exceeding the wants of
all." [143] As for the Christian system, which has produced "in nine
cases out of ten only vicious and deteriorating circumstances for human nature . . . I rejoice to say, that no very formidable obstacle now
interposes, to prevent these degrading circumstances from being withdrawn, and replaced by others of the most delightful and beneficial
character." [144] Owen hoped that this achievement could be had in
another generation. He postulated "three distinct states of society."
The first, common all over the world, was one in which human character had been compulsorily formed by religious belief; the second
was a kind of agitated and negative "gulph" caused by the destruction of previous false belief—a critical period to be shortened as
much as possible; the third and final state would see all individuals
disabused of errors, with "everything that savors of irrationality . . .
withdrawn." [145] Here Owen's language grew rhapsodic and, so to
speak, evangelical: "This change is absolutely necessary before you
can be born again. This is the regeneration which you and past gener-

ations have been looking for; and this change can be wrought simply by acquiring a knowledge of these eternal and immutable facts."[146] Alexander Campbell shrewdly interposed: ". . . I would think he was preaching to us concerning the millennium; that he was the herald of a better day. Sceptical as my friend is, I must infer that he is a *believer* in the millennium; and, for aught I know, he may be doing as much as a thousand missionaries to induce it."[147] Further along in the debate, Owen did maintain "that we are approximating to a greatly improved period of human existence, call it, if you please, the millennium."[148]

Owen exclaimed: "When we remove the priests, lawyers, warriors, and merchants, what a happy state of society shall we enjoy! None of us shall have occasion to be employed more than two hours per day; yet we shall have an abundance of the best of everything!"[149] He proceeded to develop the constitution of a "natural government," based on a code of "natural laws" providing for the "things necessary for human happiness." Owen's polity was composed of ever-widening federated circles of locally autonomous communities, no smaller than three hundred persons each or larger than two thousand, presumably extensive, without national boundaries, to the whole of humanity.[150] Each community was to be administered by a council of all persons trained from infancy in its bosom between the ages of thirty-five and forty-five. "The business of the council," Owen declared, "shall be to govern all the circumstances within the boundaries of its own community . . . by removing continually the most unfavorable circumstances to happiness. . . . The council shall have full power of government in all things as long as they do not act contrary to the divine laws of human nature. These laws shall be their guide upon all occasions, because, when understood, they will prevent one unjust or erroneous decision or proceeding."[151] Furthermore, persons were not legitimate subjects of praise or blame.[152]

Campbell's general riposte was, of course, that rationality implied freedom of choice and the condition "that man is constitutionally responsible."[153] Earlier on he had challenged Owen to prove that all men were independent beings; now it was evident that Owen's institutions "require[d] man to have [no] more control over his own actions than a mill-wheel has over its own revolutions." But responsibility, for Campbell, was not a consequence of independence. It is in this sense that we grasp his interconnected ideals of social and sacred relationships inserting themselves into the debate:

The basis of all obligation or responsibility, I hold to be *dependence*. A being, independent of any other, has no rule to obey, but that which his own reason or will prescribes. But a state of dependence will, inevitably, oblige the inferior to take the will on whom he depends, as the rule of his conduct, at least, in all those points wherein his dependence consists; consequently, as man depends absolutely upon his Creator for every thing, it is necessary that he should, in all points, submit to his will. This I do hold to be the true and immoveable basis of natural, social, and religious obligation, and responsiblity.[154]

In Campbell's view, sacred obligation was the source and legitimation of profane bonds of authority, which were, nevertheless, though still tied to the principles of dependence and responsibility, of a contractual and voluntary character. In the following extended passage Campbell expressed his political theory, which, in both its particulars and deep structure, is no different from liberal democracy or from the Tocquevillian sense of the American republican ideology:

> No society has ever existed, or ever can exist, without some sense of responsibility or obligation. We talk of *lawless banditti,* but this is to be understood *sub modo.* They are not without laws, and rigorous ones too, among themselves; they well know that they could not exist without them.[155]

> No social compact has yet existed, without the doctrine of responsibility, obligation, or accountability. Mr. Owen's scheme is the most Utopian project in the annals of society. He lays the axe at the root of all obligation and accountability, and yet would have society hang together without a single attraction, save animal magnetism, if such a thing exist. The doctrine of *no praise, no blame,* is to be taught from the cradle to the grave; and yet all are to live in accordance with the most virtuous principles. They are to have no principle of responsibility suggested; and yet, under the charm of social feeling alone, they are to be more firmly bound then any wedded pair! Among the visions of the wildest enthusiasm, this one appears to be a rarity.

> I am yet at a loss to know what Mr. Owen means by *society.* A society without a social compact to me is unintelligible. Society is not a number of persons covering a certain piece of ground, like the trees in our forest. They must congregate upon some stipulations expressed or implied. These stipulations are to be performed, and consequently, responsibility or accountability forces itself upon Mr. Owen, in defiance of the powers of his imagination. In all other societies, except Mr. Owen's imaginary one, the people and the magistracy, whether elective or hereditary, are mutually accountable to each other. The people owe *allegiance,* which they promise in electing their rulers; and the magistracy owe *protection,* which they promise in being elected. In entering into society, man surrenders a part of his natural liberty for other benefits, which he could never enjoy as a hermit. This surrender he must never recall, nor those benefits must they withhold: they are, therefore,

under continual obligations to each other. Whenever any person feels himself absolved from these obligations he is either dangerous to, or unfit for, society. And certainly, Mr. Owen's system of training children would naturally lead them to feel themselves absolved from all such obligations. His system directly unfits them for society.[156]

Sixty-five more pages of debate follow the last citation. At the end Campbell was predictably greeted by thunderous ovations, while only three brave souls rose for Owen.

For Campbell, a contractual sense of authority, obligation, and allegiance confirmed the performance and cohesion of society and the institution of civil government. That vision of politics was undergirded by an absolute condition of dependence in the sacred sphere—but the one sphere merely authorized the other, it did not dominate it. In the profane sphere, the notion of compact and obligation asserted freedom and responsibility against utopian determinism and rationalistic human engineering. It was also implicitly hostile to messianic universalism of any sort, for it described the grounds of a tolerable condition that was neither in the strong sense perfectible nor prone to imperializing zeal, unless by example alone. It was perhaps, as Campbell seems to have believed, compatible with millennium, as a "tent" is to a "temple." No doubt it was no substitute for "Christocracy." But the Second Coming, although a central article of Christian faith, was neither highly urgent nor predictable. While the Lord's people waited, they had at least given themselves the blessings of responsibility and self-government.

The crucible of the Civil War flamed up like an eruption of premillennial apocalypse and subsided. It permanently marked American mythology and rhetoric, creating a chasm of tragedy and martyrdom in the bosom of the "holy experiment." But this mixed mood of doom, exaltation, and fratricidal fury abated in a changed and changing nation whose providence could not long be seen in the image of self-purgation. A desire to get on with progress swelled in the victorious North. Restraint vanished. In 1865 President Andrew Johnson called on the whole people to join in "confession of our national sins" and ask God to show the way to the future.[157] But by 1868 this sorely pressed president-by-default had reverted to the more traditional rhetoric: "The conviction is rapidly growing ground [sic] in the American mind that with increased facilities for intercommunication between all portions of the earth the principles of free government as embraced in our constitution . . . would prove sufficient strength and breadth to comprehend within their sphere and influence the civilized nations of the world."[158] Grant's First Inaugural Address expressed the view that "the Great Maker" would ready the world for America's political institutions.[159] The American holocaust seemed merely to have confirmed America's destiny; that was how "the judgments of the Lord are true and righteous altogether." Walt Whitman now declared: "America, if eligible at all to downfall and ruin, is eligible within herself, not without; for I see clearly that the combined foreign world could not beat her down."[160]

Just before the eve that Lincoln was shot, the clergyman Henry Ward Beecher, who had little of the fibre of his ancestors, could signal a preoccupation of the new era by declaring: "It is better for religion; it is better for political integrity; it is better for industry; it is better for money—if you will have that ground motive—that you should educate the black man, and, by education, make him a citizen."[161] Henceforward corruption and unrestrained capitalism transformed the face of the nation even as it flexed its continental muscles. Ancient pieties survived as the shell of a once-exuberant faith, but we may accept Sidney Mead's contention about the remaining years of the nineteenth century that "there occurred a virtual identification of the outlook of . . . denominational Protestantism with 'Americanism' or 'the American way of life' and . . . we are still living with some of the results of this ideological amalgamation."[162] By 1890, in Ahlstrom's words: "To mainstream Protestants a denial of America's manifest destiny bordered on treason. The American was a fully convinced 'post-millennialist.' He believed that the Kingdom of God would be realized in history, almost surely in American history."[163] The expansion and fulfillment of the Hamiltonian "continental system," abetted by a strongly consensual Protestant ideology, provided for a kind of perverse and parochial civil religion. The Christian heroes of the nation were men like Andrew Carnegie; the pulpits cultivated and coddled the rich and soothed them with theologies of success and duties of liberality.

Henry Adams described contemporary politics as a "systematic organization of hatreds" no longer frustrated by Madison's judicious remedies.[164] In his novel *Democracy* he commented acidly: ". . . the hopes of mankind are staked on [democracy] and if the weak in faith sometimes quail when they see humanity floating in a shoreless ocean, religion long since condemned as rotten, mistake or not, men have thus far floated better by its aid than the popes ever did with their prettier principle so that it will be a long time yet before society repents."[165] Yet this plutocracy harbored a great, if illusionary, binding force, every day authenticated in new conquests of nature, the creation of wealth, and conspicuous and vulgar monumentalism, for almost all—except utopians, mortgaged dirt farmers, voiceless immigrants, forgotten Blacks, and a few appalled aesthetes—were agreed on the irreversible thrust of national progress. Presidents Cleveland and McKinley outdid each other in sounding this note with conviction.[166] "Our faith," said the pious McKinley, "teaches us that there is no safer reliance than upon the God of our fathers, who has so singularly favored the American people in every national trial."[167] It was at this time that George Burton Adams wrote that "a new era of history" was at hand that had rendered Washington's Farewell Address obsolete;[168] and that John Henry Barrows, president of Oberlin College, declared: "God has made us a world power."[169] The providentialism of world example had become the providentialism of world destiny in a burst of *hubris* taught by Christians but scarcely faithful to the Christian assumptions of the founding. Reinhold Niebuhr describes the Spanish War episode as "hypocrisy," overdone "because a youthful and politically immature nation tried to harmonize the anti-imperialistic innocency of its childhood with the imperial impulses of its awkward youth."[170] But the innocence was already in tatters.

This atmosphere provoked the rise of the rather shapeless movement called the Social Gospel, which, appalled at the prideful and greedy travesties of the Gilded Age, had tried to summon Americans back to a care for their neighbor. The Social Gospel, which was thoroughly nondenominational in temper, "did not represent Protestant ministers as a whole; certainly they did not represent the Protestant congregations. Often they spoke only for a handful, were disavowed by more, and were ignored by most."[171] Encompassing men like Washington Gladden, Francis Peabody, Richard Ely, Josiah Strong, and Walter Rauschenbusch, this impetus for a social Christianity that would reach out to the poor, and especially the urban poor, took shape in the 1880s. Protestantism was badly placed to deal with slums and sweatshops.[172] The Social Gospel had no particular theological coherence except a propensity to liberal "modernism"; its great innovation was in the field of pastoral care and in its conflation of religious and public issues. This evangelism differed radically from the conversion efforts of the Second Great Awakening, for it announced a "commitment to restructure society actively and directly . . . rather than adopting the circuitous route of the revivalists who sought to alter society by converting men one by one."[173] Thus it had a political doctrine that verged toward collectivism (and sometimes socialism) and intimate contacts with the American secular reform movements that could be classified as "progressivism." As Meyer writes: "Pastors confronted politics directly, as the means to victory.

In so doing they exposed themselves to the pressures that every idea faces in action. Politics was to be not only a means, but a testing of the ends."[174]

The power of both postmillennialism and American providentialism was so unchallenged that it stamped this radical creed as deeply as the adversary one. Before the Civil War one could unite the themes of progress and providence and be a comfortable bourgeois or a William Ellery Channing. No doubt there were different signs of progress, but each sought its American affirmation. In a still more immanentist religious sense, the Social Gospel animated this same tradition. This was indeed, as Ahlstrom says, "a form of millennial thought."[175] It was a religion that could accommodate its preaching to democracy and social science, but it could not, without ceasing to be a religion in America, burst free of nationalist *élan* and providential enthusiasm. The underprivileged and unchurched were to enter the kingdom; but—at least in the prolific writings of Josiah Strong— the nativism of Beecher and Bushnell was descanted in more secular but shriller tones:

> In this era mankind is to come more and more under Anglo-Saxon influence, and Anglo-Saxon civilization is more favorable than any other to the spread of those principles whose universal triumph is necessary to that perfection of the race to which it is destined; the entire realization of which will be the kingdom of heaven fully come to earth.[176]

However, Walter Rauschenbusch, the most intellectual and theological of the group and of German descent besides, spoke in relatively hushed words of the American mission and took the pacifist side in World War I, shortly before his death. His millennialism had only the faintest odor of ethnocentricity:

> Perhaps these nineteen centuries of Christian influence here have been a long preliminary stage of growth, and now the flower and fruit are almost here. If at this juncture we can rally sufficient religious faith and moral strength to snap the bonds of evil and turn the present unparalleled economic and intellectual resources of humanity to the harmonious development of a true social life, the generations yet unborn will mark this as that great day of the Lord for which the ages waited, and count us blessed for sharing in the apostolate that proclaimed it.[177]

Rauschenbusch preached a politics of equality verging on socialism and to be redeemed in love, a love achieved by Christian action in the social system. His providentialism shared certain features with the hope of another major figure, Woodrow Wilson, who is not commonly remembered as an apostle of love. Though Rauschenbusch endorsed a more radical politics than Wilson, both were deeply infused with the ideals of humanitarian salvation and unyielding in their commitment of the United States to that purpose. Both were, in Reinhold Niebuhr's terms, naive idealists: they proposed America as hope and example, rather than as a wielder of world power. Yet Wilson, like Gladstone and other liberal politicians, came to believe that providential power could be used unambiguously by moral politicians for the good.

A few citations from Wilson will set the context: "I love this country," he told the G.A.R., "because it is my home, but every man loves his home. . . . That does not suffice for patriotic duty. I should also love it, and I hope I do love it, as a great instrument for the uplift of mankind." [178] To some newly sworn citizens he cautioned: "My urgent advice to you should be, not only to think first of America, but always, also to think first of humanity." [179] A year earlier he had professed: "A patriotic American is a man who is not niggardly and selfish in the things that he enjoys that make for human liberty and the rights of man. He wants to share them with the whole world." [180] In the same speech, he added: "The way to success in this great country, with its fair judgments, is to show that you are not afraid of anybody except God and his final verdict. If I did not believe that, I would not believe that people can govern themselves. If I did not believe that the moral judgment would be the last judgment, the final judgment, in the minds of men as well as the tribunal of God, I could not believe in popular government." [181] This is the essential ideology that carried Wilson into, through, and past World War I. While an old civilization was cracking into fragments, Wilson was ever ready to designate the path of those fragments to "man's best hope." That is why, despite his initial popularity on the Old Continent, discerning critics began to chide the native simplicity of his millennium:

> His thought and his temperament were essentially theological, not intellectual, with all the strength and weakness of that manner of thought, feeling, and expression. . . . He had no plan, no scheme, no constructive idea whatever for clothing with the flesh of life the commandments he had thundered from the White House. He could have preached a sermon on any of them, or have addressed a stately prayer to the Almighty for their fulfillment, but he could not frame their application for the actual state of Europe. [182]

In the meantime, American democracy's *alter ego* William Jennings Bryan was proclaiming: "A man can be born again; the springs of life can be cleansed instantly. If this be true of one, it can be true of any number. Thus a nation can be born in a day if the ideals of the people can be changed."[183] No doubt there was something stubbornly holy and admirable in these kinds of ingenuousness, especially when set against the greed of the plutocrats and the calculating coldness of the *Realpolitiker:* but they were criticizable in both American and Christian terms. Their dissection would be the major mission of Reinhold Niebuhr.

In one of Niebuhr's last books, he discussed "the irony of American history."[184] When Niebuhr touched on the ironic mode, he implied some of the ironies we have already witnessed or will take up. To claim that irony is probably the proper rhetorical trope for understanding our history is neither seditious nor disrespectful. It is crucial that national self-esteem not be embalmed in the pickling juice of indulgence. Naive assumptions of grace and worthiness might best be replaced by a more Stoic fortitude in the face of sobering experience. Supplications for forgiveness, when warranted, are more seemly than a babble of innocence. More realistic attitudes can create a spirit of freedom amid the recalcitrant roadblocks of necessity, instead of building prisons from the conviction that most of the profane world is there for the human appropriation—of Americans. That is what I mean by the vein of irony.

Some of the same irony attended the career of Reinhold Niebuhr (1892-1970). He was unquestionably the best-known American-born theologian of his century and possibly the finest since Jonathan Edwards. Yet if, for a generation, Reinhold Niebuhr—a skilled exegete, a genuine philosopher of history, and one of the only American political theorists worthy of the name in his time—was the theologian in vogue, it cannot be said that he dictated the direction in which the American churches or, more specifically, the American religious consciousness would travel. Both as a propagandist, based from 1928 on at the Union Theological Seminary, and as the indefatigable author of scholarly lectures and books, Niebuhr enjoyed eminent standing as an intellectual prophet, but his impact on the nation was not overwhelming.

This should not cause surprise. As Niebuhr's own thought evolved —generally from radical to more moderate positions in politics and from prophetic castigation to lofty reflection in theology—he ran the gauntlet of competing positions and flailed out at almost all of them. Most of these were the entrenched Protestant tendencies—perhaps more a cacophony than a consensus—whose frustrations were reflected in the responses of most American church members: fundamentalism, with its defensive suspicion of all treatments of Scripture that did not invoke its literal inerrancy; sugar-coated liberal modernism that forsook dogmatics for a soft and safe bourgeois ethic; self-righteous pacifism and quietism; sectarian extravagance; and Social Gospel extremism that reduced Christianity to a kind of idealistic case work. Niebuhr's erudition, combined with his comfortless criticism, annoyed more Americans than it converted. To all this must be added Niebuhr's militancy in the left-wing politics of the postdepression years, his measured appreciation of class struggle, and his conviction that American society was digging itself into an ever-deeper crisis. It might have appeared superficially from Niebuhr's early—and more radical—period that politics and religion were a collaborative project, earth-bound and earth-tormenting. In this respect he might have seemed an unsentimental and rather revolutionary revisionist of the Social Gospel. But even while Niebuhr deplored the social conditions that had brought capitalist culture to the brink of chaos, he was creating his fundamental tension between the imperatives of Christian-centered moral action and the tragic realism of world politics. His *Moral Man and Immoral Society* (1932) went to the heart of this ambiguity; ". . . it will never be possible to insure moral antidotes sufficiently potent to destroy the deleterious effects of the poison of power upon character. The future peace and justice of society therefore depend upon, not one but many social strategies, in all of which moral and coercive factors are compounded in varying degrees." [185]

For Niebuhr the ultimate Christian value remained love. But love was usually possible only within a very small compass, given the realities of the world. It was therefore the task of politics, partly through the appropriate uses of power, to strive for justice, a difficult enough goal and one presently conceivable only within the nation-state, for all its travesties and dangers, for

> what lies beyond the nation, the community of mankind, is too vague to inspire devotion. The lesser communities within the nation, religious, economic, racial and cultural, have equal difficulty in competing with the nation for the loyalty of its citizens. The church was able to do so when it had the prestige of a universality it no longer possesses.[186]

Religion, of course, set a high premium on justice and peace, and on the law (no doubt this is what led Niebuhr, though not in the manner of Barth, back to the fundamentals of St. Paul and St. Augustine), but only a shrewd and realistic politics was in a position to secure justice. Niebuhr wavered over support of Roosevelt's New Deal in the late 1930s not because he failed to appreciate many of its social motives but because he distrusted its sentimentality and lack of realism. When he finally endorsed Roosevelt, it was in part because he himself felt the need for a greater pragmatism.[187]

Even before World War II (revulsed by Munich, Niebuhr lent his strong voice to the allied cause),[188] Niebuhr's anomaly of politics and religion did not prevent him from appreciating the compelling role of eschatology:

> There is a millennial hope in every vital religion. The religious imagination is as impatient with the compromises, relativities, and imperfections of historic society as with the imperfections of individual life. . . . The gospel conception of the kingdom of God represents a highly spiritualised version of [the] Jewish millennial hope, heavily indebted to the vision of the Second Isaiah. Whenever religion concerns itself with the problems of society, it always gives birth to some kind of millennial hope, from the perspective of which present social realities are convicted of inadequacy, and courage is maintained to continue in the effort to redeem society of injustice.[189]

Nevertheless, by 1940, the theologian's tone had perceptibly shifted from the utopistic and normative idea of millennium in the service of the struggle for justice to its reality as a transhistorical judgment upon pride and self-idolatry:

> If there is not some transcendent reference from which a particular historical mission is judged, the executors of divine judgment in history vainly imagine themselves to be God, even if they do not believe in God—or perhaps particularly if they do not believe in God. The struggle between the prophets and the pride of Israel, in which the prophets sought vainly to prove to Israel that a nation might have a special mission and yet not be immune to the divine judgment, contains ultimate insights which are completely lost in modern life.[190]

The focus of castigation had not changed, for Niebuhr was still attacking "the unbelievable optimism in American political life [caused by the] degree the perspectives of the Enlightenment and Sectarianism had been united in America";[191] but the emphasis was now on the proper view of man as "creature" as well as "creator" of historical destiny. This motto would be more searchingly affirmed in Niebuhr's later writings: "The conception of a divine sovereignty over history which is not immediately apparent in the structures and recurrences of history establishes a dimension in which there can be meaning, though the facts of history are not related to each other in terms of natural or logical necessity. The freedom of God over and beyond the structures of life makes room for the freedom of man."[192]

World War I, according to Niebuhr, had "made me a child of the age of disillusionment." [193] His intellectual progress through the depression, the New Deal, a second great war, and the ensuing confrontation with global responsibility in an adversary nuclear world may be described as a coming to terms with limits, prudence, faith, and history. In this progress, while religion was surely never made an alternative to society, there was a cultivation of the sober recognition that religion's ideal function was to preserve itself as a pure medium in which the anxieties of society and history could be made intelligible without giving rise to fatuous optimism. The state of war, if not war itself, was an everpresent condition. Naive America, especially, with its comfortable beliefs in progress and idealistic moral conversion had to be educated in the pragmatic arts of statesmanship and shown the hollowness of some of its pretensions: "Escape from our ironic situation obviously demands that we moderate our conceptions of the ability of men and nations to discern the future; and of the power of even great nations to bring a tortuous historical process to, what seems to them, a logical and proper conclusion." [194] This involved an acceptance of responsibility and an acknowledgment of "the idea that guilt accompanies responsibility," a notion difficult for Americans. [195]

For some Niebuhr was an arrogant intellectual who failed to make contact with the true sources of gospel evangelism; for others he was a parlor radical turned "cold warrior." In any case, his spirit has largely evaporated. He made, I think, a preponderate contribution to the subject we have been canvassing, for never had a prominent American religious figure, speaking in entire good faith and indeed prophetically, made such a blunt and reasoned attack on the holy image of America and its conviction of providential fulfillment. While professing great love for his country and its better ideals, Niebuhr reduced America to being a nation among nations. Niebuhr declared that American hopes were frustrated by the very conditions imposed by the sacred on the profane. He warned that "the opulence of American life and the dominant position of American power in the world create the illusion of a social stability which the total world situation belies." [196] He concluded: "If we should perish, the ruthlessness of the foe would be only the secondary cause of the disaster. The primary cause would be that the strength of a giant nation was directed by eyes too blind to see all the hazards of the struggle." [197] And he reminded Americans that "there is . . . no possibility of a final judgment within history but only at the end of history," charting us back to a premillennial humility. [198] If this was a sober riposte to the different vagaries of the American faith, it was also, in another sense, a rebuttal to the republican and religious settlement that Tocqueville had proposed. Niebuhr did not see religion as a prime component of civic culture; he came to regard it as judging that culture—ironically. For him, the fates of the sacred and the secular were not, so to speak, linked. Against Niebuhr it might be argued that, in stark contrast to his own belief in an Augustinian God of history—unnaturalized at Ellis Island—the messianic-millenarian belief had waned greatly in the Western world. As Peter Berger writes:

> It is very instructive to note that the immeasurably greater horrors of World War II did not [lead to a theodicy debate]. Insofar as these events (particularly those connected with the Nazi atrocities) raised metaphysical questions, as against ethical or political ones, these were typically anthropological rather than theological in character: "How could men act this way?" rather than, "How could God permit this?" [199]

Perhaps this was some deeper irony of ironic history and perhaps it bespoke the separation between democratic reality and Christian ultimacy that Niebuhr conceded. But perhaps it meant the end—a critique—of all providence. This would sustain Hannah Arendt's absolute positing of the values of politics against religion: "The important historical fact is that an overwhelming majority has ceased to believe in a Last Judgment at the end of time." [200] Arendt had pinned down an inescapable tendency of our high culture and indeed of our social rationale. It was nonetheless probably true at the time she wrote those words that forty or more American sects with a combined membership of over a million and perhaps three million other fundamentalist denominational Christians regarded premillennialism as a central doctrine. [201] If we refer to the table given in the last chapter and note sectarian progress over the past generation, it is not too wild a guess to say that this number might now have risen by at least two million. What seems to have deteriorated greatly is postmillennial optimism.

Notes

1. *Diary of Cotton Mather,* Collections of the Massachusetts Historical Society, 2 vols., Seventh Series, vols. 7-8 (Boston, 1911-1912), II, 366.
2. Woodrow Wilson, *The New Democracy: Presidential Messages, Addresses, and Other Papers,* ed. Ray S. Baker and William E. Dodd (2 vols., New York, 1926), II, 414.
3. *Democracy in America,* I, 450.
4. Peter Dennis Bathory, "Tocqueville on Citizenship and Faith: A Response to Cushing Strout," *Political Theory* 8 (February 1980): 33.

5. Robert Baird, *The Christian Retrospect and Register* (New York, 1851), p. 188.
6. *Democracy in America, II,* 351. One wonders here if Tocqueville was not ironically echoing the elder Cato's famous remark: "Victrix causa deis placuit, sed victa Catonis" ("The victorious cause is pleasing to the gods, but the losing one to Cato.").
7. Fourteenth address, in J.G. Fichte, *Addresses to the German Nation,* ed. G.A. Kelly (New York, 1968), p. 215.
8. Ibid., p. 227.
9. Jules Michelet, *Introduction à l'histoire universelle* (Paris, 1898), p. 467; and *La Prêtre, la femme et la famille* (Paris, 1898), p. 280.
10. Fyodor Dostoievsky, *The Diary of a Writer* (trans. B. Brasol, 2 vols., New York, 1949), II, 575.
11. Fyodor Dostoievsky, *The Possessed* (New York, 1936), p. 256.
12. Ernest Tuveson, *Redeemer Nation* (Chicago, 1968), p. 51.
13. See Ahlstrom, *Religious History,* pp. 807-12. Dispensationalism tended to "claim that all Christian history was a kind of meaningless 'parenthesis' between the setting aside of the Jews and the restoration of the Davidic kingdom" (p. 811).
14. Furniss, *Fundamentalist Controversy,* p. 23.
15. Davidson, *Logic of Millennial Thought,* p. 16.
16. Ibid., p. 18.
17. See above, p. 81.
18. Jonathan Edwards, "The Great Design God is Pursuing" (Miscellanies No. 547), in Ahlstrom, ed., *Theology in America,* p. 189.
19. Davidson, *Logic of Millennial Thought,* p. 79.
20. Youngs, *God's Messengers,* pp. 110-12.
21. Davidson, *Logic of Millennial Thought,* p. 241.
22. See John R. Howe, Jr., "Republican Thought and the Political Violence of the 1790s," *American Quarterly* 29 (Summer 1967): 147-65; J.F. Maclear, "The Republic and the Millennium," in Elwyn A. Smith, ed., *The Religion of the Republic* (Philadelphia, 1971), pp. 188-200; Nathan O. Hatch, "The Origins of Civil Millennialism in America: New England Clergymen, the War with France, and the Revolution," *William and Mary Quarterly,* Third Series, 31 (July 1974): 407-30; Marshall Smelser, "The Jacobin Phrenzy: Federalism and the Menace of Liberty, Equality, and Fraternity," *Review of Politics* 13 (October 1951): 457-82; James W. Davidson, "Searching for the Millennium: Problems for the 1790s and the 1970s," *New England Quarterly* 45 (June 1972): 241-61.
23. Samuel Hopkins, *A Treatise on the Millennium* (Boston, 1793), pp. 57-60.
24. Timothy Dwight, *A Sermon Delivered in Boston . . . Before the American Board of Commissioners for Foreign Missions* (Boston, 1813), p. 32.
25. William Ellery Channing, "The Essence of the Christian Religion," from *The Perfect Life,* in *Twelve Discourses* (Boston, 1873). Quoted in Ahlstrom, *Theology,* pp. 206-8.
26. Mark Hopkins, *"The Law of Progress of the Race,"* An Address Delivered before the Society of the Alumni of Williams College . . . (Boston, 1843), p. 23.

27. Smith, "Righteousness and Hope," p. 21.
28. Ibid.
29. H.R. Niebuhr, *Kingdom of God in America,* p. 49.
30. John Wise, *A Vindication of the Government of New-England Churches* (1717).
31. Strout, *New Heavens,* pp. 26-27.
32. Ibid., p. 65.
33. Nathaniel Whitaker, "An Antidote Against Toryism; or, The Curse of Meroz," in Frank Moore, ed., *The Patriot Preachers of the American Revolution* (New York, 1862), p. 201.
34. A key text was Abiel Abbot, *Traits of Resemblance in the People of the United States of America to Ancient Israel* (Haverhill, Mass., 1799).
35. Just a few years ago, the theologian Herbert Richardson warned: "It is urgent that America understand this ideological bias within her traditional identification with Israel's history and religion—and repudiate it." "Civil Religion in Theological Perspective," in Richey and Jones, eds., *American Civil Religion,* p. 174.
36. Bernard Bailyn, "Religion and Revolution: Three Biographical Studies," *Perspectives in American History* 4 (1970): 85-169.
37. Nathan Hatch, *The Sacred Cause of Liberty* (New Haven, 1977), p. 17.
38. Jonathan Mayhew to James Otis in 1766, quoted in Albanese, *Sons of the Fathers,* p. 54.
39. Ibid., pp. 88-94.
40. Davidson, *Logic of Millennial Thought,* p. 234.
41. J.G.A. Pocock, *The Machiavellian Moment* (Princeton, 1975), p. 513.
42. Strout, *New Heavens,* p. 63.
43. Ibid., p. 48.
44. "Farewell Address," in *Orations of American Orators,* I, 46.
45. Ibid., p. 33.
46. Ibid., p. 54.
47. Ibid., p. 51.
48. Ibid., p. 143.
49. In John Adams, *Works* (ed. Charles Francis Adams, 10 vols., Boston, 1850-1856), X, 223.
50. "Oration at Plymouth," 22 December 1802, in *Orations of American Orators,* I, 327.
51. Ibid., pp. 340-41.
52. John Quincy Adams, *An Oration Delivered Before the Inhabitants of the Town of Newburyport . . . July 4, 1837,* quoted in Albanese, *Sons of the Fathers,* p. 192.
53. Lyman Beecher, *Works* (2 vols., Boston, 1852), I, 189f.
54. Mead, *Old Religion,* p. 112.
55. Lyman Beecher, *Sermons Delivered on Various Occasions* (Boston, 1828), p. 159.
56. Ahlstrom, *Religious History,* p. 422.
57. Beecher, *Sermons,* p. 268.
58. Ibid., pp. 184, 363.
59. Ibid., p. 298.
60. Ibid.
61. For American nativism, see especially Ray A. Billington, *The Protestant*

Crusade, 1800-1860: A Study of the Origins of American Nativism (New York, 1938).

62. Archbishop Ireland, "Peace in the Wake of Victory," 10 July 1898, in *Orations of American Orators,* II, 491, 493, 498.
63. "The Principle of National Greatness," An Oration Pronounced Before the Society of Phi Beta Kappa (1837), in Clark Sutherland Northrup, William C. Lane, and John C. Schwab, eds., *Representative Phi Beta Kappa Orations* (2 vols., Boston, 1925; New York, 1927), I, 2-23.
64. Horace Bushnell, *Barbarism the First Danger* (New York, 1847), p. 32.
65. Ibid., pp. 4-5.
66. See Barbara M. Cross, *Horace Bushnell: Minister to a Changing America* (Chicago, 1958), pp. 136-37.
67. Quoted in Marty, *Righteous Empire,* p. 88.
68. Horace Bushnell, *Nature and the Supernatural as Together Constituting One System of God* (New York, 1877), p. 112.
69. Horace Bushnell, "Popular Government by Divine Right" (Hartford, 1865).
70. Ibid., pp. 4-5. And see "Reverses Needed," in W.S. Hudson, ed., *Nationalism and Religion in America* (New York, 1970), pp. 79-81.
71. Bushnell, "Popular Government," p. 5.
72. Ibid., p. 11.
73. Bushnell, "Reverses Needed," p. 80.
74. Bushnell, "Popular Government," p. 15.
75. Bushnell, "Reverses Needed," p. 81.
76. Bushnell, "Popular Government," p. 7.
77. R.T. Ely, *The Social Law of Service* (New York, 1897), p. 162.
78. Quoted in Nagel, *Sacred Trust,* p. 49.
79. Ibid., p. 80.
80. See Ahlstrom, *Religious History,* pp. 858-67.
81. Charles Hawley, *The Advantages of the Present Age* (Rochester, 1850), p. 13.
82. Nathaniel Chipman, *Principles of Government: A Treatise on Free Institutions* (Burlington, Vt., 1833), p. 16.
83. R.W. Emerson, "Lectures on the Times," *The Dial,* July 1842 (4 vols., New York, 1961), III, 15.
84. Emerson, notes from Missouri, 19 April 1853, in *Essays: Second Series,* p. 343.
85. Ralph Waldo Emerson, "American Civilization," in *Works* (12 vols., Boston, 1888), XI, 179.
86. Ralph Waldo Emerson, *Journals,* ed. E.W. Emerson and W.E. Forbes (10 vols., Boston and New York, 1909-1914), VIII, 226.
87. Rep. Presley Ewing (Whig-Ky.), *Congressional Globe,* 32d Cong. 1st Sess., H.R. (24 April 1852).
88. Joseph Story, "Characteristics of the Age," delivered to the Harvard Phi Beta Kappa Society, 31 August 1826, in *Orations of American Orators,* I, 381, 407.
89. Edward Everett, "Festival of the Alumni of Harvard" (1852), in *Orations and Speeches on Various Occasions* (4 vols., Boston, 1850-1859), III, 120.
90. "Four Sermons Preached at the Pennsylvania Yearly Meeting of Pro-

gressive Friends," *Proceedings of . . . Progressive Friends* (New York, 1858), p. 50.

91. See Nagel, *Sacred Trust,* p. 62. Among other patriotic primers of the time: William McCary, *Songs, Odes, and Other Poems on National Subjects* (Philadelphia, 1842); William H. Ryder, *Our Country; or, The American Parlor Keepsake* (Boston, 1854); John Henry Hopkins, *The American Citizen* (New York, 1857).

92. See Edwin De Leon, *The Positions and Duties of Young America* (Charleston, 1845).

93. James K. Polk, "Second Annual Message to Congress" (8 December 1846), in Richardson, ed., *Compilation of Messages and Papers,* V, 2322.

94. "Young America," in *New York Mirror* 20 (20 October 1842): 338.

95. Walt Whitman, "American Futurity," 24 November 1846, in Cleveland Rogers and John Black, eds., *The Gathering of the Forces* (New York, 1920), I, 4.

96. *New York Herald,* 25 September 1845.

97. See Donald S. Spencer, *Louis Kossuth and Young America: A Study of Sectionalism and Foreign Policy, 1848-1852* (Columbia, Mo. 1977), p. 13.

98. Quoted in Smith, *Revivalism and Social Reform,* p. 226.

99. Quoted in Arthur A. Ekirch, Jr., *The Idea of Progress in America, 1815-1860* (New York, 1944), p. 173.

100. The material that follows is largely indebted to Spencer, *Kossuth.*

101. Ibid., p. 6.

102. Ibid., pp. 47, 90.

103. Ibid., p. 61.

104. Ibid., pp. 125-27.

105. Ibid., p. 62.

106. Ibid., pp. 50-51.

107. Richardson, ed., *Compilation of Messages and Papers,* VI, 2614.

108. Ibid., VI, 1717.

109. Thomas Hudson McKee, ed., *The National Conventions and Platforms of all Political Parties, 1789 to 1900: Convention, Popular, and Electoral Vote* (Baltimore, 1900), p. 79.

110. See above, re John Wise, p. 130.

111. See Dennis Thompson, "The Education of a Founding Father: The Reading List for John Witherspoon's Course in Political Theory, as Taken by James Madison," *Political Theory* 4 (November 1976): 523-29.

112. Alexander Campbell, *The Christian Baptist* (3 vols., Buffaloe, Va., 1824-1826), II, 2.

113. See Robert Frederick West, *Alexander Campbell and Natural Religion* (New Haven, 1948), p. 10.

114. Ibid., pp. 17, 24, 28, 110-11.

115. Alexander Campbell, *The Millennial Harbinger* (41 vols., Bethany, Va., 1830-1864), IV, 155.

116. Alexander Campbell, *The Christian Baptist* (3 vols., Bethany, Va., 1827-1829), IV, 38-40, 79.

117. See West, *Campbell,* pp. 177, 184.

118. Ibid., pp. 194-96.

119. Alexander Campbell, *Popular Lectures and Addresses* (Philadelphia, 1863), pp. 2-45.
120. Campbell, *Christian Baptist,* VII, 1.
121. See Campbell, *Millennial Harbinger,* XIV, 64; XV, 360.
122. See, on this, Leroy Garrett, "Alexander Campbell and Thomas Jefferson: A Comparative Study of Two Old Virginians" (Dallas, 1963), passim; and West, *Campbell,* pp. 204-5.
123. Campbell, *Millennial Harbinger,* XXVII, 89.
124. Ibid., XV, 145-47.
125. Ibid., XXV, 550.
126. Ibid., III, 110.
127. West, *Campbell,* p. 137.
128. Campbell, *Millennial Harbinger,* XI, 413.
129. Ibid., XVII, 4-5.
130. Ibid., XVII, 20.
131. West, *Campbell,* p. 206; and see Campbell, *Millennial Harbinger,* XXIV, 487.
132. W.E. Garrison, *Religion Follows the Frontier: A History of the Disciples of Christ* (New York, 1931), p. 147.
133. Campbell, *Popular Lectures and Addresses,* pp. 372-74.
134. Tuveson, *Redeemer Nation,* p. 79.
135. West, *Campbell,* p. 66.
136. Ibid., p. 67.
137. *Debate on the Evidences of Christianity: Containing an Examination of the Social System, and of All the Systems of Ancient and Modern Times, Held in the City of Cincinnati, for Eight Days Successively, between Robert Owen, of New Lanark, Scotland and Alexander Campbell, of Bethany, Virginia . . .* (London, 1839), p. 241.
138. Ibid., p. 21.
139. Ibid.
140. Ibid., p. 22.
141. Ibid., p. 28.
142. Ibid., p. 37.
143. Ibid., p. 54.
144. Ibid., p. 92.
145. Ibid., pp. 102-3.
146. Ibid., p. 103.
147. Ibid., p. 104.
148. Ibid., p. 200; cf. p. 216.
149. Ibid., p. 174.
150. Ibid., p. 127.
151. Ibid., p. 128.
152. Ibid., p. 129.
153. Ibid., p. 130.
154. Ibid., p. 66.
155. Cf. St. Augustine, *The City of God,* bk. xix, p. 687.
156. *Debate,* pp. 376-77.
157. Andrew Johnson, in Richardson, ed., *Compilation of Messages and Papers,* VIII, 3530.

158. Cited by Reinhold Niebuhr, *The Irony of American History* (New York, 1952), p. 71.
159. Grant, Second Inaugural Address, in Richardson, ed., *Compilation of Messages and Papers,* IX, 4176.
160. Whitman, "Democratic Vistas," in *Leaves of Grass and Democratic Vistas* (London, n.d.), p. 334.
161. Henry Ward Beecher, "Raising the Flag Over Fort Sumter," 14 April 1865, in *Orations of American Orators,* II, 332.
162. Sidney E. Mead, "From Denominationalism to Americanism," *Journal of Religion,* January 1956, p. 1.
163. Ahlstrom, *Religious History,* p. 845.
164. Henry Adams, *The Education of Henry Adams* (New York, 1931), p. 7.
165. Henry Adams, *Democracy* (New York, 1968), p. 96.
166. See Nagel, *Sacred Trust,* pp. 273-77.
167. William McKinley, "Inaugural Address, 1897," in *Orations of American Orators,* II, 459.
168. G.B. Adams, "The United States and the Anglo-Saxon Future," *Atlantic Monthly,* July 1896, 35.
169. Barrows's speech is in Robert L. Fulton and Thomas C. Trueblood, eds., *Patriotic Eloquence* (New York, 1900), pp. 11-16.
170. Reinhold Niebuhr, *Moral Man and Immoral Society* (New York, 1960; orig. 1932), p. 99.
171. Donald B. Meyer, *The Protestant Search for Political Realism, 1919-1941* (Berkeley and Los Angeles, 1961), p. 1.
172. Handy, *Christian America,* p. 144.
173. Garrett, "Politicized Clergy," p. 389.
174. Meyer, *Protestant Search,* p. 3.
175. Ahlstrom, *Religious History,* p. 786.
176. Josiah Strong, *The New Era; or the Coming Kingdom* (New York, 1893), p. 80. Despite his insatiable desire to Anglo-Saxonize mankind, Strong often had more sensible things to say than this. His type of rhetoric was widespread in both England and America, in liberal as well as conservative circles, e.g., Lord Rosebery and Joseph Chamberlain.
177. Walter Rauschenbuch, *Christianity and the Social Crisis* (New York, 1907), p. 422.
178. Woodrow Wilson, address at G.A.R. celebration, Washington, 18 September 1915, in Wilson, *Great Speeches and Other History Making Documents* (Chicago, 1917), p. 69.
179. Woodrow Wilson, address to new citizens, Philadelphia, 10 May 1915, ibid., p. 172.
180. Woodrow Wilson, at Independence Hall, Philadelphia, 4 July 1914, ibid., p. 200.
181. Ibid., p. 202.
182. John Maynard Keynes, *Essays and Sketches in Biography* (New York, 1956), p. 186.
183. Quoted by Richard Hofstadter, *The American Political Tradition* (New York, 1954), p. 186.
184. R. Niebuhr, *Irony of American History.*
185. R. Niebuhr, *Moral Man and Immoral Society,* p. 21.
186. Ibid., p. 91.

187. See Meyer, *Protestant Search,* pp. 266-68.

188. Ibid., pp. 359-60.

189. R. Niebuhr, *Moral Man and Immoral Society,* pp. 60-61.

190. Reinhold Niebuhr, *Christianity and Power Politics* (New York, 1940), p. 137.

191. Ibid., p. 56.

192. Reinhold Niebuhr, *Faith and History* (New York, 1949), p. 27.

193. R. Niebuhr, "What the War Did to My Mind," *Christian Century* 45 (27 September 1928): 1161.

194. R. Niebuhr, *Irony of American History,* p. 140.

195. R. Niebuhr, *Faith and History,* p. 100.

196. Ibid., p. 161.

197. R. Niebuhr, *Irony of American History,* p. 174.

198. R. Niebuhr, *Faith and History,* p. 232.

199. Berger, *Social Reality,* p. 79.

200. Hannah Arendt, in "Religion and the Intellectuals," *Partisan Review,* No. 2 (1950), p. 115. Western Europeans do not mainly believe in a life after death; but survey after survey shows that Americans do, however confusedly. See "67% said to believe in afterlife", *Baltimore Sun,* 18 May 1982; précis of George Gallup, Jr. and William Proctor, *Adventures in Immortality* (New York, 1982).

201. Stow Persons, "Religion and Modernity, 1865-1914," in Smith and Jamison, eds., *The Shaping of American Religion,* p. 398.

6

Disenchantment

Max Weber's now classic coinage "disenchantment" *(Entzauber-ung)* has stressful mood-connections with *fin de siècle* and the holo-caust of World War I. It was exploited in a public lecture where Weber counseled his audience stoically that they must not seek emo-tional adventure in science. There are also obvious affinities with the various portraits of alienation of man from nature proposed by Rous-seau, Schiller, Hegel, Marx, and their successors, with a particular link to Novalis, who had written in *Christenheit oder Europa* (1799) with regard to the Enlightenment: "In Germany . . . attempts were made to give the old religion a more modern, rational, and universal sense by carefully divesting it of everything wonderful and myste-rious." [1] Novalis had added: "No historically minded person can doubt that the age of resurrection has arrived. . . . In Germany . . . the traces of a new world can be pointed to with complete cer-tainty." [2] But for Weber disenchantment is not reversible. It ex-presses more than a vanishing of the religious or supernatural justification of human purposes and existence; more than the sur-render of public spirit and leaderly energy to bureaucratic routine: "It means that, in principle, there are no mysterious incalculable forces that come into play, but rather that one can, in principle, master all things by calculation." [3] It is the philosophy of Hobbes finally en-shrined in the spaces of society, and perhaps *in foro interno* besides: "the world's transformation into a causal mechanism." [4] This ten-dency is not unrelieved by pathos and resistance, for, according to Weber, the more the external world is rationalized, the more some men will attempt to escape from that world into mystical and salva-tionary solutions. [5] Science has the unavoidable capacity to stimulate sects. We would be hard-pressed to call this procedure "dialectical" (for it is increasingly a tension of mechanical and irrational extremes without mediation or higher resolution, also describable as a tension between matter-of-factness and disillusion). It was vivid in Weber's intellectual ambiance. As his great predecessor Dilthey had expressed it:

> Fill yourself completely with this realism, this worldliness of interest, this dominance of science over life! They represent the spirit of the last [eighteenth] century and, however the future may be, it will retain these basic features. This earth must become the stage for free action ruled by thought and no repression will hinder it.

> But when, today, we ask what is the final goal of action for the individual or for mankind, the deep contradiction which pervades our time emerges. We face the enigma of the origin of things, the value of our existence, the ultimate value of our actions no wiser than a Greek in the Ionian or Italian colonies or an Arab at the time of Averroës.[6]

The struggle between "realism" and "meaning" was doomed, in Weber's view, to "succumb in the end to the world dominion of unbrotherliness," mastered by "the technical and social conditions of rational culture."[7] Throughout Weber's complicated and sometimes ugly locutions a pervasive ostinato could always be heard, a heavy tread of the impersonal upon the vanquished corpse of the personal. There was also tragic irony: prophetic Calvinism begets rationalistic progeny; religious election establishes a doom in which the new elect "commit" themselves to a calling in which all passion is dangerous and, in the case of science, to a charisma routinized by "methodology"; modern life must memorialize the capitalist as its last hero. For him disenchantment was not only a collective state of mind or an institutional fatality; it was also a history of Western man's spiritual closure. That history was long, laborious, and inexorable, a process cadenced by an intellectualism that "has continued to exist in Occidental culture for millennia."[8] By the mid-nineteenth century (despite Romanticism's abortive attempts at reenchantment), it had driven daggers to the heart of the religious impulse, rebuffed only, so to speak, in literature like Tolstoy's. It had canceled out in advance Tillich's "matters of ultimate concern": "Since death is meaningless, civilized life as such is meaningless."[9]

We have some trouble in recognizing an earlier America in these forebodings, for if we accept Weber's treatment at face value (the ideal-type method has errancies of hyperbole), this means that disenchantment for Americans has been inseparable not only from the gaudy advertisements of providential progress discussed in the last chapter but also from secularist tendencies that shaped the federal republic and from characteristics imputed by Tocqueville to democratic society at large. Yet, naively or shrewdly, most Americans—despite conspicuous intellectual and artistic alienations—seem to have remained "enchanted" with the results of their "experiment in the wilderness" up to the present century and, although in decreasing numbers, well beyond. They discerned transcendental, conceivably magical, properties in prosperity and the conquest of nature. Both religion and politics were charged with the symbols of an optimistic, even redemptive, sense of nationhood guided by a wise providence in which God was a hearty collaborator. That providence, it seemed, could accommodate Weberian calculation and still remain free, open, and enchanted. Indeed, rationalization had become revelation itself: part of the continuing aura of romance, part of the field of faith. America had no need of Europe's fabricated "positivistic" religions. Was there not abundant evidence that Jehovah was doing the job?

This seems more substantial than mere "false consciousness." Whereas in Europe (especially Weber's Central Europe) the enchantment collapsed with Bismarck and Königgrätz, the rise of naturalism and positivism, and the submission of a class society to a more common, urban, and utilitarian struggle for power and privilege, these tensions were muted in America. America had scarcely known ascriptive privileged orders; her elites were secure as well as mobile; and for a long while the burden was on constructing, not reutilizing, cities. Moreover, America—a creation or "fragment" of the world of Bacon, Hobbes, and Locke—was also a virgin continent whose remaining *vacua loca* still evoked the magical.[10] Even in the present days of disenchantment, if one flies transcontinentally, especially in winter, one looks down over great forests (more abundant in the Northeast than a century ago) and, in mid-nation, wide tracts of unrelieved land that the snow's delicate traceries transform into spidery wash drawings of road, rail, town, and farm, capturing a vision that one might still dare to identify with a mixed magic of human and natural design. No less pleasing in their way are the cramped patches of village, pasture, and windbreak encountered in Flanders and Holland, but these are, without ambiguity, *entzäubert,* steeped in the logic of mundane fabrication and use.

Thus, all at once, America was a geographical reservoir of the mystery that inspires hope and faith, a mental image begotten in part by salvationary and redemptive impulses, and yet, not least, a crucible for the unalloyed casting of the profane behavior of self-interest. There are several reasons that Weberian disenchantment made a tardy appearance. First, for much of American history the geographical and spiritualistic tendencies outpropagandized rational-technical behavior: Emersonianism warded off Taylorism. Second, the politico-religious settlement allowed for a relatively free flow of values—not always the highest—between the political, societal, and private spheres of life (fructified, perhaps later petrified, by "denominationalism"). Or, as Thomas Luckmann has written: "Comparing the European and American findings on the social location of church religion and owing for the differences in character of church religion in European and American society, we are led to the conclusion that traditional church religion was pushed to the periphery of 'modern life' in Europe while it became more 'modern' in America by undergoing a process of internal secularization." [11] Third, the insulation from international strain and the tragedy of war damage and defeat (other than internal) sustained belief in the constancy of providence. Finally, the resolute alienation of intellectual values from the mainstream of the American cultural experience deferred the ideology, if not the practice, of instrumental rationalism as well as the irrational intellectual currents that, *a contrario,* promote it.[12] While America's enchantment was in many ways neither enchanting nor profound, a fact rarely missed by foreign observers (e.g., Harold Laski or André Siegfried),[13] this very inhibition to flights of the intellect helped to make disenchantment a highly un-American enterprise, appropriate to solitude or exile. Pragmatism, technicism, and plain mediocrity played some part in sedating the American soul from the pains of any unmysterious world, although they would later be poor guardians against its encroachment.

The specific causes of the retardation are perhaps less important than the nature of the disenchantment that has, by stages, visited our shores.

Disenchantment is porous: its social connectedness or social location is extremely hard to pin down because of its unmediated play of oppositions. It owes as much to success as to nemesis; it relates to trend-setting middle classes as well as to the despairing poor; and it has deviantly branching historical roots in America. Some modern writers feel that it receives a part of its dynamics from the ascendancy of a predominantly secularizing force—sometimes called the "knowledge class"—the values it imposes, and the antagonisms it elicits in the wider society. It seems also to be a result of a more generalized conflict between imperatives of production and patterns of distribution and consumption that we are now experiencing.

While it would be imprudent to neglect the elements of degree and detail that make our situation singular, it seems beyond dispute that all of Western civilization is affected by similar tensions and a com-

mon malaise. The features by which disenchantment can be objectively analyzed are transnational. So, to a considerable degree, is the
collective sensing of disenchantment by articulate persons. Perhaps,
as a late bloomer, the United States might be expected to resist better. But it could also be argued that a relative complacency makes
American jeopardy greater than that of nations trained in adversity.
Probably the lag is both sorts: our "backwardness" might give us a
kind of psychological and institutional resilience. This was, for example, the sort of argument that Paul Tillich used in 1938 to explain how
Calvinist religion still buffered (and humanized) American capitalism
against the danger of revolution.[14] Such resilience may be Tocquevillian; but not the imputation of backwardness. Is America a "new"
nation or a "young" nation? Here we recover Hegel's observation
that "North America will be comparable with Europe only after the
immeasurable space which that country presents to its inhabitants
shall have been occupied, and the members of the political body shall
have begun to be pressed back on each other."[15] This also seems a
precondition for Weberian disenchantment. It is an aspect in which
the United States now rejoins Western Europe, a measure of their
common politico-religious fate as well as an attestation of Reinhold
Niebuhr's ironic realism.

I have already discussed parallels and differences between politics
and religion. Neither as belief systems nor as embodied institutions
are they analytically or functionally interchangeable. They depend on
different mechanisms of conviction and different communities of purpose. They have also disputed prerogatives of both secular power and
moral control, while for the most part preserving their distinctiveness.
Yet they have likenesses as belief systems, as institutions, as competitors, and as organizing forces susceptible to vitality or decline.[16] I
believe that they are best seen as distinct *and* comparable, as "control systems" pursuing separate but collaborative ends. I attempted to
show earlier that we required the distinction of *sacred* and *profane* in
order to grasp the functions of religion and politics as ultimate control
systems.[17] This distinction lacks some conceptual clarity today—
after a barrage of versions of "the withering away of the state" and a
displacement of the central idea of religion from that of transhistorical
judgment to that of existential life-adjustment, both of these being, as
we shall see, symptoms of disenchantment. The character of the distinction I intend can, I think, be explored by reference to two very
different theorists.

For John Locke the controls of sacred and profane were meticu-
lously distinct and balanced. In the first instance, Locke notes:

"every man has an immortal soul, capable of eternal happiness or misery; whose happiness [depends] upon his believing and doing those things in this life, which are necessary to the obtaining of God's favor, and are prescribed by God to that end. . . ." "There is nothing in this world," he continues, "that is of any consideration in comparison with eternity." In parallel, there is the profane sphere: "Besides their souls, which are immortal, men also have their temporal lives here upon the earth; the state whereof being frail and fleeting, and the duration uncertain; they have need of several outward conveniencies to the support thereof." The preservation of these "conveniencies" and of a secure liberty "obliges men to enter into society with one another; that by mutual assistance and joint force, they may secure unto each other their proprieties, in the things that contribute to the comforts and happiness of this life." The profane system has no license to control the sacred, its proper business being only "to provide . . . for the safety and security of the commonwealth, and of every particular man's goods and persons." [18] Locke's method of specifying the sacred and the profane was appropriate to his mission of obtaining toleration for all Protestants. [19] He was not so disturbed by the prospect of religious sectarian warfare as by the inefficacy and immorality of mandated religious beliefs. In Tocqueville's description of the voluntary, yet common, religious morality achieved in America, Locke's fundamental analysis would seem to be vindicated. But Locke did not conjure with the basic question of the waning of faith, in public or in private. And what has happened in the meantime is, of course, a mutation in our common interpretations of religion and politics. Our *commitments* are not the same, as they are offered or withheld respectively by *believers* and *citizens*.

Another way of examining the relationship between the two control systems concedes the separation of the things of God and of Caesar (in effect disestablishment carries us back to the Pauline situation of Christianity), but it would also use the morally compelling ordinances of the one to temper the physically coercive immediacy of the other, and the legitimate coercive restraints of the second as an armature for the practice of a free and conscientious spirituality in the first. This is essentially the Augustinian solution. In this sense, the profane may be said to allow the sacred a buffering span of human time to shape itself and the sacred may be said to bestow moral legitimacy and a kind of dignity on the profane. Karl Barth has expressed this reciprocity particularly well: "political systems create and preserve a space for . . . the fulfillment of the purpose of world history, a space for faith, repentance, and knowledge," while members of the religious (Christian) community within the state "bring [the Kingdom of God] to man's attention . . . reminding the state of those things of which it is unlikely to remind itself." [20] Barth's version is noteworthy, not because his ideas are prevalent in America today, but because, better than Tocqueville, he expresses the religious-public continuum as it was more or less understood by the New England Puritans, who found a positive value in community-oriented action since it spiritualized the span of human time in which the Kingdom of God might arrive. Obviously, though, in fair weather or foul, the Augustinian theory has had little appeal for liberal society. In such a quandary one might want to ponder Montesquieu's blunt alternative: "the less religion disciplines, the more the civil laws ought to."

Both religion and politics have been trapped in the disenchantment process: religion has not been saved by becoming private and close to us; politics was not so much disenchanted by its separation from religion (which was proper) but by its own crisis of faith that bears comparison with the religious. Here I would like to reintroduce the notion of "lag" or "gap" that has characterized the decline of these systems in their faith-content and in their matching of conviction to forms of order. It seems that this gap has closed to a degree that one would not have thought possible at the beginning of this century, when the anguishes of religion (challenged by Darwinian science or profane spiritualism) seemed in no way to implicate the destiny of the political sphere. Reason, it was held by some, would stabilize politics and dispel religion, the latter being replaced by some vague doctrine of social benevolence. Or, as others proclaimed, *Grosspolitik* would provide enchantment for all.

One theory of the "closing of the gap" can be extracted from Marx's early writings, especially the *Critique of Hegel's Philosophy of Right* and the essay *On the Jewish Question*. In a first motion, a diremption of theology by anthropology (as announced by Feuerbach) is accompanied by the banishment of religion to "civil society" (i.e., the realm of the relationships of private individuals). "The criticism of religion ends with the doctrine that *man is the supreme being for man*. It ends, therefore, with the *categorical imperative to overthrow all conditions* in which man is an abased, enslaved, abandoned, contemptible being." [21] Religion will be overcome totally through the reintegration of the individual to a nonalienating social and public existence. But, as a preliminary, "the criticism of heaven is transformed into the criticism of the earth." [22] Marx now asserts that previous theories of politics—and especially Hegel's—were theological in character, essentially like religion: "The political constitution was until now the religious sphere, the religion of a popular life, the heaven of its universality in opposition to the earthly existence of its actuality. . . . Political life in the modern sense is the scholasticism of a popular life.''[23] Finally, then, even the agnostic bourgeois-democratic regime, after privatizing religion and making it coequal with commercial society, would be transformed, via the proletarian revolution into a nonstate or true communist community.

Marx clearly discerned some of the parallelisms between religion and politics, and he was perceptive enough about his own cultural climate and the one to follow to foresee that what was happening in the religious sphere would have its counterpart in politics pursuant to a series of mediations. He saw the Hegelian ''rational state'' as the highest political expression of a concrete theology; in America, informed by Tocqueville's book, he perceived the first phase of its dismemberment.[24] He believed that his own philosophy at the service of the proletariat would provide a ''catharsis'' (in the Gramscian sense)[25] by which the bourgeois republic would be nullified. The Marxist program corresponds (or has corresponded in ''vulgar'' practice) to a good many of Weber's ''disenchantment'' agenda, although in other respects it violates those agenda—especially in the early writings—with its powerful criteria of ''meaningfulness,'' its project of collective human *metanoia*, and its eschatological drive.[26] Marx erred, however, in prophesying an *Aufhebung* of both religion and politics. Though privatized, the former was scarcely eradicated; the latter waxed, but on an unhealthful diet. His critique of the two pathologies seems, paradoxically, to have stimulated both messianic and political energies, now all but moribund in the West, though virulent in the ''Third World.'' As I have suggested, the career of Marxism itself can probably be studied by means of the ''Protestant paradigm.'' This is grimly appropriate; for Marx and Engels, in some moods, saw themselves as completing the work of Luther by destroying ''the priest within.''[27] We may take it from as qualified an analyst as Kolakowski that Marxism's current result is not simply or chiefly due to some gross perversion of its original materials.[28] Marx gives us valuable clues about the relationship of politics and religion, but not necessarily in support of his own vision.

My scheme may be challenged on empirical grounds. I leave this to the critic. The simpler task is to attack it on formal grounds. Here, two objections come to mind. Either politics and religion may be viewed as incomparable concepts or they may be sociologically assigned to impermeable structures with different patterns of performance. In the first instance, for example, if we were to be guided by the

Hegelian system, we might find it illicit to correlate politics and religion. With Hegel politics clearly finds its place within the range of collective human activity called "objective spirit," while religion manifests an ineffable and higher order called "absolute spirit." Although Hegel assigns a function to each that could be accommodated by Barth's formulation, he pointedly separates the institutional and spiritual aspects of religion, while leaving politics integral and reconciled in that realm of freedom that is the state. Positive religion is, moreover, subordinated to politics in the world of historical event and religion as "ultimate concern" is tributary to philosophy in a world that, though compelled to appear in time, is beyond time.[29] Religion seems to be a second-class transience and a second-class permanence. However, our focus on the notion of sacred and profane control systems helps to bridge the gap between spirit and its embodiment, and to restore religion and politics to a correlation.

We need not take a position here on the implications of the philosophical *Aufhebung* of religion in Hegel.[30] However, there is a gap in Hegel's practical argument itself. Philosophy is not for the mass of men: most people, according to Hegel, receive their intimations of higher truth through the representations (*Vorstellungen*) and sentiment (*Gefühl*) of religion. This shifts the burden of the problem (for all but the few) to the critical question of adequate symbolization. Since there is a recurrent insistence in much late-twentieth-century writing (some of it by American theologians) that the traditional symbols of Christianity are unable to command conviction (Hegel had said of Christian art that "we no longer bow our knee") or that "liberal" religion has consummated the abstraction of ethical faith from its religious graphics, it is quite plausible that the conviction of the "many" has been greatly disturbed by a garbled symbolic communication of *sophia*. We can scarcely venture to analyze this problem here. There is a pathos of symbolization in the age of disenchantment that encompasses such phenomena as private and immanent experiences (à la William James), "positivistic" reconstructions (like Comte's or perhaps Teilhard's), syncretistic or scientific cultism, the discovery of worshipful meaning in the bosom of the profane (à la Harvey Cox, and surely with premonitions in the writings of Simone Weil), or "civil religion." Moreover, modern philosophy has not gotten very far with superseding religion (surely not on the scale achieved in Hellenistic and Roman culture). Either it has launched *pointiliste* adventures in the philosophies of language and mind or it has solemnly celebrated the advent of a totally profane cosmos, often borrowing archaic religious symbolism and vocabulary.

The "majesty" of Hegelian politics—and its tension with religion—[31] has also been debased into reproducing the pathology of religion. Whereas it had previously been believed that the growth of
democracy in an ever-widening social perimeter (Dewey's "Great
Community") was axiomatically "public" and susceptible to absorbing much of the energy of the "religious," it has become common
today to regard politics, too, as being "privatized," reduced toward
indifference or to a bureaucratic stimulus lethal to public energy. But
long before this had seemed the case, Dilthey made the major methodological move by conflating the "objective" and "absolute" spirits
of Hegel into his category of *Geisteswissenschaften*.[32] This represented a step toward disenchantment, but it also created proper cor-
respondences in the wake of an idealism that had failed to explain the
world. By this means Hegelianism leads to a politics-religion parallel-
ism that is neither that of Locke nor of St. Augustine, but that equally
confirms our view.

Another kind of interpretation, also with German roots, trades on a
stipulated dichotomy of *society* and *culture*. It can probably be traced
back to the conflicting views of Herder and Kant and to concepts
swirling in German Romanticism. Society, in this view, is dynamic,
linear, and extensive, while culture is nurturant, spatially bounded,
and inclusive. From the earlier sources, updated by Tönnies, or so it
seems to me, the distinction made its way into American social
thought through the categories of Talcott Parsons.[33] One wonders
whether this line can be drawn either within or between politics and
religion. The useful concept of "political culture" is well known.
Similarly, the social character of religion is one of the staples of anthropology. Even if we arbitrarily assigned religion to "culture" and
politics to "society," is it really possible to distinguish culture from
society?

Yet this is done, for example, by Daniel Bell in a recent essay on
"the return of the sacred."[34] In Bell's view, society is subject to the
process of "secularization," which is expressed through "differentiation" of authority and through "rationalization." The process is represented as a linear and irreversible trend. Society apparently
englobes the sphere we have been treating as "politics," without
much autonomy to the latter—although Bell had given it special privilege in his earlier writing.[35] Culture, on the other hand, which not
only includes religion but is defined as the sacred, has been subject to
"disenchantment" or "profanation."[36] However, as opposed to society, "culture . . . is always a *ricorso*."[37] This means, *a fortiori*, that
although the sacred may be profaned, it can never disappear. "Re-

ligion is not an ideology, or a regulative or integrative feature of society—though in its institutional forms it has, at different times, functioned in this way. It is a constitutive aspect of human experience because it is a response to the existential predicaments which are the *ricorsi* of human culture."[38] Bell's predication of "new religions" need not concern us here, except that he significantly insists on their "moralizing," "redemptive," and "mythic" features—all things seemingly trivialized in modern mainstream religion.

The separation of religion from "society" seems to obey a counterintuitive classification and to follow from the notion held by William James and others that religion flourishes only in the recesses of privacy. This suggests not only that churches and sects are readily disposable containers of an imperishable sacred but that the condition of their appearance and vanishing (so important to Hegel or Weber) is unproblematic. Moreover, culture—whether understood by *littérateurs* or anthropologists—is not merely an "existential" response; it is a collective emanation where the sacred can repose just as easily as in the individual ego. Finally, Bell's rather odd definition of the sacred is susceptible to encouraging the same modern aestheticism that he denounces as a "profanation."[39] The conviction of inevitable *ricorsi* may be consoling to religiously inclined persons; but the *ricorsi* are no more certain than is the possibility of an entirely secular culture allowed for by Bryan Wilson, even though we have never experienced one.[40]

It does not seem that politics is distinguishable from religion in this way. We may rationalize politics while emotionalizing religion, but it is still likely that the "preservative control system in the realm of the profane" is based on a range of values that cannot be removed from "culture" and peremptorily assigned to "society," in the sense that these ideas are displayed in opposition. Politics is an art and a sequence of acts of creativity or imitation that, like science, is guided by rules embodied in a community of practice. Politics is linked to science not as a body of theories but as a practice. Religion is not so very different—its theories (theology) are esoteric to science; its practice, as sect or church, is comparable.

The age in which science could assail either religion or politics with irresistible credentials is ending. This does not staunch disenchantment because the faculties of reason appropriate to describing the relations of the three cannot reach a stage of disinterestedness or productive collaboration in the realm of practice. If religion shrinks or gives way to profane substitutes, this does not seem to be exactly a prolongation of the travails religion faced in the nineteenth century, when it was confronted by the absolute claims of a positivistic natural science. Many residues of this line of thought still exist, to be sure: we continue to read articles affirming that the "big bang" theory of cosmic creation supports the Scriptures. But the reason is rather to be sought in the problematic symbolic adequacy of man to his cosmos. The new problem lies not primarily in the "historicization" of scientific truth as expressed in the works of Kuhn, Lakatos, and Feyerabend (for these recondite interpretations do not reach the ordinary man) but rather in the conceptual exoticism of contemporary "normal science" and its inability to convey a cosmos in which most people recognize themselves. Is it easier to believe in four hundred elementary particles (many of them merely theorized) than in the Holy Trinity? As A. J. Ayer has written: "The scientific world-picture which was current in the nineteenth century was reasonably simple and coherent. . . . But by now the situation of science itself has changed. . . . Its basic concepts are further removed from those of common sense; they make no immediate appeal to the layman's imagination. Thus, to the uninitiated, its account of the world, though more precise, is hardly less fantastic than the religious account."[41] Biogenetics has intervened since Ayer wrote this. As a consequence of that new discovery and of the perpetual threat of nuclear weapons, science has acquired a less benign visage in the average person's mind: it is seen as a threatening as well as an ameliorating force—a dualistic faith. Consequently, the decline of religious institutions and convictions must be attributed to processes in which science is involved but no longer decisive.

Politics has not been affected by science in the same way. For a long time—at least since Condorcet—there has been the optimistic assumption that they could be partners. This fraternization was encouraged by the fact that politics had often battled religion and that politics, like science, was of this world and not the next. In the case of politics, a profane metaphysics colonized a profane practice; in the case of religion, it confronted a sacred cosmos. However, in its struggle to free itself from theological principles, politics had theorized its own transcendence—natural law—where it grounded its unifying concepts of justice, social peace, liberty, legitimacy, and the like. Science had to conquer natural law with new procedures and values before it could reduce politics to a version of itself. Even with this transformation partly achieved, politics—prudential and "preservative" at its core—could only suffer from the corrosive effects of scientific criticism, for, as Habermas writes, "a scientistic self-affirmation of the sciences can promote a positivistic common consciousness that sustains the public realm. But scientism also sets standards by which it can itself be criticized and convicted of residual dogmatism.''[42] A free method of experimental criticism (let us grant for the sake of argument that it was appropriate to political objects) could not but, on the one hand, encourage uncritical self-certainty in politics where political practices seemed to achieve verification or, on the other, wreak havoc where it counseled hasty revisions in authoritative institutions that were not subject to the same kind of correction that one might bring to a body of research. Neither the scientific confrontation of religion nor the scientific colonization of politics was a blessing; in each case it became impossible to produce "theory" in an effective way. Theology withered, and political theory fell into history while history itself was being altered as a practice by the scientific impetus. "Grand sociology" and psychoanalysis helped to cover the traces.

Thus science played its role in stimulating disenchantment. That role may be less as time proceeds. The "loss of religion" has been felt since the seventeenth century; a landmark is Tennyson's touching poem *In Memoriam*. No one has yet written a poem of stature about the loss of politics, but it is not excluded: an anti-Virgil. We should at this point, however, make a critical distinction about disenchantment. We should acknowledge a difference between what I will call "formal" and "substantial" disenchantment. Generally speaking, the formal mechanisms of modern life—institutions, collective mental processes, sources of authority, etc.—have become "disenchanted," as described. However, formal disenchantment does not immediately affect the person and the wellsprings of his character and conduct. Substantially, ordinary people share many of the "enchanted" impulses of their ancestors. As Novalis put it, with immoderate irony, "It is a pity that nature remained so wonderful and incomprehensible, so poetical and infinite, defying all attempts to modernize it."[43] People do harbor poetic, aesthetic, playful, and superstitious impulses. But because they are increasingly constrained to function within instrumental and depersonalized surroundings, they inevitably internalize their routines, and carry these to their private relations. As Zbigniew Brzezinski has written: ". . . social life tends to be so atomized . . . that group intimacy cannot be recreated through the artificial stimulation of externally convivial group behavior."[44] Even if spontaneity holds out in the private sphere, it can less easily be translated into or communicated in a public language.

In the remainder of this chapter I shall illustrate how, albeit without Procrustean uniformity, disenchantment has affected both politics and religion in contemporary life. Consonant with earlier remarks, my references will pertain to Western Christendom and Western democracy, with conditions specific to the United States brought forward where they require emphasis. The categories I will treat are: privatization, secularization, immanentism, bureaucratization, indifference, dissociation, and nostalgia. A certain cross-referencing will be unavoidable.

Privatization means essentially the withdrawal of an understanding or a practice from the public space of collective inspection and choice to the microcosm of individual choice, passing perhaps by way of the restricted group of friends and kin with whom one has "private relations."[45] Choices become valued precisely because they are generated from personal ("authentic") conviction rather than because they affirm the expectations of authority or tradition. Often the movement of choice in this direction has been interpreted as an expansion of autonomy; today it is increasingly felt by some that convictions driven inward are, by that token, unfree. Here, either what was once conceived and organized as public acquires the rhetoric and justifications of the inner life, or, more characteristically, a phantom public is fabricated from an aggregate of diffuse private wills and opinions—as in survey research. Privatization should be distinguished from the more familiar notions of individualism and subjectivism: from the former, because it appears and is felt as a mass phenomenon ("the lonely crowd") and is not "rugged" in the slightest; from the latter because it is not a philosophical position from which the world is to be reconstituted but rather a recoil from that understanding. Since I do not mean to imply that identical privatistic tendencies are reproduced indiscriminately in the areas of religion and politics, my method will be to show the forms they take in each, with the suggestion that the appearances are not coincidental.

In religion, we might begin with the phenomenon of shopping around or "consumerism." In Berger's words: "Since the socially significant 'relevance' of religion is primarily in the private sphere, consumer preference reflects the 'needs' of this sphere. This means that religion can more easily be marketed if it can be shown to be 'relevant' to private life than if it is advertised as entailing specific applications to the large public institutions."[46] Of course Berger does not mean here *radically* private in the sense of Pascal's wager; he means open to competitive choice for private reasons. The quest need not simply be for a cozy, undemanding faith. It may imply a serious pursuit of "situated" meaning that leads, as Harvey Cox notes approvingly, to a relativized condition where religion is "accepted as the peculiar prerogative and point of view of a particular person or group."[47] Thomas Luckmann connects privatism with the fragmentation of sacred coherence: "The 'autonomous' consumer selects . . . certain religious themes from the available assortment and builds them into a somewhat precarious private system of 'ultimate' significance. Individual religiosity is thus no longer a replica or approximation of an 'official' model."[48] This might seem to be the happy outcome that John Dewey was contemplating when he wrote: "The opposition between religious values as I conceive them and religion is not to be bridged. Just because the release of these values is so important, their identification with the creeds and cults of religion must be dissolved."[49] But, contrary to what Dewey thought, the weakening of the meaning and validity of corporate worship appears to have been accompanied by a loss of corporate identity in general.[50] The theologian Frederick Sontag has commented: "A church must show its people that God is to be found and experienced and obeyed best through the procedures and doctrines which it keeps alive rather than by individualistic search." "But," he adds glumly, "the revolt of millions has placed this claim in doubt too."[51] Although privatization, understood as a release from denominational and theological constraints, may appear to represent "a historically unprecedented opportunity for the autonomy of personal life for 'everybody,'"[52] it partakes of narcissism and passively accepts encroachments of "the technical and social conditions of rational culture."[53]

It is also present in the devaluation of the religious element of public legitimation. That decline is, to be sure, often regarded as liberating, and it is swaddled in the language of rights—the secular or profane rights of a disestablished polity. But the absence of the sacralization of the public power by the faith of groups and communities is as much a warrant of pessimism as of freedom. The irony is that we have often and increasingly sensed freedom as an indiscriminate escape from useful controls (castigated as "the system") and have thereby contrived an escape from freedom itself. To a certain degree, *lares* and *penates* still people our world with local magic, but the Olympian Jehovah fails increasingly to serve the function of concord. Although it has been often enough said that "the American state is . . . emphatically *not* separated from religion in general,"[54] it seems unlikely—except at high moments—that "a vague and somewhat sentimental religious syncretism," further described as "a sort of state Shinto,"[55] whose panpluralist capacities have surely waned in the twenty years since the phrases were composed, disputes privatism or fulfils a Tocquevillian design. We must notice, too, that secularism itself is largely privatized in America.

The notion of legitimation furnishes a key bridge to the privatization of politics.[56] That phenomenon should be examined both from the base and from the pinnacle. In the first instance, in the words of Sheldon Wolin, it consists in "reducing citizenship to a cheap commodity."[57] Indeed, it is unremarkable that we speak naturally of "the private citizen." Any public commodity that is both universalized and trivialized—and to which no particular merit is attached—might be expected to suffer this fate. "Citizenship," T. H. Marshall wrote, "is a status bestowed on those who are full members of a community. All who possess this status are equal with respect to rights and duties with which the status is endowed. . . . The urge forward along the path thus plotted is an urge towards a fuller measure of equality, an enrichment of the stuff of which the status is made and an increase in the number of those on whom the status is bestowed."[58] However, the multiplication of "social rights" does not appear to have enriched the status of citizen in the United States with its "great extension of the area of common culture and common experience."[59] Nor perhaps could it have been expected to do so in a situation where "social integration [has] spread from the sphere of sentiment and patriotism into that of material enjoyment."[60] Two centuries ago, Adam Ferguson wrote of peoples that "even when they have for a while acted on maxims tending to raise, to invigorate, and to preserve the national character . . . have, sooner or later, been diverted from their object, and fallen prey to misfortune, or to the neglects which prosperity itself had encouraged."[61] Benjamin Constant brilliantly argued in his lecture "De la liberté des anciens comparée à celle des modernes" (1819) that "modern liberty" was not, in the first instance, public or participatory, but an instrument for the protection of the private enjoyment of goods from the invasion of others, including the state.[62] The new possessors of "social rights" are assuredly not guilty in any direct sense of the debasement of citizenship, for the demoralization is structural and citizenship is reinterpreted as clientage. But clients do not make good patriots. Some writers, like Habermas, maintain that the stability of the modern welfare state depends on "civic privatism."[63] In any case, citizenship itself is not legitimated.

The state has suffered a corresponding fate. No longer is one apt to say, with Matthew Arnold, that "a State in which law is authoritative and sovereign, a firm and settled course of the public order, is requisite if man is to bring to maturity anything precious and lasting now, or to found anything precious and lasting for the future."[64] A down-to-earth skepticism is beautifully captured in some dialogue from Remarque's *All Quiet on the Western Front:*

"Ach, man! he means the people as a whole, the State—" exclaims Müller.

"State, state"—Tjaden snaps his fingers contemptuously, "Gendarmes, police, taxes, that's your state; if that's what you are talking about, no thank you."

"That's right," says Kat, "you've said something for once, Tjaden. State and home-country, there's a big difference."

"But they go together," insists Kropp, "without the State there wouldn't be any home-country."[65]

Remarque's cheeky irreverence toward the Wilhelmine colossus turns out, in a sense, to sustain Arnold's pompous rhetoric. To be a citizen and enjoy a home-country one must have a state. But the state, too, has become privatized, not only in the horizons of the citizen but also in the scrutiny of reigning political doctrine.[66] Even as the state has become bloated with new functions and has forged or forced new contacts with the citizen, it has become less focal as a center of loyalty. It has been gelded by the normative supremacy of civil society, with its segmented interests and passions. As a consequence, Wolin writes, "the political has been transferred to another plane, to one that formerly was designated 'private' but which now is believed to have overshadowed the old political system."[67] He adds appositely, in view of Weber's analysis: "This is a world that Hobbes might have enjoyed: one created by human wit, where rational action has become a matter of routine, and magic has been banished."[68] One may wonder whether human wit does not veil a certain amount of chaos. But the Leviathan is indeed, it seems, a "mortal God."

Such trends, by inducing privatization, also undermine legitimacy and loyalty. In America, far more resoundingly than in Europe (for historical reasons), conceptions of public life and public preference arise that are increasingly unmediated by parties or other standard agents of the political structure, the important exception being the constitutional courts, which, it should be remembered, hear chiefly individual pleas. Concomitantly—and this is no doubt partly a consequence of living in the age of Freud, a Freud overdetermined by the primacy of the private—people have cultivated a psychologistic manner of assessing leadership, representation, functional hierarchy, and political authority in general, a "political Donatism" that ignores the public rite or office for the private image of the *pontifex*. This is expedited by the otiose way in which information is distributed and digested. And, in the demise or neglect of other criteria, a "political Protestantism" infects citizens, a pretension to bestow legitimacy privately *via* the individual conscience. As Robert Coles writes: "When the self becomes our transcendence, politics becomes, along with everything else, a matter of impulse, whim, fancy, exuberant indulgence, bored indifference, outright angry rejection." [69] That self, that conscience, is at the antipodes of Rousseau's ideal of the reason of each one deliberating in the silence of the passions within a public space.[70] Finally, in a complex society where economic issues command most attention but seem almost as mysterious to the experts as to the laymen, "pressures of legitimation can be mitigated only through structures of a depoliticized public realm. A structurally secured civic privatism becomes necessary for continued existence because there are no functional equivalents for it" (this means roughly that norms affecting stability and duration must be externally generated.)[71] If privatism has pushed religion out of the public sphere, it is currently turning politics into either an I-Thou relationship or a sphere of indifference.

Secularization is not just a progress of worldliness but an application of worldly techniques to establish the valuation and directedness of all problematic change. It is a rationalization of all value-oriented activity as an unmysterious obedience to the scientific world view. This process has, of course, been going on for a very long time. In a first phase, beginning in the seventeenth century, the knowledge of revelation was made inferior to the mathematical explanation of the physical world. Though flattering to the amour-propre of the human intellect, this value shift toward cognitive rigor also had the result of limiting claims of human understanding to the changing and the measurable, and hence (in older language) to the perishable. In a second phase, mechanistic arguments commenced to reduce men and society to their presumably calculable and predictable traits. Although at first glance it would seem—to use familiar terms—that man was coping with a challenging and "open" universe such as he had never known before, methodological and practical restraints on the openness closed it to previous forms of action and imagination. Its mysteries were abstract; its daily fare was all too human. There were, of course, Promethean resistances to these trends, and there were also cases in which the trends themselves were proclaimed in Promethean form. Above all, modern man attempted to deny death by ignoring it or sublimating it.[72] As James Agee wrote a generation ago regarding what has since proved to be a rather faddish turn of intellectuals to religion: "The 'modern mind' denies [evil's] existence. There must be sufficient indication to the contrary in any person's experience, outward and secret, to account alone for many conversions."[73] Denying evil was the accompaniment to denying death.

In America, disenchantment has been very much conditioned by the way in which secularization was received. In the eighteenth century one had a rather neat dialectic between millennial biblicism and the rational religion of the American Enlightenment that weighed so heavily on the republican founding. Although this first secularization was later engulfed in the political invasions of denominational ideology, it served as a brake on the latter until after the Civil War. Tocqueville interpreted this country at a time of relative harmony between the two dispositions and elevated that harmony to a democratic norm. Later, a more Promethean secularization affected both politics and religion, tainting both orthodoxy and liberalism. Harmony was increasingly tilted toward profane abuses of the sacred, until "evangelicals were convinced that theirs was a Christian civilization on the way to victory and perfection."[74] More recently, with the stirrings of genuine disenchantment, there has been, as countless observers have noted, "far more insistence . . . not upon faith in a future life, but upon religion as a help to success" and a religious "acquiescence in the habitual."[75] The other side of the coin was an existential and private form of brooding. Both have ultimately produced a predictable political reaction, either in the prophetic tones of Bellah's *The Broken Covenant* or in the slick transposition of the sacred to the sphere of politics proper in Cox's *Secular City:* "Theology today must be that reflection-in-action by which the church finds out what this politician-God is up to and moves in to work along with him. In the epoch of the secular city, politics replaces metaphysics as the language of theology."[76] Although Bellah's return to jeremiad is surely more in the American grain than Cox's sacred ward-politics, it will later be argued that his "civil religion" is part of the problem, not the pathway to a solution.

With regard to religion, it is sometimes held that "secularization is the tendency or process by which sectarian religious movements become 'worldly.'"[77] That is not false, but it is a very small part of the question. For us it is important to see how secularization acts on all religious feeling and agency. Essentially it does this by redefining the role of religion, by detheologizing it (ridding it of theory), by "differentiating" it, and by demystifying it.

The secularization process has featured two principal moments in which the traditional role of religion (transcendent judgment) was redefined. First, religion was turned into a useful, perhaps indispensable, sociological construct: a regulator in the profane sphere of society. Tocqueville, as we know, was vastly interested in how Protestantism conditioned liberty in the profane world, but he did not take this to be its exclusive value. Second, there was the development of a vision of religion as personal therapy for mundane purposes. In Berger's words: "Religion is highly beneficial, perhaps even essential, to the psychological integration of the individual . . . conducive to mental health."[78] For, as Coles writes of our society: "The self is the only or main form of (existential) reality."[79] For Clebsch, religion is some kind of amniotic fluid: "To train oneself to be sensitive to one's own personhood and personal relations with other human (or transhuman) selves is to fight off the gnawing sense of insignificance and aimlessness that complex social institutions seem to foster."[80] Secularization advances these incomplete renderings of religion. Although neither of the positions is false, religion is more than social utility because it is also an impending judgment from beyond society, and it is more than life-adjustment because it is also unceasing disquietude.

Secularization removes theology from religion on the grounds that it is a metaphysical trapping well discarded and that it is provocative of discord and intolerance. Whereas it was once believed that religious thought could construct a global synthesis of the sacred that reconciled particularities (somewhat in the same way that divine law was held to encompass natural law, but without infringement), this was now denied by the appeal to experience. Even "natural theologies" finally became suspect. Of course, experience itself could not create a coherent world view, and it was just as possible for differing theologies to coexist peaceably as it was for scientific truth-claims. But, as Vahanian has put it, "gradually, theological liberty, which at first meant freedom from dogmatic restraint or constraint, more and more imperturbably signified freedom from theology."[81]

In the mid-nineteenth century Philip Schaff was convinced that "America will no doubt produce . . . a classical theology of its own, that shall rise superior to the sectional and denominational schools, which so far have mostly prevailed amongst us, and be truly catholic in spirit and influence."[82] Though theology did not vanish and it did become less denominational (cf. the theology of Bushnell), Schaff's program was never fulfilled. The ecclesiologist Frank H. Foster was later to write that "theology must become *the explanation of Christian experience*."[83] That was still a demand for theory, but it could be interpreted in a Jamesian sense, where, as Berger has put it, "cosmology becomes psychology."[84] In more privatized times theology has been reduced to a spiritual exposition of the states of selfhood, with "revelation . . . now thought of, not in terms of propositions of doctrine . . . but in terms of a personal encounter with God which elicits an affirmative response of trust and commitment."[85] The last stage of this process (but endemic in the earliest impulses of Protestantism) is the emergence of a "layman's religion" that "does not consist of definite articles of faith such as might be embodied in a credo and expounded in a theology. Though it is not necessarily anticlerical or antichurch, it is antitheological."[86] Or else, as with earlier Cox, theology is translated into political metaphors. The tendency has been for religion to be deprived of its theory, the categories in which the sacred has been thought of as a prelude to collective belief and action.

Attempts to surmount traditional theologies with what has been called a "political theology" are not, of course, the invention of Harvey Cox. They have been more especially the project of contemporary German writers, particularly Catholics touched by Marxism as well as by some Protestants like Friedrich Gogarten. Gogarten's linguistic move is to regard "secularization" as a positive value—the working out of man's spiritual predicaments in *his* world—and to set it against "secularism," the false vanity of secular progress. In this view, "secularization" transcends and ought to abolish "secularism" (cf. "modernization" and "modernism" in nonreligious writing). However, Gogarten sharply divides the secularization of the world from the realm of faith, stressing the traditional Protestant contempt for salvation by works and inviting the criticism from more radical theologians that his scheme discloses bourgeois ideology.[87] This is not the strategy of the ostensibly neo-Marxist substitution of *orthopraxis* for *orthodoxy* in the work of Johann Baptist Metz (influenced by the *Hoffnungsprinzip* of Ernst Bloch and, I suspect, more distantly by the elder Fichte), which reduces theology to a kind of *on s'engage et puis on voit*.[88] What is important to note in Metz, Moltmann, and some Latin American "liberation theologists," and even in the "secular city" phase of Cox, is that they posit "secularization" as an affirmative value against "privatization": political theology is intended, above all, to involve the militancy of communities of human suffering. Does this succeed? It works through the replacement of theory by self-testing action modeled on a historicist Messianism. The move does little to controvert the disenchantment hypothesis, for it applies a political objective (Frankfurt-style) to religious understanding and denies the independent generative properties of the sacred.

Secularization also "differentiates" religion. The word is a monster, worse even than the stipulative distinction between "secularization" and "secularism." In a first sense, the differentiation of religion simply means that the sacred is consigned to its proper realm by understanding and practice. To this there can be little objection. In a second sense, as used by Talcott Parsons and some of his followers, the increasing specialization of the functions of modern society—the economy, the political system, science, education, and so forth—has also situated religion, retracting but not diminishing its power as a focal integrating element. Rather it has reinforced religion by consolidating its function. This was especially argued in an important article by Bellah.[89] "Parsons," Greeley puts it, "thinks that religion does, at least indirectly, affect much of what goes on in the other corporate structures. . . . My own inclination is to side with Parsons."[90] Greeley sharply distinguishes "differentiation" from "secularization," regarding the latter as a false issue, at least in America: "My problem is not whether religion can live with secular man, but whether he exists; and I will contend that save in senior faculty positions in some universities and in certain places in the communications industry, secular man is not common in the United States and does not seem to be growing more common."[91] This barb is intended mainly for writers like Luckmann and Berger, who take differentiation to operate in a third context, a situation where the retreat of religion from previous positions has caused it to lose its "reality potential" as a value-giving or legitimating force in the public sphere.[92] Indeed, according to Luckmann, this has been the common fate of all control institutions, leaving "wide areas in the life of the individual unstructured."[93] Richard K. Fenn argues, even more radically, that in secular, pluralistic, and instrumentally organized societies all meaning systems are relativized, questions of administration predominate, and "duly established priorities, effectiveness, and propriety become the primary sources of legitimacy."[94] This debate is seen to hinge on the substantive question of whether religion continues to provide public legitimation (for it can scarcely integrate if it does not legitimate) and whether there is an irreducible core of religious influence that resists privatization. My contention is that although religion still possesses public resources (not simply as a secular pressure group), it is losing them; that "differentiation" proves to be a function of secularization (with feedback) and that it fosters an incoherent perception of the sacred.

Demystification seems obvious, but it is difficult to pin down. As we have seen, sacred interpretations have been ceding to utilitarian ones over a long period of time. As a prime instance, death is consoled only by remembrance and the good works left behind. Since it is unproblematic, the burden of problems is shifted to life, which cannot bear them. Still—in the realm of "substantial disenchantment"—there are resolute resistances to the supremacy of the transient and perishable, which accounts for the incorrigible superstitions of "people who ought to know better." We also note the appeal of varieties of cultism based on science fiction or the authority of non-Western mysticism.[95] The private often claims its own truth, which is not apt to be "the road of patient, cooperative inquiry operating by means of observation, experiment, record, and controlled reflection."[96] It may be that demystification can result only in another mystification: "Secularism [as Vahanian calls it] . . . is an expropriation of religion, not for the sake of shaking off the tyranny of its supernaturalism as it is claimed, but really for the sake of another mystique and another fundamentalism or fanaticism."[97] And as Reinhold Niebuhr maintained: "Strictly speaking, there is no such thing as secularism. An explicit denial of the sacred always contains some applied affirmation of a holy sphere. . . . The avowedly secular culture of today turns out upon close examination to be either a pantheistic religion . . . or a rationalistic humanism."[98] It is plausible that demystification is, at most, a limiting concept. But it would be hard to deny that the demystifying thrust of secularism has become increasingly persuasive.

A "secularized politics" as well? It seems obvious that politics is secular to the core, for it is the "control system of the profane." However, politics as a well-delineated mode of theory and conduct long before the tests we have applied to secularization could have been conceived. Classical politics, whose legacy we share, was rooted in the imagery of cycles and duration: the political art stood against time and corruption.[99] In Christian civilization politics, although corrupt and perishable, was regarded as the necessary buffering of the earthly city against chaos, a temporal space to be protracted as long as needed for the kingdom to come. In Judaism Moses created a people and invested them with a politics that found its adequate earthly symbolization in the covenant and the law. It is therefore quite plausible to speak of a "secularization" of politics, implying not only its separation from religion but also its submission to similar external influences.

Secularization in politics refers especially to the will to master the recurrently fortuitous in the control system of the profane; that is why Machiavelli is "modern." The deconstruction of personalized politics (i.e., the establishment of role- and rule-governed hierarchies and the separation of morality and legal justice) represented the loosening but not the secularization of the profane order. Secularization, however, made a giant step in the proposal to substitute administration for government in the interest of science, predictability, and rational control. We ought not to think of such a temper as proceeding unproblematically from the desire to control conduct, because it was only necessary that human conduct should be known and tractable in the aggregate for an order to be built according to its tendencies and needs. For a time, at least, the liberal could join the technocrat in this adventure. The idea, prefigured as long ago as Bacon, received its crystalline expression in the work of Henri de Saint-Simon:

> We are weary of all political principles which do not aim at returning the destinies of the peoples to the hands of devotion and genius. We shall cast off our fearful mistrust when we reflect calmly for one moment about the pitiful results [the prevailing system] brings about. And we shall joyfully return to that great virtue, so disregarded—we may even say, misunderstood—to that easy and gentle virtue among beings who have a common aim they wish to attain; a virtue so painful, so revolting when it stoops to egoism. We shall return lovingly to obedience.[100]

The belief that politics might be dispossessed of troublesome passions or that it might organize them scientifically led to a rejection and defamation of theories compatible with politics, appropriate to specific political knowledge and the art of practicing it, in ways altogether parallel with the excising of theology from religion. Because politics—as opposed to the practical content of other "social sciences"— is a universal field of everyone's transactions, the responsibility of translation from theory to practice is very great. Theories appropriate to politics are obliged to recognize this basic condition. In seriousness and scope politics lies beyond other intellectual practices with which it is frequently yoked. For instance, when economics grows deadly serious, this simply means that it has acquired a political dimension.

Secularized politics seeks to deny this. It is the politics of both the "end of ideology" and of the most rampant ideologies. The debunking of the idea of the "common good" is a familiar example. "In the end," writes d'Entrèves, "the common good is perhaps nothing else than the bond of solidarity and loyalty which holds the State together."[101] Since, he points out, "none of us is free to do anything he wishes . . . whether we like it or not, the State is one of the chief artificers of these limitations."[102] Secularized political theory had the mission of destroying the notion of the state, for that notion is based on a chiefly legal conviction of order that can no more be reduced to a calculus of social forces than it can be interpreted as a play of electrical charges or of hormones. Although it is not terribly easy to say what the "common good" is as soon as preservation has been secured, political theory is impoverished without this regulative idea. Without it, we not only can say little about the state but cannot say much either about revolution viewed as a response to the corruption of the common good. In this perspective, secularization is quite close to what Judith Shklar described as "the decline of political faith" and analyzed so acutely.[103]

Secularized politics abolishes the sense of our processes of becoming without resubscribing to eternal verities. The value of *history*, according to Hannah Arendt, "owes its existence to the transition period when religious confidence in immortal life had lost its influence upon the secular and the new indifference toward the question of immortality had not yet been born."[104] Then the myth of history was perverted into the vulgar secularity of "modernization" or absorbed in the self. As Henry Kariel has written of his response to the writings of Nietzsche, Freud, and Mannheim: "The logic of their work has the effect of removing a good deal of traditional political philosophy from the public scene. . . . At the same time it summons man to establish himself. It summons him to form or re-form the infinite potentialities which are truly his. . . . The individual person is expected to make his own truth, thereby satisfying his own diverse needs."[105] Even Robinson Crusoe was not compelled to make his own truth; perhaps he did not possess "infinite potentialities." It is in precisely such a conception that secularization joins privatization in the political thought of our time. Though Kariel's sophisticated *homo creator* may seem a universe distant from the pseudo-science of technical values, both are terms of the dialectic of disenchantment.

I shall be briefer with *immanentism* and the other categories, since much of this develops out of the logic of what has just been said. I take immanentism explicitly to mean the transplantation of the source of values from a point external to the world (or the body) to a site within. I do not employ this idea in the far more restricted sense of Swanson, when he writes: ". . . alone among the world's major religious traditions, Protestantism—most dramatically Calvinist Protestantism—rejects all beliefs in immanence and particularly the Catholic belief in God's immanence in the visible church, the sacraments, and the soul transformed by sacramental grace."[106] Indeed, I take his formulation to be misleading. Immanent stands over against transcendent in somewhat the same way as public-private, subjective-objective, profane-sacred, and psychic-cosmic: it enriches, without reduplicating, these other relationships. As against privatism, for example, immanentism does not imply restricted communication. Immanentist systems are commonly defended as clarifications of a delusive transcendence. And although immanentism can mean a kind of solipsism, it more commonly refers to a group's self-projection of desires, beliefs, and interests.

In religion, immanentism especially designates the long development from theocentrism to anthropocentrism. It may either assume the radical form of the Feuerbachian "transformative method" by which God is made the result of man's capacity to idealize himself,[107] or it may reflect the tepid American liberal theology described by André Siegfried: "The current of American religious thought has been so strongly directed from transcendence to immanence, from the other world toward this one, from God-centeredness to man-centeredness, from dualism to monism that it has become unstoppable."[108] In other words, immanentism can be either profound or trivial. In either form, it is destructive of theology. As William R. Garrett writes: "Any religious movement which defines God as immanent in the world . . . breaks down the dichotomy between sacred and secular in a manner which obfuscates the reality of the sacred; and when its sacred center has been emptied of content, theological systems simply cannot retain vitality."[109] This criticism implicates all profane symbolization of the sacred as well as the temptation to interpret theology as a sacred history of "human suffering" in place of incarnate divine sacrifice.[110] For Cox, according to one critic, "the transcendence of God is identified with the stubbornness of historical (and perhaps also natural) facticities."[111]

Immanentism undoubtedly has special appeal for radical religious reformers. But it is no less easily manipulated by the Bruce Bartons. Though it might seem that a radical and immanent doctrine could bring "meaning" and "history" closer together, Reinhold Niebuhr has clearly seen that this world's justice—for which higher religion is obliged to work—cannot preempt the sacred judgment that is at the limit of profane history.[112] It is not easy to sustain a modern gnosticism: "understanding" the world will not "change" it in the ways one could desire, and the primacy of action is less apt to create theory than mischief and melancholy. In the nineteenth century we had varieties of optimistic and militant immanentism, powered by faith in "history as the story of liberty." Today that design pulsates only faintly.

The frustration of sweeping world views has a certain tendency to politicize theology and religious thought, for if providence as a collective project is cast in doubt, guerrilla warfare fills the void. Sectarian quarrel takes over. I do not mean to say that religious precepts cannot be glossed politically—indeed, that is one of our obvious forms of access to them: the struggles of God, Moses and Aaron, and the people of Israel during the forty years in the wilderness is a good example.[113] Profane justice depends on spiritual sanction. But we are no more privileged, from an immanent understanding, to regard our situated political acts as sacred than were the medieval theorists of the "two swords."[114] Nor can we, without some *Schadenfreude,* juggle the word *secular* to signify what the sacred has become for us.

Immanentism in politics itself is basically a rejection of the whole for the notion that a part or certain parts are a substantively valid expression of the whole. This is not a criticism of representative or majoritarian proceduralism. Nor is it to be confused with "holism" or any doctrine that would make the parts mere modes of the substance of the whole. Immanentism is not pluralism per se; it is only the kind of pluralism that is pretentiously self-destructive and destructive of the preservative control system. *Liberum veto* is the classic example. The immanently derived claims of various groups in the nineteenth century—the middle classes, the state bureaucracy, the proletariat— to be a "universal class" were focal stages in the modern process of disenchantment. They may be compared with denominational claims to the truth. Religious denominations have not, however, recently disposed of the coercive power of the state or forces adequate to challenge that power.

Modern political immanentism has worked especially in four modes. The first of these has been the functional usurpation of the sphere of the sacred (especially in legitimation) by way of "'society' . . . the source of a new *mystique,* the *Magna Mater* of an age that wanted desperately to commune."[115] In attributing to society "the transcendence denied God," modern politics also attacked the state, confusing immanence with transcendence as well as profane with sacred. There ensued a second error: the self-legitimation of politics through its own values, which have ranged from power to educative participation. A third kind of immanentism was national self-idolatry, where evanescent advantages of will, resources, or military strength, abetted by xenophobic propaganda and mobilization, violated the objectives of a profane control system. While concentrating on the American form of self-idolatry, we have noted its attraction for other nations.[116] The fourth mode has been the revolutionary, where confused ideas of the sacred come closest to touching the profane, especially when combined with the nationalistic impulse. As John Dunn writes: "For a revolution to be a *real* revolution it is necessary for the revolutionaries who seize power to be genuinely more capable of handling the problems of the society in which they win power than were their immediate predecessors—and above all it is necessary that it should not turn out that the only problem which they are capable of handling more deftly than those whom they replace is the single problem of social control." [117] Virtually all revolutions fail by this standard.

Finally, a word needs to be added about the politics of the self, the smallest but in some ways most legitimate of political authorities. The person is evidently crucial to any interpretation of political legitimacy, because the person is ultimately the object of all politics and only the person is empirically real. Souls are more obviously real than corporate supersouls. The person is also the most purely immanent source of political values, although this is mitigated by the fact that persons embody and project corporate, national, or even universalistic convictions. Our position is that while requiring both protection and political voice and being, as it were, the primordial agent of politics, the self, with its wants and preferences, cannot be regarded as the oracle that determines what passes for profane truth any more than it can for sacred truth. The self may be a plaintiff for human justice but it cannot embody a system of justice—not only because it lacks the power to establish one but because legitimate positive political rights are collective ones. The proper politics of the self in the authoritative sense is self-regulation.

There is a vast literature on *bureaucratization,* and it cannot be reviewed here. Bureaucratization is a double-edged concept in modern usage, and this in two regards. In the first place—more or less following Weber's pioneering treatment—it is seen as an effective and redoubtable means of organization while at the same time being a reprehensible instrument that stifles will and creativity. Second, while in popular language bureaucracy, as a repository of garbles, errors, and red tape, becomes the butt of bitter jokes, and "beating the bureaucracy" is a source of pride, there is an equally strong tendency to confuse bureaucracy (the rule of offices) with technocracy (the rule of technique), which implies an end to all joking and an imposition of glacial and involuntary norms. All these features are no doubt arrayed in the process of disenchantment.

In customary religious structures—but also within religious groups normally regarded as voluntaristic or even cultish (one need cite only the Salvation Army or the Church of the Latter-day Saints or the Reverend Falwell's Baptist church in Lynchburg, Virginia)—there has been a pronounced increase in what sociologists are fond of calling "functional rationality." In other words, such diverse factors as the revolution in technology, the geographical collapse of congregational and parish lines, and ecumenical attempts to reforge religious unity from least-common denominators have tended to produce a much wider division of labor in church organizations, even at a time when the morally legitimizing capacities of religion have been shrinking. These activities have become more routinized, yet more complex and less susceptible to responsible control. Thus cleavages have been created between the worldly and spiritual activities of churches, promoting standards of professionalism more appropriate to a welfare agency (liberal) or to a sales force (fundamentalist) than to a house of worship. Luckmann attaches this trend directly to privatization: ". . . the primary public institutions no longer significantly contribute to the formation of individual consciousness and personality, despite the massive performance control exerted by their functionally rational 'mechanisms.'"[118] Swanson interprets it as part of the secularization process: "Rather than employing rules that govern the exact procedures by which work is carried out [as was presumably done by more traditional hierarchical forms supported by collective conviction], the complex organization specifies the work to be accomplished, leaving to the employees many decisions about how best to obtain objectives. . . . What in the religious sphere we call secularization seems to be of the same order as professionalization and bureaucratization, and to have similar roots and consequences."[119] To this it needs only to be added that while bureaucratization seems to be a predictable tendency of a liberal religion increasingly absorbed in the "secular city," it may also be regarded as a providentialist technique adapted to the forwarding of God's purposes by fundamentalists.

Bureaucratization is of course primarily a political—or antipolitical—tendency. Its link with religion is presumably that in proportion as it neutralizes belief systems in the profane sphere, it similarly inhibits corresponding forms of "value absolutism" in cultural and spiritual matters and reduces religion to an aggregate of personalized meanings without integrative force in society. However, there is another view according to which such a state of affairs provides a negative or acquiescent basis for technocratic domination. "I recognize that privatization processes are occurring," Robert E. Stauffer writes, "but would argue that they are occurring in part *because* people have accepted the ideas of technocracy and thus accepted their own political impotence."[120] He draws attention, perhaps too glumly, to "kinds of awe and devotion inspired by expertise." This recalls Brzezinski's rather bone-chilling prediction of "special opportunity for the singularly talented few"[121] and Habermas's "structurally secured civic privatism."[122] There is, however, no need for bureaucracy/technocracy to be awe or devotion inspiring to work in support of political disenchantment. It need not spawn "myths or stories . . . to serve as instruments of unification."[123] It may simply be the drab truth of the matter. A less apocalyptic, but no less productive, result of bureaucratization may instead lie in the substitution of the internal politics of large organizations for the politics of a public. As Crozier has written: "The resulting difficulties [from 'the rigidity of task definition, task arrangements, and the human relations network'], instead of imposing a readjustment of the model, are utilized by individuals and groups for improving their position in the power struggle within the organization. Thus a new pressure is generated for impersonality and centralization, the only solution to the problem of personal privileges."[124] And, above all, bureaucracy encourages a spread of techniques of decision-making that veil or defeat the imputation of responsibility, which is the normal test of politics.

Indifference in itself would scarcely be worth treating as a distinct category if it did not have a serious philosophical pedigree. In the West its roots are post-Socratic and Hellenistic. I should be inclined to say monastic as well, were it not for the fact that thoroughgoing indifference rejects the values of both the sacred and the profane. Christian anchorites or monastic communities acted in full commit-ment to the sacred. The model is really to be found in Cynicism and, especially, Epicureanism, where an absorbing *ataraxía* (i.e., the absence of worry, fear, or pain)[125] was held to inculcate peace of mind through the banishment of supernatural sanctions and through obedience to the maxim: "We must free ourselves from the prison of affairs and politics."[126] It is, I think, no accident that a philosophy that evenhandedly censures the control systems of the sacred and the profane should rest on a materialist metaphysics and psychology. The effects that such a belief bestows upon its modern progeny are extremely varied. However, taken together in the understandings and practices that we are discussing, they imply either the congenital detachment of the strong from "base pursuits" or the denigration of the human being as a central and privileged part of matters both pervading and transcending the all-too-human, or negative feelings of powerlessness in either of the spheres. If we recognize the affinity of these effects, we shall have no difficulty in understanding how the modern portmanteau word "alienation" has come to refer indifferently to outraged intellectuals and to social marginals who are past caring.

Most persons are not, of course, self-reliant enough to cultivate

Epicurean *ataraxía* amid the events that shape their lives. Thus they either practice a hedonistic self-indulgence (degenerate Epicureanism) encouraged by the temptations of "modern liberty," submit to a profane sectarianism that is parasitic on the corrupt order they are shunning, oscillate between phases of withdrawal and abrupt spasms of militancy, or they abandon all hope. Negativity in itself can be a virtue, but only as a reorientation for new departures, as fruitful outrage.

Dissociation means, as the word suggests, both a loss of focus and the tendencies of a pluralism out of control. Of the features of disenchantment cited here, it is possibly the one that best illustrates the fissionable tendency of the "Protestant paradigm." Dissociation may be justly contrasted with the properties attached to the phrases "civil association" or "voluntary association" in the Tocqueville sense. One example of its effect in American religion is a confused clash of sacred and profane norms. I do not mean simply that men and women almost always experience such clashes within their life expectations and patterns of conduct. I mean that the contradictions have become explicit within the sphere of religion itself, so that the specific functions of religious life cease to have much particularity and are also heavily cross-pressured. This of course makes it extremely difficult for religion to legitimate or authorize any kind of social practice. The notion that religion (as opposed to a more universal and authentic force called "morality") should not do this is endemic in liberal theories going back to the Enlightenment and well expressed by Wilhelm von Humboldt: ". . . although the influence of religious ideas unmistakably harmonizes and cooperates with the process of moral perfection, it is no less certain that such ideas are in no way inseparably associated with that process." [127] In contemporary America, "morality" is generally apolitical, areligious, and permissive. But religion as a source of conduct is scarcely more coherent in the major denominations. To use sociological jargon, there is a benumbing conflict of different "plausibility structures" within traditional systems of belief; religion fails to be, in Tillich's words, "a whole of symbols in which our relation to the ground and meaning of existence is expressed." [128] Nor does it easily penetrate those areas where people are obliged to make serious moral choices. In particular, there is a hiatus between the destiny of persons and the destiny of the religious community in a fragmented pluralism. As O'Dea writes: "Institutional religion displays two kinds of irrelevance. Either it has maintained some significant personal meaning for its adherents, but has lost a relationship to man's larger history; or it struggles to attain historical relevance and exhibits little personal significance for ordinary men." [129] Once upon a time these ruptures were managed by the oligopolistic consortium of the denominations. Today, despite deceptive ecumenicalism, a far greater relativism with a warehouse of symbolic materials ranging from witchcraft to fractured orthodoxies, have made the religious map almost illegible.

The same kind of fragmentation has struck at politics for reasons that may in part be sought in the parallel developments of church and state in America—the experiences of filling up a continent, of federalism, of sectionalism, and of the opportunity for initial diversity advanced in the earliest times of settlement. We should not, of course, ignore a significant counter-trend where, in the breakdown of an evangelical religious conformity that had been pronounced in the nineteenth century, a greater sense of political unification appeared, notably in the days of the New Deal. Yet from today's perspective in both politics and religion there seems to be a centrifugalism at work, a Balkanization of moral claims, and this despite the fact that the Hegelian "saturation" has ensued. Our present situation makes the time-honored strategy of coalition-building more difficult, for there are more nonnegotiable issues as well as an overload of approved diversity. If politics is, in Wolin's words, "what is general and integrative to men, a life of common involvements," [130] and if, as Arendt maintains, traditions, religion, and authority were the keystones of our common world, [131] we can measure our malaise in terms of their breakdown. One might point especially to the increased mismatch between the images and substance of politics—or between politics as a practice and politics as a spectator sport. If, as Michael Novak claims, "for many politics is *deeper* than religion," neither of them would seem to have remarkable profundity. [132]

Finally, we must mention *nostalgia*. Nostalgic reactions can take essentially three forms: that something which is gone is to be deeply regretted or memorialized; that something which is gone can be resurrected; that something which never was can supply the image for what is gone. There was a nostalgia of all three kinds in the response of Novalis and other German Romantics to the Newtonian world of the eighteenth century. [133] But the political conditions of Novalis's time lent nostalgia a remote realism that has never been characteristic of any reliable reading of American history. If nostalgia seems currently to have gripped America, it may be, as I have suggested, that our "young" country is no longer in the nursery. Or, as Harold Laski put it ambiguously, "America as the 'young' nation is at once both a defensive and a prophetic concept." [134] Nearly all the currents of dis-

enchantment that I have analyzed disclose piquant ironies, but none
is perhaps so close to the ironic quick as our contemporary nostalgia
for a simpler, more simply pious world where ugliness and scarcity
and insecurity would have their fangs drawn.

Nostalgia includes both privileged and anxious reactions to change
within the movement of disenchantment. It has its militant and quies-
cent modes of expression. It sometimes reveals an authentic provincialism. In some senses, it is obviously a countercurrent to other
agencies of disenchantment. But we should recall that Weber's concept allowed not only for specific—and even heroic—resistances but
for their incorporation into its very fabric. Nostalgia has touched
America, not for the first time, in religion and politics—both in the
uneasy common ground that they occupy and in the jeremiads of the
one against the other, which are basically appeals to the founding
virtues of the republic. There is no need to specify what these currents are (some are fanatic and others prudential) or to take a partisan
position toward them, for we are engaged in a theoretical investigation. Clearly there is much pent-up frustration in this country, and
there are opposing frustrations that are not reciprocally endured with
very much civility. This is nothing new in our history, or in the relations of politics and religion. Our movements and slogans, as well as
our intellectual worries, betoken both a hostility to the symbolic
worlds we live in and a disenchanted mistrust of symbols. We have
fairly much ceased to believe in the New Atlantis; it does not follow
that we have placed our faith in Arcadia. None of today's restiveness
carries us beyond our problem: how are we to be spiritual, free, and
committed to common purpose—all at the same time, and in American terms? There has surely been a breakdown of Tocqueville's common democratic morality inspired by religion. Nostalgia dissipates
both "faith" and "loyalty" with its consummate suspicion of the present and the present's real links with the past.

In religion, nostalgia induces, in the first place, an attempt to replenish archaic vehicles of belief (and archaic prophecies) in the hope
of salvaging the symbolic supports they once gave to national pride
and faith. Often this is related to a kind of "ruralism," which has
been a component of evangelical discourse ever since Dwight
Moody's excursion into cities a century ago; Moody, it is related, was
"effective because he appealed to the traditional and familiar in the
religious realm."[135] Second, there has emerged a kind of moral Man-
ichaeanism that is intended to give battle to relativism and sloppy
pluralism, but probably leads to even worse fragmentation. Essentially, this has been a new way of carrying the liberal-fundamentalist

split into politics in vastly changed conditions. We now run the risk of substituting for a manageable religious pluralism a condition of hostile and incompatible moral ideologies, the antipodes of what Tocqueville had seen as our greatest strength. That is of course not solely the fault of Manichaean nostalgics but also of the secularists who had been goring them. Third, there is a reluctance to confront the moral map of society as it exists, either in order to validate it or reject it; we often suspect that our deepest moral dilemmas are being teased by bad faith. Some see shortcuts to salvation; but salvation means victory and the problem of what to do with the vanquished. In politics we first of all discern the return of a kind of tepid anti-intellectualism (Hofstadter's "paranoia" is too severe) that accepts unexamined expertise but is not inclined to ask for its credentials. Second, there is a rise of scatter-shot individualistic utopianism of various sorts, bred indifferently on right or left, in cramped cities or in the wide-open spaces. Utopianism is admittedly an exaggerated term for it, because in all its shapes it compromises incessantly with powers that be and is nurtured by a world we know all too well. Finally, there are a good many unfounded presumptions about how the sacred and the profane interact. There are excessive imputations or denials of evil that ignore the necessity of evil in the profane sphere while misunderstanding the ways in which a reverence for the sacred might temper it. The nostalgic reaction tries to reintroduce not just faulty remembrances but also the ancient notions of guilt and sin into a society that has become morally ill equipped to receive them. There is a confused straining for both freedom and moral absolutes, which, as James Agee wrote many years ago, is "hardly surprising among those who have witnessed, suffered or perpetrated enough pragmatism and moral relativism—above all in their customary degraded use in public and private life." [136] There is also much hypocrisy; moral absolutism is difficult to reconcile with "secular man's concern with the question, 'Will it work?'" [137]

This is the anatomy of disenchantment. Is it also decadence? We have held out little hope that it is not. But we have thus far neglected any serious treatment of the much-heralded phenomenon of the "American civil religion." That civil religion—if it exists—might take a number of shapes. It might be an arrogant, profane, and politicized form of the postmillennialism of a "favored nation." It might also be a warrant that Tocqueville's thesis was alive and well in America. It might be the most bovine materialism. Or it might be a nostalgic element of disenchantment itself. In the following chapter I will try to deal with these questions.

Notes

1. Novalis, "Christianity or Europe," in H.S. Reiss, ed., *Political Thought of the German Romantics* (Oxford, 1955), p. 134.
2. Ibid., pp. 135, 136. And cf. Adam Müller, "Elemente der Staatskunst" in ibid. (p. 161): "all affairs of the heart, of conscience and of death which could not be calculated have been left to religion."
3. Weber, *From Max Weber: Essays in Sociology,* p. 139.
4. Ibid., p. 350.
5. Ibid., p. 357. And cf. Karl Mannheim, *Ideology and Utopia* (trans. Louis Wirth and Edward Shils, New York, 1936), p. 41: "The process of exposing the problematic elements in thought which had been latent since the collapse of the Middle Ages culminated at last in the collapse of confidence in thought in general. There is nothing accidental but rather more of the inevitable that more and more people took flight into scepticism or irrationalism."
6. Wilhelm Dilthey, "Present-day Culture and Philosophy" (1898), in H.P. Rickman, ed., *Dilthey: Selected Writings* (Cambridge, 1976), p. 111.
7. *From Max Weber,* p. 357.
8. Ibid., p. 139.
9. Ibid., p. 140.
10. Also, as Louis Hartz, who developed the "fragment" thesis, reminds us, a "culture of flight," evocative of the divine or the demonic. *Liberal Tradition in America,* p. 65.
11. Luckmann, *Invisible Religion,* pp. 36-37.
12. See Hofstadter, *Anti-Intellectualism,* pp. 38, 44.
13. See Laski's *The American Democracy* and Siegfried's *Tableau des Etats-Unis* for recurrent instances.
14. Paul Tillich, *The Religious Situation* (New York, 1956), pp. 199-200.
15. See above, p. 63.
16. See above, pp. 29ff.
17. See above, pp. 11-22.
18. All citations are from John Locke, *A Letter Concerning Toleration,* in Maurice Cranston, ed., *Locke on Politics, Religion, and Education* (New York, 1965), pp. 134-35.
19. Locke qualified his toleration to forbid forms of worship injurious to public peace and he denied civil status to Catholics, Mohammedans, Antinomians, and Levellers.
20. Barth, *Community, State and Church,* pp. 31, 33, 80.
21. Karl Marx, "Contribution to the Critique of Hegel's Philosophy of Right: Introduction," in Bottomore, ed., *Karl Marx: Early Writings,* p. 52.
22. Ibid., p. 44.
23. Karl Marx, *Critique of Hegel's Philosophy of Right,* ed. Joseph O'Malley (Cambridge, 1970), pp. 31-32.
24. Karl Marx, "On the Jewish Question," in Bottomore, ed., *Karl Marx: Early Writings,* pp. 8-9.
25. For discussion, see Walter L. Adamson, *Hegemony and Revolution: Antonio Gramsci's Political and Cultural Theory* (Berkeley, 1980), p. 153.

26. Some of these qualities allow Charles Taylor to classify him as an "expressivist" thinker: see Taylor, *Hegel* (Cambridge, 1975), pp. 547-48. Weber repressed this tendency.
27. See, e.g., Karl Marx, "Introduction to Critique," in Bottomore, ed., *Karl Marx: Early Writings,* pp. 52-53.
28. Leszek Kolakowski, *Main Currents of Marxism,* Vol. I: *The Founders* (trans. P.S. Falla, Oxford, 1978), pp. 416-20.
29. See Kelly, *Hegel's Retreat from Eleusis,* p. 227.
30. Treated by Karl Löwith, "Die Aufhebung der christlichen Religion," in *Hegel-Studien* 1 (1962):196-236.
31. Kelly, *Hegel's Retreat from Eleusis,* pp. 115, 118-19.
32. Dilthey, *Selected Writings,* pp. 194-95.
33. Talcott Parsons, "The Intellectual: A Social Role Category," in Philip Rieff, ed., *On Intellectuals* (Garden City, 1969), p. 3f.
34. Daniel Bell, "The Return of the Sacred? The Argument on the Future of Religion," *British Journal of Sociology* 28 (December 1977):419-49.
35. Ibid., p. 427; but cf. his treatment in *The Cultural Contradiction of Capitalism* (New York, 1976).
36. Bell, "Return," p. 427.
37. Ibid., p. 428.
38. Ibid., p. 444.
39. Ibid., p. 433.
40. Wilson, *Religion in Secular Society,* p. 227f.
41. A.J. Ayer, in "Religion and the Intellectuals," *Partisan Review,* No. 2 (1950), p. 218. Cf. Richard Rorty, *Philosophy and the Mirror of Nature* (Princeton, 1979), p. 5: ". . . by the early twentieth century the scientists had become as remote from the intellectuals as had the theologians."
42. Habermas, *Legitimation Crisis,* p. 84.
43. Novalis, "Christianity or Europe," p. 134.
44. Zbigniew Brzezinski, "America in the Technetronic Age," *Encounter* 30 (January 1968):19.
45. There is an ambiguity of privatism, because it might mean "familial" or "small-group" relations or it might mean the determinations of the "independent individuality" (a notion virtually incomprehensible until the seventeenth century). For a lucid exposition, see Oakeshott, "Moral Life in the Writings of Thomas Hobbes," pp. 76-77. Today these distinctions are perhaps slightly less critical than in the past two centuries; if so, this is a measure of our "privatization." But it is extremely important to preserve different categorial notions of what passes for "autonomy" and what passes for the "language of the tribe."
46. Berger, *Social Reality,* p. 146.
47. Harvey Cox, *The Secular City* (New York, 1965), p. 2.
48. Luckmann, *Invisible Religion,* p. 102.
49. Dewey, *Common Faith,* p. 28.
50. Wilson, *Religion in Secular Society,* p. 34.
51. Frederick Sontag, *The Crisis of Faith: A Protestant Witness in Rome* (Garden City, 1969), p. 114.
52. Luckmann, *Invisible Religion,* p. 114.
53. See above, n. 7.

54. Berger, *Noise of Solemn Assemblies,* p. 59.
55. Marty, *New Shape,* pp. 86-87.
56. On the ambiguous proximity of Habermas and Berger, see William M. Sullivan, "Shifting Loyalties: Critical Theory and the Problem of Legitimacy," *Polity* 12 (Winter 1978):260, and n. 6.
57. Sheldon Wolin, *Politics and Vision* (Boston, 1960), p. 353.
58. T.H. Marshall, "Citizenship and Social Class," in *Class, Citizenship, and Social Development* (New York, 1963), p. 92.
59. Ibid.
60. Ibid., p. 106.
61. Adam Ferguson, *Essay on the History of Civil Society* (London, 1768), p. 316.
62. Constant, however, recognized that excessive privatism could threaten the modern commonwealth. See "De la liberté des anciens comparée à celle des modernes," in Marcel Gauchet, ed., *De la Liberté chez les modernes: Ecrits politiques* (Paris, 1980), pp. 512-13.
63. Habermas, *Legitimation Crisis,* p. 37.
64. Matthew Arnold, "Culture and Anarchy," in *Culture and Anarchy and Friendship's Garland* (New York, 1912), p. 197.
65. Erich Maria Remarque, *All Quiet on the Western Front* (New York, 1960), p. 180.
66. For further analysis, see Kelly, "Who Needs a Theory of Citizenship?" pp. 21-22, 30-31.
67. Wolin, *Politics and Vision,* p. 353.
68. Ibid., pp. 354-55.
69. Robert Coles, "Civility and Psychology," *Daedalus:* "The End of Consensus," 109 (Summer 1980):140.
70. Rousseau, *Contrat social,* II, iii.
71. Habermas, *Legitimation Crisis,* p. 58.
72. See Ernest Becker, *The Denial of Death* (New York, 1973).
73. In James Agee, "Religion and the Intellectuals," *Partisan Review,* No. 2 (1950), p. 109.
74. Handy, *Christian America,* p. 115.
75. Laski, *American Democracy,* pp. 302, 321.
76. Cox, *Secular City,* p. 255.
77. W. Seward Salisbury, *Religion in American Culture: A Sociological Interpretation* (Homewood, Ill., 1964), p. 280.
78. Berger, *Noise of Solemn Assemblies,* p. 90.
79. Coles, "Civility and Psychology," pp. 136-37.
80. Clebsch, *American Religious Thought,* p. 8.
81. Gabriel Vahanian, *The Death of God* (New York, 1961), pp. 140-41.
82. Schaff, *Germany,* p. 8.
83. F.H. Foster, *The Modern Movement in American Theology* (New York, 1939), p. 211.
84. Berger, *Social Reality,* p. 66.
85. Kenneth Cauthen, *The Impact of American Religious Liberalism* (New York, 1962), p. 245.
86. Franklin L. Baumer, *Religion and the Rise of Scepticism* (New York, 1960), p. 273. The author cites Troeltsch, Toynbee, Whitehead, and

Jung as his heroes (p. 276f.) and recommends a religion of "inwardness" (p. 291).

87. See Friedrich Gogarten, *Despair and Hope for Our Time* (Philadelphia, 1970).

88. See J.B. Metz, "Political Theology," in *Sacramentum Mundi: An Encylopaedia of Theology*, V (London, 1970). For a discussion of Metz, see Marcel Xhaufflaire, *La "Théologie politique": Introduction à la théologie politique de J.B. Metz* (Paris, 1972).

89. Bellah, "Religious Evolution," 358-74.

90. Greeley, *Religion in the Year 2000*, pp. 85-88.

91. Andrew M. Greeley, "An Exchange of Views," in Daniel Callahan, ed., *The Secular City Debate* (New York, 1966), p. 101.

92. See Berger, *Social Reality*, pp. 128-32.

93. Luckmann, *Invisible Religion*, pp. 39, 90-92.

94. Richard K. Fenn, "Toward a New Sociology of Religion," *Journal for the Scientific Study of Religion* 11 (1972):16-32.

95. See above, pp. 108.

96. Dewey, *Common Faith*, p. 31.

97. Vahanian, *Death of God*, p. 67.

98. Niebuhr, *Christianity and Power Politics*, p. 204.

99. See especially Pocock, *Machiavellian Moment*, pp. 53-54.

100. G.G. Iggers, ed., *The Doctrine of Saint-Simon: An Exposition, First Year, 1828-1829* (New York, 1972), pp. 199-200.

101. Alexander Passerin d'Entrèves, *The Notion of the State* (Oxford, 1967), p. 228.

102. Ibid., p. 9.

103. Judith N. Shklar, *After Utopia: The Decline of Political Faith* (Princeton, 1957).

104. Arendt, *Between Past and Future*, p. 73.

105. Henry Kariel, *In Search of Authority* (Glencoe, 1964), p. 5.

106. Swanson, *Religion and Regime*, p. 8.

107. Ludwig Feuerbach, *The Essence of Christianity* (trans. George Eliot, New York, 1854), pp. 24-30.

108. Siegfried, *Tableau des Etats-Unis*, p. 98.

109. Garrett, "Politicized Clergy," p. 396.

110. See Charles Davis, *Theology and Political Society* (Cambridge, 1980), pp. 45, 51-53.

111. Steven S. Schwarzschild, "A Little Bit of Revolution?" in Callahan, ed., *Secular City Debate*, p. 151.

112. R. Niebuhr, *Faith and History*, p. 27.

113. For a somewhat overdone instance of this, see Steven J. Brams, *Biblical Games: A Strategic Analysis of Stories in the Old Testament* (Cambridge, Mass., 1980).

114. See H.X. Arquillière, *L'Augustinisme politique* (Paris, 1934), pp. 93-104.

115. Wolin, *Politics and Vision*, p. 361.

116. See above, pp. 124-25.

117. John Dunn, *Modern Revolutions* (Cambridge, 1972), p. 15.

118. Luckmann, *Invisible Religion*, p. 97.

119. Swanson, "Modern Secularity," in Donald R. Cutler, ed., *Religious Situation,* pp. 803-4.
120. Robert E. Stauffer, "Civil Religion, Technocracy, and the Private Sphere: Further Comments on Cultural Integration in Advanced Societies," *Journal for the Scientific Study of Religion* 12 (December 1973):416.
121. Brzezinski, "America in the Technetronic Age," p. 22.
122. Habermas, *Legitimation Crisis,* p. 58.
123. Précis from Emmanuel G. Mesthene, "Technological Change and Religious Unification," *Harvard Theological Review* 65 (January 1972): 29-51, in *Harvard University Program on Technology and Society, 1964-1972: A Final Review* (Cambridge, Mass., 1972), p. 169.
124. Michel Crozier, *The Bureaucratic Phenomenon* (Chicago, 1969), p. 194.
125. Also defined as: "a variety of hedonism, a form of the theory that the end is pleasure . . . the distinguishing feature is that pleasure equals freedom from pain combined with safety, whether from fear of the gods or of death or of any other mortal affliction, or from the purely 'fleshly' inconveniences of life." J.M. Rist, *Epicurus: An Introduction* (Cambridge, 1972), pp. 125-26.
126. Epicurus, *Gnomologium Vaticanum,* V, lviii.
127. W. von Humboldt, *The Limits of State Action,* ed. J.W. Burrow (Cambridge, 1969), p. 58.
128. Paul Tillich, in "Religion and the Intellectuals," *Partisan Review,* No. 2 (1950), pp. 255-56.
129. Thomas F. O'Dea, "The Crisis of the Contemporary Religious Consciousness," *Daedalus* 96 (Winter 1967):129.
130. Wolin, *Politics and Vision,* p. 434.
131. Arendt, *Between Past and Future,* pp. 93-95.
132. Michael Novak, *Choosing Our King,* p. 17.
133. See above, notes 1, 2.
134. Laski, *American Democracy,* p. 399.
135. James F. Findlay, Jr., *Dwight L. Moody, American Evangelist, 1837-1899* (Chicago, 1969), p. 186.
136. James Agee, in "Religion and the Intellectuals," p. 108.
137. Cox, *Secular City,* p. 60.

7

Civil Religion

Machiavelli, whose contempt for the civic utility of Christianity was virtually boundless, nonetheless praised the religion that Numa had given the Romans as "the most necessary and assured support of any civil society."[1] "This religion," he continued, "gave rise to good laws, and good laws bring good fortune."[2] Since, as Pocock has put it, Machiavelli saw religion as "the control of fortune,"[3] his general maxim cannot astonish us: "Princes and republics who wish to maintain themselves free from corruption must above all things preserve the purity of all religious observances, and treat them with proper reverence; for there is no greater indication of the ruin of a country than to see religion condemned."[4] Rousseau, at his most civic and pugnacious, agreed with Machiavelli: "No state was ever founded without having a religious basis . . . and the law of Christianity is at bottom more harmful than useful to the strength of the constitution of the state."[5] Rousseau, who explicitly provided us with the term "civil religion" (the idea of "political theology" goes back to Varro), concluded the importance of a "purely civil profession of faith of which the Sovereign should fix the articles, not exactly as religious dogmas, but as social sentiments without which a man cannot be a good citizen or a faithful subject."[6] He also admired the festival aspects of the civic faith—its pageant and imagery—both as ongoing patriotic education and as the manifestation of a people's integrity and freedom.[7] We shall return to these classical examples in due course.

The contemporary "civil religion debate" in America was inaugurated by a famous article by Robert Bellah in 1967. As we shall presently see, Bellah's conceptualization did not come out of thin air, although it served powerfully to redirect the search for an American normative faith and to define the critique of that faith. It will be useful here to state just enough of Bellah's thesis to establish a context for our exploration. "What we have," Bellah wrote, "from the earliest years of the republic is a collection of beliefs, symbols, and rituals with respect to sacred things and institutionalized in a collectivity. This religion—there seems no other word for it—while not antithetical to and indeed sharing much in common with Christianity, was neither sectarian nor in any specific sense Christian. . . . The civil religion expressed what those who set the precedents felt was appropriate under the circumstances. It reflected their private as well as public views."[8] Several things are to be noted about Bellah's earliest attempt to define the American civil religion. First of all, it was an institutionalization of ritual and discourse. Second, it had "much in common with Christianity"; in other words, it was neither explicitly pagan (in the Machiavellian sense) nor a "religion of the republic" (in Sidney Mead's theist sense). Indeed, Bellah has emphasized its prophetic and biblical attachments.[9] Third, we have had it "from the earliest years of the republic" and have it still; this appears to challenge both the "secularization" hypothesis (Bellah had always preferred the Parsonian notion of "differentiation")[10] and the contention that American religion has been fundamentally altered by the new pluralism issuing from the implantation of the cultures of the 1880-1920 immigrations.[11] Fourth, the forms of the religion have been largely due to "those who set the precedents" (i.e., certain of our presidents). Fifth, the civil religion has not merely been a matter of outward political expediency but of an expression of the inner convictions of these elites. Finally, the Durkheimean-Parsonian sociological hypothesis lurks wistfully in the background: "It would seem that the problem of a civil religion is quite general in modern societies and that the way it is solved or not solved will have repercussions in many spheres."[12] However, in Bellah's later lectures, *The Broken Covenant,* this sociological imperative appears also as a moral-political one: "The substitution, in an effort to demythologize the political system, of a technical-rational model of politics for a religious moral one does not seem to be an advantage."[13] We shall later examine the relationship between analysis and exhortation in the work of Bellah and others. However, enough groundwork has now been laid regarding one version of "civil religion" for us to turn our attention to a specific historical episode that bears on the problem.

On 15 August 1824 (coincidentally the Feast of the Assumption), Gilbert du Motier, Marquis de Lafayette, the "hero of two worlds," came back to the world where he had first won his spurs. The former major-general of the American Continental Army, who had been granted our citizenship, arrived in the port of New York aboard the

Cadmus as an official state guest at the invitation of President Monroe. Having been defeated for parliamentary reelection and temporarily eclipsed in the cramped politics of the Bourbon restoration, Lafayette was able to tarry among his idolatrous American hosts for over a year. Since he was in financial straits, the national government and the various municipalities provided for him lavishly.

Lafayette's attachment to the spirit of '76 had not been feeble. He had named his son after his surrogate father George Washington and had sent the boy to Mount Vernon to be educated as a republican. Now, after forty years' absence from our shores, the French patriot received the expanding nation's acclaim, not only in each of the thirteen original states but also in the vast lands to the West and South that the Treaty of Paris and the Louisiana Purchase had procured. It was a triumphal and exhausting tour for a man well past the prime of life. Lafayette called forth the last energies of the "era of good feelings," for the domination of the Virginia dynasty was about to close. The year of his visit coincided with a presidential election hotly contested by John Quincy Adams, Jackson, Crawford, and Clay. Its outcome would be settled only after postelectoral negotiations between Adams and Clay, whereupon the republic of the oligarchs and old heroes effectively ended. Lafayette's presence was not unfavorable to the fortunes of his friend Adams, who was also Monroe's candidate. But what is more striking is that the news of Lafayette's comings and goings usurped interest from the national election.[14] The ideology of the Revolution and its passing from actuality into memory were concentrated in this man.

Lafayette's third visit to our country[15] is an excellent moment in time to grasp the character of an "American civil religion" if one existed. American public opinion was not only firmly set against the remarriage of Throne and Altar that shaped European politics at this time but was proud to consecrate a hero who, stigmatized for professing American political values, had been made almost an outcast in his own country. Lafayette was like a monument. By dint of his youth, he had outlived almost all the Founders (Adams *père* and Jefferson would both die on 4 July of the year following his visit; the last living signer of the Declaration of Independence, Charles Carroll, would be mourned by the tolling of the Liberty Bell in 1832). Everywhere Lafayette traveled he had a tumultuous reception, with each town trying to outdo its neighbor.

When Lafayette first disembarked in New York, a newspaper proclaimed him the "distinguished friend of civil liberty." It went on: "At every step he will meet with some object familiar to his memory:

objects which must awaken in his ardent mind the most grateful feelings, and fill his soul with the purest enjoyment. He left us weak, unorganized, and tottering with infancy; he returns to us, and finds our shores smiling with cultivation, our waters white with the sails of every nation, our cities enlarged, flourishing, and wealthy, and our free government, for whose establishment he himself suffered, perfected in beauty, union and experience. He finds, too, a remnant remaining, of the great and patriotic men of '76, to welcome him to the land of freedom.'' [16] The word "remnant" is biblical, but was this conceivably a religious flight of emotion? When a rainbow parted the storms menacing Lafayette's passage of Staten Island and "as it were, the very Heavens both wept and smiled for joy," the comment was that "in a superstitious age and country, [this] might have been regarded as a happy omen.'' [17] In Providence, Rhode Island, Lafayette was told that "the light of history shows us nothing like it; and we have heard no such event from the voice of tradition. . . . Might the Potentates of Europe but behold this Republican spectacle in America!'' [18] In Hartford, Connecticut, "about *eight hundred* children between the ages of six and twelve years, the girls dressed in white, and all wearing badges with this motto '*Nous vous aimons Lafayette*'" greeted the hero. "At the upper section of the Yard, the Deaf and Dumb pupils of the Asylum were stationed, wearing badges with this inscription *WE FEEL what our country EXPRESSES.*'' [19] The acclaim, the crowds, the banquets, the odes, and the ritual were entirely secular (republican rococo) in a country, as one will recall, still preoccupied by the Second Great Awakening. All this was received with a secular modesty by the lionized guest. As Miss E. S. Quincy, daughter of the mayor of Boston, relates: ". . . whenever the tenor of an oration showed that a compliment was about to be paid to [Lafayette], he had a conscious apprehensive, yet pleased expression which seemed to say 'now it is coming.'" [20] The evidence of Lafayette's tour encourages us to think of it as a prolonged festival in which the profane and the sacred were kept at a seemly distance, where profane celebration expanded its limits without breaking into the sacred sanctuary.

Bellah has written: "The Roman facade of the new republic was singularly cold and unhomelike to the great majority of the American population. There was a brief flurry of republican religion, a stoic, rational deism . . . but . . . [generally] it had no appeal.'' [21] It may easily be granted that republican religion had little appeal for Americans (David and Robespierre could not have touched them), but republican secular imagery—not to be confused with sacred things—

had quite a lot, as the decorative arts of the period remind us. The motifs of the heroic architectural tableaux that greeted Lafayette are a case in point. At Castle Garden, in New York, "no roof, supported by pillars, can ever cover such a space as was here peopled by fashion, beauty, and grace. In this particular the Castle Garden fete possessed an advantage over every other similar scene of modern times. —The groups of dancers looked like fairies moving in the distance to mellowed music." [22] In Newark,

> the base of the temple covered an area of about 35 feet diameter, and was formed of thirteen arches, representing the thirteen original states, surmounted by a dome, representing the western hemisphere. The pillars which sustained the dome were fifteen feet in height, and of due proportion. On either side, extending directly back, were colonnades, of twelve arches each, intended as arbors for the ladies. But the front was the most imposing.—The portico was lofty and formed four grand triumphal arches, supporting what might be called a tower. On the top of this stood a large and finely wrought golden Eagle, with a crown of laurel in his beak, and on one side a cornucopiae [sic], and the olive branch and cap of liberty in his talons. [23]

At New Brunswick there was "an arch at each of the four streets. From the centre rose a sort of spire, on which perched with wings extended, a beautifully carved Eagle, below the eagle were four banners, on the one was '1777,' on another 'France and America,' on a third '1787,' and on the fourth 'Friend of Washington.'" [24] The triumphal progress was now approaching the severe orthodoxies of the Princeton Seminary, founded at just about this time. But the Reverends Alexander and Hodge appear to have raised no eyebrows as Lafayette passed on his way to Trenton and Philadelphia. In Trenton he was greeted by "24 beautiful young ladies representing the several states, the waists of each encircled with white satin belts, on which was inscribed in conspicuous characters, the names of the states that they respectfully [sic] represented." Those of the original thirteen states "broke forth in concert." [25] Lafayette altered the trip slightly here to visit Joseph, the "good Bonaparte," at his retreat in Bordentown.

When he arrived in Philadelphia, he was greeted by a "civic arch" whose "plan and general features are somewhat similar to the triumphal arch of Septimus Severus, at Rome. Its dimensions are 45 feet front by 12 feet in depth, embracing a basement story of the doric order . . . from which the great arch springs, to the height of 24 feet above the pavement of the street." [26] In Baltimore, Lafayette encountered a "noble *civic arch,* of thirty-six feet span in the clear, raised upon square Doric columns, fifteen feet high," decorated in oil painting with the names of the original thirteen states and those of the outstanding revolutionary generals—including portraits of Washington, Warren, and Lafayette himself.[27] So it went, throughout the new nation.

Lafayette's tour of America was not simply a celebration of civic pomp. Religious sensibilities were balanced unconfusedly with profane enthusiasm. On 26 September 1824 he attended services at the Presbyterian Church of Trenton;[28] on 2 October, in Philadelphia, he went to Christ Church (Anglican) in the morning and in the afternoon to vespers at St. Augustine's Roman Catholic Church (his own official faith, like Tocqueville's).[29] On Sundays he generally attended Protestant services, as, for example, in Richmond, on 31 October.[30] In Baltimore he worshipped in a Roman Catholic church; the archbishopric has no record to clarify whether the priest in charge addressed him in his sermon.[31] Intermixed with Lafayette's religious observances was his ardent Masonic practice; he visited lodges wherever possible (e.g., in Cincinnati), and was escorted to Episcopalian worship in Fredericksburg, Virginia (20 November 1824), by the local Masons.[32] Masonry had long been for Lafayette a kind of substitute devotion in a Catholic country.[33]

The great theatrical climax of Lafayette's travels was his descent into Washington's tomb at Mount Vernon. This is best described in the words of his French aide:

> Simple and modest as he was during his life, the man [Washington] buried here and his tomb are barely recognized amid the surrounding cypresses. A burial mound scarcely raised and covered with grass, a wooden entry without inscription, a few wreaths already dry and some still green indicate to the traveller the place where the man whose powerful arm broke his country's chains reposes. As we drew near, the door opened and General Lafayette went down first alone into the cavern. Several minutes later he reappeared, his face bathed in tears; he took us by the hand, his son and me, made us go with him, and with a gesture he pointed to the coffin of his paternal friend. He tarried near his lifetime companion, now forever joined to him by death. We all bowed before that coffin and kissed it respectfully. On rising we threw ourselves into the arms of General Lafayette and mingled our tears with his grief.[34]

Twenty-five years after Washington's death, Lafayette visited his friend's remains. Like any ordinary mortal he was deeply moved by recalling his association with a beloved older comrade. American journalists treated the event in this vein. Catherine L. Albanese is using a good deal of poetic license when she writes that "Lafayette's descent into the tomb of the dead father seemed a collective ritual of initiation in which the patriots reimmersed themselves in the meaning of the Revolution in order to be born anew as sons."[35] This retrospective Romanticism is shaky anthropology: "rededication" is the word Americans customarily used for such events. And, as another writer correctly observes, "the subject of death had not yet reached the zenith it would in the later nineteenth century."[36]

There is no intention of suggesting that Lafayette's visit was not an extraordinary happening in the lore of the young republic. Wherever the French hero went he was besieged by crowds, hailed, dined, and toasted. In Fayetteville, N.C., he was told: "Dispose of all—everything is yours."[37] With a single concordant voice the United States acclaimed him. But it did so civically, not religiously. When he was welcomed by the House of Representatives, its speaker Henry Clay proclaimed that he was "in the midst of posterity."[38] When Lafayette took leave of America in September 1825, President Adams declared that antiquity itself had nothing quite so noble to offer as his deeds.[39] A man whose name was inseparable from that of Washington had riveted the entire nation's attention for over a year. But there is nothing in any of this high excitement to signify "rituals with respect to sacred things." As for religion, Lafayette made his devotions privately on Sundays. The white-robed girls who graced his passage through American towns and sang profane odes to his glory modestly changed to less conspicuous clothes to join their proud parents for church worship. American civil religion is thus not to be found in one of the places where we would most expect it.

The notion I shall pursue is that the concept "civil religion" as it tends to have been used since Bellah's article (and here it is proper to warn that the usage has been vaporous and not even entirely consistent in Bellah's own writings) could not have been present at the creation of the American republic and was probably instantiated only during the Protestant denominational hegemony of the latter half of the nineteenth century, if at all. The early Puritans had had a civil religion, but it was of the "state church" variety and thus not relevant to our particular line of discussion. Our Revolutionary patriots were of course inbred with the notion of a "publick religion"—to use Franklin's phrase,[40] that is, a religion Protestant or Unitarian in tone, congregational in form, and integrative in substance that, as taught through families, schools, and churches, would inculcate a morality where public virtue and collective republicanism could be anchored, a notion hardly distinct from what Tocqueville professed to find when he visited America. If less aggressive and flamboyant in method or in claim than the Christianity that appeared in concert with the great westward movement, this religion nevertheless also dedicated private faith to the nation.

It was not so much, I think, a "religion of the republic" as a religion favorable to republicanism and adaptable to the practice of republicans. "Publick" did not in those time square off against "private" in the sense that we think of them today. "Privatization" would have been a gibberish idea in colonial or revolutionary times. Even the insulated or exclusive sects practiced a very public and, within their perimeters, political form of devotion. "Private" was not so much opposed to "public" as "sacred" was to "profane" in earlier American communities. Most of the ways of divine adoration—even Anglicanism—were effectively "civil" in the sense that they posed no insuperable barriers to republican conduct: they did not need to be ground into a common grist. Despite the unquestionable tendency to associate the new national venture with God's will and providence and (especially as an outgrowth of Puritan theology and imagery) to associate America with the Exodus and to preach against corruption in the sentences of Elijah and Elisha as well as in a preformed "classical republican" language, it is difficult to see how the easy coexistence of these lexical and rhetorical traditions had to produce a *tertium quid* known as civil religion. Of course it was natural for American leaders in times of great tribulation and rejoicing (prominently James Madison) to call upon a common stock of ideas familiar to a nation with deep religious roots. It was equally natural for them to do this—given the temper of their times and the pluralism of their constituency—by nonsectarian supplications of the sacred. These resourceful and practical men, not being idealist philosophers, had no inclination to connect the tripartite separation of powers with the doctrine of the Holy Trinity or to associate the reserved powers of the states with the ancient privileges of the twelve tribes of Israel. Moreover, as Gordon Wood has brilliantly shown, the majority of persuaders in the Constitutional Convention of 1787 had reached the conclusion that the virtue inspired by religious belief was not adequate to guarantee the stability of a federal republic; a new "political science," based on man's more ordinary and profane tendencies, was also necessary.[41] Since all nations are steered by ideas or pronouncements connected by legend or text with their birth, the ideology of the Revolution had important repercussions on the future of America's collective religious practice. But the *novus ordo seclorum* was not a new religion: it modified already implanted ones to fit a new circumstance. It wanted them docile and willing to underwrite its needs; it did not profane them.

Here it might be argued from social theory that since all national communities require an abiding source of integrating strength and ritual, it was incumbent on a sectarian federation to fabricate one. It might then further be argued that America's prosperity meant that one had been fabricated successfully. We would then only need able modern scholars to decipher the substance and qualities of this faith. But this is to fly in the face of the fact that America rose in a world of dominant-church states that presumably provided for their civil religion by means of this interwoven texture. Even today, in a very secularized realm, the queen of England recurrently performs "civil religious" ceremonies of ancient origin that would be considered not only quaint but rather absurd in America.[42] For America was to be something resoundingly different from these other countries: not only a republic but a polity where, at least on the federal scale, guarantees for free religious practice and observance were to be provided as a positive achievement and not as a *politique de pire*. Is it therefore likely that the agenda of the new disestablished nation prominently included the construction of some elusive religious creed to which all might subscribe? Is it likely that such an enterprise would have been so subtly carried out by our first generation of elites that their intention can be disclosed only by contemporary scholarly decipherment? Is it not somewhat suggestive that the notion of this primordial civil religion should only have been put forth by writers of the past generation? What has wiped the scales from our eyes? When Catherine L. Albanese (1976) confides ingenuously that "one indication of the vigor of the myth [of civil religion] in the present has been scholarship concerning civil religion on which the present essay rests,"[43] might we not suspect that some contemporary volition compels us to see the past in this way? Sidney Mead's statement of the issue is historically more upstanding, since he implicitly concedes the answer to our rhetorical questions: "the species of religion incarnated in the denominations, with their massive institutional inertia, is not the religion that actually sets and legitimates the norms of our society. . . . *The* theology of the Republic is that of 'Enlightenment' in Crane Brinton's sense [i.e., Jefferson, Madison]. And it is not clear that this mainspring is broken."[44] As an ardent advocate, Mead has every right to set the ideal of "Enlightenment" against the forms of religion that he dislikes, to pose "the cosmopolitan, universal theology of the Republic" against "the particularistic theological notions of the sects."[45] What is exceedingly questionable in his account is the confidence that his preferred faith actually provides the backbone of "public piety" or possesses the sacred capacities to do so. But this is far different from Albanese's claim that a "religion" that can be hazardously reconstructed from texts going back to the late eighteenth and early nineteenth century has subterraneously come to "civil" self-awareness only in our own time.

More likely the closest approximation that the United States has had to a "civil religion" was prepared in the evangelistic convergence of Calvinism and Wesleyanism described in my third chapter, reinforced in turn by a commingling of sacred and secular postmillennial themes as described in chapter 5. Although the Civil War converted deep-set way-of-life differences and constitutional anomalies as well as fundamental issues into a gory sectional scar, it did not stifle the impulse toward a potent, if variegated, Protestantized political hegemony. Bryce commented on this feature in *The American Commonwealth* and attached special importance to the widespread participation of Protestant Americans in church affairs: "The country which most resembles America is Scotland, where the mass of people enjoy large rights in the management of their church affairs, and where the interest of all classes has, ever since the Reformation, tended to run in ecclesiastical channels."[46] Of course southern fundamentalists and northern theological liberals like Bushnell might entertain the most violent political antipathies toward each other. In the rural and *gemeinschaftlich* view of the southern evangelicals, the clerical spokesmen of the North were godless prophets of industrial wage-slavery and transgressors of the inerrancy of Scripture. According to the political theology of Bushnell, the "atheistic" character of the Constitution, victimized by the need of compromising with the contractual and states' rights dogmas of the South, had prevented America from becoming truly one nation under God. Lincoln's religious pathos mediated these extremes—especially in the language of the Second Inaugural Address; thus it is not astonishing to find Lincoln, "our greatest, perhaps our only, civil theologian,"[47] at the center of Bellah's general argument, even if civil religion was held to have existed "from the earliest years of the republic." After all these intricacies are acknowledged, it remains true that both the victorious and defeated parts of the nation, though corrupted in victory and shamed in defeat, felt themselves moving toward the consummation of a Christian and Protestant commonwealth.

By Lincoln's time, Hudson writes, "the ideals, the convictions, the language, the customs, the institutions of society were so shot through with Christian presuppositions that the culture itself nurtured and nourished the Christian faith."[48] War sundered these arrangements—made perhaps two civil religions—but the next forty years restored the common undertaking, just as it was about to be threatened by secularization, urbanization, and immigration. Protestants were consoled by believing that the future of the globe belonged to America, England, and Germany: "The old promise is being fulfilled; the followers of the true God are inheriting the world."[49] Even the social radicals subscribed to this general premise: "On the whole the social gospel had a high estimate of the civilization it wished to make more fully Christian."[50]

I do not want to argue that all of this was a true, or a good, American civil religion. Indeed, one must be of two minds about whether it was one at all in the sense in which the term is commonly understood. However, I am persuaded that if the notion is useful, it is most useful between the Union victory and the Gilded Age. Contrast the customary rhetoric of this period with the cautious formulations of the Founders, who had every reason to be exhilarated but, being both modest about dogma and classically constrained, came to pin their hopes on "political science." Contrast even the separation between profane and religious observance attending the visit of Lafayette in 1824-1825 with the far more volatile religious upswelling that Kossuth orchestrated for several months as a refugee from the Hungarian Revolution of 1848-1849 (see chapter 5). Contrast the hegemonic Protestant vision of the era of the Spanish-American War with the situation that pertained when Bellah was writing his *Daedalus* article. Woodrow Wilson was perhaps the last genuine articulator of the American civil religion.[51]

Robert T. Handy's *A Christian America* is a good guide to these events. I do not share Handy's winsome conclusion that Protestant America's dream has been dissolved in religious and ethnic pluralism (Protestants now being something like Louis Hartz's "liberal fragment," ill-equipped to operate in a wider spectrum of ideologies), for, as I expressed it earlier, I find that America remains Protestant (or "post-Protestant") at its bedrock. While, in the words of Sidney Mead, "many theologians of the sects continued to talk as if they were the exponents of the normative 'cultural system' of the commonwealth, while actually they represented only that of, at best Christianity in general, at worst their exclusive sect,"[52] there was, for at least a half-century, an ability for them to talk the commonwealth line and there is still a sense in which Protestant themes dominate public religious discourse.

I should now like to pass to a critique of the notion of civil religion as it came into recent American recognition and debate. As a background, texts from Machiavelli and Rousseau have already been cited. Let me go a bit further back in time to a quintessential expression of what the congruence of politics and religion looked like in antiquity:

> In the classical epoch religion has the appearance of being firstly a social or more exactly a civic matter. Religion and the city are inseparably joined. They are joined in the very structure of the city. Family, phratry, tribe are essentially defined by the common cults, the cults of common ancestors, an eponymous hero, of Zeus and Apollo Patroös. At the examination (δσκιμασία) of magistrates of Athens it was established that the candidate was born of Athenian parents, that he had family tombs in Attica and that he shared in the worship of Zeus Herklios and Apollo Patroös (Aristotle, *Ath. Pol.*, 55). Religion and city were so closely linked that there were no professional clergy in Greek cities; the magistrates of the city as such were entrusted with the prayers and sacrifices. It is hardly necessary, on the other hand, to mention the sincerity and intensity of the civic religion of Athens in the fifth century.[53]

This is the pagan polis in its most austere, nonsacerdotal form, the municipal ultimate in civil-religious practice. With the Romans there was a division between the magistracy and the priestly function in form, although every schoolboy used to know that a term as *pontifex maximus* was no hindrance to Julius Caesar's becoming a consul and later a god. Machiavelli and Rousseau well understood that both the Christian ethic and the cosmopolitan pretensions of a "world religion" posed difficult, perhaps insurmountable, obstacles to placing religious strength at the full service of the commonwealth. At the same time it should be remembered that Christianity's inheritance of a vast pagan empire and its astute adaptation of imperial pomps and rituals, as well as the numinous powers of local superstition, gave it much of the binding force of a civil religion so long as a compact "Christendom" could be sustained. Then, conversely, at the time when the unity of the Western Christian world was being shattered by dogmatic schisms and dynastic politics, it was briefly possible—as in Greece—to enroot civil religions within the walls or environs of small territorial enclaves like Geneva or Zurich.

However, both social fact and Christian theological predisposition ordained that the realms of the sacred and the profane would be pulled apart ("differentiated"), not necessarily with any great or obvious sacrifice of social cohesion. I think it is one of the errors of the recent "civil religion" school of analysts as well as of the sociology inspired by Durkheim to focus people around some common set of religious symbols and practices and proclaim it as the *sine qua non* of the corporate life. It is surely important to cohesion, tacit understandings, and reciprocal behavior that religion should favor this, but often we find other "primary institutions," more secular than numinous— kinship patterns, societies, guilds, and the like—that perform integrating functions side by side with, but exclusive of, collective religious devotion. These will be expected to coexist amicably with prevailing religious practice and even to join with it in festivals and other public events, but they surely should not be seen as some indiscriminate facet of civil religion itself. In brief, religion ("the gods of the city") helps shape and uphold the polis or *Gemeinschaft,* but it is not solely responsible for the nexus of solidarity. The ideal of common striving and face-to-face relationships is, in a sense, one thing and the religious bond is another. Predictably, however, they will be mutually reinforcing: heaven and earth, as Tocqueville put it, will be "harmonized" by the balance pertaining between the profane and sacred systems of control and their ramifications.

A good case in point would be the so-called home towns of post-Westphalian southern and western Germany, as brilliantly described by the historian Mack Walker.[54] These imperial or "free" urban settlements, with populations ranging from about five to fifteen thousand each, enjoyed a high degree of self-sufficiency, municipal autonomy, and civic cohesion. Participation was both extensive and densely structured by local law and by economic organization and practice. In their heyday these "home towns" (Möser's Osnabrück being the most famous) displayed most of the salubrious elements that a civil religion is held to provide, albeit in a repetitive and static manner, as a consequence of the fit they achieved between society and politics. It is a good guess that their solidarity was reinforced by religious compatibilities that went back to the days of *cuius regio, eius religio,* although by the seventeenth century they could not have been exclusive religious enclaves. Very strikingly, however, neither the word "church" nor the word "religion" is indexed in Walker's lengthy treatment of the matter. This may be an omission (it is at least conceivable that some work remains to be written on the civil religion of the "home towns"), but it is indicative of the possibility that civil religion as a binding force can be overstressed.

Whatever we may think of Rousseau's advocacy of the civil religion solution, he had at least the merit of putting the question in extremely clear and decisive terms: "Everything that fractures social unity is valueless. All institutions that set man in contradiction with himself are also valueless."[55] It was a summons to relieve an aching tension between the claims of the two cities, though not by the "cosmopolitan" means that Sidney Mead recommends. However, Rousseau's notion of how to deal with the "double eagle" must seem either exotic or repugnant in American terms. Already unrealistic in a Europe of "Christian commonwealths" with monopolistic ecclesiastical arrangements, was it not even more so in the experimental land of "free religion"? Was it not Tocqueville who showed how religion and politics might work for us and Cavour who gave the indicated European solution ("a free church in a free state") its crystalline, though fragile, formulation? We must wait a bit before concluding. However, even Rousseau did not avoid ambiguity. Why was his "civil religion" chapter placed at the end of a recapitulation and interpretation of Roman republican institutions? What was Rousseau's motive in not simply advocating Locke's style of toleration (which he does), and stopping at that? The answer has been well put by a recent writer: "The ideal of civil religion is . . . a radical, even desperate, attempt to provide the State with an ultimate sanction capable of putting the law above men."[56] Rousseau, who combined a passionate commitment to his ideas with some of the more detached fascination of problem-solving, was not a man to shrink from impracticality. His problem, interestingly, was the exact opposite of that faced by the American conventionals of 1787. Rousseau suspected that secular civic institutions might not alone do the job of maintaining the solidarity he desired; his surrogate would be the "civil profession of faith." Americans like John Adams and Madison, on the other hand, had come increasingly to the view that republican virtue, taught chiefly though not entirely by a latitudinarian Protestant religion, would not be sufficient to the task of regulating the divisiveness of the civil community; a political science was also needed that would, in Rousseau's phrase, "take men as they are."[57] The American republicans did not thereupon create a civil religion; they conjured with its probable inadequacies, and they determined to leave existing Christianity "free" and subject to its own play of checks and balances.

Now, where does all this leave us in approaching Bellah's seductive hypothesis and the immense influence it has had over current debate? Martin Marty fingered the question with politic but pointed skill when he said of civil religion (in 1974, seven years after the term had first been mooted) that "it somehow now 'exists'. . . . It functions chiefly as what Peter Berger and Thomas Luckmann call 'a social construction of reality.' So far it remains chiefly the product of

the scholar's world; the man on the street would be surprised to learn
of its existence."[58] This is the fact of the matter: while American
scholars were debating, *inter alia,* the secularization hypothesis
(which the present writer accepts in his own formulation), the tor-
pidity of "American mainstream religion" (an old subject),[59] the
"death of God" theologies, and, finally, civil religion, the country
was responding with cultism and privatized mysticisms, with varieties
of secularist religiosity (liberal and radical), and, most vigorously,
with an updated and aggressive fundamentalism. To be sure, all these
approaches to the sacred—especially when combined with political
issues like civil rights, war, welfare, public support of abortion, bureaucracy, self-help, drugs, nativism, and a host of other things—
touched a nerve in the civic body and threatened sometimes to rend
it. In that sense, a concentration on civil religion was not inappropriate. Yet, as Marty suggests, it was mostly a pastime of the intellectual
elites, themselves beleaguered in specific precincts of academia.

If the half of the country that, *grosso modo,* goes to church did not
hear about the miraculous existence of civil religion from their priests
and pastors, this means neither that such a thing did not exist nor
that, even if it did not, the concept was fabulous. In the first instance,
it was plausible that there could be civil religion without its having
come to the consciousness of most ministers and congregations; after
all, they were the analysand on which the intellectual community was
imposing its "social construction of reality." The concept also had
the advantage of joining the unchurched to the religiously subscribed
in a lexicon of meanings. In the second place, if intellectuals do not
always explain us to ourselves very well, they have the added function of prodding us to see forthcoming problems that would little occur to the ordinary person going about his business. The focusing of
religious style and religious predicament on civil religion late in the
decade of the 1960s had the advantage of uniting intellectuals around
a concept they could redefine or contest, and it restored Rousseau's
problem to our consciousness at a time when it had become far more
relevant than it had been for those gathered in Philadelphia in 1787.
Above all, it linked bodies of research and interpretation—heretofore
isolated—that were axiomatically important to American self-understanding as the bicentennial year 1976 came upon us: the "true" ideological roots of the American republic, and an assessment of the
roles of religious and secular symbols and motivations in our personal
lives and common culture. Yet it is no less an irony that an intellectually generated doctrine of solidarity, passionately debated in confer-
ences and journals from Cambridge to California, remained so remote

from the general population that was supposed to be its quickening proof.

By 1974 it was possible to organize a trade volume—not unique—around the topic of civil religion. This might be regarded as unexceptional; religious publishing adapts to this kind of anthological format with easy know-how, whether it be "secular city," "death of God," "situational ethics," "religion of the republic," or whatever. What is notable is that scholars of distinction who had themselves coined alternate formulas such as "religion-in-general," "the American Way of Life," "political theology," "national religion," "religion of the republic," "public religion," and "public piety" were willing to come to grips with the concept chosen by Bellah, even if, in the process, they may have disfigured it with their own revisions, deconstructions, and addenda. Bellah later wrote, with some pride, that civil religion had "turned out to be far more tendentious and provocative than I at first realized. I think now that the choice of the term was fortunate and that the controversies that it generated are fruitful." [60] In any case, the editors of the 1974 volume were committed to choosing civil religion as their point of reference and, in so doing, identified in their introduction no less than five variants of the type: (1) "folk religion"; (2) "the transcendent universal religion of the nation"; (3) "religious nationalism"; (4) "democratic faith"; and (5) "Protestant civic piety." [61] A glance at this nomenclature, without further comment, should suffice to indicate that civil religion, as anthologized, becomes almost anything that was earlier meant by "public religion," any apprehension of the sacred grounded in national traditions or values that is not existentially private or confined to a sect. Another point worth mentioning is that with the possible exception of the fourth category (in which secularist humanisms and cosmopolitanizing ideologies find their place) there is little on the list that cannot be accounted for, aggregatively, by the public postures of the main denominations.

What we have is a diffused concept that was both *zeitgeistig* and invented by elites for themselves. However, it is of great interest to trace the germination of that concept as Bellah chose it and adapted it. Bellah's own formal training and research dealt not only with the sociology of American religion but also with that of Eastern religions, especially the Japanese—where of course an institutionalized state worship had long existed side by side with Mahayana Buddhism. This led this scholar to be exceptionally sensitive to the veiled existence of parallel situations. Interestingly enough, more than a half-century earlier the important American philosopher of "community" Josiah Royce had been similarly impressed by the capacities of the Japanese

ethos to command "loyalty."[62] In the second place, Bellah's sociological orientation was functionalist. In a line proceeding back
through Parsons to Durkheim, this predisposed him to look for sacred
significance and sacred symbols at the core of society. In his much-
noted article "Religious Evolution," he identified also a progression
whereby, after millennia of "primitive" and "archaic" religions, "the
historic religions discovered the self; the early modern religion found
a doctrinal basis on which to accept the self in all its empirical ambiguity; modern religion is beginning to understand the laws of the
self's own existence and so to help man take responsibility for his
own fate."[63] In this perspective Bellah argued forcefully that "the
very situation that has been characterized as one of the collapse of
meaning and the failure of modern standards can also, and I would
argue more fruitfully, be viewed as one offering unprecedented opportunities for creative innovation in every sphere of human action."[64] It
may seem a far cry from "religious evolution" to Orientalism to
"civil religion," but by 1975 Bellah, whose theoretical virtuosity is
tempered by a complex consistency, could write that "the still small
voice that is heard only by the spiritually sensitive may portend seis-
mic changes for the society as a whole" and had pointed especially to
"interest in oriental religion."[65] Bellah has always seen religious
meaning as emanating from the vitality of social practice. Where he
becomes prescriptive the issue takes on a different coloration, and we
must reserve comment on this for the present. There is another problem: the linkage of civil religion (which is obviously "public religion") with Bellah's rather constant emphasis on "the laws of the
self's own existence" (recalling remarks made earlier about "privatization"). This confusion appears to partake of the modern quandary
in which liberal politics and liberal religion find themselves. Bellah
complicates the difficulties by seeking a way out or a way back: at the
same time that he is commending the liberation of the self from theological tyrannies, he is finding its corrective in a meeting of East and
West, a kind of global religious republicanism that he identifies with
the destiny of American religion itself.

Now, having commented on the intellectual strains influencing
Bellah, let us turn to the wider milieu of American religious interpretation in which he advanced his fertile concept. For many years it
had been alleged that mainstream Protestant religion in America was
complacent, shallow, and at the service of Mammon. If it was liberal,
it bracketed out the power of dogmatic faith and endorsed the norms
of modern society uncritically. If it was conservative, it ignored the
church's mission to participate in social reality as a critical witness

and preached conventional nostrums of salvation fifty years out of date. Conservative religion shot its bolt in the Volstead Act and the fundamentalist controversy. Liberal religion, sometimes allied with intellectuals, sometimes with powers-that-be, failed to renew its ancient ties with evangelism, could not cope with the creeping despair of urban life, and failed to produce a revival to match the economic recovery of the late 1930s. Then war came, and as a concomitant to war "there were no atheists in foxholes." Religion, like labor and industrial capitalism, had to be mobilized around a conflict more ideological (except the Civil War) than any our country had ever endured, although it experienced those four years with exemplary unity. With the peace confirmed in 1945 if not exactly settled, liberal and conservative churchmen alike—though with different vocabularies and nuances—agreed in the transfer of ideological animus to "the Communist enemy." The internal democratic consequences of the peace allowed for a much fuller entry of non-Protestants to an equal sharing in American life and values, and especially in an aspiration to the profane benefits of a society that, for the time being, had no rival in affluence. Churches of all sorts reflected this lax secularity (although their "suburban flabbiness" has sometimes been overstated); secular critics and a few religious ones sensed an unwholesome continuity with the Gilded Age and the Prohibition Era that seemed to make a mockery of the social combats of the 1930s. Religion was felt to be an avenue to social respectability and upward-boundness. The sacred pie swelled with the profane pie, with appetizing slices for more and more.

It was in this age (roughly coincident with the Eisenhower administration) that religious observers began to record and criticize the flaccid ways of the Protestant churches, while secularist forces mustered their battalions for the conquest of a humanist spirituality. Sociologists and theological liberals joined forces. This was not a new coalition; it dated from the Social Gospel, but its sociology was now far more sophisticated and it was no longer restricted to Protestants. Moreover, what we currently call the "communications industry" was poised for its spectacular takeoff. President Eisenhower made a crafty and much-publicized statement that it did not greatly matter what faith Americans believed in, as long as they *believed*. He was not considered by the intellectuals to be a powerful civil theologian. The emphasis was then, as it has remained, on "symbols," symbols as a supercharging or a refinement of reality. Indeed, symbols were both appearance and reality. If one could agree on them, and receive them with a proper respect, one could agree on substance and procedure at the same time. As the sociologist Robin Williams wrote: "Symbols . . . can constitute an overarching set of referents for enormously varied orientations throughout the society."[66] This fixation with symbols could reach the heights of intellectual power, as in Ernst Cassirer's great work on the subject,[67] or descend to the lowest depths, as in the new science of "image-making." Top and bottom of the trend spoke to different universes.

The first major book of the civil-religious analysis was Will Herberg's *Protestant, Catholic, Jew* (1955). Reflecting on the expanded status of the "ethnics" in American society, Herberg professed to discover a pluralistic "American Way of Life," with no great attachment to biblical dogmas, functioning as a common American public religion. He was bittersweet about this occurrence: on the one hand, the "American Way of Life" was an effective, not ignoble, way of uniting the polyglot pluralisms of our melting pot into a semblance of morality and reverence; on the other hand, its secularist and materialist character doomed it to heresy and irreverence as compared to the great transcendent religions from which it had sprung. Herberg set a pattern by expressing what he saw as the sociological facts of the case and then by criticizing them in terms of normative traditions and beliefs.

The second influential writer in this vein was the Protestant cultural historian Martin Marty, who in 1958 published a book professing to identify a fourth American religion, which he named "religion-in-general," no doubt somewhat influenced by General Eisenhower's statement about faith.[68] Marty did not exactly subscribe to the melting-pot thesis: he visualized American culture as "post-Protestant."[69] But he continued the campaign of earlier critics of American church religion. "We have been seeing," he wrote, "the maturation of several processes: the erosion of particularity, the smoothing of the edges of witness, the loss of religious content. Particularity is challenged by a blurry, generalizing religion; distinctive witness is confronted by sentiments . . . about religion. . . ."[70] He wrote acerbically of "the cultural discrepancy between ethic and practice."[71] However, Marty, like Herberg, walked the tight line; in a later book he realistically predicted continuing conflict between the major strains of "individualistic" and "social" (sc., fundamentalist and liberal) religion, although he did not then grasp the revitalized social capacities of fundamentalism.[72]

These kinds of arguments were a partial setting for the notion of civil religion, but a more radical injection was required. The war had produced not only retracted liberalism and conservative conformity but a continuation of postmillennial optimism and democratic and secularized faith in the mode of John Dewey. In brief, democracy was to become a genuine civil religion, a sacralized political way of life, apt not only for America but extensive to the globe (William Ellery Channing without God). This was bluntly put in J. Paul Williams's book of 1952: "The democratic ideal accords with ultimate reality."[73] That was surely a controversial statement to be dropped into a religious environment where the Pauline doctrine of the separation of *imperium* and *sacerdotium* still carried a certain weight and where, more prudentially, the American Founders had chosen to leave religion and politics to their separate devices, hoping that this would muffle conflict. Williams went on to present the issue in terms that Rousseau might have admired: "Systematic and universal indoctrination is essential in the values on which a society is based, if that society is to have any permanence or stability. The only way we can preserve our liberties in 'private religion' is to forgo some 'liberties' in 'community religion.'"[74] Some of what Williams wanted had been voiced in progressive Protestant declarations a century earlier, but in his environment America no longer had "no enemies on the Left." Moreover, in the America of his time civil-religious indoctrination had become an unpleasant thought for most people.

Sidney Mead's alternative was more moderate, more genteel, and more historically tangible. He maintained that the historically unifying American public religion had been the faith of the Founders and of some subsequent New Light New England Congregationalists (especially Lyman Beecher); he called this "the religion of the republic." However, despite the coincidence of Mead's normative faith with an illustrative time in American history and a bias that many civic Americans might share with his heroes, Mead himself had to concede that his version of Jeffersonianism and Enlightenment had most often been honored in the breach in the reality of American history, having been cast down by the denominations and sects that it liberated. Mead's interpretation of American history is thus a series of chidings, and an exhortation to break new ground in old soil. Like Williams (and like Marty and Bellah, and liberals in general), Mead has proposed an eschatological cosmopolitanism and a geographical, if not an extramundane, transcendence. In other words, his notion of the American faith is ideal and not empirical, which is the case with virtually everyone discussed here, except possibly Herberg.

From the cultural-religious side, then, it can be fairly stated that Bellah's genius was to integrate the findings and convictions of humanistic secularists, modern theologians, liberal patriots, and religious critics of privatism and the "American Way of Life." His astuteness in clarifying these convergences gave his notion of civil religion a wide currency and focused the trends I have mentioned with certain others that remain to be discussed.

Americans had pondered over their religious experience as a nation long before the subject became a matter of sociological discourse. In these inquiries the formative character of Puritanism and the Puritan ethic, whether this was admired or disliked by the researcher, was often foremost. H. Richard Niebuhr's *The Kingdom of God in America* (1935) was a kind of classic of the Protestant story. But we owe the most serious investigations of Puritanism to historians like Edmund S. Morgan and especially to the prolific Perry Miller. In Miller's work colonial history began to link up with Revolutionary history. As we have seen, Miller insisted on the centrality of the Great Awakening and the importance of religious rhetoric in the events leading up to the Revolution, especially in Massachusetts.[75] Other recent work has tended to confirm that there is far less disparity between the religiosity of New England and the cooler secularism or deism of the South than had once been supposed.[76] Miller's student Alan Heimert produced a prodigious book in 1966 that argued not only for the religious inspiration of Massachusetts patriotism but for the pronounced evangelical quality of the most patriotic preaching and for the comparative reticence of liberal Congregationalist elites touched by the Enlightenment.[77] Subsequently this impression has been somewhat rebalanced in works by Henry F. May,[78] James West Davidson,[79] Nathan O. Hatch,[80] and Mark A. Noll,[81] among others. The gist of these studies—if I may abbreviate—has been to rejoin disparate elements of pre-Revolutionary Massachusetts in a common patriotism fed by both profane and sacred rhetoric, to postulate a rapprochement of secular and religious millennialisms that touched fundamentalists and deists alike, and to argue for a state of mind that might justly be called religious nationalism.[82] Davidson took partial exception to this conforming of all the influences,[83] and so do I. The purpose is not, however, to criticize specifics of these excellent studies but to locate a certain mind-set of modern scholarship that favored the emergence of the concept of civil religion or retrospectively traded on it. It seemed from this work that conventional political notions of the American Enlightenment had to be reinterpreted, that providentialism was not just propaganda, and that, from the beginning, both religion and politics were central categories of the American mind. Catherine L. Albanese (1976) perhaps went a little over the edge, however, by suggesting that the American Revolution was in itself a religious experience upon which our fundamental civil religion was established.[84]

The works mentioned above span a generation that opened with serious inquiries into the "national purpose" and the glamor of the Kennedy inauguration and then quickly produced assassinations, racial tensions, the quagmire of an ill-advised foreign war, the "youth rebellion," the onset of economic troubles, shocking corruption in high places of government, and nasty and divisive political quarrels over "style issues." All this was sandwiched around the rather wan celebration of the national bicentennial. That is another context for appreciating the fortunes of the idea of civil religion. While it would be improper to impute intentional biases to the work of contemporary Revolutionary historians (although such biases are undisguised in the hortatory writings by Bellah and Mead), it is not plausible that any of these authors could have escaped their milieu; as Hegel puts it: "Whatever happens, every individual is a child of his time."[85].

Finally, at roughly the same time that these other intellectual influences were being shaped and debated, other scholars were engaged in a searching reappraisal of the republican political tradition as it had come down to us from antiquity. Essentially this inquiry was conducted by historians and not by political scientists or philosophers; it concentrated on a thorough textual examination according to the organizing principles of "traditions of discourse," "languages," or "ideologies," and not primarily on the great works of the great thinkers (although names like Aristotle, Polybius, Machiavelli, Harrington, Montesquieu, and Rousseau would be prominent). The most sweeping volume of this sort was J.G.A. Pocock's *The Machiavellian Moment* (1974), which traced republican language and concepts from Renaissance Florence and Venice to the Anglo-American cultures. More apposite to American eighteenth-century debate, however, were Caroline Robbins's *The Eighteenth-Century Commonwealthman: Studies in the Transmission, Development and Circumstances of English Liberal Thought from the Restoration of Charles II until the War with the Thirteen Colonies* (1959),[86] Bernard Bailyn's *The Ideological Origins of the American Revolution* (1965), and Gordon S. Wood's *The Creation of the American Republic, 1776-1787* (1969).

Aside from the intrinsic merit of these studies—which is great—their most obvious impact on our subject had been of the following sort. America's foundations had been conventionally thought "liberal," with little or no disparity felt between that word and "republican." Louis Hartz's enormously influential *The Liberal Tradition in America* (1955) prolonged this identification, but with the sharp warning that (Lockean) liberalism was in many ways a narrow ideology. By the 1960s liberalism had come under fire in America, both politically and philosophically. It was connected by its critics to capitalist greed (an old Parringtonian theme), to self-centered utilitarianism, to "possessive individualism," and to a mechanical (i.e., Madisonian) view of constitutional proceduralism. "Liberal" religion, as it had evolved in the mainstream faiths, also took its lumps: either it favored obscure secularist theologies with existentialist or scientistic overtones, or it became associated with the undiscriminating shallowness of "religion-in-general." In political science American liberalism was held to encourage a vulgar positivist or "value-free" interpretation of American institutions—often described as "pluralist interest-group politics"—that seemed to rob the nation of its soul (never mind whether it was a "nation with the soul of a church") and to sponsor the complacencies of the "end of ideology."

"Republicanism" could be effectively opposed to such a view of liberalism in America in a way that—and here Hartz seems to have been absolutely right—socialism or conservatism could not. The idea was useful to the left of our political spectrum because it had populist and participatory connotations and a revolutionary lineage. It was no less attractive to the right, for at least as understood in America, it implied an emphasis on self-help and the "free market," an attack on the Keynesian welfare state and big government, an inspiration to political devolution, a preference for "virtue" (as rooted in the Christian faith) over "self-interest" (as glorified in liberal political science), and a return to earlier moral standards (especially with regard to sexuality and the family life). It goes without saying that there was more than a little *Schadenfreude* in all of these "republican" ventures. But the term and the tradition were of significance, both intellectually and as they filtered down into the common culture. It was probably true that liberalism American-style had, at least temporarily, discredited itself with its war in Vietnam, its counter-productive "war on poverty," and its apparent glorification of politics-as-usual, bureaucratic centralism, waste, and a national morality running out of hand.

Neither Pocock, nor Robbins, nor Bailyn, nor Wood was an oracle of the extreme left or right. Their own orientation was probably "liberal" (if the word still makes any sense), but the thrust of their project commended such notions as "civic virtue," "civic humanism," and "classical republicanism," which had become detached from the current understanding of liberalism. It is significant also that none of these writers was proreligious; each tended to assert a primacy of politics in interpreting the tradition of republican virtue. Thus they have no direct role in any translation of their secular republicanism to religious republicanism. However, the "civic humanist" tradition of ideology and discourse identified virtue as its animating principle, i.e., the "willingness of the individual to sacrifice his private interests for the good of the community."[87] This facet of human self-sacrifice was posed without hesitation against the tradition of self-interest: both seemed to have been active in the founding of the United States. According to this new history of political thought, a republicanism stressing virtue had crossed the Atlantic and later been sustained by a persistent "Whig ideology" dating back to the Commonwealth. In other words, one could, by meticulous historical research, find "virtue" in the creation of the republic—for had not Montesquieu, among others, said that virtue was the mainspring of democratic republics?[88] Virtue might have battled utility and "political science" and lost, as in Wood's rendition of the period 1776-1789, but was it not always there at least as a living example of our country's coming to birth? Was it not a challenge to the degraded "liberalism" of the present?

From here it was but a logical step, though a major move, toward a syntheses between republican virtue and Protestant spirituality. The learned documents of the two scholarly approaches I have just described had their meeting ground in the notion of a coalition between classical humanism and Protestant Christian piety against secularist and utilitarian liberalism. In a previous generation the coalition had gone against Christianity, or Christianity had been allied with mundane utility: *de gustibus*. . . . However, by the 1960s the changing taste was clear. On the left Wilson Carey McWilliams wrote: "Ours is a polity dominated by exchange relations and shaped in the image of those modern theories that informed the Framers. But in value and desire, to say nothing of institutions, America has never completely accepted the liberal tradition."[89] On the right a putative "moral majority" with its appeal to fundamentalism and "simpler values" was already hard at work. And, spanning the chasm, Robert Bellah pronounced that "the revitalization of the revolutionary spirit of the young republic . . . [requires] a major shift in the established biblical religions, a shift away from an uneasy alliance with utilitarian individualism and toward a profound reappropriation of their own religious roots."[90]

Why was it so important to reference all our current public problems and the nature of our discontent to battles over the foundation of the republic and the religious and moral tendencies present at the creation? Aside from the fact that we were caught up in both the majesty and the economics of bicentennialism, there were other influences at work. One of them is always active in the life of nations: when a received tradition, suddenly seen as banal, falters, some other explanation with ancient credentials must be revived, and historically dignified, to take its place. Another is that America, described variously as "man's last, best hope" and as "the first new nation," sorely needed spiritual fertilizer from its sources that would remind people of an essential continuity and distinctiveness. A third is the battle of symbols in which a great deal of modern life is transfixed, although not very enduringly. A fourth has to do with the specific vagaries of the intellectual enterprise, which is exclusive though not ignorant of the nuances of ordinary public opinion. But finally there is the contemporary requirement in America for a vast distancing of value judgments and a refurbishing of symbols, which is characteristic of a disillusioned nation that has come of age, not only because of world power, responsibility, and empire but also because of a loss of unquenchable faith in its own uniqueness. In other words, America has been inquiring, probably for the last time, whether it is *sui generis* and how this might be shown.

Bellah composed all these strains genially and simply. If we review the materials of his several pertinent essays and lectures—self-realization, Japanese Shinto, Parsonian sociology, prophetic witness, elite civic consciousness, national tradition, religiously inspired virtue, anti-utilitarianism, and transcendent judgment—we can perceive why he made such a potent synthetic impact on scholarship. His message arrived in the right midst and at the right time. An attractive feature of Bellah's work is that its intellectual foundations command respect, while at the same time its expression is clear and seemingly uncomplicated. However, Bellah has merged exceedingly complex signals, scholarly traditions, and ideological motives into a dubious blend.

Bellah began his 1967 article with an ontological proposition: although "few have realized it," there is "rather clearly differentiated from the churches an elaborate and well-institutionalized civil religion in America," with its own "seriousness and integrity."[91] The lineage of this statement with Bellah's own sociological tradition and with the earlier formulations of "the American Way of Life" and "religion-in-general" is clear. In other words, civil religion in some sense *had* to be there: it remained to identify it. It remained also to formulate it in such a way that, while admitting that "it has suffered various deformations and demonic distortions,"[92] it could also be presented as a faith of more dignity, worth, and potential than the somewhat shallow religions described by Herberg and Marty. Civil religion had to be invested with "powerful symbols of national solidarity and [had to be able] to mobilize deep levels of personal motivation for the attainment of national goals."[93] These goals, Bellah went on to say, included generous social values, held humanisms as well as Judaism and Christianity within their scope, and aimed—in the sense of "religious evolution"—toward "some kind of viable and coherent world order" that was in keeping with "the eschatological hope of American civil religion from the beginning."[94] "At its best civil religion would be realized in a situation where politics operates within a set of moral norms, and both politics and morality are open to transcendent judgment."[95]

How did Bellah find civil religion "institutionalized"? In later writing he calls it "marginal, though very securely institutionalized."[96] It is the liberalism of self-interest and competitive individualism that makes it marginal, but the institutionalization is still somewhat mystifying, unless we regard civil religion as thus secure in the "civil religion literature." Apparently Bellah had something more important in mind. First, I would judge, is the sociological imperative from which he began, a *petitio principii*: "Every community is based on a sense of the sacred and requires a higher context of meaning"[97] or "all politically organized societies have some sort of civil religion."[98] Empirically, however, it seems that civil religion is enshrined for us in our Declaration of Independence and in various presidential messages and documents (Lincoln's Second Inaugural and Kennedy's Inaugural receive special attention). There are also scattered references to tone, tradition, opinion, and symbolization, for Bellah probably does not wish to suggest that civil religion is renewed only by being handed down from high places. Despite the modern sociology, the universalism, and the positive valuation of existential selfhood in Bellah's intellectual brew, the inevitable simile that grips one is the Mosaic politics of the Exodus carried on with the people, on one hand, and God, on the other. Still, the "transcendent source of judgment" remains rather murky. Is it a God of all nations? Is it some moral law of Kantian proportions? Is it the eschatological ideal of America as true progressives, both religious and humanist, would conceive of this? Is it the tribunal of history? These discriminations tend to be brushed aside. They are important to our inquiry not so much for their theological implications as for their impact on the proper relations of the sacred and the profane in Bellah's conception.

The institutionalization difficulty can be further illustrated by the notion common among secularizers as well as among those who reserve to God a constitutional place above all politics. This is the very familiar idea that the consensual civil ethos of the American republic is grounded in the pronouncements and developing constitutional case law of the Supreme Court. In this regard it is generally recognized that the Constitution of 1787 as amended is not a "dead" document, that it expands according to evolving conceptions of not only justice but society and politics, and that it has taken on functions, and indeed a sanctity, that were not envisaged by the Framers. At least until very recently some might have described *it* as "the religion of the republic." That much was once implied by Max Lerner in terms perfectly compatible with religious sociology: "Every tribe clings to something which it believes to possess supernatural powers, as an instrument for controlling unknown forces in a hostile universe. . . . In fact the very habits of mind begotten by an authoritarian Bible and a religion of submission to a higher power have been carried over to an authoritarian Constitution and a philosophy of submission to a 'higher law.'"[99] Today, for complicated reasons that cannot be gone into here (except to note, inter alia, controversies regarding the public privilege of organized religions and the definition of religion itself), Constitution and Court are less the focal point of our civil theology than they were in the past. They were at least a highly institutionalized focus, which civil religion is not; and we might hazard the guess that a need to speak of civil religion was more urgently felt by some in the measure that the sanctuary of our Twelve Tablets was being breached by more and more hostile petitioners and by a mood of desanctification.[100]

The concept of civil religion as Bellah developed it, and as it took hold in intellectual debate and discussion, was heavily freighted with the problem of how people create unity and share values through symbolic communication. Our culture is pervaded by the notion that man is, above all, a symbol-making and symbol-using animal. All our arts, our sciences, and our games reflect this presupposition. It helps powerfully in explaining baseball, politics, computers, air travel, abstract art, and a host of other matters; it seems neither vulgarly materialistic nor archaically metaphysical. Indeed we cannot escape it. It was therefore predictable that once civil religion had been discovered, devotees of the idea would incorporate it to the science of symbology. As Michael Novak wrote: "[Civil religion] *is a public perception of our national experience, in the light of universal and transcendent claims upon human beings, but especially [sic!] Americans; a set of values, symbols, and rituals institutionalized as the cohesive force and center of meaning uniting our many peoples.*"[101] In reading such a passage one might be easily tempted to inquire what had become of eccentricity; the "oversoul" of Emerson was evidently a more tolerant receptacle of the civic faith. Roderick Hart puts it this way: "All [scholars] seem to agree that civil religion constitutes what Kenneth Burke might call a system of symbolic, dramatic action and that its motivating force emanates from man's need for those hagiographic elements so crucial in a nation's emotional life." [102] It is certainly not true that "all scholars" took this position, but, aside from that, it was preposterous to elevate our political theology to a kind of multi-media event when its raw material was at the time more fitted to the theater of the absurd.

A more serious criticism is that although we seem to be living in an age of the theory of symbol, ritual, and liturgy, there has really been no hard evidence of either public or religious vigor in this regard. Amid the civil religion debate Lloyd Warner's old and touching vignette of Memorial Day in Newburyport, Massachusetts, in the 1930s was resurrected, in which he had written of "a cult which partially satisfies this need for common action on a common ground." [103] Memorial Day is, to be sure, a "civil" holiday with religious overtones par excellence, for death is preeminently consoled by religion. But was it celebrated in Warner's fashion in many communities in the 1970s? Are our civil holidays as passionately subscribed to as they once were? Need not we only point to the convenient modifications of our calendar that make Washington's Birthday, Memorial Day, Columbus Day, and Veterans' Day movable feasts falling only on Mondays so that privatistic desires may be quenched? Our public theology would seem to be more adequately expressed in rock concerts and professional sports. With the conspicuous exception of tragic public funerals, has American civil liturgy been well served by recent inaugurations of presidents or by the variety of Hollywoodish or art-deco political arrangements that we have become accustomed to? We cling to a curious civil religion.

Of course one can overstress the novelty of impoverished liturgy and ritual. People have talked about this for a long time. Over seventy years ago former President Grover Cleveland wrote a magazine article deprecating the shallowness of patriotic observance among Americans, their general lack or loss of community harmony in the throes of industrial life, and their substitution of extravagance for frugality—in short, their betrayal of republican mores. [104] As the philosopher Josiah Royce put it almost simultaneously:

> Once the Fourth of July was a day for training patriotic loyalty; it has now degenerated, and is probably irretrievably lost to the cause of true loyalty. Memorial Day and our national Thanksgiving Day are our best

holidays for expressing loyalty to the community and to the nation. Let us cherish them, and preserve them from desecration. But with us both holidays and public ceremonials have a certain democratic tendency to degeneration. We need more means for symbolizing loyalty, both in public monuments and in ceremonials, as well as in forms of common public service to our community.[105]

Tastes change: today's living ritual is proper fare for tomorrow's paleologist. But, on balance, it seems that the visible symbols that we would naturally attach to the common practice of a civil devotion have been more and more emptied of substance, commitment, and participation.

Since, as Bellah and most of those who subscribe to his position freely acknowledge, there are at least resemblances if not congruities between American civil religion and church religion, we would expect a ritualistic emphasis in the former to have some repercussions on the latter. It is true that there has been an expansion of the ritual of the fringe cults,[106] but this is scarcely the stuff that public theology is made of. In the more conventional (and even evangelical) churches, our era has experienced transverse impacts of secularization, ecumenicalism, more formless though perhaps more spontaneous worship, and especially a preoccupation with encouraging the individual to participate in the divine ceremony. The only thing we have not had (and there are few signs of it on the horizon, although they could be found a generation ago) is a liturgical revival, as opposed to "liturgical experiment." "High church" is not what the religious consensus is seeking. In the traditionally liturgical churches—the Catholic, the Episcopal, and the Lutheran—a movement mostly inspired by the clergy (spearheaded by the "new breed") has lowered the pomp and consistency of ritual by experiment, retranslation, and confusion of symbolic substance. Many of the laity have objected, to little avail or with the result that specific services and offices have become contentiously pluralized.[107] No doubt there is a good argument to be made for the refurbishing of church worship in a time when so much else has changed; and the liturgical alterations have produced only a moderate amount of schism. But one wonders whether a liturgical crisis in church religion is not linked to similar confusions in civil religion or is indicative that the much-heralded "force and center of meaning" of the latter has not been greatly exaggerated. Whether or not one likes repetitive liturgies that hearken to a distantly imaginable agricultural and sacred biblical cycle with minimal surprise and novelty, they are the stuff of collective social cohesion. This is apt to be true of civil religion as well.

Bellah did not emphasize "republicanism" in his earliest presentation of civil religion. It is surely not that he was unaware of the classic doctrines and texts of that tradition. Probably Bellah felt that the introduction of unabashedly political matter in an essay arguing that religion of a certain sort was alive and here to stay might promote a confusion of themes; or else he preferred to sidestep the ideological cavils between "republican" (conservative) and "democratic" (liberal-radical) that marked the political language of that time. But by 1975, in a darker mood, he was writing of "a third time of trial at least as severe as those of the Revolution and the Civil War," [108] invoking the historical "convergence of the Puritan covenant pattern [all Puritanism had been absent from the 1967 essay] and the Montesquieuan republican pattern," [109] connecting religion with "myth and ritual," [110] pondering whether pluralism and ethnicity might not have produced "many civil religions," [111] and finally despairing that "today the American civil religion is an empty and broken shell." [112] How would that shell be mended and filled since, by sociological *a priori,* it was irreplaceable? The answer was in the move to republicanism. Here Bellah's interests fully joined those of Bailyn and Wood, explicitly extolling "that inner spirit of republican character and mores that makes for republican citizenship." [113]

Bellah's *bête noire* had become a godless and heartless liberalism of utility, self-servingness, anomie, and the politics of interest. Without much nuance, he posited the republican truths of the Declaration of Independence against the agnostic mediocrity of the Constitution. [114] He found this contradiction endemic in American life and still vital in its befuddled political faith. "From the point of view of republicanism," he argued, "civil religion is indispensable. . . . A republic must attempt to be ethical in a positive sense and to elicit the ethical commitment of its citizens. For this reason it inevitably pushes toward the symbolization of an ultimate order of existence in which republican values and virtues make sense." [115] "And yet," he conceded, "the religious needs of a genuine republic would hardly be met by the formal and marginal civil religion that has been institutionalized in the American republic." [116] This did not prevent him from insisting that "civil religion and public theology in our national history . . . have been absolutely integral to . . . our existence as a republican people." [117]

In some ways we can see Bellah driving toward a "renewing impulse, the rebirth," [118] with almost Rousseauian tones of hope and despair. Ironically he had also returned to the strictures against the Constitution launched by Bushnell in the 1860s. However, his objection was neither as lucid nor as unacceptable as Bushnell's, largely because Bellah veiled God and transcendence with the ambiguities of symbolism.[119]

As I pointed out earlier, there is an intriguing anomaly in the coalition Bellah forged with the historians of republican virtue. If the Revolutionary historians had a bias, it was certainly in favor of *virtue,* but it was not for a virtue fueled by Bellah's kind of civil religion. It was the classical virtue of *dulce et decorum est.* Bailyn and Wood of course recognized the implication of religion in American civic development (cf. the Samuel Adams ideal of "Christian Sparta"), but they did not give it pride of place in their rendition of "Whig ideology," which depended on secular political figurations. Some language of Wood is revealing on this score: "In place of individual self-sacrifice for the good of the state as the bond holding the republican fabric together, the Americans began putting increasing emphasis on what they called 'public opinion' as the basis of all governments." [120] In this regard, "the Americans of 1787 shattered the classical Whig world of 1776." [121] The terms "individual self-sacrifice" and "public opinion" are especially significant. Whatever else civil religion is, with its penchant for communicative symbols and collective ceremony, it is not an indicator of the self-sacrifice of individuals. Similarly, the "public opinion" held by Wood to be the essence of the Madisonian world of 1787 (which Bellah castigated) was also Rousseau's "fourth most important law . . . graven in the hearts of the citizens," [122] and no doubt for him intimately linked with the inculcation and binding force of civil religion, not a "volonté de tous." In other words, Rousseau's republic and the American republic were quite distinct, both *in nuce* and in flight, as Tocqueville clearly perceived. Provincialism might have created some contact between the two conditions, but this linkage had vanished long before Bellah took up the question. Rousseau's project was an impossible mission for America.

Thus it was far from assured through Bellah's formula—even as modified by revision and criticism—that one could find or rekindle what Sidney Verba has described as the "primordial emotional attachment that is necessary for the long-term maintenance of a political system." [123] That religion is "public" or "civic" in some of its manifestations there is no reason to doubt. To argue otherwise would be to subscribe, as William James did, to the total privatization of religion—I and Thou. The speed with which scholars rushed to the "civil religion" banner no doubt reflects an awareness of this fact, together with a repugnance for purely private devotion and a sense of the corporate importance of public worship. Herbert Richardson called civil religion "an inevitable social structure," while warning, like Herberg, of its dangers.[124] J. Milton Yinger, like Bellah, a functionalist, wrote: "By ritual, by symbol, by its system of beliefs, its doctrines of rewards and punishments, religion may help to produce the socialized individuals who accept the dominant values as to legitimate means and ends. This aids the political authorities, but also has an influence upon them."[125] Most writers agreed that religion should "come out of the closet," that it should exert a greater impact on public morality, and that it should rally the public to ideals more generous than the "self." Yet none of them wanted religion to exceed its boundaries; they wanted it to stabilize pluralism, not to abolish it. This is why, on the whole, their criticisms of secularity were rather restrained, their definitions of a *truly* religious morality rather nebulous, and their faith in present institutions (except possibly suburbia or the market economy) remarkably constant. Now the civil religion craze has waned greatly: it continues mainly as a challenge to what is perceived as a growing administrative technocracy in the profane sphere. Conservative evangelicals or specific movements like the Reverend Moon's Unification Church may continue some of these themes in ways totally repellent to Bellah, Mead, and other writers; but theirs is not the same "quite broad conception of God as a reality providing a sanction for morality, a more than human foundation for the rights of man, and issuing a call to the active spirit of America to carry out a divine will or purpose in man's history."[126]

The civil religion avatar has not been without worth or substance, but its value, I think, was in responding critically to a specific, perplexing set of historical circumstances. As Bellah's arguments moved from the sociologically axiomatic to the fiercely prescriptive, sweeping in a whole baggage of historical ratiocination, political polemic, and prophetic hope, their impressiveness lay more in their witness than in their science. The discovery of civil religion was indeed almost unnoticed by the nation at large. As one observer wrote: "I am convinced for myself that 'civil religion' is a problematical category under which to view American society. The conception is itself a product of recent American history."[127] Herberg accepted civil religion (apparently in place of his own etiquette) as "an organic structure of ideas, values, and beliefs that constitutes a faith common to Americans as Americans."[128] But he still saw no tension between this and ordinary church religions,[129] and he regarded the exaltation of civil religion above ordinary faiths as "idolatry."[130] John M. Cuddihy shrewdly pointed to the likelihood that civil religion was a kind of attempt to extend Protestant (or post-Protestant) values beyond their endurable limits in America—which was probably true, and neither heroic nor deplorable, but inevitable.[131] Finally, Herbert Richardson warned that civil religion was an inappropriate way to restrict the state's control over the lives of citizens: "The national form of civil religion in America is not inevitable—and it is certainly wrong."[132] He also used the same essay to take a whack at the primacy of privatized belief on the same grounds: "It is *institutionalized ecclesiastical religion* that is the real limitation on the state's claim to a general sovereignty over society, not mere individual beliefs."[133]

Despite all the cawing and crowing about the affirmative stature of religion in America and its fortunate influence over our politics and society, it is clear (1) that we are not sure what religion is; (2) that our conceptions of the relation among religion, politics, and morality vary greatly and increasingly in our public debates; (3) that laissez faire in this area of conflict no longer suits us very comfortably; and (4) that our political factionalism is once again more tied to religious factionalism. I do not mean by this last point that there is any simplistic correspondence between evangelical religion and conservative politics; they have been subject to a transient crossing of interests—a nostalgic reaction against secularization and bureaucratization that conceals some of their own disharmonies. They are certainly not about to create a new "civil religion"; more likely they will negotiate a new pluralism with their opponents.

I should like to conclude with two citations, no more privileged than any other ironies in this book, that express my own impression of the evanescence of civil religion. The first of them comes from the noted Episcopalian William Reed Huntington, who was writing at a time when another "moral majority" opposed his interpretation:

> These vestiges of Christianity, as we may call them, are printed on the sand. The tide has only to crawl up a few inches further to wash them clean away. There is nothing in the theory of the Republic that makes such usages an essential part of the national life. . . . The moment popular opinion sets against them, all these relics of an established religion must go by the board.[134] They are not the natural fruit of our system; they are but reminders of an old order of things that has passed away.[135]

The second is from Reinhold Niebuhr: "To speak of our Western civilization as 'Christian' is to analyze it on a different level than when we speak of it as 'democratic.' It may die as a Christian civilization and yet live as a democratic one, or vice-versa."[136] That, I suspect, is the fact of the matter. It is not that we must choose between having our politics or having our religion, opting for the one against the other. Nor can we afford to ignore or neglect their transactions. But the genius of our civilization is in holding the two distinct. Religion needs to be social and private, and political, too, when it can, without forfeiture of its soul, enter the political arena. But civil religion, as it has been analyzed in this chapter, seems a fiction, if not quite an "idolatry." Lafayette would not have recognized it in 1824 despite his experiences in Revolutionary France. The civil religion talked about for the past fifteen years in academic conventicles is a species of *docta ignorantia,* of disenchantment.

Notes

1. Niccolò Machiavelli, *Discourses,* Bk. I, chap. xi, in *The Prince and the Discourses* (New York, 1950), p. 148.
2. Ibid., p. 146.
3. Pocock, *Machiavellian Moment,* p. 202.
4. Machiavelli, *Discourses,* Bk. I, chap. xii, p. 149.
5. Rousseau, *Contrat social,* IV, viii.
6. Ibid.
7. E.g., *Gouvernement de Pologne, Oeuvres complètes,* 4 vols., ed. M. Raymond and B. Gagnebin (Paris, 1959-), III, 956-59, 962-70.
8. Bellah, in America, "American Civil Religion," p. 18.
9. Ibid., p. 18.
10. See above, p. 190.
11. This feature, so increasingly manifest in American politics and social mobility, is a prime factor lying at the base of the "pluralism hypothesis" of "American Way of Life" religion and allied interpretations. It graciously compliments our melting-pot capacities, but it ignores the residual strength of the Protestant ethos and its inflexibilities.
12. Bellah, "American Civil Religion," p. 13.
13. Robert N. Bellah, *The Broken Covenant: American Civil Religion in Time of Trial* (New York, 1975), p. ix.
14. See A. Levasseur, *Lafayette en Amérique en 1824 et 1825, ou journal d'un voyage aux Etats-Unis* (2 vols., Paris, 1829), II, 43.
15. He came to fight in 1776 and stayed till 1781; later he briefly revisited the American confederation between August and December 1784; see Claude Manceron, *Le Vent d'Amérique* (Paris, 1976), pp. 418-500, passim.
16. *The Commercial Advertiser,* 17 August 1824. Quoted in Edgar Ewing Brandon, ed., *Lafayette: Guest of the Nation: A Contemporary Account of the Triumphal Tour of General Lafayette* (2 vols., Oxford, Ohio, 1950), I, 36.
17. Ibid., I, 41.
18. *Providence Gazette,* 25 August 1824, in ibid., I, 88.
19. *Hartford Times,* 7 September 1824, in ibid., I, 168.
20. Marian Klamkin, *The Return of Lafayette, 1824-1825* (New York, 1975), p. 34.

21. Bellah, *Broken Covenant,* p. 44.
22. *New York American,* 15 September 1824, in Brandon, ed., *Guest of the Nation,* I, 207.
23. *New York Commercial Advertiser,* 24 September 1824, in ibid., II, 21.
24. *New Brunswick Times,* 29 September 1824, in ibid., II, 35.
25. *The True American,* 2 October 1824, in ibid., II, 41.
26. *United States Gazette,* 1 October 1824, in ibid., II, 72.
27. *Niles Register,* 16 October 1824, in ibid., II, 126.
28. Klamkin, *Return of Lafayette,* p. 76.
29. Ibid., pp. 84-85.
30. Ibid., p. 101.
31. Brandon, ed., *Guest of the Nation,* II, 155.
32. Klamkin, *Return of Lafayette,* p. 103.
33. Freemasonry (Loge du Grand Orient) was swiftly becoming the vogue in French military circles at the time of the French intervention in the American War of Independence: there were sixty-eight military lodges (see Pierre Chevallier, *Histoire de la Franc-Maçonnerie française,* Paris, 1974, I, 197). Their orientation was one of free discussion, a certain lowering of class barriers, and a discreet liberty. Masonry had also a wide connection in the American independence leadership, without offense to organized religion. Lafayette freely partook of both influences. Being a man of *lumières,* he was not particularly enamored of the dogmas of his official Catholic faith, and he found a spiritual substitute in Masonic practice.
34. Levasseur, *Lafayette en Amèrique,* I, 392-93.
35. Albanese, *Sons of the Fathers,* p. 170.
36. Klamkin, *Return of Lafayette,* p. 95.
37. Ibid., p. 124.
38. Levasseur, *Lafayette en Amèrique,* II, 20.
39. Ibid., 593.
40. See above, p. 44.
41. Gordon Wood, *The Creation of the American Republic, 1776-1789* (Chapel Hill, 1969), pp. 611-12.
42. Cf. *New York Times,* 13 April 1979, "Elizabeth Hands Out Alms [on Maundy Thursday] Amid the Glitter of History."
43. Albanese, *Sons of the Fathers,* p. 223.
44. Mead, *Old Religion,* pp. 68, 71.
45. Mead, "The Nation with the Soul of a Church," in Richey and Jones, eds., *American Civil Religion,* p. 64.
46. Bryce, *American Commonwealth,* p. 702.
47. Bellah, "Religion and the Legitimation of the Republic," p. 21.
48. Winthrop S. Hudson, *The Great Tradition of the American Churches* (New York, 1953), p. 108.
49. Lewis French Stearns, *The Evidence of Christian Experience* (New York, 1890), p. 366.
50. Handy, *Christian America,* pp. 180-81.
51. As when he said to the Senate on 10 July 1919 regarding the Treaty of Versailles: "The stage is set, the destiny is disclosed. It has come about by no plan of our conceiving, but by the hand of God, who led us into this way. . . ."
52. Mead, *Old Religion,* p. 79.

53. A.J. Festugière, *Epicurus and the Gods* (Oxford, 1955), p. 1.
54. Mack Walker, *German Home Towns: Community, State, and General Estate, 1648-1871* (Ithaca, 1971).
55. Rousseau, *Contrat social,* IV, viii.
56. Charles M. Sherover, "Rousseau's Civil Religion," *Interpretation,* VIII, 2/3 (May 1980), 114-22.
57. See Wood, *Creation,* esp. pp. 596-606.
58. Marty, "Two Kinds of Civil Religion," in Richey and Jones, eds., *American Civil Religion,* p. 140.
59. Cf. "Why No Revival?" editorial, *Christian Century* 52 (18 September 1935): 1168-70. For current analysis, see Roof, "America's Voluntary Establishment," pp. 165-84, passim.
60. Bellah, "Legitimation," p. 16.
61. Introduction, in Richey and Jones, eds., *American Civil Religion,* pp. 14-17.
62. Royce, "The Philosophy of Loyalty," in *Basic Writings,* II, 949.
63. Bellah, "Religious Evolution," p. 372.
64. Ibid., pp. 273-74.
65. Bellah, *Broken Covenant,* pp. 156-57.
66. Robin Williams, *American Society: A Sociological Interpretation* (New York, 1951), p. 530.
67. Ernst Cassirer, *The Philosophy of Symbolic Forms* (3 vols., trans. Ralph Manheim, New Haven, 1953-1957).
68. Marty, *New Shape,* pp. 32, 86.
69. See ibid., pp. 2-4, 32.
70. Ibid., p. 2.
71. Ibid., p. 18.
72. Marty, *Righteous Empire,* p. 177.
73. J. Paul Williams, *What Americans Believe and How They Worship* (New York, 1952), p. 488.
74. Ibid., p. 372.
75. See above, p. 44.
76. See, for example, Donald G. Mathews, *Religion in the Old South* (Chicago, 1977), chap. 1.
77. *Religion and the American Mind* (1966).
78. *The Enlightenment in America* (1976).
79. *The Logic of Millennial Thought* (1977).
80. *The Sacred Cause of Liberty* (1977).
81. Mark A. Noll, *Christians in the American Revolution* (Grand Rapids, 1977).
82. See, e.g., May, *Enlightenment,* pp. 153-76; Hatch, *Sacred Cause,* pp. 6-17; Noll, *Christians,* p. 62.
83. Davidson, *Logic of Millennial Thought,* p. 216.
84. Albanese, *Sons of the Fathers,* p. 6.
85. Hegel, Preface to *The Philosophy of Right,* p. 11.
86. Cambridge, Mass.
87. Wood, *Creation,* p. 68.
88. Montesquieu, *De l'Esprit des lois,* III, iii.
89. W.C. McWilliams, "On Equality as the Moral Foundation for Commu-

nity," in Robert R. Horwitz, ed., *The Moral Foundations of the American Republic* (Charlottesville, 1977), p. 212.

90. Bellah, "The New Religious Consciousness and the Crisis in Modernity," in Charles Glock and R.N. Bellah, eds., *The New Religious Consciousness* (Berkeley, 1976), p. 352.
91. Bellah, "American Civil Religion," p. 1.
92. Ibid., p. 12.
93. Ibid., p. 13.
94. Ibid., p. 16.
95. Bellah, "American Civil Religion in the 1970s," in Richey and Jones, eds., *American Civil Religion,* p. 270.
96. Bellah, "Legitimation," p. 19.
97. Bellah, "American Civil Religion in the 1970s," p. 270.
98. Ibid., p. 257.
99. Max Lerner, "Constitution and Court as Symbols," *Yale Law Journal* 46 (1937): 1294.
100. See, in general, Sanford Levinson on "religious" divisions in constitutional jurisprudence in " 'The Constitution' in American Civil Religion," *The Supreme Court Review* 21 (1980): 123-51.
101. Novak, *Choosing Our King,* p. 127.
102. Roderick P. Hart, *The Political Pulpit* (West Lafayette, Ind., 1977), p. 2.
103. W. Lloyd Warner, "An American Sacred Ceremony," in Richey and Jones, eds., *American Civil Religion,* p. 103.
104. Grover Cleveland, "Patriotism and Holiday Observance," *North American Review* 184 (April 1907), 683-93.
105. Royce *Philosophy of Loyalty,* p. 961.
106. See above, p. 108.
107. Paul Seabury, "Trendier Than Thou," *Harper's,* October 1978, pp. 39-52.
108. Bellah, *Broken Covenant,* p. 1.
109. Ibid., p. 27.
110. Ibid., p. 85.
111. Ibid., p. 107.
112. Ibid., p. 135.
113. Bellah, "Legitimation," p. 18.
114. Ibid., p. 19.
115. Ibid., p. 20.
116. Ibid.
117. Ibid., p. 21.
118. Ibid., p. 23.
119. See above, p. 234.
120. Wood, *Creation,* p. 612.
121. Ibid., p. 606.
122. Rousseau, *Contrat social,* II, xii.
123. Sidney Verba, "The Kennedy Assassination and the Nature of Political Commitment," in B.S. Greenberg and E.B. Parker, eds., *The Kennedy Assassination and the American Public* (Stanford, 1965), pp. 359-60.
124. Richardson, "Civil Religion in Theological Perspective," p. 165.
125. Yinger, *Scientific Study of Religion,* p. 118.

126. John E. Smith, "Royce and Dewey on Community," in *America: Manifest Destiny and Historical Judgment* (Carlisle, Pa., 1973), p. 49.
127. John F. Wilson, "The Religious Basis for American Social Life," in ibid., p. 33.
128. Herberg, "America's Civil Religion: What It Is and Whence It Comes," in Richey and Jones, eds., *American Civil Religion,* p. 77.
129. Ibid., p. 85.
130. Ibid., p. 87.
131. John Murray Cuddihy, *No Offense: Civil Religion and Protestant Taste* (New York, 1978).
132. Richardson, "Civil Religion in Theological Perspective," p. 167.
133. Ibid., p. 181.
134. Marvin Zetterbaum comments pointedly: "For a religion to be effective at all its adherents must have a faith resistant to temporal stresses and strains. If that faith has no support but majority opinion, it must inevitably decay." *Tocqueville and the Problem of Democracy* (Stanford, 1967), p. 121.
135. William Reed Huntington, *The Church-Idea: An Essay Towards Unity* (New York, 1884), pp. 128-29.
136. R. Niebuhr, *Faith and History,* p. 217.

8

Faith and Loyalty

Civil religion compresses spheres of control and conviction that history and theory counsel us to keep separate. It may be, in Herberg's word, an "idolatry" and it may not even be a reality. After all is said and done about American civil religion, it seems to be an artifact of the secularizing process, cloaking profane practices with a sacred terminology and mock-sacred justifications and repudiations. This study makes it quite clear that Americans have, at moments in their history, gone to absurd lengths to equate divine intentions with national desires. They have also visualized the divine as a projection of the self-purifying ego, and have sectarianized their "common faith" by the pluralization and privatization of worship. Civil religion cannot be obtained by concluding disenchantedly that some historic result with transmundane implications can be recaptured from the principles of our settlement and founding, for, as I wrote earlier, those principles are more memorabilia than memories. Moreover, politics and religion are grounded in different varieties of conviction, preludes to empirically hybrid actions, but distinct as accesses to the profane and sacred. I have called these types of conviction "faith" and "loyalty." Loyalty might be linked with *allegiance,* and faith with *piety.* The latter part of this chapter will be a comment on the conceptual relations between these two animating principles. First, however, it will be useful to review the major disclosures of our study thus far.

A secularization process (not exactly the same as that of the Enlightenment, where deists still insisted that the *Dieu caché* should be worshipped) has increasingly—although not without lively reactions and jolts—shaped the public morality that feeds into politics. It is a complex process that gives signs of continuity, at least within our present cultural parameters.[1] Paradoxically, that seems like nonsense to many committed religious believers, who wage a fierce rear-guard action that carries into politics, another control system now seemingly fraught with weaknesses. However, our sober conclusion must be that the world works against religious revival. It is a rather widespread assumption in modernist theology that the divine (whether Christian or not) must perish if people cease to believe in it. There is absolutely no reason to suppose that this is true, nor does this account for the destiny described here. Under a total secularism mankind would simply have annulled one of the dimensions of human understanding, with consequences for politics, art, cosmology, and other fields, that we can well imagine in the broad sense. I am most surely not arguing that this *cannot* happen; indeed I think that it *is* happening. The result, I think, must be a profound change in how our secular life will be controlled and disciplined: a stricter and more resolute politics than our civilization has ever seen.

Secularization has not, in most respects, provided a common workable ethic superior to Judaeo-Christianity. Even "religiosity" cannot do the work of religion, because it is hostile to collective institutions and, *a fortiori,* to the communal ties that bind people to firm conceptions of good and bad action—in private or in public. Religiosity allows the poet his flower, the gifted scientist his theorem, the thief his theft in a good cause, but it does not make a meaningful cosmos of permission and prohibition out of these multiple events. The most drastic result of the private legitimation of the spiritual has been to drive conviction inward, anchoring it in the wishes or hopes of the self, rather than in a more extensive magnanimity or even in the prudence of "self-interest rightly understood." Unfortunately, neither public virtue nor collective practicality can be effectively achieved without institutionalized norms and values that are repetitively practiced, perhaps even sacramentally, though not for us in mixtures of civil religion.[2]

Another consequence of this trend has been the cultivation of a utilitarian view of action and manners, which is not so much vicious because it is individually goal-oriented as because it conceals the specificity of the sacred. Self-creation of spirituality (sometimes described as "autonomy") and utilitarian prudence are of course not the same thing. Yet the prevailing pressures in modern society (including criteria of self-esteem and self-worth) have driven the two into fantastic combinations, whose common denominator is subjectivity and, in an altogether pathetic sense, self-preservation. The success story of "inner lives," and the publicity that broadcasts them, provide a miraculous outcome that is supposed to leave one feeling "free" and profanely resourceful at the same time, often in disregard of one's neighbor or one's community.

Exactly the same tendencies are to be observed in politics, with perhaps an even greater degree of confusion, since politics is at least presumed to occupy a public space with public issues. The current clamor for new "political self-determination" (highly frustrating when it cannot achieve efficacy or locate any other object to represent but the self) often complements dysarchy in the moral or religious life. It is sometimes described as a demand for "expressivity." Just as transcendent religions are taxed with tyranny and mystification, politics transacted at a distance through the filtration of representatives, hierarchies, and institutional procedures is felt to be deadening and demeaning. Without exaggerating this condition, it is fair to say that a once-moderate pluralism has become centrifugal—partly because the self is afraid of the travesties of the bureaucratic state or all too ready to declare social, but antipolitical, values—and that past procedures (elections, majority rule, balancing of rights with the ethos of the community, redress of just grievances) for eliciting consensus and operative government have been challenged by the demands of autonomous legitimation. Here again, utopian, egocentric, and utilitarian motives mingle. There is a desire to overthrow formalities rather than to find better ones, to make "great refusals" rather than "great challenges," or to set the clock back to things people might once have agreed on but that now mainly serve—in Bentham's phrase—"sinister interests" (a hypocrisy slightly worse than the "primacy of the self" because its culpability is harder to trace). It is little wonder that some concerned intellectuals have sought solace in the idea of civil religion—a bridging concept that might infuse the national consciousness with morale or succor.

Yet politics does not drift into religion or religion into politics so easily, at least in our culture. There is an intervening area called *morality,* where much of the trouble takes place. Though not specifically public in the sense of "official," morality is, if nothing else, "other-regarding." Morality takes at least two. To speak of "private morality" is simply to refer to the protections of law and nondisclosure that keep a person or persons from the nuances of bigoted opinion or arbitrary government. However, people need moral codes and systematic expectations of mutual behavior to live by. These may be plural, but they are scarcely unlimited and far from a matter of caprice. The most moral society is not that which has the greatest possible number of moral options or moral experiences but that which most perfectly understands itself in moral terms.[3] Tocqueville was well aware that a consistency of moral practices legitimated by the separate religious sects was a warrant of freedom in the sphere of political and economic life. But for many today the sphere of morality ("what ought I to do?") is so fluid and ill defined that it is no longer even confused with civil freedom ("doing anything that the laws allow"). It is coextensive (short of the major crimes and most reprehensible deceits) with what one judges necessary to his own fulfillment. In brief, ethics comes to be confused with mere action (as opposed to thought): since human beings are, by definition, ethical beings, it follows that all human action, even gratuitous, and often cruel or antisocial, is, in some sense, ethical. Parts of our society now confront each other over the gravest moral issues of life and death (capital punishment, abortion, genetic manipulation, euthanasia, etc.), things that politics is badly equipped to settle in its profane routine, except in drastic cases of self-preservation. And yet morality, rightly understood, is the perplexing minefield where we all live. Traditionally, religion has animated it, law has given it a shell to inhabit, opinion has calibrated it, and politics has been domesticated by its force and persuasion.

Morality has been described by Oakeshott as "a vernacular language . . . [that] intimates considerations to be subscribed to in making choices, in performing actions, and in pursuing purposes." A moral education is obtained by learning "how to speak the language intelligently."[4] If this is so, our predicament is partly involved in how we communicate and in the relationship of the language of morals to the languages of faith and knowledge. It has frequently been remarked that America, once thought to be a nation temperamentally rooted in mundane and intensely practical affairs, has grown overly fond of abstract concepts. Several accounts of this might be given. First of all, it is true that many of our earliest settlers had an incorrigible metaphysical bent: difficult words such as *election, salvation, grace,* and *atonement* came easily to their lips. Second, one might argue that the penchant for abstraction is the natural consequence of the postindustrial organization of multiple empirical activities and processes. However, a third reason is probably the most valid: the linguistic shift is directly related to the increase in size and importance of the "knowledge estate" and the imposition of its dialect upon the general population. In other words, we are speaking of what is in large part a sociological phenomenon related both to the new needs of communication and to imperatives of dominance and social control. Some might count this a blessing and a coming of age: a vulgarization of intellectual resources in the best sense, an expanded capacity of Americans to deal with the serious issues of the world, an instrument for nationalizing a widely dispersed continental people, and a crosscutting agent of democracy. Unfortunately, it is none of these things. Hobbes's famous sovereign was the wielder of not only the sword but the dictionary;[5] we seem gradually submitted to a sovereign newspeak.

Quite aside from the abstract vocabularies needed for working at the creative frontiers of knowledge and the coinages of living argot (where the "big words" are used ironically), we have gone far toward developing a *koiné* disembodied from concrete institutions and practices, loaded with clumsy solecisms and vagrancies of definition, alien to civil discourse, and, most certainly, "disenchanted." What is more, this medium of expression, both pallid and periphrastic, has become an essential tongue for those who wish to make waves in the world. It debases politics, religion, and most of what it touches.

The new language tends to sedate a culture for the most part already weary of literacy. In so doing, it probably smooths or settles many of the quarrels that arise in a situation of fragmented moral pluralism. At least the angriness of the American self or selves is muted by the forms and phrases in which people now learn to communicate. The blandness of common "intelligent" discourse is not totally inane; it is also preservative, functioning in place of the waning communities of family, school, church, and state and their specific tongues. That is why rebellious attacks against both primary and inclusive institutions customarily have a language dimension: stuttering ambiguity, "filthy speech," ethnic dialects proclaimed as normative, "female" improvements on "chauvinistic" grammatical constructions, glossolalia in the "charismatic" religious movements, and so forth (the appearance of an acronym like *est* in minuscules at the head of a scholarly sentence says it all). Those resistances are both plaintive and plausible. Their target is not really Shakespeare, the King James Bible, Dr. Johnson, or Jane Austen. It is the language of the modern academy, bureaucracy, and communications industry. It is the "unhappy consciousness" of modern life itself. This accounts also in part for the power of fundamentalism and nostalgia. Why should "scriptural inerrancy" be less privileged and persuasive than the jargon of a government ordinance? Why should truth be discovered more readily in the *Washington Post* than in the *Wealth of Nations?* A Harvard professor once told me without any twinkle in his eye that it was foolish to read Aristotle, since one could capture his insights in modern texts while avoiding his many mistakes.

Has "bourgeois reason" then failed? It has failed only to the extent that reason *tout court* (which is far more venerable than the modern industrial class and its courtiers) was restricted to "cognition" or else naively charged with having created the illicit dominance of some over others, with having despoiled nature (our ancestors feared bears, now we pat them), with having dehumanized the "person" (a Latin word meaning first actor's mask and then a subject of law), or with having inaugurated the despotic reign of mass society ("masses" is a term used by decent intelligent members of the middle class to designate inferiors or by communist ideologues as a term of strength and approbation). Although leading academics have defined intellectuals as all those involved in any way in the processing of culture as opposed to material goods[6]—akin to calling the Kellner "Herr Ober-kellner"—a sharp distinction should be made between true intellectuals—persons of wit, culture, and devotion to ideas—and the so-called knowledge estate. John Stuart Mill once wrote: "No progress at all can be made toward obtaining a skilled democracy unless the democracy [i.e., the less educated and fortunate] are willing that the work which requires skill should be done by those who possess it."[7] This seems to be a basic argument for having a knowledge estate and for distinguishing between it and the "democracy" in capacity and service. Perhaps it is: except that Mill assigned his experts an intensive role of educating the public and concluded that "participation should everywhere be as great as the general degree of improvement of the community will allow; and that nothing less can be ultimately desirable than the admission of all to a share in the sovereign power of the state."[8] Mill's faith in education and participation was, we may judge, naive on the evidence—partly because, unlike Tocqueville, he saw organized religion as a barrier, not an aid, to the civic effects he wished to achieve. In fact, however, while like most other liberals (Constant is another example) seeing "ideas" and "principles" as the main forces that move the universe,[9] Mill most certainly did not want a supercilious class of knowledge-therapy experts to dominate men's thoughts. That, however, has become a part of the problem in America and other Western countries. It has happened, most obviously, because a class was needed to service and promote exaggerated political promises of the "good life" and because temptations of translating knowledge into power were hard to resist. But it has also come about because of the demolition of traditional restraints, conspicuously religious, that might have unmasked the futility, and even the emptiness, of such expectations. Constant, who came to appreciate personal religion while continuing to dislike all organization or "sacerdotalism," wrote, in anticipation of Tocqueville: "We detest an intolerant power, but we fear the philosophical power."[10] His point—like Rousseau's—was that secular knowledge was just as apt to become a fanaticism as religion and, given the spirit of the age, with even harsher consequences.[11]

Kant's three famous epistemological questions are relevant here: "What can I know?" "What ought I to do?" "What may I hope?" In Kant's formulation, the questions were employed to distinguish the spheres of theoretical reason (science), practical reason (ethics), and rational faith (religion). We can use them for a somewhat different sociological purpose. Hope, as Tocqueville pointed out, is the common currency of the human being and is closely connected with faith.[12] It is presumably shared by the most brilliant theoretical physicist and the humblest manual worker. It is the anchor-point of both thought and action. In the case of the "new class" of postindustrial society, however, the questions "What can I know?" and "What may I hope?" are so intimately linked in the procurement of esteem and favorable life-chances that they have a tendency to exclude the ethical inquiry. Conversely, the lot of the humble is to remain in drastic ignorance of much of the "new knowledge" and the possibilities of knowing it; for this vast majority of people there is an instinctive connection between the questions "What may I hope?" and "What ought I to do?" Hope is a prelude to action, and it is substantially through action that the objects of hope must be procured. Multiple consequences follow from this fact. For many people imperatives of action are blended with a sufficiency of practical knowledge, and thus hope is stabilized, although, even here, work processes are sometimes so routinized or drained of ethical content as to bring on demoralization. For others, hope and action must be sustained by the kind of faith taught by a church or sect that promises supernatural reward for the just life. For still others, the hopeful plunge into action means resistance or revolution, based on a mixture of despair and visions of a profane *parousia*. This is one of the ways that lines tend to be drawn in our world, and we might append to Kant's first question that other one of T.S. Eliot: "After such knowledge, what forgiveness?"[13]

Two of the greatest abstractions that mankind has been called on to wrestle with are *freedom* and *truth*. One of the functions of the higher religions has been to disclose a cosmos of truth in which, sometimes against all appearances, a human felicity akin to the feeling of freedom is sustained. Christianity affirmed this most strikingly: "The truth shall make you free."[14] Behind that word "free" is a whole congested memory of previous bondages: in Egypt, in Babylon, to false gods, to the dried-up letter of the law. In Christianity freedom is

alleged to flow from a vast single complex truth that is too discursive
for human reason to capture, one that is validated finally by faith,
"the evidence of things not seen."[15] Protestantism, in revolt against
the peculations of a corrupt papacy, took faith to be the condition of
salvation rather than the chief access to truth through freedom ("the
liberty wherewith Christ has made us free"),[16] thereby creating a
dogmatism of its own.

The relativistic modern mind has stubbornly refused to give up
these words, although it has made them mean so many different
things that it toils amid this rich, dark incoherence. "Truths" are
multiple and probabilistic: in the last analysis, since life-chances and
individual talents never make us equal, egalitarianism dictates that
"your truth is as good as my truth." A "truth" of science is defined
as something capable of refutation; otherwise it is a sort of faith.
"Freedom," from at least the eighteenth century on, was subdivided
into "metaphysical," "civil," and "political."[17] Subsequently we became acquainted with "ancient" (political) and "modern" (civil) liberty,[18] translated by way of Kant's moral philosophy[19] and the usage
of T.H. Green[20] into "positive" and "negative." And all the while,
with roots reaching deep into the feudalistic Middle Ages, we have
been accustomed to dealing with specific freedoms (rights, privileges,
and exemptions granted exceptionally by a higher power) as well as
freedom *tout court* (perceived as a constant necessity of the human
condition, especially as opposed to slavery). It is hardly the place
here to begin coping with these complications, except to note that
while exercising our mental capacities, the profusion of ways in
which freedom and truth are understood, analyzed, and related reduces us almost to a psychological self-definition of these terms: *truth*
is what I am most convinced of; *freedom* is what I experience when I
feel most directly able to supply my wants.

Of course the problematic of freedom and truth does not stop here.
In the first place, our feelings of freedom change with mood and situation, and our notions of truth can be altered by experience and evidence, or even persuasion. Second, the possession of *my* freedom
and *my* truth is usually prudentially attached to a concession that others may have *theirs*, which are distinctly not mine, so long as they do
not try to extinguish my freedom and my truth. Third, we have the
inescapable feeling that truth (whose actuality we must at least opera-
tionally accept—in family life, in business dealings, in the law courts,
in the laboratory) lies essentially beyond our competence and control
(hence the needs for faith and conciliation), whereas freedom is some-

thing we can immediately experience, perhaps even shape, if not "know," and is a matter of perceived gradations, as truth is not.

Freedom and truth in the sacred sphere are supposed to be one. The suspicion that they are not, that "truth" can be obtained only by the exercise of multiple and conflicting "freedoms" or that "freedom" is a condition of admitting or accepting multiple "truths," is a strong argument to deny the sacred altogether, to regard it as a ruse by which the powerful extract their pound of flesh from the weak. The alternative is then to reduce sacred freedom and sacred truth to being merely a tiny portion of competing claims in the profane marketplace, in full expectation that these claims will compete dismally against the others. The scriptural version of pluralism is somewhat different: "Now there are diversities of gifts, but the same Spirit. And there are differences of administration, but the same Lord."[21] And theology competently parries the secularist charge by denying the modern definition of freedom, according to which he who feels most unconstrained in a world of self-created meaning, or at least feels most genuinely responsible to himself, is freest. The political theory spun off by a religious culture may indeed foster human freedoms in the profane sphere that accept the trial-and-error of personal morality and the prudential practices of public morality. It is not, however, in a position to absolve the errors of "situation ethics," for that is the task of the sacred. And no sacred theology can regard its own view of freedom—other than the undoubted freedom to err—as situational; for it, freedom involves a transcending of law and politics that incorporates worship, service, love, and even supererogatory performances that are not what ethics calls "strict duties." Moreover, sacred freedom is in part a determinism, at least as seen from the viewpoint of profane voluntarism. It reminds man, in the words of the psalm, that "it is he that hath made us, and not we ourselves."[22] This should not seem so very strange, since the secular world also imposes all manner of authorities and obligations on us, which we accept, even as part of the tradeoff of "free" societies. It was the modern liberation from crude secular bondages that culminated in Kant's spectacular demonstration that, in order to preserve a universal foundation of liberty, the sacred had to be proposed as the result rather than the source of our free moral action.[23] However, sacred determinism can also be seen as the *juste milieu* of freedom and control. As Reinhold Niebuhr has written: "The traditional debate between voluntarism and determinism in the history of thought has been aggravated in modern culture by the fact that modern forms of determinism have annulled human freedom more completely than Christian ideas of Providence; and modern forms of voluntarism have asserted the freedom of man more absolutely than either classical or Christian theories."[24] The condition for having truth at all, as opposed to "interested" truths that must be negotiated or truths ranked by their usefulness to the commodity of mundane life, is that truth is radically exclusive of us, precedes our discovery of it, and, while invested by us with its highest value, is not created by man's free acts of intellect and will. And clearly both faith and loyalty place entailments on freedom. One does not ask here: What is it to be truly free (in the sense that one might fly)? One asks: What qualities of freedom are compatible with faith and loyalty?

Truth and freedom are quite otherwise in the profane sphere. There they are fluctuating and always open to challenge; they must be excavated from original meanings and retranslated as the centuries pass and as culture collides on culture. They go through trends and cycles. In some epochs they are stringently controlled; in others they are released to the centrifugal imagination of "open societies." Their sullen imposition breeds frustration and tyranny; their relaxation inspires feverish creativity and, carried too far, a kind of paralytic schizogenesis and a moral night where all cats are gray. Plato described such a process typologically in the eighth book of the *Republic*. In that regard, it is common to damn Plato for endorsing the rule of the wise and deprecating democracy. Rarely, however, is it noticed that it required a democracy to produce and educate a Socrates, and that the flagrantly individualistic polity of this text would scarcely have bothered to condemn Socrates for offending religion and corrupting the youth (who would have given it a thought?). It is not Plato's regime preferences but the remorselessness of his cycle that fascinates us in this remarkable passage.

In the profane sphere truth and freedom also constantly bump into each other. We cannot for long reconcile truth and freedom in ourselves without committing some deceit, for we are always accosted by social responsibilities and decisions that revise our views of them. Scarcely are we out the door and five blocks down the street when we happen on some occasion that poses these alternatives. Our freedom to take the bus is thwarted by the undoubted truth that we do not have the correct change. Our freedom to enjoy the pleasures of grand opera tonight is thwarted by the truth that an admired soprano has laryngitis. The truth that we are bored out of our wits at a party does not activate the freedom to leave, since our spouse is having a good time. Our freedom to vote for whomever we choose does not produce truth in the outcome of the election. The truth that is widely felt to inhere in the abolition of chattel slavery still permits us the freedom of acting slavishly. I have given deliberately banal examples because the contest between truth and freedom in profane existence, besides being indecisive, is frequently banal.

Sometimes, however, it is not. That is most likely to be so in politics, the ultimate control system of the profane. From Hesiod's time to the Renaissance it was believed that the deviance of a ruler from the ways of truth could so miserably afflict a society that the pleasures of the tyrant himself would be made nugatory.[25] Although King David was free to seduce Bathsheba and to have her husband Uriah killed in battle, the failure of truth in his act cost his people dearly. King James II of England followed truth as he perceived it, with consequences for the public definition of freedom that led to his involuntary abdication. The absolute truth of the French Jacobins was the denial of freedom, and often life, to those suspected of opposition. The Gulag has taken care of persons whose exercise of freedom collided with "objective truth." The most poignant examples, however, are those in which rulers or magistrates must deliberately violate some factual or moral truth in order to protect the freedom of the governed. The most recent case, as I write these words, is the Israeli air strike against the nuclear reactor outside Baghdad. But examples proliferate in all instances of civil war and international crisis. This is the famous problem of "dirty hands." It is most profoundly explored by Max Weber in his notion of an "ethics of responsibility,"[26] and has been much debated of late by philosophers who either grant or refuse to grant a greater component of "consequentialism" to official public actions than would seem permissible in private relations.[27] In all these ways, freedom and truth, as we understand them, collide in our profane existence. The perils of imposing what we take to be sacred standards on events in our far-from-perfect world are evident, and our loss of confidence in secularized postmillennialism chastens us. We must then take justice to be a problem constantly raised, and never a self-fulfilling historical prophecy. At very least, the power to achieve the good no longer seems an unqualified attribute of the species, as the Enlightenment had taught. Conversely, the humanistic profanation of the sacred provides us only with a familiarity that breeds contempt, transferring all the profane dilemmas of freedom and truth to what survives of the sacred sphere. Reaching toward the good through profane discovery is not the way of the world. Such optimism denies all reason by making the world—our "postindustrial" world of the late twentieth century—the standard for judging not only all history, all memory and expectation, but also the unimaginable space and time of the cosmos itself.

A significant separation of the sacred and the profane returns us to the reality of this earth, but it does not privilege the earth against the mysterious, unforeseeable, and remote sources of hope and truth. The profane order has its own established, but alterable, ways of preservative control. These have usually been influenced, balanced, and moderated by the conceptions we have formed of the sacred. On the other hand, the organization of the profane does not lie within a sacred bondage, as our deep sense of free will and choice teaches us. We are therefore collectively responsible for the preservation of civilized life—for the civility—we have arduously created since we were all hominids, and later nomadic food-gatherers. That is essentially the task of politics. The task of religion is to provide us with a collectively persuasive pattern of cosmic meaning, a common ethic that transcends both self-interest and the prescriptions of public law, and a set of rituals that discipline our memory and give us a place of action in the precincts of the sacred. It goes without saying, then, that religion requires institutionalization over as wide a space as there is a common preservative impulse and a common moral territory. This is the means by which the control system of the sacred enters our affairs and persists in the world.

Since sacred institutions are obviously corruptible, much like the profane ones, pious souls have often felt that they should be abolished or at least restricted to very small and pure communities of believers. The "positivity" of religion has often been seen as involving impediments to faith.[28] There is some truth in the argument. On the other hand, as our exploration of American religious culture and the "Protestant paradigm" has tried to show, there are dangers in fissionable sectarianism where moral territories are multiplied, especially within a single political unit, and there are even worse consequences in an atomized faith that enshrouds the individual in privacy and solitude. For all its smug and arrogant forfeitures, denominationalism was a better solution than these others, for, while denying the belligerent doctrine of *extra ecclesia nulla salus,* it could negotiate a moral compact that suited a moderately pluralized political and social system.[29] It could also accommodate a variety of internal ecclesiastical constitutions, ranging from rather strict hierarchy, through mixed government, to a good deal of congregational democracy. I have nowhere in this study bedecked American Protestantism with flowery compliments. Rather, I have not been only critical but pessimistic regarding its affiliated political and religious tendencies in this country. But I cannot be cheered by the indictments made of this same history by *terribles simplificateurs,* or by the accelerated fragmentation of our political culture and its spiritual supports.

I believe I have said enough about the "secularist" option. Might there not, however, be a Catholic or "Catholicizing" option for America? In many respects—especially given substantial, though anguished, revisions in Catholic exclusivity made since Vatican II—this is an attractive idea or at least a basis for negotiating a moral community founded on the presence and distinctiveness of the sacred. Gallup polls currently show that, as never before in our history, Catholics and Protestants have a reciprocal tolerance for each others' beliefs.[30] Moreover, the Catholic, and more tolerant, population of America inches up, year by year, toward numerical equality. In my judgment, one of the advantages Catholicism possesses in our time of stress is its seminal skepticism toward the superior virtues of any sort of nationalistic postmillennialism and its practiced and realistic concentration on the here-and-now, without capitulation to secularism. Another is its Molinist subtlety in treating contrition and forgiveness in the profane context of human events. Casuistry aside, Catholicism acknowledges that men are of this earth and that sacred absolution is incessantly ready to restore them to earthly efficacy if they have not transgressed abominably.

There are, however, several stumbling blocks in the way. They do not preclude forthcoming Catholic contributions to the American resolution, but they make the project difficult. One of these is that we do not live in an even remotely Catholic culture, taken in the large. The power of certain eminent Catholic prelates in the past to affect outcomes in American politics (notably during the New Deal) has ebbed with the increased independence of the laity from church politics, a result of rising status. Moreover, even in the nineteenth century, leaders of the Catholic hierarchy had themselves been partly Protestantized, i.e., liberalized and inclined to denominationalism and compromise with the prevailing culture. Archbishop Ireland and Cardinal Gibbons shocked the Vatican with their transparent "Americanism," which was thereupon castigated with respect to "modernist" developments in the French Church.[31] This pattern was not abolished by the multiple absorptions of "ethnicity" or by the mobilization of Catholic voting blocks, and it has been reaffirmed more recently by progressive ("post-Protestant") declarations on both politics and ecclesiastical issues by influential Catholic churchmen, seconded by many in the regular clergy and orders, and among the intellectuals. At very least, the days of Cardinal Spellman and Cardinal McIntyre are over. I do not mean to suggest that these developments have no logic within the internal debates of Catholicism itself or that their rapprochement with certain liberal Protestant positions is injurious to religious concord. However, there is some evidence that American Catholicism has embarked on its own versions of privatization and secularization—even its dress rehearsal of the "Protestant paradigm," minus the fundamentalist ferocity that one finds in extreme Protestant evangelicalism (which is of course precluded by the whole Catholic emphasis on mediation by authority and traditional interpretation). Also, in striking similarity with the mainstream Protestant denominations, the American Catholic laity is less modernist than the clergy, as well as less devout. The point is, then, that Catholicism will probably, as time passes, be in less of a position to contribute distinctive solutions of its own, especially in the sphere of faith, to the American problematic of the sacred. Catholics indeed have their developed views on questions of war, capitalism, the family, communal life, and political competence to offer the nation, but the major difference lies in the rationale, not in the pragmatic consequences; and that rationale is often inaccessible to the Protestant mind.

A second feature, linked to the foregoing, is that beneath the surface of an ancient and time-tested uniformity of sacred institutions and processes, the Roman Catholic Church, here as elsewhere, is experiencing wider pluralization. It is not just, or even chiefly, an ethnic pluralization, stimulated by the repudiation of the Latin mass, but a pluralization of vital elements of belief, of questions of autonomy and obedience, of ways of leading the moral life, and of the relations of the sacred and the profane. Here as well, the lines are differently drawn than those within Protestantism, but it is becoming increasingly difficult to speak in America on basic issues with an integral Catholic voice.

The intellectual substructure of the Catholic view on moral, social, and political concerns was traditionally an adaptation of the great synthesis of St. Thomas Aquinas, "the angelic doctor." Neo-Thomism—articulated forcefully in the writings of Jacques Maritain, Yves Simon, John Courtney Murray, and others—proved resilient enough seven hundred years removed from its source to provide a humane theory of community and democracy and compelling enough to attract the interest of some non-Catholic intellectuals. It was not, however, a doctrine that could capture the fidelity of liberal Protestants or secularizers, for its mediation of the realms of grace and nature suggested a church-state solution that was not in the American grain. Furthermore, it fitted badly with all postmillennialist ideologies—nativist, liberal, or Marxist. *Qua* Catholic, it could not suit Protestant premillennialism, either. It harbored suspicions about capitalist profit-taking, but it could not manage to nourish a Christian socialism in a country hostile to affixing religious labels to political movements. Today, within Catholicism, neo-Thomism is challenged, and sometimes beaten, by new theologies (ranging from the radical Christology of Hans Küng to the Marxist-influenced "liberationists") and, in this country, by a variety of existentialist, evangelical, secularizing, and "post-Protestant" influences. Even had the neo-Thomists been able to conduct any sustained dialogue with Protestants a generation ago, such an opportunity has now virtually disappeared.

The closest linkage between the Catholic and Protestant minds in America is in the Pauline and Augustinian traditions. That, too, is not an easy reunion because post-Tridentine as well as post-Vatican II Catholicism both submerge these currents of doctrine, while liberal Protestantism (except for the flurry of "neo-orthodoxy" that came and went in the past generation) tends to disregard it, too, although not for the same reasons. The plunge of the church into the world and the judgment of the church by the world are not conspicuously welcoming to this current of thought. It obviously cannot form the basis for any religious entente if it is subscribed to literally or "fundamentally." Indeed, a great deal of Protestant fundamentalism, if I understand it correctly, is hostile to this doctrine. St. Paul never aspired to write the Gospel into law. He encouraged the church to encamp and spread its message in an adversary world regulated by civil observances, not to spend vital energies by opposing those powers but by creating a parallel and more compelling sphere of action. St. Augustine wrote his greatest work not only to show that we are agents of some ultimate design toward which reason draws us while leaving us unsatisfied at the portals of faith but to diminish our expectations of the millennium and to cast back these disappointments on our ongoing earthly performances, especially our political ones.[32]

America was, I think, founded on this kind of understanding, although it also abounded in expressions of millennial catastrophism and millennial optimism that have surfaced often in our history. Of these two options, both well removed from the central doctrines of St. Paul and St. Augustine, the second has been the more pernicious because it easily flowed over into secularity and convinced generations of Americans that their personal successes in business, sports, sexuality, or worldly reputation were pleasing to the divine plan, and that these successes, as well as being signs of favor, were instances of human evolution toward divinity. In the last analysis, the least destructive of exclusivisms is that of the invisible moral community connected with hope and uncertainty. But it is very difficult to see how different strains of Americans could become united on this notion and use it as both an instigation and a foil to their politics.

This is, however, the version of a sacred control system that is most apt to keep controls from sliding into what Tocqueville called a "soft despotism" in a period when Americans are being compelled to learn that they are like the others. Tradition and situation preclude that *vivere civile* in its intense republican connotation can be more than a nostalgic storm warning: it was hardly much more than that at the Constitutional Convention of 1787. However, it is on the margin of possibility that some reconstructed theory of the sacred and profane could ease our bewilderment in the world.

There is quite obviously no "Judaic option" in this country, but there is an ineradicable Judaic ingredient. Aside from the fact that American Jews have had an intellectual and commercial impact on the United States far beyond their numbers, it is of great significance that Judaism survives in the world—and most vigorously in America—because it has known how to combine integralism with pluralism. Here we should distinguish the empirical situation of various groups of Jews from the spirit that animates them. With regard to political and social life, the Jews, more so than the Catholics, have entered a Protestant culture and been torn by it. Some are resolutely secular and agnostic in belief either because this has seemed the most effective way to move in the forefront of a threatening world or because it is the best insulation from historic Christian bigotry. Others authentically cleave to the *mores* of a chosen remnant, and emphasize it to the discomfort even of other Jews. Many shades of attitude and practice exist between these extremes. The important fact to grasp, however, is that in the great diaspora following Titus's destruction of the Second Temple of Jerusalem in 70 A.D., the majority of stricken Jews accepted the Pharisaic doctrine that the temple was now to be found in the hearts of true believers, that it was movable like the ark of ancient times, but was now internalized in the person if only his faith could be sustained by wisdom, interpretation, and unity, and in a constancy of hope and expectation.[33] Although most Christians regard Pharisaism as a narrow belief that was strictured in the Gospels and overcome in the preaching of a converted Saul of Tarsus, its historic function was actually to make an insular nation fit for living abroad under the worst conditions, while remaining in enduring possession of its faith. This extraordinary adaptation recalls both the

Protestant dispersion from the sacred authority of Rome and the Catholic respect for interpretation and tradition. Since the Judaic experience has incorporated both these elements and has, above all, instructed its faithful in how to commemorate the sacred while living in the toils of the profane, Jews rejoin Christians in a deeper and wider version of the Pauline and Augustinian traditions, sensed with an acuity that goes beyond any motley civil religion or shallow vision of the "American Way of Life." Or at least, if this is not the present fact of the case, it, too, reposes, historically and experientially, on the margin of the possible.

The major problem is not, then, in the incongruity of the American strains of faith in a sacred perspective, but the susceptibility of all of them to disenchantment and the unsettled balance—the destruction of Tocquevillian "harmonization"—between the ultimate control systems of the sacred and the profane. As widely noted, this has come about in an age when politics was never more dangerous, when competence to devise and direct political strategies was never rarer or more difficult for laymen to judge, and when free political life itself was never more threatened by its own "impracticalities."

If we have such vexations in understanding the existing manifold of pressures and events, we are even more confused by the placement of that manifold in time and in the conquest of its dynamic meaning. It is not outrageous to say that we are becoming a people without a history, fulfilling that trait which Tocqueville noticed when he came here in 1831.[34]

The traditional form of sacred history ceased to be written toward the end of the seventeenth century in England, France, and Germany. Attempts by American Calvinist theologians like Edwards to continue the project were not of far-reaching influence in Western civilization. Neither the Bible nor the speculation of early Church fathers like Augustine and Orosius were any longer felt to be plausible guides to man's collective self-understanding. Aside from the critical onslaught by Bayle and others, sacred history was undermined in two directions: first, by the substitution of the profane ideologies of liberalism, positivism, and Marxism as total explanations of the course of the world (all of these retaining some obviously metaphysical elements); and second, by a comparative history of civilizations stressing variety and uniqueness and downplaying the likelihood or desirability of moral or religious convergence.

Today it is almost equally impossible to write profane world history, with or without any reference to transhuman goals. The achievement of Arnold J. Toynbee has been regarded mainly as a *beau geste*. While we may pride ourselves in our historical sensitivity, tools, and training—in brief, our aptitude for research and recovery—we are less able to write the total story of ourselves in any convincing pattern of creative or mythic development than at any time since Herodotus. The great secularist ideologies have been mostly shattered and the value of variety has been confused with that of incoherence. Philosophy of history tends to become an analytic or rhetorical examination of how people have written history. Our last, and weakest, attempt to propound the way of the world has been called the "comparative history of modernization," a spiritless effigy of the secular enthusiasms of the nineteenth century. This is the world history that America has rejoined. Perhaps it is a fulfillment of Emerson's *boutade* that all history is biography.[35] Where centrifugal pluralism sweeps away established institutional focuses without being able to replace them, the evidence is that it proceeds to further fragmentation. It is the same with historical patterns, as indeed it is with all landmarks of conviction.

Conviction is, however, at the base of both the religious and the political enterprises. It is not, in the last analysis, convenience that brings politics to birth and gives it its milk, nor is religion some simple extrapolation of biorhythms or a genial production of the poetic and dramatic impulses. What matters is communities bound together by conviction. The other factors are secondary, arising when persons gain the aptitude to raise the question: what kind of religious or political structure really suits us and pleases us? To that extent, politics and religion are alike. As concrete practices of conviction, they are also, to turn the coin over, systems of control, for shared beliefs demand that persons act in such a way and create institutions to the end that deviancy will not threaten to tear the fabric apart. I have already shown how, for purposes of the set of problems presented here, the controls of politics and religion meet in the field of public morality. There is no need to retort that this is, rather, the function of *opinion:* What shapes opinion?

At this point the exigencies of the sacred and the profane and the particularities of their control systems take over. From the primal source of conviction, we now become aware of dichotomies that distinguish politics from religion. They are of the order that I conveyed earlier in my comments on John Locke and Karl Barth.[36] Thus discriminated, politics and religion are in a position to compete or collaborate (both in the realm of conviction and in the play of institutions, which are themselves a sort of congealed conviction). Their relation will never be frictionless, but ideally the community is soundest when they share the burden of preserving it. As vehicles of conviction, they are mutually in a position not only to conjugate self-interest but to demand sacrifice. The essential mechanisms by which religion and politics operate on members of a community are, respectively, faith and loyalty.

Faith is a conviction that may be subject to a reasonable doubt, but that overweighs that doubt with its own evidence. Faith is not totally unreflective, for it is a conviction experienced in a world of living, moving, and untrustworthy objects: it is the passion that survives these confrontations after they have been reflected on. Whether it partakes of a higher order of reality than reason is not the subject of this book. All I shall have to say on that score is that faith is a real presence in human life. Because faith tests itself against the world and not just against some omnipotent and numinous force, its content and meaning are social and not merely personal. The faithful are a *we*. Although faith "may be defined as fidelity to our own being—so far as such being is not and cannot become an object of the senses,"[37] this fidelity is meaningless without earthly application. Fidelity, as Gabriel Marcel has expressed it, incorporates two elements: constancy and presence. "It may even be said," he writes, ". . . that I am constant for myself, in my own regard, for my purpose—where I am *present* for the other, and more precisely: for *thou*."[38] This *thou* may, of course, be several or many, although not multiplied infinitely. Faith, mixed with piety and also many of the same bonds that unite secular communities, is the appropriate form of religious conviction. Its opposites are *incredulity* and *faithlessness*. It is a contribution of the Judaeo-Christian heritage; one may rummage through all the ethical writings of Aristotle without finding any conception remotely resembling it.

Loyalty is the basic positive conviction of politics.[39] *Allegiance* is its close synonym. Its opposite is "treason"; but we will immediately notice that because the properties of the profane control system have evolved differently from those of the sacred, loyalty is not tested with such ultimacy as the faith of the religious believer. This is made explicit by the notion of a "loyal opposition," which, from the eighteenth century on, was developed in the Western constitutional states.[40] Nonetheless, the sectarian impulses of Protestantism have also, in their way, allowed for "faithful" oppositions. As Hegel wrote about congregationalism, with special reference to the faith preached by Schleiermacher:

Every moment the groupings alter like the patterns in a sea of sand given over to the play of the winds. Yet at the same time—as is only fair—every group regards the private and distinctive peculiarity of its view as something as otiose and even unremarkable that it does not mind whether it is acknowledged or not, and gives us all claims to objectivity. All these little groups can stay peacefully side by side in a pervasive atomism; and certainly the enlightened separation of church and state fits in here very nicely.[41]

Hegel's irony could easily have been a comment on the fortunes of the "Protestant paradigm" in America, where, however, the diffusion of faith, attached, as Tocqueville remarks, to a common morality and sustaining, at least for a time, political loyalty, seemed to render the question of "objectivity" moot. Loyalty was indeed built around a common feeling of novelty and distinctiveness. In Bancroft's words: "In the fullness of time a republic arose in the wilderness of America. . . . From whatever there was of good in the systems of former centuries she drew her nourishment; the wrecks of the past were her warning."[42] But loyalty, unlike faith, is preservative in the profane sphere and subject to its many fluctuations. It is not pure, and it is in part calculating, because the state is not the only profane institution to which it may be extended.

Albert O. Hirschman has, I think, expressed this difference particularly well with reference to "firms, organizations, and states":

> The intimation of some influence and the expectation that, over a period of time, the right turns will more or less balance the wrong ones, profoundly distinguishes loyalty from faith. A glance at Kierkegaard's celebrated interpretation of Abraham's setting out to sacrifice Isaac makes one realize that, in comparison to that act of pure faith, the most loyalist behavior retains an enormous dose of reasoned calculation. . . . Loyalty, far from being irrational, can serve the socially useful purpose of preventing deterioration from becoming cumulative, as it so often does when there is no barrier to exit.[43]

Hirschman, as an economist, might disagree with my view that there is something value-specific about a state (as opposed to a firm or a supermarket) that conditions loyalty in a particularly profound way (legal, territorial, and ancestral), and that disloyalty is not a light position to take with regard to one's country. That aside, there is much truth in the way he presents the profane conviction as against the sacred one. In point of fact, faith and loyalty often become confused. But conceptually they are quite specific. Their characteristics also help to define the resources of the institutions they create.

There is no more succinct, though paradoxical, interpreter of this distinction than David Hume. Hume, it will be recalled, distinguished radically in his philosophy between "relations of ideas" (mathematical and logical deductions) and "matters of fact" (experience). Since "the contrary of every matter of fact is still possible,"[44] it follows that their veridical standing is always probabilistic. Reasoning concerning matters of fact is taken to include "moral reasoning, or that concerning matter of fact and existence. . . ."[45] Virtually all of Hume's philosophy is concerned with this latter (probabilistic) branch of inquiry, whose dignity he rescues in the end from extreme skepticism by declaring that "Nature will always maintain her rights, and prevail in the end over any abstract reasoning whatsoever."[46] This appeal to nature or, more properly, "human nature," is the method by which Hume sets out to rebuild the shattered fortress of causal reliability in our experience.

However, Hume divides his investigation in both his first major volume *(A Treatise of Human Nature)* and the subsequent reworking of its parts *(An Enquiry Concerning the Understanding* and *An Enquiry Concerning the Principles of Morals)* into two separate kinds of treatment. The "understanding" parts are intended to deal with normal causal expectation in conditions of high (be they scientific or homely) probability or of low (and hence vulnerable or refutable) probability, i.e., religious dogmas. But the "morals" parts are additionally supported by a theory of the genesis and maintenance of morality: human nature's possession of an intrinsic faculty of benevolence that oscillates between the standards of utility (by which Hume means an overcoming of narrow self-interest in view of a common interest) and the pleasure of approbation (which human beings seek and their fellows are willing to grant for virtuous actions). Otherwise, both operations repose on a similar epistemological structure, the likelihood of beliefs that are sustained, objectively and socially, by "custom and habit,"[47] or, put more scientifically, by the experience of phenomena joined in constant conjunction. In this respect, Hume critically divides phenomenal sequences considered to be mere "probabilities" from those he dignifies with the label of (probabilistic) "proofs."

It is under this former rubric (and also under the treatment of the "understanding") that he delivers his withering critiques of rational religion and that he disputes the truth of miracles, prophecies, and metaphysical claims such as the existence of God and the immortality of the soul.[48] This leads Hume to summarize: ". . . upon the whole, we may conclude, that the *Christian Religion* not only was at first attended with miracles, but even at this day cannot be believed by any reasonable person without one. More reason is insufficient to convince us of its veracity. And whoever is moved by Faith to assent to it, is conscious of a continued miracle in his own person, which subverts all the principles of his understanding and gives him a determination to believe what is most contrary to custom and experience."[49] His intention is, moreover, to return philosophy "to her true and proper province, the examination of common life. . . ."[50] Hume concludes, rather wryly: "Divinity or Theology . . . has a foundation in reason, so far as it is supported by experience [which, having already reduced reason to reasonable human expectation, he finds it not to be]. But its best and most solid foundation is in *faith* and divine revelation [i.e., certainly not the business of philosophy]."[51] He then writes significantly: "Morals and criticism are not so properly objects of the understanding as of taste and sentiment."[52] In other words, even though Hume is occasionally guilty of a phrase such as "the rules of morality and religion,"[53] he nowhere attempts to argue that their rules have anything in common. Religion does not appear to derive from any "natural" instincts of humanity (it is probably a primitive deception to be outgrown); and it is best dealt with in terms of the understanding, rather than in the more liberal and welcoming precincts of morals. Yet once Hume, facetiously or earnestly, posits a realm of faith (which to him was probably quite analogous to political fanaticism in the profane sphere), he also opens the door to fideistic interpretation. Curiously enough, Hume, for whom "rational beliefs (which in his somewhat loose fashion, he tended to identify with custom, habit, experience, nature, and the like) are to be distinguished from mere fantasy or guesswork or prejudice or superstition,"[54] gave ammunition to German proponents of faith over reason (Hamann, Jacobi, Schleiermacher), and thereby fed into the Protestant (and American Protestant) view of personal religion, described by Hegel as a "subjectivity for which beauty and truth present themselves in feelings and persuasions, in love and intellect."[55] What Hume at least did was to define a realm of faith *per hiatum*.

When we turn to *loyalty* (Hume's preferred term is usually "allegiance"), we see that it is quite differently grounded. In seeking this different grounding, Hume's analysis agrees with our general argument and with the distinction made by Hirschman. This matter is most thoroughly pursued in the *Treatise of Human Nature*. Here loyalty depends upon all the artifice or "artificial virtues" (refined on top of "natural" virtues or passions that keep human beings equidistant from Arcadia and the state of war) needed for intersociability. This mechanism takes in all that Hume intends by promises, justice, and government. However, as he argues, the mere invention of promises (i.e., contracts) is not sufficient to create a government or to endow one's allegiance to it; similarly, "imitation and custom" are not adequate to found and sanction political authority.[56]

> Though there was no such thing as a promise in the world, government would still be necessary in all large and civilized societies; and if promises had only their own proper obligation, without the separate sanction of government, they would have but little efficacy in such societies. This separates the boundaries of our public and private duties, and shows that the latter are more dependent on the former than the former on the latter. *Education* and *the artifice of politicians* concur to bestow a further morality or loyalty, and to brand all rebellion with a greater degree of guilt and infamy.[57]

This last is not meant sarcastically by Hume, as some might take it today: he was not worried about "hidden persuaders" but about the all too visible ones. Fatigued by Whig mythic exuberance and by Jacobite threats to the settlement of 1688, Hume endorsed a moderate form of political training and thought it to be in the interest of incumbent politicians to provide it. Most of all, he conceived of political loyalty as something to be imagined in a broader, more impersonal way than any intimate pledge of faith.[58] Government, and the conditions of allegiance, were not created from some kind of personal trust, but rather from an interest susceptible to stimulating loyalty, and furthermore not dependent on the form of the regime:

> This interest I find to consist in the security and protection which we enjoy in political society, and which we can never attain when perfectly free and independent. As the interest, therefore, is the immediate sanction of government, the one can have no longer being than the other; and whenever the civil magistrate carries his opposition so far as to render his authority perfectly intolerable, we are no longer bound to submit to it.[59]

That Hume is cautious about the *interest* of rebellion is made clear by his references to the uncontroversial cases of Dionysius, Nero, and Philip II. That he theorizes a doctrine of loyalty that is not blown away by appeals to individual conscience or subjective interpretations of *faith* is also clear. It is equally evident that he attempts to establish civil order by defusing faith.

Hume's division between faith and loyalty seems more substantially persuasive to the modern secularized mind than that, say, of St. Paul. The problem is that the realm of faith is claimed, or at least seems to be claimed, nugatory by a process of rational corrosion (and this by an "impure" reason): this is the face of most present anthropological evidence. A lesser problem is that the realm of loyalty is made rather cool, also against a good deal of evidence. The virtue in Hume's solution is that a division is at least made.

If Hume had framed his argument to concede (on the basis of experience) that religion was not simply a question of relative proofs and disproofs involved in processes of the "understanding," but that it was an "enracinated" cultural phenomenon on a par with morality and government, he would have been nearer the universal case. In a different social environment—one not so obsessed with the travesties of ecclesiastical control—he might have been less pugnacious on this issue. Be that as it may, Hume obviously did not give a latitude to religion that he gave to morality in his philosophical reconstruction from the depths of skepticism.

America has produced one thinker of stature who dealt with these issues urgently and seriously in his writings: Josiah Royce. Unfortunately, he cannot be presented here as a *deus ex machina,* for Royce made, in my judgment, the wrong move of assimilating faith and almost every other virtue to loyalty. In fact he laboriously constructed a "philosophy of loyalty," Protestant and neo-Calvinist in design.[60] Royce did not see the problem in the perspective of the present study and had little awareness of the specificity of politics. He wrote, in a scarcely original vein: "The good are still in the majority [disagreeing here with Robespierre and other intellectual revolutionists]. The heart of society is still healthy. . . . [But] the great limitation of our thoughtful public in America remains its inability to take sufficient control of affairs."[61] A bit later on in this meandering essay he confessed: "If I tried to formulate a political theory, it would be a very poor one; for I have no scientific comprehension of politics, no philosophy adequate to directing my choice of parties."[62] Royce was politically a kind of technocrat; this was not so menacing in his time when set against the "sinister interests" of robber barons and city bosses (L.T. Hobhouse, Sidney Webb, and other leftists also subscribed to this belief). "Only the expert," Royce wrote, "can decide . . . with clearness, whether the new is good."[63] And yet Royce managed to appeal to the wellsprings of "human sympathies" above the "narrow range" of "expertness." In order to ground his ideal of a community of loyalty, he developed a theory of a "community of interpretation" that owed much to C.S. Peirce's logic and has been carried forward in our own day in Habermas's concept of "communicative competence."[64] Thus, in the evolution of his notion of loyalty, it would be altogether wrong to accuse Royce of making some obscure leap of metaphysical faith or of resting his theory on the presence of an immediate, almost sensuous presence of *Glaube,* like Jacobi and other German Romantics. Royce was too steeped in Hegel to let subjectivity take over. Indeed, by way of his theory of interpretation he had reached the ontological conclusion that "a community behaves like an entity with a mind of its own,"[65] and that if "all experience must be *at least* individual experience," it is impoverished unless "it is also *social* experience."[66]

Royce's spiritual collectivism was in no sense consanguinous as it had been for Aristotle, who had written at the dawn of Western moral speculation, "The attachment of cousins and other relatives is an extension of the affection between brothers going back to their common ancestry, and their mutual sympathy is greater or less according as they are more nearly or more distantly connected with the common ancestor," and had accorded less value to "utilitarian friendship."[67] Nor did Royce ever stop at a narrow nationalism, but instead held that "the logical development of the loyal spirit is . . . the rise of the consciousness of the ideal of an [*sic*] universal community which, despite all warfare and jealousy, and despite all varieties of gods and of laws, is supreme in value, however remote from the present life of civilization."[68] These attitudes both locate him and distance him from other interpretations of collectivism and organicism in his time, which ranged from neo-Hegelianism to the religious commitments of the Social Gospellers. What Royce especially rejected were the rapacious commercialism of the "American Way of Life" and the different individualisms of men like James and Spencer. Perhaps his bearings come most directly from the Anglo-American legacy of Coleridge: "Each man in a numerous society is not only coexistent with, but virtually organized into, the multitude of which he is an integral part. His *idem* is modified by the *alter.* And there arise impulses and objects from this synthesis of *alter et idem,* myself and my neighbour."[69]

Although, as we shall presently see, Royce took as his fundamental communal model the brotherhood of faith and loyalty preached by St. Paul to the early Christians, which he called the "Beloved Community,"[70] his illustrations of the master virtue, meaning "the *practically devoted love of an individual for a community,*"[71] have so many social and political applications that we can touch on them briefly without moving into the field of theology.

Without canvassing the deeper problems of Royce's idealist philosophy, we can commence by describing him as a hierarchical pluralist, once again resembling Hegel in this regard. As Smith has written: ". . . although loyalty seems to be inseparably connected with religion for Royce, he continually emphasized the wealth and variety of concrete enterprises in which the spirit of loyalty plays an all-important part."[72] Greater loyalties were constructed out of smaller social building-blocks. This was in some ways not unlike the position John Dewey came to hold some twenty-five years later in his conceptual effort to construct the "Great Community,"[73] but there is a manifest gulf between the two thinkers: the one pragmatic, egalitarian, rather contemptuous of *esprit de clocher,* and, above all, secular; the other idealist, hierarchical, appreciative of provincialism, and religious to the core. Because Royce placed such a premium on loyalty—not convenience, not consent, not obligation in the secular sense—as the cement of community, he was deeply attuned to the damning perils of treason. "Our theory of evil," he remarked, "is indeed no 'shallow optimism.'"[74] He held that "the breaking of the once plighted faith is always a disloyal act, unless the discovery that the original undertaking involves one in disloyalty to the general cause of loyalty requires the change."[75] This is not a type of analysis with which Dewey would have felt at all comfortable. There is also a dogmatism of loyalty in Royce that tends to repress the Christian mechanisms of forgiveness and charity. As MacIntyre writes: "What is the condition of forgiveness? It requires that the offender already accepts as just the verdict of the law upon his action and behaves as one who acknowledges the justice of the appropriate punishment; hence the common root of 'penance' and of 'punishment.' The offender can then be forgiven, if the person offended against so wills. . . . The virtue exhibited in forgiveness is charity."[76]

Royce did speak of charity, nevertheless. His loyalty entailed "justice, charity, industry, wisdom, spirituality,"[77] and could attach itself to any form of association so long as it involved *"the willing and practical* and thoroughgoing devotion to a person to a cause"[78] and a truly social bond: "You can love an individual. But you can be loyal only to a tie that binds you and others into some sort of unity, and loyal to individuals only through the tie."[79] However, the political first stage of Roycean pluralism is the "province" or region of one's birth or domicile, a subject on which his rhapsodies reach almost Burkean proportions and might seem peculiar for a Californian who made his mature career in Cambridge, Massachusetts. Royce wrote a long essay on provincialism. A province was to be cherished for its "customs and ideals" objectively, and also for the "love and pride" that lead inhabitants to choose those "traditions, beliefs, and aspirations" for their own.[80] "The man of the future," Royce declared, "must love his province more than he does today. . . . Provincialism, like monogamy, is an essential basis of true civilization."[81] His fear of the propensity "to read the same daily news, to share the same general ideas, to submit to the same overmastering social forces, to live in the same external fashions, to discourage individuality, and to approach a dead level of harassed mediocrity,"[82] might strike one as not terribly different from criticisms of "mass society" written fifty years later. For Royce, provincialism meant "self-respect" and "individual initiative."[83] It was also the surest haven of freedom: "Freedom, I should say, dwells now in the small social group, and has its securest home in the provincial life. The nation, by itself, apart from the influence of the province, is in danger of becoming an incomprehensible monster, in whose presence the individual loses his right, his self-consciousness, and his dignity."[84] The province has a regulatory role in cultivating freedom, for "the individual is naturally wayward and capricious. The waywardness is a constant source of entanglement and failure. But the community which he loves is rendered relatively constant in its will by its customs; yet these customs no longer seem, to the loyal individual, mere conventions or commands."[85]

What, then, of the nation-state? Although Royce's chain of loyalties extended as far as a cosmopolitan universalism, he was well aware that loyal attachment grew weaker as it grew more extensive, and he felt that "there can be no true international life unless the nations remain to possess it."[86] But he was dissatisfied with the conditions of loyalty in the American state of his time. "We have," he wrote, "been neglecting to cultivate [loyalty] in our social order. We have been making light of it. We have not been training ourselves for it. Hence we, indeed, often sadly miss it in our social environment."[87] Royce accused superficial education, irrational individualism, social conflict, cynicism, as well as the cultivation of false loyalties for the American distress.[88] He was far less chauvinistic than many contemporaries: "[Loyalty] has no joy in national prowess, except in so far as that prowess means a furtherance of universal loyalty."[89] Without my taking the space to demonstrate it, it can be shown that postmillennial cravings were quite alien to Royce, a consequence both of the idealist philosophy he had developed and of his Pauline-Augustinian Christian heritage.[90]

Royce knew as well as we do that a plural society begets conflicting loyalties: ". . . it is obvious that nobody can be equally and directly loyal to all of the countless social causes that exist. . . . Moreover, different loyalties may stand in mutual conflict, wherever their causes are opposed."[91] The "complication of the moral world" made greater "the chances that the loyalties of various people will conflict with one another."[92] He had no easy way out of this dilemma, obviously. However, he had several useful suggestions. The one, methodological, was a test of the stuff of loyalty as "essentially a *loyalty* to *loyalty*, that is . . . an aid and a furtherance of loyalty in my fellows" as opposed to a cause that "despite the loyalty that it arouses in me . . . is destructive of loyalty in the world of my fellows."[93] Aside from this almost Kantian formalism, moderately helpful perhaps in distinguishing true from false loyalties and in locating the sentiment more objectively, Royce felt that one must intellectually defeat those philosophies or codes that make sport of loyalty for the benefit of individual self-advancement. He perceived improvements that might be made in education and institutions to foster his version of the moral life. And he hinted at a kind of dialectic by which "high social cultivation," which has trained "individualism" and bred "spiritual enmities" and "conscious independence of spirit and deeper inner opposition to all mere external authority," can by means of "intelligence" and "self-will" reach a social revelation, a "consciousness of one who loves a community as a person."[94]

If Royce's analysis of his society—and ours—is valid, it cannot frankly be said that he has given us the magic answers for recovery. His grasp of politics was nebulous, probably derivative from Burke and Coleridge; his notion of the structural complexities of changing a society was naive; and he packed too much into his concept of loyalty. Despite these weaknesses, he was fundamentally correct and hard-headed in recognizing the centrality of loyalty and in linking it to rational commitment within a coherent philosophical outlook. He did not reduce loyalty to mere emotion or *Glaube:* "Loyalty is never mere emotion. . . . Loyalty without self-control is impossible. . . . Loyalty is social. . . ."[95] He constructed a problematic that it would be more than useful to carry further, one that, in my opinion, promises greater rewards at America's present stage of life than the deep research in the rules of liberal egalitarianism, the minute examination of the exact conditions of political obligation, and the renewed paeans of praise to a self-justifying "natural order" preached by Rawls, Barry, Dworkin, Ackerman, Walzer, Nozick, Hayek, et al. that compete for the attention of the scholarly community. I am of course here speaking only of the development of Roycean ideas in the sphere of the profane. The fear will be that of Toryism. A limited Tory corrective in our view of society might be the spice that made the pudding fit to eat.

As for the sacred, which Royce, with his systematic idealist holism (not to be confused with his social pluralism), tended to conflate with the profane within the general rubric of loyalty, it is clear that the term "faith" can function, with judicious substitution, in the Roycean vocabulary. After all, Royce had the boldness to declare, à la Jonathan Edwards, "We need a new heaven and a new earth."[96] He went on to add: "I do not like that mere homesickness and spiritual estrangement, and that confusion of mind about moral ideals, which is nowadays too common."[97] Royce dwells a great deal on St. Paul, in passages I have not quoted from *The Problem of Christianity*. Here, while defending the moral integrity of the small community of believers—seemingly sectarian and rambunctious—he also writes of "an expression of the life and the spiritual significance of the whole universe"[98] and defines Christianity not as simple, "fundamental," Gospel truth, but as "an interpretation of the Master and of his religion in the light of some doctrine concerning his mission, and also concerning God, man, and man's salvation."[99] Religion is, then, not merely the burden but the possession of the community, which it is an act of faith both to seize in meaning and bring into the world collectively through a community of interpretation. That act is a warrant of truth as well as a control that is operative and understood in the world we call home, a world where we may fear treason as "the hell of the irrevocable"[100] and yet dwell not only in a "community of memory" but a "community of hope."[101]

If a further analysis of what Royce intends by "loyalty" could be consolidated with what Reinhold Niebuhr means by "justice" and Oakeshott means by morality as a "vernacular language," some progress might be made toward organizing the profane for tasks complementary to, but discrete from, ideals proper to the sacred. Those ideals, in turn, are connected not only with the conviction called faith but with the wholesome fear of judgment—a judgment that is to be had neither at the polls nor in the press, nor as any consequence of extortionate behavior by organized sectors of the public. For it is a demanding and ongoing judgment that our greatest statesman once described as "true and righteous altogether." In any case, a reorientation of theoretical debate and of the way persons look at these issues is a first order of business if we want to restore realism and replenish morale.

America, as I have tried to show, has historical resources and traditions relative to its place in the world and in a sacred cosmos that allow for this reformulation. Alongside such hopeful possibilities there are, however, many more abusive factors; and there is a widespread misunderstanding of the central problems of politics and religion altogether. Frustrated by the constraints that eventually check, or can overwhelm, any nation's abundance and its fantasy of freedom (Spinoza wrote that if a stone flung in the air suddenly gained consciousness, it would believe that it was moving of its own free will), a people needs some inner Stoicism. It needs a just appraisal of the given and the chosen. It also needs the tool of irony for understanding itself from a distance—a historical distance—outside itself. In other words, it needs two selves, call them if we like sacred and profane, for a comprehension of its meaning.

The distinctiveness of the sacred and the profane—denied even in a great deal of modern theology, not to mention by the daily commerce of society—does not mean that state and church are quarantined from each other or that true religion is a private affair. To the extent that religion is apprehended only privately, it is likely that these same private impulses will also work to erode the integrity of the state and of civic commitment. Private judgment will then dictate the conditions and obligations of public action or be used as a commonplace excuse for indifference. Patriotism, which Hegel defined as "the sentiment which, in the relationships of our daily life and under ordinary conditions, habitually recognizes that the community is one's substantive groundwork and end,"[102] will then itself fall prey to the internecine combats of moral pluralism.

Let me repeat once more: this is a pessimistic account, although it nowhere counsels surrender to the trends that currently dictate our frame of mind and scope of action. However, nothing can be solved by a few reformist daubs and splashes. We must regain the skill of conceiving experience, especially moral experience and historical experience, in a different, undoubtedly more Stoic, way. The strengths of the Protestant idea of the visible and invisible communities have been fairly ravaged by the sectarianism and postmillennial secularism of the "Protestant paradigm" in our traditions of religion and politics, our grasp of faith and loyalty. Understanding how this came about, how profoundly rooted it is in our assumptions, how our controls have gone out of control, is a first step for doing anything about it. Deliberate architects, athletes of a civilization no longer well kept up, will now need to rummage in these ruins.

Notes

1. See Berger, *Sacred Canopy*, pp. 151-55.
2. The whole question of the meaning, inauguration, and spontaneity of civil-religious events is interestingly dealt with in Mona Ozouf, *La Fête révolutionnaire, 1789-1799* (Paris, 1976).

3. In describing liberal society, P.F. Strawson writes (in "Social Morality and Individual Ideal," G. Wallace and A.D.M. Walker, eds., *The Definition of Morality,* London, 1970, p. 118): "There are variant moral environments but in which no ideal endeavours to engross, and determine the character of, the common morality." Bruce Ackerman, in his much-noted *Social Justice in the Liberal State* (New Haven, 1980), p. 11, goes far beyond Strawson's variant moral environments to a kind of manipulated anarchy of preference. See also Ronald Dworkin, "Liberalism," in Stuart Hampshire, ed., *Public and Private Morality* (Cambridge, 1978), p. 127.
4. Oakeshott, *On Human Conduct,* pp. 78-79.
5. Cf. Thomas Hobbes, *Leviathan,* ed. Michael Oakeshott (New York, 1962), chap. iv, pp. 39-49; chap. xviii, pp. 137-38.
6. Cf. Seymour Martin Lipset, *Political Man* (Garden City, 1960), who defines as intellectuals "all those who create, distribute, and apply *culture,* that is, the symbolic world of man, including art, science, and religion in general" (p. 311). A remarkably democratic definition of the word.
7. J.S. Mill, *Representative Government* (Indianapolis, 1958), p. 91.
8. Ibid., p. 53.
9. J.S. Mill, *Philosophy of Scientific Method* (ed. Ernest Nagel, New York, 1950), Bk. V, chap. viii, pp. 350-51; Constant, "De la perfectibilité de l'espèce humaine," in Gauchet, ed., *De la Liberté chez les modernes,* p. 592.
10. Benjamin Constant, *De la Religion, considérée dans sa source, ses formes et ses développements* (5 vols., Paris, 1826-1828), I, 108.
11. E.g., Rousseau, *Confessions,* in *Oeuvres complètes,* I, 435.
12. See above, p. 12.
13. T.S. Eliot, "Gerontion."
14. *St. John,* viii, 32.
15. *Hebrews,* xii, 1.
16. *Galatians,* v, 1.
17. Locke carefully distinguishes civil liberty from the "metaphysical liberty" discussed in the *Essay* in *Second Treatise,* iv, 22; Montesquieu explores the different meanings of liberty in *De l'Esprit des lois,* xi, 2-4, 6.
18. Constant, in Gauchet, ed., *De la Liberté chez les modernes,* pp. 509-10.
19. Cf. Kant, *Critique of Practical Reason,* ed. L.W. Beck (Indianapolis, 1956), "Analytic of Practical Reason," pp. 28-30.
20. T.H. Green, *Principles of Political Obligation* (London, 1955), pp. 2-27.
21. *1 Corinthians,* xii, 4.
22. *Psalms,* c, 2.
23. Cf. Kant, *Practical Reason,* pp. 137ff.
24. R. Niebuhr, *Faith and History,* p. 79.
25. See Hesiod, *Works and Days,* ll. 248-66.
26. Gerth and Mills, eds., *From Max Weber,* pp. 120-28.
27. See esp. the essays by Stuart Hampshire, Bernard Williams, Thomas Scanlon, and Thomas Nagel in Hampshire, ed., *Public and Private Morality.*
28. Cf. Hegel, "The Positivity of the Christian Religion," in T.M. Knox, ed., *Friedrich* [sic] *Hegel on Christianity: Early Theological Writings* (New York, 1961), pp. 86-87, 169-72, and passim.

29. On special aspects of "moderate" and "polarized" pluralism in political competition, see Giovanni Sartori, *Parties and Party Systems: A Framework for Analysis* (Cambridge, 1976), pp. 131-84.
30. See Princeton Religion Center, *Emerging Trends* 3 (April 1981): 1-2.
31. Ahlstrom, *Religious History,* pp. 835-41.
32. See Herbert Deane, *The Political and Social Ideas of St. Augustine* (New York, 1963), pp. 239-41.
33. See Jacob Neusner, *From Politics to Piety: The Emergence of Pharisaic Judaism* (Englewood Cliffs, 1973), esp. pp. 152-54.
34. See above, chap. 2, p. 41.
35. See above, chap. 4, p. 91.
36. See above, chap. 6, pp. 173-75.
37. Samuel Taylor Coleridge, "An Essay on Faith," in *Aids to Reflection and the Confessions of an Inquiring Spirit* (London, 1893), p. 341.
39. It is acknowledged that to the degree that politics is pluralistic, loyalties are apt to be plural, perhaps deeply conflicting. Sometimes a "procedural" loyalty is deemed sufficient to accommodate substantive moral conflict. However, "if the values supporting the procedures are not present, the procedures alone will certainly fail to produce compromise. . . ." G.A. Kelly, "Mediation versus Compromise in Hegel," *NOMOS XXI: Compromise in Ethics, Law, and Politics* (New York, 1979), p. 90.
40. However, as a straw in the wind, the Catholic reformer Hans Küng has been speaking of "loyal opposition which, without illusions but with a readiness for dialogue, seeks to plead for more sincerity, frankness, pluralism, and tolerance within the Catholic Church." *New York Times,* 13 December 1981.
41. G.W.F. Hegel, *Faith and Knowledge,* ed. Walter Cerf and H.S. Harris (Albany, 1977), pp. 151-52.
42. George Bancroft, *Memorial Address on the Life and Characteristics of Abraham Lincoln* (Washington, 1866), p. 6.
43. Albert O. Hirschman, *Exit, Voice, and Loyalty: Responses to Declines in Firms, Organizations, and States* (Cambridge, Mass., 1970), pp. 78-79.
44. David Hume, *Enquiries Concerning the Human Understanding and Concerning the Principles of Morals,* ed. L.A. Selby-Bigge (Oxford, 1962): *Understanding,* sect. IV, pt. 1, p. 23.
45. Ibid., sect. IV, pt. 2, p. 35.
46. Ibid., sect. V, pt. 1, p. 41.
47. Ibid., p. 43.
48. Esp. ibid., sect. VIII, pt. 2, p. 103f; sect. X, pt. 2, p. 116f.
49. Ibid., sect. X, pt. 2, p. 131.
50. Ibid., sect. VIII, pt. 2, p. 103.
51. Ibid., sect XII, pt. 3, p. 165.
52. Ibid.
53. Ibid., sect. VIII, pt. 2, p. 98.
54. Isaiah Berlin, "Hume and the Sources of German Anti-Rationalism," in *Against the Current: Essays in the History of Ideas* (London, 1979), p. 174.
55. Hegel, *Faith and Reason,* p. 57.

56. Hume, *A Treatise of Human Nature,* bk. III, sect. viii, in H.D. Aiken, ed., *Hume's Moral and Political Philosophy* (New York, 1948), p. 113.
57. Ibid., p. 107.
58. Ibid., p. 109.
59. Ibid., sect. ix, p. 111.
60. On Royce's Calvinism, see John E. Smith, *Royce's Social Infinite: The Community of Interpretation* (Archon Books, n.p., 1969), p. 129.
61. Royce, "On Certain Limitations of the Thoughtful Public in America," *Basic Writings,* II, 1121.
62. Ibid., 1129.
63. Ibid., 1133.
64. Habermas does not, for very plausible reasons, claim Royce as a source, but he devotes a short chapter to Peirce in his *Knowledge and Human Interests* (trans. Jeremy Shapiro, Boston, 1971), pp. 91-112.
65. Josiah Royce, *The Problem of Christianity* (Chicago, 1968), p. 82.
66. Ibid., p. 41.
67. Aristotle, *Nicomachaean Ethics,* bk. viii (trans. J.A.K. Thompson, Harmondsworth, 1962), pp. 251, 253.
68. Royce, *Problem of Christianity,* p. 84.
69. Coleridge, "An Essay on Faith," p. 347. The passage has overtones of Hegel's *Phenomenology of Spirit* (cf. p. 227), although Coleridge was not closely familiar with Hegel.
70. Royce, *Problem of Christianity,* p. 45.
71. Ibid., p. 41.
72. Smith, *Royce's Social Infinite,* p. 132.
73. John Dewey, *The Public and Its Problems* (Chicago, n.d.; orig. 1927), p. 157.
74. Royce, *Philosophy of Loyalty,* p. 1011.
75. Ibid., p. 937.
76. Alasdair C. MacIntyre, *After Virtue* (South Bend, 1981), p. 162.
77. Royce, *Philosophy of Loyalty,* p. 860.
78. Ibid., p. 861.
79. Ibid., p. 862.
80. Royce, "Provincialism," in *Basic Writings,* II, 1069.
81. Ibid., p. 1071.
82. Ibid., p. 1074.
83. Ibid., p. 1076.
84. Ibid., pp. 1083-84.
85. Royce, *Problem of Christianity,* p. 84.
86. Royce, "On Certain Limitations," II, 1155.
87. Royce, *Philosophy of Loyalty,* p. 899.
88. Ibid., pp. 942-46.
89. Ibid., p. 939.
90. He called St. Augustine an "apparently extreme partisan of authority" (together with Plato and Aristotle), ibid., p. 865, but shared his anti-chiliasm.
91. Ibid., p. 897.
92. Ibid., p. 898.
93. Ibid., p. 901.
94. Royce, *Problem of Christianity,* pp. 113-18.

95. Royce, *Philosophy of Loyalty,* pp. 861-62.
96. Ibid., p. 858.
97. Ibid.
98. Royce, *Problem of Christianity,* p. 45.
99. Ibid., p. 66.
100. Ibid., p. 162.
101. Ibid., pp. 248ff.
102. Hegel, *Philosophy of Right,* para. 268, p. 163.

Bibliography

Abbot, Abiel. *Traits of Resemblance in the People of the United States of America to Ancient Israel* (Haverhill, Mass., 1799).

Ackerman, Bruce A. *Social Justice in the Liberal State* (New Haven, 1980).

Adams, G.B. "The United States and the Anglo-Saxon Future," *Atlantic* 78 (July 1896): 35-44.

Adams, Henry. *Democracy* (New York, 1968).

————. *The Education of Henry Adams* (New York, 1931).

Adams, James Thurlow, ed. *Dictionary of American History*. 5 vols., suppl. (New York, 1940).

Adams, John. *Works,* ed. Charles Francis Adams. 10 vols. (Boston, 1850-1856).

Adamson, Walter L. *Hegemony and Revolution: Antonio Gramsci's Political and Cultural Theory* (Berkeley, 1980).

Adler, Margot. *Drawing Down the Moon* (New York, 1979).

Agresto, John T. "Liberty, Virtue, and Republicanism," *Review of Politics* 39 (October 1977): 473-504.

Ahlstrom, Sydney E. "The American National Faith: Humane, Yet All Too Human," in J.M. Robinson, ed., *Religion and the Humanizing of Man* (Ontario, Canada, 1973).

————. *A Religious History of the American People* (New Haven, 1972).

————, ed. *Theology in America* (Indianapolis, 1967).

Albanese, Catherine L. *Sons of the Fathers: The Civil Religion of the American Revolution* (Philadelphia, 1976).

Alley, Robert S. *So Help Me God: Religion and the Presidency* (Richmond, Va., 1972).

Andreski, Stanislav. *Elements of Comparative Sociology* (London, 1964).

Anthony, Dick, and Thomas Robbins, eds. *In Gods We Trust: New Patterns of Religious Pluralism in America* (New Brunswick, 1981).

————. "Spiritual Innovation and the Crisis of American Civil Religion," *Daedalus* 111 (Winter 1982): 215-34.

Arendt, Hannah. *Between Past and Future* (New York, 1967).

Ariès, Philippe. "La mort inversée," *Archives européennes de Sociologie* 8 (1967): 165-95.

281

Aristotle. *Nicomachaean Ethics* (trans. J.A.K. Thompson, Harmondsworth, 1962).

Armstrong, Maurice W., Lefferts A. Loetscher, and Charles A. Anderson, eds. *The Presbyterian Enterprise* (Philadelphia, 1955).

Arnold, Matthew. *Culture and Anarchy and Friendship's Garland* (New York, 1912).

Arquillière, H.X. *L'Augustinisme politique* (Paris, 1934).

Auer, J. Jeffrey, ed. *The Rhetoric of Our Times* (New York, 1969).

Bachrach, Peter. *The Theory of Democratic Elitism: A Critique* (Boston, 1967).

Baechler, Jean. "Mourir à Jonestown," *Archives européennes de Sociologie* 20 (1979): 173-210.

Bailyn, Bernard. *The Ideological Origins of the American Revolution* (Cambridge, Mass., 1967).

———. "Religion and Revolution: Three Biographical Studies," *Perspectives in American History* 4 (1970): 85-169.

Baird, Robert. *Religion in America; or An Account of the Origin, Relation to the State, and Present Condition of the Evangelical Churches in the United States, with Notices of the Unevangelical Denominations* (New York, 1844).

———. *The Christian Retrospect and Register* (New York, 1851).

Balitizer, Alfred. "Some Thoughts About Civil Religion," *Journal of Church and State* 16 (Winter 1974): 31-50.

Bancroft, George. *Memorial Address on the Life and Character of Abraham Lincoln* (Washington, 1866).

Barlow, Joel. *The Vision of Columbus* (Paris, 1793).

Barry, Brian. *The Liberal Theory of Justice* (Oxford, 1973).

Barth, Karl. *Community, State, and Church* (New York, 1960).

———. *The Knowledge of God and the Service of Man* (New York, 1939).

Bates, Ernest S. *American Faith* (New York, 1940).

Bathory, Peter Dennis. "Tocqueville on Citizenship and Faith: A Response to Cushing Strout," *Political Theory* 8 (February 1980): 27-38.

Baumer, Franklin L. *Religion and the Rise of Scepticism* (New York, 1960).

Bayle, Pierre. *Dictionnaire historique et critique.* 16 vols., (Paris, 1820).

———. *The Great Contest Between Faith and Reason,* ed. K. C. Sandberg (New York, 1963).

Becker, Ernest. *The Denial of Death* (New York, 1973).

Becker, Howard, trans. and adapt. *Systematic Sociology on the Basis of the Beziehungslehre and Gebildelehre of Leopold von Weise* (New York, 1932).

Beecher, Lyman. *Autobiography, Correspondence, etc.,* ed. Charles Beecher. 2 vols. (New York, 1865).

———. *Sermons Delivered on Various Occasions* (Boston, 1828).

———. *Works.* 3 vols. (Boston, 1852-1853).

Bell, Daniel. *The Cultural Contradiction of Capitalism* (New York, 1976).

————. "The Return of the Sacred? The Argument on the Future of Religion," *British Journal of Sociology* 38 (December 1977): 419-49.

Bellah, Robert N. "The American Civil Religion," *Daedalus* 96 (Winter 1967): 1-21.

————. "American Civil Religion in the 1970s," *Anglican Theological Review* 1 (July 1973): 8-20.

————. *Beyond Belief: Essays on Religion in a Post-Traditional World* (New York, 1970).

————. "Religion and Legitimation in the American Republic," *Society* 15 (May-June 1978): 16-23.

————. "Religious Evolution," *American Sociological Review* 29 (June 1964): 358-74.

————, and Phillip E. Hammond, eds. *Varieties of Civil Religion* (San Francisco, 1980).

Bennett, John C. *Christians and the State* (New York, 1958).

Bercovitch, Sacvan. *The Puritan Origins of the American Self* (New Haven, 1965).

Berens, John F. "Religion and Revolution Reconsidered: Recent Literature on Religion and Nationalism in Eighteenth-Century America," *Canadian Review of Studies in Nationalism* 6 (Fall 1979): 233-45.

Berger, Peter L. *The Noise of Solemn Assemblies* (Garden City, 1961).

————. *The Precarious Vision* (Garden City, 1961).

————. *The Sacred Canopy: Elements of a Sociological Theory of Religion* (Garden City, 1967).

————. *The Social Reality of Religion* (London, 1967).

————. "The Sociological Study of Sectarianism," *Social Research* 21 (Winter 1954): 467-85.

————, and Thomas Luckmann. *The Social Construction of Reality: A Treatise in the Sociology of Knowledge* (Garden City, 1966).

Berlin, Isaiah. *Against the Current: Essays in the History of Ideas* (London, 1979).

Beth, Loren P. *The American Theory of Church and State* (Gainesville, 1958).

Billington, Roy A. *The Protestant Crusade, 1800-1860: A Study of the Origins of American Nativism* (New York, 1938).

Booth, Harry F., ed. *Civil Religion in America: Manifest Destiny and Historical Judgement* (Carlisle, Pa., 1973).

Bowden, Henry Warner. *Church History in the Age of Science: Historiographical Patterns in the United States, 1876-1918* (Chapel Hill, 1971).

Braden, Charles. *These Also Believe* (New York, 1949).

Brams, Steven J. *Biblical Games: A Strategic Analysis of Stories in the Old Testament* (Cambridge, Mass., 1980).

Brandon, Edward Ewing, ed. *Lafayette, Guest of the Nation: A Contemporary Account of the Triumphal Tour of General Lafayette*. 2 vols. (Oxford, Ohio, 1950).

Brinton, Crane, "Many Mansions," *American Historical Review* 69 (January 1964): 309-26.

Browne, Henry J. "Catholicism in the United States," in J.W. Smith and A. Leland Jamison, eds., *The Shaping of American Religion* (Princeton, 1961).

Bryce, James. *The American Commonwealth*. 2 vols. (New York and London, 1895).

Brzezinski, Zbigniew. "America in the Technetronic Age," *Encounter* 30 (January 1968): 16-26.

Bultmann, Rudolf. *The Presence of Eternity* (New York, 1957).

Burdeau, Georges. *Traité de Science politique:* Vol. II: *L'Etat* (Paris, 1949); Vol. V: *L'Etat libéral et les techniques politiques de la démocratie gouvernée* (Paris, 1953); Vol. VI: *La Démocratie gouvernante: son assise sociale et sa philosophie politique* (Paris, 1956).

Burke, Kenneth. *The Rhetoric of Religion: Studies in Logology* (Berkeley and Los Angeles, 1970).

Bushnell, Horace. *Barbarism the First Danger* (New York, 1847).

———. *Nature and the Supernatural as Together Constituting One System of God* (New York, 1877).

———. "Popular Government by Divine Right" (Hartford, 1865).

Callahan, Daniel, ed. *The Secular City Debate* (New York, 1966).

Campbell, Alexander. *The Christian Baptist*. 3 vols. (Buffaloe, Va., 1824-1826).

———. *The Christian Baptist*. 3 vols. (Bethany, Va., 1827-1829).

———. *The Millennial Harbinger*. 41 vols. (Bethany, Va., 1830-1864).

———. *Popular Lectures and Addresses* (Philadelphia, 1863).

Campbell, Colin. *Toward a Sociology of Irreligion* (New York, 1971).

Camus, Albert. *The Rebel* (New York, 1956).

Cappon, Lester J., ed. *The Complete Correspondence Between Thomas Jefferson and Abigail and John Adams*. 2 vols. (Chapel Hill, 1959).

Carr, Albert H. *The Coming of War* (New York, 1960).

Carroll, Jackson W., Douglas W. Johnson, and Martin E. Marty, eds. *Religion in America: 1950 to the Present* (New York, 1979).

Cauthen, Kenneth. *The Impact of American Religious Liberalism* (New York, 1962).

Channing, William Ellery. *Unitarian Christianity* (New York, 1957).

Chaunu, Pierre. *Mourir à Paris, l6e, 17e, 18e siècles* (Paris, 1973).

Cherry, Conrad. *God's New Israel: Religious Interpretations of American Destiny* (Englewood Cliffs, 1971).

———, and John Y. Fenton, eds. *Religion in the Public Domain* (University Park, Pa., 1966).

Chevalier, Michael. *Society, Manners, and Politics in the United States* (New York, 1969).

Childress, James F., and David B. Harned, eds. *Secularization and the Protestant Prospect* (Philadelphia, 1970).

Chinard, Gilbert. *L'Amérique et la rêve exotique dans la littérature française aux XVIIᵉ et XVIIIᵉ siècles* (Paris, 1913).

Chipman, Nathaniel. *Principles of Government: A Treatise on Free Institutions* (Burlington, Vt., 1833).

Clark, Elmer T. *The Small Sects in America* (New York, 1949).

Clebsch, William A. *American Religious Thought* (Chicago, 1973).

Cleveland, Grover. "Patriotism and Holiday Observance," *North American Review* 184 (April 1907): 683-93.

Cole, William A., and Phillip E. Hammond. "Religious Pluralism, Legal Development, and Societal Complexity: Rudimentary Forms of Civil Religion," *Journal for the Scientific Study of Religion* 13 (June 1974): 177-89.

Coleridge, Samuel Taylor. *Aids to Reflection and the Confessions of an Inquiring Spirit* (London, 1893).

Coles, Robert. "Civility and Psychology," *Daedalus* 109 (Summer 1980): 133-42.

Condorcet, Nicolas de Caritat, Marquis de. *Esquisse d'un tableau historique des progrès de l'esprit humain* (Paris, 1933).

Constant, Benjamin. *De la Liberté chez les modernes: Ecrits politiques,* ed. Marcel Gauchet (Paris, 1980).

————. *Du polythéisme romain considéré dans ses rapports avec la philosophie grecque et la religion chrétienne.* 2 vols. (Paris, 1833).

————. *De la Religion considérée sans sa source, ses formes et ses développements.* 5 vols. (Paris, 1824-1831).

Cornelison, J.A. *The Relation of Religion to Civil Government in the United States of America* (New York, 1895).

Costanzo, Joseph F. *This Nation Under God* (New York, 1964).

Cox, Harvey. *The Secular City* (New York, 1965).

Cragg, G.R. *From Puritanism to the Age of Reason* (Cambridge, 1950).

Craven, Wesley French, ed. *The Legend of the Founding Fathers* (New York, 1956).

Crèvecoeur, J. Hector St. John. *Letters from an American Farmer* (Gloucester, 1968).

Cross, Barbara M. *Horace Bushnell: Minister to a Changing America* (Chicago, 1958).

Cuddihy, John M. *No Offense: Civil Religion and Protestant Taste* (New York, 1978).

Curti, Merle. *The Roots of American Loyalty* (New York, 1967).

Cutler, Donald R., ed. *The Religious Situation* (Boston, 1968).

Davidson, James West. *The Logic of Millennial Thought: Eighteenth-Century New England* (New Haven, 1977).

————. "Searching for the Millennium: Problems for the 1790s and the 1970s," *New England Quarterly* 40 (June 1972): 241-61.

Davis, Charles. *Theology and Political Society* (Cambridge, 1980).

Davis, David B. "Some Ideological Functions of Prejudice in Ante-Bellum America," *American Quarterly* 15 (Summer 1963): 115-25.

Deane, Herbert. *The Political and Social Ideas of St. Augustine* (New York, 1963).

Debate on the Evidences of Christianity: Containing an Examination of the Social System, and of All the Systems of Ancient and Modern Times, Held in the City of Cincinnati, for Eight Days Successively, between Robert Owen, of New Lanark, Scotland and Alexander Campbell, of Bethany, Virginia . . . (London, 1839).

De Leon, Edwin. *The Positions and Duties of Young America* (Charleston, 1845).

Demerath, N.J., III, and Phillip E. Hammond. *Religion in Social Context: Tradition and Transition* (New York, 1969).

Dewey, John. *A Common Faith* (New Haven, 1934).

———. *The Public and Its Problems* (Chicago, n.d.; orig. 1927).

Dilthey, Wilhelm. *Selected Writings,* ed. H.P. Rickman (Cambridge, 1976).

Dostoievsky, Fyodor. *The Diary of a Writer,* trans. B. Brasol. 2 vols. (New York, 1949).

———. *The Possessed* (New York, 1936).

Douglas, Mary, *Cultural Bias* (London, 1978).

———. "The Effects of Modernization on Religious Change," *Daedalus* 111 (Winter 1982): 1-19.

Dumont, Louis. *From Mandeville to Marx: The Genesis and Triumph of Economic Ideology* (Chicago, 1977).

Dunn, John. *Modern Revolutions* (Cambridge, 1972).

Durkheim, Emile. *The Elementary Forms of Religious Life,* trans. J.W. Swain (New York, 1947).

———. *Montesquieu and Rousseau: Forerunners of Sociology* (Ann Arbor, 1960).

Dwight, Timothy. *A Sermon Delivered in Boston . . . Before the American Board of Commissioners for Foreign Missions* (Boston, 1813).

Dworkin, Ronald. *Taking Rights Seriously* (Cambridge, Mass., 1977).

Eddy, Sherwood. *The Kingdom of God and the American Dream* (New York, 1941).

Edwards, Jonathan. *Representative Selections,* ed. C.H. Faust and T.H. Johnson (New York, 1962).

———. *Works.* 4 vols. (New York, 1868).

———. *Works,* ed. Perry Miller and John E. Smith. 5 vols. (New Haven, 1957–).

Eidelberg, Paul. *The Philosophy of the American Constitution* (New York, 1968).

Eisenach, Eldon. *Two Worlds of Liberalism* (Chicago, 1981).

Eister, A.W., ed. *Changing Perspectives in the Scientific Study of Religion* (New York, 1974).

Ekirch, Arthur A. *The Idea of Progress in America, 1815-1860* (New York, 1944).

Elliott, Jonathan, ed. *The Debates in the Several State Conventions.* 5 vols. (Philadelphia, 1901).

Ellis, John Tracy. "American Catholics and the Intellectual Life," *Thought* 30 (Autumn 1955): 351-88.

Ellul, Jacques. *The Theological Foundation of Law* (Garden City, 1960).

Ellwood, Robert S., Jr. *Religion and Spiritual Groups in Modern America* (Englewood Cliffs, 1973).

Ely, Richard T. *The Social Law of Service* (New York, 1897).

Emerson, Ralph Waldo. *The Dial.* 4 vols. (New York, 1961).

————. *Essays: First Series* (Philadelphia, n.d.).

————. *Essays: Second Series* (Boston, 1857).

————. *Journals,* ed. E.W. Emerson and W.E. Forbes. 10 vols. (Boston, 1909-1914).

————. *Representative Men* (Boston, 1850).

————. *Society and Solitude* (Boston, 1904).

Engels, Friedrich. *Socialism: Utopian and Scientific* (New York, 1935).

d'Entrèves, Alexander Passerin. *The Notion of the State* (Oxford, 1967).

Everett, Edward. *Orations and Speeches on Various Occasions.* 4 vols. (Boston, 1850-1859).

The Federalist, ed. Henry Cabot Lodge (New York, 1894).

Fenn, Richard K. "Toward a New Sociology of Religion," *Journal for the Scientific Study of Religion* 11 (1972): 16-32.

Ferguson, Adam. *Essay on the History of Civil Society* (London, 1768).

Festugière, A.J. *Epicurus and His Gods* (Oxford, 1955).

Feuerbach, Ludwig. *The Essence of Christianity,* trans. George Eliot (New York, 1854).

Fichte, Johann Gottlieb. *Addresses to the German Nation,* ed. G.A. Kelly (New York, 1968).

Findlay, James F., Jr. *Dwight L. Moody, American Evangelist, 1837-1899* (Chicago, 1969).

Finney, Charles Grandison. *Lectures on the Revival of Religion* (New York, 1835).

————. *Memoirs* (New York, 1876).

Fletcher, Joseph. *Situation Ethics: The New Morality* (Philadelphia, 1966).

Foster, Frank H. *The Modern Movement in American Theology* (New York, 1939).

Frankfort, Henri, et al. *The Intellectual Adventures of Ancient Man* (Chicago, 1946).

Franklin, Benjamin. *Papers,* ed. Leonard W. Labaree. 21 vols. (New Haven, 1959–).

Frazier, E. Franklin. *The Negro Church in America* (New York, 1964).

Freud, Sigmund. *The Future of an Illusion* (London, 1928).

Fulton, Robert L., and Thomas C. Trueblood, eds. *Patriotic Eloquence* (New York, 1900).

Furniss, Norman F. *The Fundamentalist Controversy, 1918-1931* (New Haven, 1954).

Garrett, Leroy. "Alexander Campbell and Thomas Jefferson: A Comparative Study of Two Old Virginians" (Dallas, 1963).

Garrett, William R. "Politicized Clergy: A Sociological Interpretation of the 'New Breed'," *Journal for the Scientific Study of Religion* 12 (December 1973): 383-99.

Garrison, W.E. *Religion Follows the Frontier: A History of the Disciples of Christ* (New York, 1931).

Gaustad, Edwin S. *Historical Atlas of Religion in America* (New York, 1962).

———, Darline Miller, and G. Allison Stokes. "Religion in America," *American Quarterly* 31 (1979): 250-83.

Gellner, Ernest. *Contemporary Thought and Politics* (London, 1974).

———. *Words and Things* (Harmondsworth, 1968).

Gladden, Washington. *The Church and the Kingdom* (New York, 1894).

———. *The Nation and the Kingdom* (Boston, 1909).

Glock, Charles, and Robert N. Bellah, eds. *The New Religious Consciousness* (Berkeley and Los Angeles, 1976).

———, and Rodney Stark. *Religion and Society in Tension* (Chicago, 1965).

Gogarten, Friedrich. *Despair and Hope for Our Time* (Philadelphia, 1970).

Gouldner, Alvin. *The Coming Crisis of Western Sociology* (New York, 1970).

Greeley, Andrew M. "The Civil Religion of Ethnic Americans: The Viewpoint of a Catholic Sociologist," *Religious Education* (September-October 1975): 449-513.

———. *The Denominational Society* (Glenview, Ill., 1972).

———. *Religion in the Year 2000* (New York, 1969).

———. *Unsecular Man: The Persistence of Religion* (New York, 1972).

Green, Thomas Hill. *Lectures on Political Obligation* (London, 1924).

Gribbin, William. *The Churches Militant* (New Haven, 1973).

Grosclaude, Pierre. *Malesherbes: témoin et interprète de son temps* (Paris, 1961).

Grund, Francis J. *The Americans* (Boston, 1837).

Gusdorf, Georges. *Dieu, la nature, l'homme au siècle des lumières* (Paris, 1972).

Habermas, Jürgen. *Knowledge and Human Interests,* trans. Jeremy J. Shapiro (Boston, 1971).

———. *Legitimation Crisis,* trans. Thomas McCarthy (London, 1976).

Hadden, Jeffrey K. *The Gathering Storm in the Churches* (Garden City, 1969).

Hamilton, William, and Thomas J.J. Altizer. *Radical Theology and the Death of God* (New York, 1966).

Hampshire, Stuart, ed. *Public and Private Morality* (Cambridge, 1978).

Handy, Robert T. *A Christian America: Protestant Hopes and Historical Realities* (New York, 1971).

Hart, Roderick P. *The Political Pulpit* (West Lafayette, Ind., 1977).

Hartz, Louis. *The Liberal Tradition in America* (New York, 1955).

Hastings, James, ed. *Encyclopedia of Religion and Ethics*. 12 vols. (Edinburgh, 1917).

Hatch, Nathan O. "The Origins of Civic Millennialism in America: New England Clergymen, the War with France, and the Revolution," *William and Mary Quarterly*, third series, 31 (July 1974): 407-30.

————. *The Sacred Cause of Liberty: Republican Thought and Millennium in Revolutionary New England* (New Haven, 1977).

Hawley, Charles. *Advantages of the Present Age* (Rochester, 1850).

Hayek, Friedrich. *Law, Legislation and Liberty*. 3 vols. (Chicago, 1973-1979).

————. *Studies in Philosophy, Politics and Economics* (London, 1967).

Hazard, Paul. *La Crise de la conscience européenne, 1680-1715* (Paris, 1935).

Hegel, G.W.F. *Berliner Schriften,* ed. J. Hoffmeister (Hamburg, 1956).

————. *Briefe von und an Hegel,* ed. J. Hoffmeister. 4 vols. (Hamburg, 1952-1960).

————. *On Christianity: Early Theological Essays,* trans. T.M. Knox (New York, 1961).

————. *Faith and Knowledge,* ed. and trans. Walter Cerf and H.S. Harris (Albany, 1977).

————. *Phenomenology of Spirit,* trans. A.V. Miller (Oxford, 1977).

————. *Philosophy of History,* trans. J. Sibree (New York, 1956).

————. *Philosophy of Right,* trans. T.M. Knox (London, 1967).

Heimann, Eduard. *Reason and Faith in Modern Society* (Middletown, 1963).

Heimert, Alan. *Religion and the American Mind* (Cambridge, Mass., 1966).

————, and Perry Miller, eds. *The Great Awakening: Documents* (Indianapolis, 1967).

Henderson, Charles P. *The Nixon Theology* (New York, 1972).

Herberg, Will. *Protestant, Catholic, Jew: An Essay in American Religious Sociology* (Garden City, 1955).

————. "Religion in a Secularized Society: Some Aspects of America's Three-Religion Pluralism," in Louis Schneider, ed., *Religion, Culture, and Society* (New York, 1964).

Himmelfarb, Milton. "Secular Society? A Jewish Perspective," *Daedalus* 96 (Winter 1967): 220-36.

Hirschman, Albert O. *Exit, Voice, and Loyalty: Responses to Declines in Firms, Organizations, and States* (Cambridge, Mass., 1970).

Hobbes, Thomas. *Leviathan,* ed. Michael Oakeshott (New York, 1962).

————. *Man and Citizen,* ed. Bernard Gert (New York, 1972).

Hofstadter, Richard. *Anti-Intellectualism in American Life* (New York, 1963).

————. *The American Political Tradition* (New York, 1954).

Hoge, Dean R., and David A. Roozen, eds. *Understanding Church Growth and Decline, 1950-1978* (New York, 1979).

Hopkins, John Henry. *The American Citizen* (New York, 1857).

Hopkins, Mark. *"The Law of Progress of the Race," An Address Delivered before the Society of the Alumni of Williams College . . .* (Boston, 1843).

Hopkins, Samuel. *A Treatise on the Millennium* (Boston, 1793).

Horsman, Reginald. *The War of 1812* (New York, 1969).

Howe, Irving. "This Age of Conformity," *Partisan Review* 21 (January-February 1954): 1-12.

Howe, John R., Jr. "Republican Thought and the Political Violence of the 1790s," *American Quarterly* 29 (Summer 1967): 147-65.

Howe, Mark DeWolfe. *The Garden and the Wilderness* (Chicago, 1965).

Howlett, Duncan. *The Fourth American Faith* (New York, 1964).

Hudson, Winthrop S. *American Protestantism* (Chicago, 1961).

————. "Denominationalism as a Basis for Ecumenicity: A Seventeenth Century Conception," *Church History* 24 (1955): 32-50.

————, ed. *Nationalism and Religion in America* (New York, 1970).

————. *Religion in America* (New York, 1973).

Humboldt, Wilhelm von. *The Limits of State Action,* ed. J.W. Burrow (Cambridge, 1969).

Hume, David. *Dialogues Concerning Natural Religion,* ed. H.S. Aiken (New York, 1948).

————. *Enquiries Concerning the Human Understanding and Concerning the Principles of Morals,* ed. L.A. Selby-Bigge (Oxford, 1962).

————. *Hume's Moral and Political Philosophy,* ed. H.S. Aiken (New York, 1948).

Hunt, Gilbert J. *The Tour of General Lafayette through the United States* (New York, 1825).

Huntington, Samuel P. *Political Order in Changing Societies* (New Haven, 1968).

Huntington, William Reed. *The Church-Idea: An Essay Towards Unity* (New York, 1884).

Hutchison, John A. *The Two Cities: A Study of God and Human Politics* (Garden City, 1957).

Hyneman, Charles S. *The Study of Politics* (Urbana, Ill.: 1959).

Iggers, G.G., ed. *The Doctrine of Saint-Simon: An Exposition, First Year, 1828-1829* (New York, 1972).

Jacobi, F.H. *David Hume über den Glauben, oder Idealismus und Realismus: Ein Gespräch,* in *Werke.* 6 vols. (Leipzig, 1812-1825). II, 3-310.

James, William. *Letters,* ed. Henry James. 2 vols. (Boston, 1920).

————. *Principles of Psychology.* 2 vols. (New York, 1893).

————. *Some Problems of Philosophy* (London, 1911).

————. *The Varieties of Religious Experience* (New York, 1929).

————. *The Will to Believe and Other Essays in Popular Philosophy* (New York, 1898).

————, ed. *The Literary Remains of the Late Henry James* (Boston, 1885).

Jamison, A. Leland. "Religions on the Christian Perimeter," in J.W. Smith and A. Leland Jamison, eds., *The Shaping of American Religion* (Princeton, 1961).

Jefferson, Thomas. *Writings,* ed. Andrew A. Lipscomb and Albert Ellery Bergh. 20 vols. (Washington, 1903-1904).

Jouvenel, Bertrand de. *Power: The Natural History of Its Growth* (London, 1952).

Kant, Immanuel. *Critique of Practical Reason,* ed. L.W. Beck (Indianapolis, 1956).

————. *Fundamental Principles of the Metaphysics of Morals,* trans. Thomas K. Abbott (Indianapolis, 1949).

Kariel, Henry. *In Search of Authority* (Glencoe, 1964).

Keller, Charles Roy. *The Second Great Awakening in Connecticut* (New Haven, 1942).

Kelley, Dean M. *Why Conservative Churches Are Growing* (New York, 1972).

Kelly, George Armstrong. *Hegel's Retreat from Eleusis: Studies in Political Thought* (Princeton, 1978).

————. "Mediation versus Compromise in Hegel," *NOMOS XXI: Compromise in Ethics, Law, and Politics* (New York, 1979).

————. "Politics, Violence, and Human Nature," *NOMOS XVII: Human Nature in Politics* (New York, 1977).

————. "Who Needs a Theory of Citizenship?" *Daedalus* 108 (Fall 1979): 21-36.

Kendall, Willmoore, and George W. Carey. *The Basic Symbols of the American Political Tradition* (Baton Rouge, 1970).

Keohane, Nannerl O. "Montaigne's Individualism," *Political Theory* 5 (August 1977): 363-90.

Kessler, Sanford. "Tocqueville on Civil Religion and Liberal Democracy," *Journal of Politics* 39 (February 1977): 119-46.

Keynes, John Maynard. *Essays and Sketches in Biography* (New York, 1956).

Kierkegaard, Søren. *Journals,* trans. and ed. Alexander Dru (New York, 1959).

Klamkin, Marian. *The Return of Lafayette, 1824-1825* (New York, 1975).

Klein, Randolph Shipley. "Prismatic Patriotism During the Era of the American Revolution," *Canadian Review of Studies in Nationalism* 6 (Fall 1979): 175-92.

Knudten, R.D., ed. *The Sociology of Religion: An Anthology* (New York, 1967).

Koch, Adrienne. *The Philosophy of Thomas Jefferson* (New York, 1943).

Koch, G. Adolf. *Religion of the American Enlightenment* (New York, 1968).

Kolakowski, Leszek. *Main Currents of Marxism,* trans. P.S. Falla. 3 vols. (Oxford, 1978).

Kopelev, Lev. *To Be Preserved Forever,* trans. Anthony Austin (Philadelphia, 1977).

Lasch, Christoper. "The Narcissistic Personality of Our Time," *Partisan Review* 44, 1 (1977): 9-19.

―――. *The New Radicalism in America, 1889-1963* (New York, 1965).

Laski, Harold J. *The American Democracy* (New York, 1948).

―――. *A Grammar of Politics* (London, 1925).

Lerner, Max. *America as a Civilization* (New York, 1957).

―――. "Constitution and Court as Symbols," *Yale Law Journal* 46, 8 (1937): 1290-1319.

Levasseur, A. *Lafayette en Amérique en 1824 et 1825, ou journal d'un voyage aux Etats-Unis.* 2 vols. (Paris, 1829).

Levinson, Sanford. " 'The Constitution' in American Civil Religion," *Supreme Court Review* 21 (1980): 123-51.

Lieber, Francis. *Manual of Political Ethics.* 2 vols. (Boston, 1838-1839).

Lippmann, Walter. *Essays in the Public Philosophy* (Boston, 1955).

Lipset, Seymour Martin. *The First New Nation: The United States in Historical and Comparative Perspective* (New York, 1963).

―――. *Political Man* (Garden City, 1960).

Littell, Franklin H. *From State Church to Pluralism* (Chicago, 1962).

Locke, John. *Locke on Politics, Religion, and Education,* ed. Maurice Cranston (New York, 1965).

―――. *Two Treatises of Government,* ed. Peter Laslett (New York, 1965).

Löwith, Karl. "Die Aufhebung der christlichen Religion," *Hegel-Studien* 1 (1962): 196-236.

Long, Charles H. "A New Look at American Religion," *Anglican Theological Review* 1 (July 1973): 117-25.

Lovejoy, Arthur O. "On the Discrimination of Romanticisms," in *Essays in the History of Ideas* (New York, 1960).

Lowi, Theodore. *The End of Liberalism: Ideology, Policy, and the Crisis of Public Authority* (New York, 1969).

Luckmann, Thomas. *The Invisible Religion* (New York, 1967).

Macaulay, D. *The Patriot's Catechism, or the Duties of Rulers and Ruled* (Washington, 1843).

Machiavelli, Niccolò. *The Chief Works and Others,* ed. Allan Gilbert. 3 vols. (Durham, 1965).

―――. *The Prince and the Discourses,* ed. Max Lerner (New York, 1950).

Mackintosh, H.R. *Types of Modern Theology: Schleiermacher to Barth* (London, 1937).

MacIntyre, Alasdair. *After Virtue* (South Bend, 1981).

―――. *Against the Self-Images of the Age* (London, 1971).

―――. *Marxism and Christianity* (New York, 1968).

―――. *Secularization and Moral Change* (London, 1967).

Maclear, J.F. "The Republic and the Millennium," in Elwyn A. Smith, ed., *The Religion of the Republic* (Philadelphia, 1972).

Macpherson, C.B. *The Political Theory of Possessive Individualism* (Oxford, 1962).

Mannheim, Karl. *From Karl Mannheim*, ed. Kurt Wolff (New York, 1971).

———. *Ideology and Utopia*, trans. L. Wirth and E. Shils (New York, 1936).

Marcel, Gabriel. *Creative Fidelity*, trans. Robert Rosthal (New York, 1964).

Marin, Peter. "The New Narcissism," *Harper's* (October 1975): 45-56.

Maritain, Jacques. *Man and the State* (Chicago, 1961).

———. *The Person and the Common Good*, trans. J.J. Fitzgerald (New York, 1947).

Marsden, George M. *The Evangelical Mind and the New School Presbyterian Experience* (New Haven, 1970).

Marshall, T.H. *Class, Citizenship, and Social Development* (New York, 1963).

Martin, David. "Revived Dogma and New Cult," *Daedalus* 111 (Winter 1982): 53-72.

Marty, Martin E. *A Nation of Behavers* (Chicago, 1976).

———. *The New Shape of American Religion* (New York, 1959).

———. *Protestantism* (New York, 1972).

———. "Religion in America Since Mid-Century," *Daedalus* 111 (Winter 1982): 149-64.

———. *Righteous Empire* (New York, 1970).

Marx, Karl. *Critique of Hegel's "Philosophy of Right,"* ed. Joseph O'Malley (Cambridge, 1970).

———. *Early Writings*, ed. T.B. Bottomore (New York, 1964).

———, and Friedrich Engels. *The Marx-Engels Reader*, ed. Robert C. Tucker (New York, 1972).

Mascall, Eric L. *The Secularization of Christianity* (New York, 1966).

Mather, Cotton. *Diary*. Collections of the Massachusetts Historical Society, Seventh Series, vols. 7-8. 2 vols. (Boston, 1911-1912).

Mathews, Donald G. *Religion in the Old South* (Chicago, 1977).

May, Henry F. *The Enlightenment in America* (New York, 1976).

McAvoy, Thomas T., ed. *Roman Catholicism and the American Way of Life* (South Bend, 1960).

McCary, William. *Songs, Odes, and Other Poems on National Subjects* (Philadelphia, 1842).

McCready, William C., and Andrew M. Greeley. *The Ultimate Values of the American Population* (Beverly Hills, 1976).

McKee, Thomas Hudson, ed. *The National Conventions and Platforms of all Political Parties, 1789 to 1900: Convention, Popular, and Electoral Vote* (Baltimore, 1900).

McLoughlin, William G. "Is There a Third Force in Christendom?" *Daedalus* 96 (Winter 1967): 43-68.

————. *Modern Revivalism: Charles Grandison Finney to Billy Graham* (New York, 1959).

————. *Revivals, Awakenings, and Reform* (Chicago, 1978).

————. "The Role of Religion in the Revolution," in Stephen G. Kurtz and James H. Hutson, eds., *Essays on the American Revolution* (Chapel Hill, 1973).

McWilliams, Wilson Carey. "On Equality as the Moral Foundation for Community," in R.H. Horwitz, ed., *The Moral Foundations of the American Republic* (Charlottesville, 1977).

Mead, Sidney E. "From Denominationalism to Americanism," *Journal of Religion* 36 (January 1956): 31-50.

————. *The Lively Experiment* (New York, 1963).

————. *The Nation with the Soul of a Church* (New York, 1975).

————. *The Old Religion in the Brave New World* (Berkeley, Los Angeles, 1977).

Mesthene, Emmanuel G., ed. *Harvard University Program on Technology and Society, 1964-1972: A Final Review* (Cambridge, Mass., 1972).

Metz, Johann Baptist. "Political Theology," in *Sacramentum Mundi: An Encyclopaedia of Theology*, vol. 5 (London, 1970).

Meyer, Donald B. *The Protestant Search for Political Realism, 1919-1941* (Berkeley and Los Angeles, 1961).

Michelet, Jules. *Introduction à l'histoire universelle* (Paris, 1898).

————. *Le Prêtre, la femme et la famille* (Paris, 1898).

Mill, John Stuart. *Philosophy of Scientific Method*, ed. E. Nagel (New York, 1950).

————. *Representative Government* (Indianapolis, 1958).

Miller, David. *The New Polytheism* (New York, 1974).

Miller, Perry, ed. *The American Puritan* (New York, 1956).

————. *Errand in the Wilderness* (Cambridge, 1956).

————. "From the Covenant to the Revival," in J.W. Smith and A. Leland Jamison, eds., *The Shaping of American Religion* (Princeton, 1961).

————. *The Transcendentalists: An Anthology* (Cambridge, Mass., 1950).

Miller, William L. "American Religion and American Political Attitudes," in J.W. Smith and A. Leland Jamison, eds., *Religious Perspectives in American Culture* (Princeton, 1961).

Miyakawa, I. Scott. *Protestants and Pioneers: Individualism and Conformity on the American Frontier* (Chicago, 1964).

Moltmann, Jürgen, et al., eds. *Religion and Political Society* (New York, 1974).

Montesquieu, Charles-Louis de Secondat, baron de. *De l'Esprit des lois*, ed. G. Truc. 2 vols. (Paris, 1956).

Moore, Barrington, Jr. *Reflections on the Causes of Human Misery and Upon Certain Proposals to Eliminate Them* (Boston, 1972).

Moore, Frank, ed. *The Patriot Preachers of the American Revolution* (New York, 1862).

Morgan, Edmund J. *The Puritan Dilemma: The Story of John Winthrop* (Boston, 1958).

Morgan, Richard E. *The Politics of Religious Conflict* (Indianapolis, 1968).

Morin, Edgar. *L'Homme et la mort*. 2d ed. (Paris, 1970).

Morris, B.F. *Christian Life and Character of the Civil Institutions of the United States* (Philadelphia, 1864).

Murphy, Walter. *The Vicar of Christ* (New York, 1979).

Murray, John Courtney. *The Problem of Religious Freedom* (Westminster, Md., 1965).

———. *We Hold These Truths* (New York, 1960).

Nagel, Paul C. *This Sacred Trust* (New York, 1971.

Neuhaus, Richard J. "The War, the Churches, and Civil Religion," *The Annals* 388 (January 1970): 128-40.

Neusner, Jacob. *From Politics to Piety: The Emergence of Pharisaic Judaism* (Englewood Cliffs, 1973).

Nevin, John W. "The Sect System," *Mercersburg Review* 1 (September 1849).

Newlin, Claude M. *Philosophy and Religion in Colonial America* (New York, 1962).

Nichols, Roy. *The Religion of American Democracy* (Baton Rouge, 1959).

Niebuhr, H. Richard. *Christ and Culture* (New Haven, 1951).

———. "The Idea of Covenant and the American Democracy," *Church History* 23 (June 1954): 126-35.

———. *The Kingdom of God in America* (New York, 1955).

———. "The Protestant Movement and Democracy in the United States," in J.W. Smith and A. Leland Jamison, eds., *The Shaping of American Religion* (Princeton, 1961).

———. *The Social Sources of Denominationalism* (New York, 1929).

Niebuhr, Reinhold. *Faith and History* (New York 1949).

———. *The Irony of American History* (New York, 1952).

———. "The King's Chapel and the King's Court," *Christianity and Crisis* (4 August 1969): 211-12.

———. *Moral Man and Immoral Society* (New York, 1960).

———. "What the War Did to My Mind," *Christian Century* 45 (27 September 1928).

Nigg, Walter. *The Heretics* (New York, 1962).

Noll, Mark A. *Christians in the American Revolution* (Grand Rapids, 1977).

Northrup, Clark Sutherland, William C. Lane, and John C. Schwab, eds. *Representative Phi Beta Kappa Orations*. 2 vols. (Boston, 1925; New York, 1927).

Novak, Michael. *Choosing Our King: Powerful Symbols in Presidential Politics* (New York, 1974).

Oakeshott, Michael. *Hobbes on Civil Association* (Oxford, 1975).

————. *On Human Conduct* (Oxford, 1975).

O'Dea, Thomas F. "The Crisis of the Contemporary Religious Consciousness," *Daedalus* 96 (Winter 1967): 116-34.

————. *The Mormons* (Chicago, 1957).

————. *Sociology and the Study of Religion* (New York, 1970).

Osborn, G., ed. *The Poetical Works of John and Charles Wesley.* 13 vols. (London, 1868-1872).

Ozouf, Mona. *La Fête révolutionnaire, 1789-1799* (Paris, 1976).

Parrington, Vernon Louis. *Main Currents in American Thought: An Interpretation of American Literature from the Beginnings to 1920.* 3 vols. (New York, 1927-1930).

Parsons, Talcott, *The Social System* (New York, 1964).

————. *The Structure of Social Action* (New York, 1949).

Partisan Review, No. 2 (1950): "Religion and the Intellectuals: A Symposium."

Pascal, Blaise. *Pensées,* ed. C. des Granges (Paris, 1964).

Pelikan, Jaroslav. *The Christian Intellectual* (New York, 1965).

Persons, Stow, "Religion and Modernity, 1865-1914," in J.W. Smith and A. Leland Jamison, eds., *The Shaping of American Religion* (Princeton, 1961).

Peirce, Charles Sanders. "How to Make Your Ideas Clear," *Popular Science Monthly* 12 (January 1878).

Pocock, J.G.A. *The Machiavellian Moment* (Princeton, 1975).

Proceedings of the Pennsylvania Yearly Meeting of Progressive Friends (New York, 1858).

Ramsay, David. *The History of the American Revolution.* 2 ,ols. (Philadelphia, 1789).

Rauschenbusch, Walter. *Christianity and the Social Crisis* (New York, 1907).

Rawls, John. *A Theory of Justice* (Cambridge, Mass., 1971).

Remarque, Erich Maria. *All Quiet on the Western Front* (New York, 1960).

Reiss, H.S., ed. *The Political Thought of the German Romantics* (Oxford, 1955).

Richardson, James Daniel, ed. *Compilation of the Messages and Papers of the Presidents.* 20 vols. (New York, 1897-1908).

Richey, Russell E., ed. *Denominationalism* (Nashville, 1977).

————, and Donald G. Jones, eds. *American Civil Religion* (New York, 1974).

Rieff, Philip, "Introduction to Max Weber: 'Science as a Vocation'," *Daedalus* 87 (Winter 1958): 111-34.

————, ed. *On Intellectuals* (Garden City, 1969).

Rist, J.M. *Epicurus: An Introduction* (Cambridge, 1972).

Roberts, Octavia. *With Lafayette in America, with Illustrations from Old Prints* (Boston, 1919).

Robertson, Roland. *The Sociological Interpretation of Religion* (New York, 1972).

――――, ed. *Sociology of Religion* (Harmondsworth, 1976).

Rogers, Cleveland, and John Black, eds. *The Gathering of the Forces*. 2 vols. (New York, 1920).

Roof, Wade Clark. "America's Voluntary Establishment: Mainline Religion in Transition," *Daedalus* 111 (Winter 1982): 165-84.

Rorty, Richard. *Philosophy and the Mirror of Nature* (Princeton, 1979).

Rousseau, Jean-Jacques. *Oeuvres complètes,* ed. M. Raymond and B. Gagnebin. 4 vols. (Paris, 1959–).

――――. *The Political Writings*, ed. C.E. Vaughan. 2 vols. (New York, 1962).

Royce, Josiah. *Basic Writings*, vol. II, ed. J.J. McDermott (Chicago, 1969).

――――. *The Problem of Christianity*, ed. J.E. Smith (Chicago, 1968).

――――. *Race Questions, Provincialism, and Other American Problems* (New York, 1908).

Ryder, William H. *Our Country; or, the American Parlor Keepsake* (Boston, 1854).

St. Augustine. *The City of God* (New York, 1950).

Salisbury, W. Seward. *Religion in the American Culture: A Sociological Interpretation* (Homewood, Ill., 1964).

Salkever, Stephen G. "Virtue, Obligation, and Politics," *American Political Science Review* 68 (March 1974): 78-92.

Sanders, Thomas G. *Protestant Concepts of Church and State* (New York, 1964).

Sandoz, Ellis. "The Civil Theology of Liberal Democracy," *Journal of Politics* 34 (February 1972): 2-36.

Santayana, George. *Character and Opinion in the United States* (New York, 1920).

Sartori, Giovanni. *Parties and Party Systems: A Framework for Analysis* (Cambridge, 1976).

Schaff, Philip. *America* (New York, 1855).

――――. *Germany: Its Universities, Theology and Religion* (Philadelphia, 1857).

Schmotter, James W. "Clerical Professionalism and the Great Awakening," *American Quarterly* 31 (Summer 1979): 148-68.

Schneider, Herbert. *Religion in the Twentieth Century* (Cambridge, Mass., 1952).

Schumpeter, Joseph. *Capitalism, Socialism, and Democracy*. 3d ed. (New York, 1962).

Seabury, Paul. "Trendier than Thou," *Harper's*, (October 1978): 39-52.

Sherover, Charles M. "Rousseau's Civil Religion," *Interpretation* 8 (May 1980): 114-22.

Shklar, Judith N. *After Utopia: The Decline of Political Faith* (Princeton, 1957).

Siegfried, André. *Les Etats-Unis d'aujourd'hui* (Paris, 1927).

――――. *Tableau des Etats-Unis* (Paris, 1954).

Simon, Yves. *Freedom and Community,* ed. C.P. O'Donnell (New York, 1968).

———. *Philosophy of Democratic Government* (Chicago, 1951).

Skinner, Quentin. *The Foundations of Modern Political Thought.* 2 vols. (Cambridge, 1978).

Smelser, Marshall. "The Jacobin Phrenzy: Federalism and the Menace of Liberty, Equality, and Fraternity," *Review of Politics* 13 (October 1951): 457-82.

Smith, Elwyn A., ed. *The Religion of the Republic* (Philadelphia, 1972).

Smith, John E. *Royce's Social Infinite: The Community of Interpretation* (n.p., 1969).

Smith, Timothy L. *Revivalism and Social Reform* (New York, 1957).

———. "Righteousness and Hope: Christian Holiness and the Millennial Vision in America," *American Quarterly* 31 (Spring 1979): 21-45.

Sontag, Frederick. *The Crisis of Faith: A Protestant Witness in Rome* (Garden City, 1969).

Spencer, Donald S. *Louis Kossuth and Young America: A Study of Sectionalism and Foreign Policy, 1848-1852* (Columbia, Mo., 1977).

Stark, Werner. *The Sociology of Religion: A Study of Christendom,* vol. I: *Established Religion* (New York, 1966).

Stauffer, Robert E. "Civil Religion, Technocracy, and the Private Sphere: Further Comments on Cultural Integration in Advanced Societies," *Journal for the Scientific Study of Religion* 12 (December 1973): 415-25.

Stokes, Anson Phelps. *Church and State in the United States.* 4 vols. (New York, 1930).

Streiker, Lowell D., and Gerald S. Strober. *Religion and the New Majority* (New York, 1972).

Strong, Josiah. *The New Era; or the Coming Kingdom* (New York, 1893).

———. *Our Country: Its Possible Future and its Present Crisis* (New York, 1885).

Stroup, Herbert. *Church and State in Confrontation* (New York, 1967).

Strout, Cushing. *The New Heavens and the New Earth: Political Religion in America* (New York, 1974).

Stuart, Reginald C. "The Origins of American Nationalism to 1783: An Historiographical Survey," *Canadian Review of Studies in Nationalism* 6 (Fall 1979): 139-51.

Sullivan, William M. "Shifting Loyalties: Critical Theory and the Problem of Legitimacy," *Polity* 12 (Winter 1978): 253-72.

Swanson, Guy E. *The Birth of the Gods* (Ann Arbor, 1960).

———. *Religion and Regime* (Ann Arbor, 1967).

Sweet, William W. *Religion in the Development of American Culture, 1765-1840* (New York, 1952).

———. *Religion on the American Frontier, 1783-1840* (Chicago, 1939).

Taveneaux, René, ed. *Jansénisme et politique* (Paris, 1965).

Taylor, Nathaniel William. "Concio ad Clerum: A Sermon Delivered in the Chapel of Yale College, September 16, 1828" (New Haven, 1842).

Thomas, L.-V. *Anthropologie de la mort* (Paris, 1975).

Thomas, Mitchell C., and C.C. Flippen. "American Civil Religion: An Empirical Study," *Social Forces* 6 (December 1972): 218-25.

Thompson, Dennis. "The Education of a Founding Father: The Reading List for John Witherspoon's Course in Political Theory, as Taken by James Madison," *Political Theory* 4 (November 1976): 523-29.

Thompson, Robert Ellis. *A History of the Presbyterian Churches in the United States* (New York, 1895).

Tillich, Paul. *The Interpretation of History* (New York, 1936).

———. *The Religious Situation* (New York, 1956).

———. *Theology of Culture* (Oxford, 1964).

Tipton, Steven M. "The Moral Logic of Alternative Religions," *Daedalus* 111 (Winter 1982): 185-214.

Tocqueville, Alexis de. *Democracy in America*, trans. Henry Reeve. 2 vols. (New York, 1945).

Toynbee, Arnold J. *An Historian's Approach to Religion* (London, 1956).

———. *A Study of History*, vols. VII-X, abridged by D.C. Somervell (New York, 1957).

Troeltsch, Ernst. *The Social Teachings of the Christian Churches*, trans. Olive Wyon. 2 vols. (New York, 1931).

Tuveson, Ernest. *Redeemer Nation* (Chicago, 1968).

Ullmann, Walter. *A History of Political Thought: The Middle Ages* (Harmondsworth, 1965).

Unamuno, Miguel de. *The Tragic Sense of Life in Men and Nations*, trans. Anthony Kerrigan (Princeton, 1972).

Vahanian, Gabriel. *The Death of God* (New York, 1961).

Van Alstyne, Richard W. "Revolution and Patriotism in America, 1763-1775," *Canadian Review of Studies in Nationalism* 6 (Fall 1979): 152-74.

Van Buren, Paul. *The Secular Meaning of the Gospel* (New York, 1963).

Voegelin, Eric. *Anamnesis: zur Theorie der Geschichte und Politik* (Munich, 1966).

———. *Die politischen Religionen* (Stockholm, 1939).

Volney, Charles-Constantin de, *The Ruins* (Albany, 1822).

Vovelle, Michel. *Piété baroque et déchristianisation en Provence au XVIIIᵉ siècle* (Paris, 1973).

Walker, Williston, ed. *The Creeds and Platforms of Congregationalism* (Boston, 1960).

Wallace, G., and A.D.M. Walker, eds. *The Definition of Morality* (London, 1970).

Walzer, Michael. *Obligations: Essays on Disobedience, War, and Citizenship* (New York, 1971).

Washington, Joseph R., Jr. *Black Religion: The Negro and Christianity in the United States* (Boston, 1964).

Weber, Max. *From Max Weber: Essays in Sociology,* ed. H.H. Gerth and C. Wright Mills (New York, 1967).

———. *The Protestant Ethic and the Spirit of Capitalism,* trans. Talcott Parsons (New York, 1958).

———. *The Sociology of Religion* (Boston, 1963).

Weil, Simone. *Gravity and Grace* (New York, 1952).

Weiss, Benjamin. *God in American History* (Grand Rapids, 1966).

Wertenbaker, Thomas J., ed. *The Puritan Oligarchy* (New York, 1970).

Wesley, John. *Collected Works.* 14 vols. (London, 1879).

West, Robert Frederick. *Alexander Campbell and Natural Religion* (New Haven, 1948).

White, Morton. *The Philosophy of the American Revolution* (Oxford, 1978).

———. *Pragmatism and the American Mind* (London, 1975).

Whitman, Walt. *Leaves of Grass and Democratic Vistas* (London, n.d.).

Williams, J. Paul. *What Americans Believe and How They Worship* (New York, 1952).

Williams, Robin. *American Society* (New York, 1957).

Wilson, Bryan R. *Contemporary Transformations of Religion* (Oxford, 1976).

———, ed. *Patterns of Sectarianism* (London, 1967).

———. *Religion in Secular Society* (London, 1966).

———. "A Typology of Sects in a Dynamic and Comparative Perspective," *Archives de Sociologie de Religion* 16 (1963): 49-63.

Wilson, Woodrow. *Great Speeches and Other History Making Documents* (Chicago, 1917).

———. *The New Democracy: Presidential Messages, Addresses, and Other Papers,* ed. Ray S. Baker and William E. Dodd. 2 vols. (New York, 1926).

Wolin, Sheldon. "Paradigms and Political Theories," in P. King and B.C. Parekh, eds., *Politics and Experience* (Cambridge, 1968).

———. *Politics and Vision* (Boston, 1960).

Wood, Gordon S. *The Creation of the American Republic, 1776-1787* (Chapel Hill, 1969).

The World's Great Classics: Orations of American Orators. 2 vols. (New York, 1900).

Xhauffaire, Marcel. *La "Théologie politique": Introduction à la théologie politique de J.B. Metz* (Paris, 1972).

Yearbook of American and Canadian Churches.

Yinger, J. Milton. "Pluralism, religion, and secularism," *Journal for the Scientific Study of Religion* 6 (April 1967): 17-28.

———. *Religion, Society, and the Individual* (New York, 1957).

———. *The Scientific Study of Religion* (London, 1970).

Youngs, J. William T., Jr. *God's Messengers: Religious Leadership in Colonial New England, 1700-1750* (Baltimore, 1976).

Index